T0155781

Lecture Notes in Computer Science 11026

Commenced Publication in 1973
Founding and Former Series Editors:
Gerhard Goos, Juris Hartmanis, and Jan van Leeuwen

More information about this series at http://www.springer.com/series/7408

Amel Bennaceur · Reiner Hähnle
Karl Meinke (Eds.)

Machine Learning for Dynamic Software Analysis

Potentials and Limits

International Dagstuhl Seminar 16172
Dagstuhl Castle, Germany, April 24–27, 2016
Revised Papers

 Springer

Editors
Amel Bennaceur (iD)
The Open University
Milton Keynes
UK

Reiner Hähnle (iD)
Technische Universität Darmstadt
Darmstadt
Germany

Karl Meinke (iD)
KTH Royal Institute of Technology
Stockholm
Sweden

ISSN 0302-9743 ISSN 1611-3349 (electronic)
Lecture Notes in Computer Science
ISBN 978-3-319-96561-1 ISBN 978-3-319-96562-8 (eBook)
https://doi.org/10.1007/978-3-319-96562-8

Library of Congress Control Number: 2018948379

LNCS Sublibrary: SL2 – Programming and Software Engineering

Cover illustration: Classification of key concepts of ML for software engineering. LNCS 11026, p. 5. Used with permission.

This Springer imprint is published by the registered company Springer Nature Switzerland AG
The registered company address is: Gewerbestrasse 11, 6330 Cham, Switzerland

Preface

Machine learning of software artefacts is an emerging area of interaction between the machine learning (ML) and software analysis (SA) communities. Increased productivity in software engineering hinges on the creation of new adaptive, scalable tools that can analyze large and continuously changing software systems. For example: Agile software development using continuous integration and delivery can require new documentation models, static analyses, proofs and tests of millions of lines of code every 24 h. These needs are being addressed by new SA techniques based on ML, such as learning-based software testing, invariant generation, or code synthesis. ML is a powerful paradigm for SA that provides novel approaches to automating the generation of models and other essential artefacts. However, the ML and SA communities are traditionally separate, each with its own agenda.

This book is a follow-up of a Dagstuhl Seminar entitled "16172: Machine Learning for Dynamic Software Analysis: Potentials and Limits" that was held during April 24–27, 2016. This seminar brought together top researchers active in these two fields to present the state of the art and suggest new directions and collaborations for future research. We, the organizers, feel strongly that both communities have much to learn from each other, and the seminar focused strongly on fostering a spirit of collaboration in order to share insights and to expand and strengthen the cross-fertilization between these two communities.

Our goal in this book is to give an overview of the ML techniques that can be used for SA and provide some example applications of their use. Besides an introductory chapter, the book is structured into three parts: testing and learning, extension of automata learning, and integrative approaches as follows.

Introduction

- The chapter by Bennaceur and Meinke entitled "Machine Learning for Software Analysis: Models, Methods, and Applications" introduces the key concepts of ML focusing on models and some of their applications in software engineering.

Testing and Learning

- The chapter by Meinke entitled "Learning-Based Testing: Recent Progress and Future Prospects" reviews the fundamental concepts and theoretical principles of learning-based techniques.
- The chapter by Aichernig, Mostowski, Mousavi, Tappler and Taromirad entitled "Model-Based Testing and Learning" provides an overview of the different models that can be used for testing and how they can be learnt.

- The chapter by Walkinshaw entitled "Testing Functional Black-Box Programs without a Specification" focuses on examining test executions and informing the selection of tests from programs that do not require sequential inputs.

Extensions of Automata Learning

- The chapter by Howar and Steffen entitled "Active Automata Learning in Practice: An Annotated Bibliography of the Years 2011 to 2016" reviews the state of the art and the open challenges for active automata learning.
- The chapter by Cassel, Howar, Jonsson and Steffen entitled "Extending Automata Learning to Extended Finite State Machines" focuses on automata learning for extended finite state machines.
- The chapter by Groz, Simao, Petrenko, and Oriat entitled "Inferring FSM Models of Systems Without Reset" presents active automata learning algorithms that relax the assumptions about the existence of an external oracle.

Integrative Approaches

- The chapter by Hähnle and Steffen entitled "Constraint-Based Behavioral Consistency of Evolving Software Systems" proposes to combine glass-box analysis with automata learning to help bridge the gap between the design and implementation artefacts.
- The chapter by Alrajeh and Russo entitled "Logic-Based Machine Learning in Software Engineering" focuses on logic-based learning and its application for declarative specification refinement and revision.

While the papers in this book cover a wide range of topics regarding ML techniques for model-based software analysis, additional research challenges and related research topics still exist for further investigation.

We hope that you enjoy this book and that it will kindle your interest in and help your understanding of this fascinating area in the overlap of ML and SA. We thank the participants of the seminar for their time and their help in reviewing the chapters. Each chapter was reviewed by at least two reviewers and many went through several revisions. We acknowledge the support of Schloss Dagstuhl—Leibniz Center for Informatics and thank the whole Dagstuhl team for their professional approach that made it easy for the participants to network, to discuss, and to have a very productive seminar. And finally, we sincerely thank the authors for their research efforts, for their willingness to respond to feedback from the reviewers and editorial team. Without their excellent contributions, this volume would not have been possible.

May 2018

Amel Bennaceur
Reiner Hähnle
Karl Meinke

Organization

Program Chairs

Amel Bennaceur — The Open University, UK
Reiner Hähnle — Technische Universität Darmstadt, Germany
Karl Meinke — KTH Royal Institute of Technology, Sweden

Program Committee

Amel Bennaceur — The Open University, UK
Roland Groz — Grenoble Institute of Technology, France
Falk Howar — TU Dortmund and Fraunhofer ISST, Germany
Reiner Hähnle — Technische Universität Darmstadt, Germany
Karl Meinke — KTH Royal Institute of Technology, Sweden
Mohammad Reza Mousavi — School of IT, Halmstad University, Sweden
Bernhard Steffen — TU Dortmund, Germany
Frits Vaandrager — Radboud University, The Netherlands
Neil Walkinshaw — The University of Leicester, UK

Contents

Introduction

Machine Learning for Software Analysis: Models, Methods, and Applications

Amel Bennaceur[1] and Karl Meinke[2]([envelope])

[1] The Open University, Milton Keynes, UK
`amel.bennaceur@open.ac.uk`
[2] KTH Royal Institute of Technology, Stockholm, Sweden
`karlm@kth.se`

Abstract. Machine Learning (ML) is the discipline that studies methods for automatically inferring models from data. Machine learning has been successfully applied in many areas of software engineering including: behaviour extraction, testing and bug fixing. Many more applications are yet to be defined. Therefore, a better fundamental understanding of ML methods, their assumptions and guarantees can help to identify and adopt appropriate ML technology for new applications.

In this chapter, we present an introductory survey of ML applications in software engineering, classified in terms of the models they produce and the learning methods they use. We argue that the optimal choice of an ML method for a particular application should be guided by the type of models one seeks to infer. We describe some important principles of ML, give an overview of some key methods, and present examples of areas of software engineering benefiting from ML. We also discuss the open challenges for reaching the full potential of ML for software engineering and how ML can benefit from software engineering methods.

Keywords: Machine learning · Software engineering

1 Introduction

One can scarcely open a newspaper or switch on the TV nowadays without hearing about machine learning (ML), data mining, big data analytics, and the radical changes which they offer society. However, the layperson might be surprised to learn that these revolutionary technologies have so far had surprisingly little impact on software engineers themselves. This may be yet another case of the proverbial *cobbler's children having no shoes themselves*. Nevertheless, by examining the recent literature, such as the papers published in this workshop volume, we can see small but perhaps significant changes emerging on the horizon for our discipline.

Surely one obstacle to the take-up of these exciting technologies in software engineering (SE) is a general lack of awareness of how they might be applied. What problems can ML currently solve? Are such problems at all relevant for

© Springer International Publishing AG, part of Springer Nature 2018
A. Bennaceur et al. (Eds.): ML for Dynamic Software Analysis, LNCS 11026, pp. 3–49, 2018.
https://doi.org/10.1007/978-3-319-96562-8_1

software engineers? Machine learning is a mature discipline, having its origins as far back as 1950s AI research. There are many excellent modern introductions to the subject, and the world hardly needs another. However, perspectives on ML from software engineering are less common, and an introduction for software engineers that attempts to be both accessible and pedagogic, is a rare thing indeed. Furthermore, at least some of the ML methods currently applied to SE are not widely discussed in mainstream ML. There is much more to ML than deep learning.

With these motivations in mind, we will present here an introduction to machine learning for software engineers having little or no experience of ML. This material might also be useful for the AI community, to better understand the limitations of their methods in an SE context. Our focussed selection of material will inevitably reflect our personal scientific agendas, as well as the need for a short concise Chapter.

To structure this introductory material, we need some organising principles. Our approach is to focus on three questions that we feel should be addressed before attempting any new ML solution to an existing software engineering problem. These are:

- What class of learned models is appropriate for solving my SE problem?
- For this class of models, are there any existing learning algorithms that will work for typical instances and sizes of my SE problem? Otherwise, is it possible to adapt any fundamental ML principles to derive new learning algorithms?
- Has anyone considered a similar SE problem, and was it tractable to an ML solution?

Let us reflect on these questions in a little more detail. As depicted in Fig. 1, the presentation will be structured around three main concepts: *models*, *methods*, and *applications*.

1.1 Models

A learning algorithm constructs a *model M* from a given *data set D*. This model represents some sort of synthesis of the facts contained in D. Most machine learning algorithms perform *inductive inference*, to extract general principles, laws or rules from the specific observations in D. Otherwise, learning would amount to little more than memorisation. So a model M typically contains a combination of *facts* (from D) and *conjectures* (i.e. extrapolations to unseen data).

A model may be regarded as a mathematical object. Examples of types of models (on a rough scale of increasing generality) include:

- a list of numeric coefficients or weights, $(w_1, \ldots, w_n) \in R^n$,
- a function $f : A \to B$,
- a relation $r \subseteq B$,
- a directed graph, $G = (V, E)$,
- a logical formula, $\phi(x_1, \ldots, x_n)$,

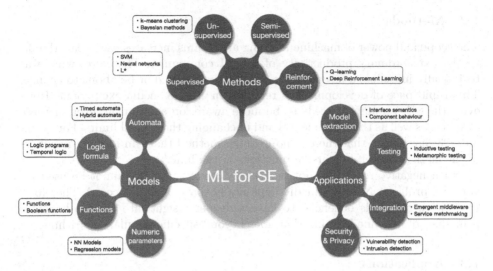

Fig. 1. Classification of key concepts of ML for software engineering

- a deterministic finite automaton,
- a timed automaton,
- a hybrid automaton,
- a first-order mathematical structure.

An important observation at this stage is that this non-exhaustive list of model types is able to support increasingly complex and structured levels of description. Our emphasis on such precise mathematical models is because for ML, a model must be machine representable. Perhaps more importantly, models are part of the vocabulary when talking about machine learning in general.

Different methods can be used to construct different models from the same underlying data set D. This is because different *abstraction principles* can be applied to form different views of the same data set. Therefore, to be able to apply ML, it is fundamentally important to understand the scope and relevance of the various model types. A learned model M never has an arbitrary structure; rather its structure, parameters and values are defined and delimited by the specific method that constructed it.

A certain type of model M (e.g. a set of numeric coefficients or weights) may provide inadequate detail for a specific SE application (e.g. testing, documentation, monitoring, timing analysis etc.). In this case, a better model type needs to be found, and after this we must consider whether there are any efficient learning algorithms for this type of model. Generally speaking, the more complex a model is, the harder it is to learn. Alternatively, a type of model may be overly complex and detailed for a specific problem. In this case, it might be better to consider simpler models, for which more efficient and scalable learning algorithms might be found.

1.2   Methods

The scope and power of machine learning algorithms increases each year, thanks to the extraordinary productivity of the AI community. Therefore, what was technically infeasible a few years ago, may have changed or be about to change. This rapid pace of development is reflected in current media excitement. However, the SE community needs to be more aware, on a technical level, of these changes, as well as the fundamental and unchanging theoretical limits. For example, [23] has shown that there is no learning method that can identify members of the class of all total recursive functions in the limit[1].

Such negative results do not necessarily mean that ML cannot be used for your SE problem. Nor does media hype imply that you will succeed. Therefore, we believe that it is beneficial to have a deeper insight into the fundamental principles of machine learning that goes beyond specific popular algorithms.

1.3   Applications

We also believe it will be beneficial for software engineers to read about success stories in applying ML to SE. Therefore, we will try to outline some SE applications (Model extraction, testing, and component integration), where ML has already been tried with some degree of success. Scalability in the face of growing software complexity is one of the greatest challenges for SE toolmakers. Therefore, information (however ephemeral) about the state of the art in solvable problem sizes is also relevant.

1.4   Overview of This Chapter

In Sect. 2 we give a brief overview of the major paradigms of machine learning. These paradigms (such as supervised and unsupervised learning) cut across most of the important types of models as a coarse taxonomy of methods. The number of relevant types of models for SE is simply too large to cover in a short introduction such as this. Therefore, in Sect. 3 we present models and methods focussed around various types of state machine models. State machine models have been successfully used to solve a variety of SE problems. Our introduction concludes with Sect. 4, where some of these applications are discussed. Our survey of the literature will be woven into each Section continuously.

2   Learning Paradigms

Machine learning is the discipline that studies methods for automatically inducing models from data. This broad definition of course covers an endless variety of subproblems, ranging from simple least-squares linear regression methods to

---

[1] Informally *identification in the limit* means that for any infinite sequence of observations $o_1, o_2, \ldots$ there exists some finite point n after which the function learned from the first n observations is longer changed by any later observations.

advanced methods that infer complex computational structures [33]. These methods often differ in their assumptions about the learning environment, and such assumptions allow us to categorise ML algorithms in a broad way as follows.

2.1 Supervised Learning

This is the most archetypical paradigm in machine learning. The problem setting is most easily explained when the underlying model (in the sense of Sect. 1.1) is a mathematical function $f : A \to B$, however the approach generalises to other models[2], such as automata.

In this setting, the learning algorithm is provided with a finite set of n labelled examples: i.e. a set of pairs $T = \{(x_i, y_i) \in A \times B : 1 \leq i \leq n\}$. The goal is to make use of the example set T (also known as the *training set*) to induce a function $f : A \to B$, such that[3] $f(x_i) \equiv y_i$ for each i, (see for example [50]). Notice an implicit assumption here that the training set T corresponds to some function: i.e. for each $1 \leq i, j \leq n$ if $x_i = x_j$ then $y_i = y_j$. If this assumption is false, we must conclude that either: (i) a function model is not appropriate for the training set T, and a relational model $r \subseteq A \times B$ should be used; (this might reflect non-determinism in the **System Under Learning (SUL)**) or, (ii) the training set contains measurement noise, and a function model could be used when combined with data smoothing[4]. Thus some domain knowledge is often needed for the best choice of model. This situation seems to be rather typical in practise.

The task of a learning algorithm is to actually construct a concrete representation of f for any given training set T. This could be, for example, in terms of coefficients for a set of simple basis functions that collectively describe f[5].

It is natural to try to evaluate the quality of f as a model. By quality, we generally mean the predictive ability of f on a data set $E = \{(w_i, z_i) \in A \times B : 1 \leq i \leq m\}$ which is disjoint from T (often called the *evaluation set*). To quantify the quality of f we can for example measure the percentage of instances i such that $f(w_i) \equiv z_i$. Of course, this is only an empirical estimate of the quality of f, and care needs to be taken with the choice of E. Generally, a larger value of m will give greater confidence in the accuracy of the quality estimate. These two steps are illustrated in Fig. 2.

A larger value of n often leads to a model f with better predictive ability on the same evaluation set E. This is because many machine learning algorithms have the property of *convergence* over increasing data sets. However, convergence is not

---

[2] Note that in general A and B can be cartesian products of sets, e.g. $A = A_1 \times \ldots \times A_n$.

[3] Here, the relation $f(x_i) \equiv y_i$ means that $f(x_i)$ is very close to y_i for some suitable metric. Of course one such relation is the equality relation on B.

[4] By data smoothing we mean any form of statistical averaging or filtering process, that can reduce the effects of noise. Data smoothing may be necessary even when a relational model is appropriate.

[5] This is done in many approaches including linear regression models, polynomial approximation, Fourier methods, simple neural networks and deep learning.

always theoretically guaranteed for every learning algorithm. This problem can be significant for algorithms based on optimisation methods, such as deep learning.

The domain A of all possible training and evaluation inputs is often very large or even infinite. Therefore, neither perfect training, nor perfect evaluation are usually practicable. Perfect and complete learning may not even be necessary for specific applications. An approximate model may already yield sufficient information, for example to demonstrate that a bug is present in a software system under learning.

When learning is incomplete, some kind of probabilistic statement about the quality of f may be adequate. A popular approach is the *probably approximately correct* (PAC) learning paradigm of [61]. This paradigm expresses the quality of f in terms of two parameters: (ε, δ), where ε is the probability that $f(w_i)$ lies no further than δ from z_i for each $(w_i, z_i) \in E$. Extensive research into PAC learning (see e.g. [36]) has shown the existence of models that are PAC learnable in polynomial time, but which cannot be exactly learned in polynomial time. So being vague may pay off!

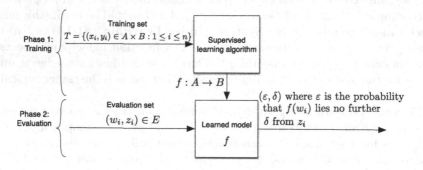

Fig. 2. Illustrating the supervised learning paradigm

A major hurdle in applying supervised learning is often the significant effort of labelling both the training and evaluation data, in order to induce a function f with sufficient quality. Fortunately, in a software engineering context, there are situations where the system under learning itself can act as a qualified teacher that can label both training and evaluation examples.

2.2   Unsupervised Learning

This is an alternative paradigm to supervised learning that lowers the entry hurdle for application by requiring only an unlabelled training set, $T = \{x_i \in A : 1 \leq i \leq n\}$. In order to be able to come up with a useful model when no supervision is provided, unsupervised learning must construct its own labelling scheme which is then used to label the training set elements x_i. The most well-known example of unsupervised learning is probably k-*means clustering*, where the learning algorithm identifies k (possibly overlapping) sub-categories $C_1, \ldots, C_k \subseteq A$

within the training set T, and assigns each object x_i to one or more such categories C_j. Thus the categories C_j are not given a-priori. This process is illustrated in Fig. 3. Obviously, the results of unsupervised learning cannot compete with those of supervised learning. For example, in supervised learning incorrect classification is not possible as the categories are identified a-priori.

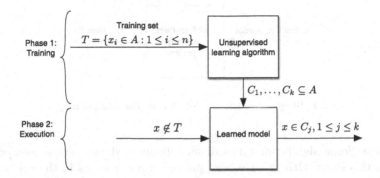

Fig. 3. Illustrating the unsupervised learning paradigm

2.3 Semi-supervised Learning

This is a pragmatic compromise between Sects. 2.1 and 2.2. It allows one to use a combination of a small labelled example set $T_s = \{(x, y)\}$ together with a larger unlabelled example set $T_u = \{x\}$. This can allow us to improve on the limited supervised learning possible with T_s only, by extending the result with unsupervised learning on T_u.

2.4 Reinforcement Learning

Reinforcement learning requires the existence of a *reward* mechanism that can be used to guide the learning algorithm toward a revised hypothesis as illustrated in Fig. 4.

The learner is in a feedback loop with the environment with which it interacts. The learner performs an action on the environment and observes the corresponding reward try to get a step closer to maximising this reward. Over time, the learner optimises for the best series of actions. Q-learning [66] is an example reinforcement learning technique in which agents learn incrementally how to act optimally in controlled Markovian domains.

3 Models and Methods

In this Section we introduce some important classes of learnable models and some of their associated learning algorithms. This survey is not meant to be

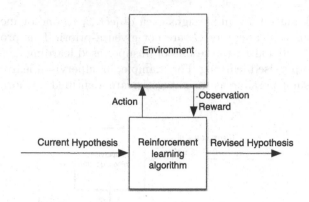

Fig. 4. Illustrating the reinforcement learning paradigm

exhaustive. Some significant types of models omitted here are presented elsewhere in this Book. Others have been presented many times in the existing ML literature.

A general category of models which are quite natural to learn for the purposes of software analysis are *models of computation* for computer software or hardware. This is because such models are able to abstract away implementation details (such as programming language syntax) while preserving important behavioural properties. For example, one application of machine learning for models of computation is to dynamically infer a model from runtime behaviour, and then apply a static analysis technique to this model.

In computer science, there is a long tradition of defining and studying various models of computation, including: Turing machines [30], Petri nets [53], deterministic finite automata (DFA) [30], pushdown automata [30], register machines [14], non-deterministic [30], probabilistic [28], and hybrid automata [4].

In this Chapter, we will mainly focus on different types of *automata models*. There is a rich literature around automata models that encompasses many variations. The explicit computational structure of such models is able to support many of the basic aims of software analysis. Furthermore, there is the advantage of traceability between the training data and the learned model, which can support SE traceability and certification needs. Thus automaton learning is largely consistent with the emerging paradigm of *explainable AI* (XAI). Model traceability is often lost in other ML statistical methods.

We have several aims. The most basic aim is to survey different classes of models which might be appropriate for different software analysis tasks such as verification or testing. Another aim is to provide simple pedagogical examples of algorithms that convey certain important ideas. These algorithms do not necessarily reflect the state of the art in machine learning, (which can be found elsewhere in this Book). However, they should equip the reader to master the literature.

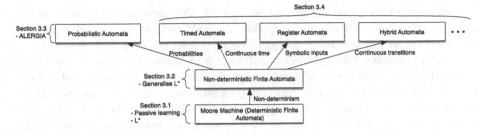

Fig. 5. Learning automata models

Finally, we wish to compare and contrast the problem of learning across different model classes (see Fig. 5). In particular we aim to identify certain common principles and techniques that can be refined and extended to new model classes.

3.1 Deterministic Finite State Machines

Pedagogically, it is appropriate to start with the simplest automata model which is the deterministic finite state machine. Then gradually we will introduce more features associated with greater complexity both in model structure and difficulty of learning.

By a finite state machine (FSM), we mean a model of computation based on a finite set $Q = \{q_0, \ldots, q_n\}$ of states, and transitions (i.e. state changes) $q_i \to q_j$ between two states, that can occur over time. A state transition is always initiated by some input and usually returns some output. This description actually applies to many different models of computation found in the literature, including some that one would prefer to call *infinite state machines*. So for the purposes of studying machine learning we will need to be more precise.

A refinement of this description is that an FSM can only accept input values from a *finite input alphabet* Σ and return values from a *finite output alphabet* Ω. Essentially, this means that the memory model of an FSM has a fixed and finite size. This property distinguishes the FSM model from other models, such as pushdown automata, Turing machines and statecharts [27]. The finite memory characteristic plays an important role for convergence in machine learning, as we shall see.

In the simplest case, a specific transition $q_i \to q_j$, from a state q_i to a state q_j, is triggered by receiving an input value $\sigma \in \Sigma$. According to whether the corresponding output value $\omega \in \Omega$ of an FSM is associated with taking the transition $q_i \to q_j$ itself, or arriving in the target state q_j, the FSM is classified as either a *Mealy* or a *Moore machine* respectively. A Mealy machine can give an equivalent but more compact representation of the same Moore machine. However, this makes Mealy machines somewhat harder to infer (as a function of their size). For simplicity, in this survey we focus on learning Moore machines.

Supposing that from any given state $q \in Q$, the same input value σ always leads to the same next state $q' \in Q$ then an FSM (Moore or Mealy) is said to be *deterministic*, otherwise it is said to be *non-deterministic*. Non-determinism is quite a pervasive phenomenon in software and hardware systems, especially where these are built up from loosely coupled communicating components. However, because of their greater complexity, non-deterministic FSMs are harder to learn. We can consider quantifying the probabilities associated with non-deterministic choices of transitions. This leads to an even more general model termed *probabilistic automata*. We shall return to these more general models in later sections of this Chapter.

In the context of models of computation, we begin then with the simplest type of learning problem, the task of learning a deterministic Moore automaton.

Definition 1. *By a **deterministic Moore automaton** we mean a structure*

$$A = (Q, \Sigma, \Omega, q_0, \delta : Q \times \Sigma \to Q, \lambda : Q \to \Omega),$$

where: Q is a set of states, $q_0 \in Q$ is the initial state, $\Sigma = \{\sigma_1, \ldots, \sigma_k\}$ is a finite set of input values, $\Omega = \{\omega_1, \ldots, \omega_{k'}\}$ is a finite set of output values, $\delta : Q \times \Sigma \to Q$ is the state transition function, and $\lambda : Q \to \Omega$ is the output function.

If Q is finite then A is termed a *finite state Moore automaton*, otherwise A is termed an *infinite state Moore automaton*. Infinite state machines are useful both for pedagogical and theoretical purposes. For example, they can inspire ideas about more general learning paradigms.

The structural complexity of A is an important parameter in studying the complexity of learning algorithms. The simplest measure here is the *size* of A as measured by the number of states $n = |Q|$.

Notice that according to Definition 1, a deterministic Moore automaton is a universal algebraic structure[6] in the sense of [45], and this observation leads to the subject of *algebraic automata theory* [29]. Algebraic concepts such as isomorphisms, congruences and quotient algebras are all applicable to such structures. These algebraic concepts can be quite useful for gaining a deeper understanding of some of the principles of learning. The following insights are particularly useful.

- Structural equivalence of automata is simply isomorphism;
- The main method for automaton construction in automaton learning is the quotient automaton construction;

---

[6] A universal algebraic structure is a many-sorted first-order structure $\langle A_i : i = 1, \ldots, n; c_j : j = 1, \ldots, m; f_k : k = 1, \ldots, p, \rangle$ consisting of data sets A_i, constants $c_j \in A_{i_j}$, and functions $f_k : A_{i_{k(1)}} \times \ldots \times A_{i_{k(n)}} \to A_{i_{k(n+1)}}$ but no relations. Thus a deterministic Moore automaton is a 3-sorted universal algebraic structure. See e.g. [45] or [44] for further details.

– The set of all possible solutions to an automaton learning problem can be modelled and studied as a lattice of congruences. The ordering relation is set-theoretic inclusion $\subseteq$ between congruences. The maximal elements in this lattice correspond with minimal models.

Unfortunately, in a short introductory chapter such as this, we do not have space to explore this rich mathematical theory in any depth.

Deterministic Moore automata properly include deterministic finite automata (DFA) encountered in formal language theory. DFA are a special case where the output alphabet Ω is a two element set: e.g. $\Omega = \{accept, reject\}$. Automaton learning algorithms found early applications in the field of natural language processing (NLP), where they were used to infer a regular grammar empirically from a corpus of texts. The sub-field of DFA learning is therefore also known as *regular inference* [28]. For software analysis, the generalisation from two outputs to multiple outputs $\Omega = \{\omega_0, \ldots \omega_{k'}\}$ is important, and not always trivial.

Suppose that we are given as an SUL a software artifact that we wish to model and learn as a deterministic Moore automaton. We can imagine that this SUL is encapsulated within a black-box, so that we can communicate with it, without being aware of its internal structure, or even its size. This is the paradigm of *black-box learning*. Black-box learning is appropriate in software analysis for learning problems involving third-party, low level, dynamically changing, and even undocumented software. In practise, even when we do have access to the SUL (e.g. its source code), its explicit structure as a state machine is often far from clear. Nor is it always clear which type of state machine best captures the SUL behaviour (e.g. a deterministic or a non-deterministic machine).

To learn the SUL as a deterministic Moore machine, we observe its behaviour over time, and for this we need to be given an explicit protocol to communicate with the SUL. In practical applications, defining and implementing this protocol can be quite challenging. For example, we might communicate with the SUL in a regular synchronous fashion, or an asynchronous (event-driven) manner. We may also need to map between the abstract symbolic representation of an input set Σ and specific structured and complex input values (such as lists, queues, objects etc.). The same mapping problem applies to the outputs of the SUL and Ω.

By a *query* on the SUL we mean a finite string or sequence $\bar{\sigma} = \sigma_1, \ldots, \sigma_l \in \Sigma^*$ of length $l \geq 0$ over an appropriate input alphabet Σ derived from its API. Notice that even the empty string ε can be a legitimate query for returning the initial state of the SUL on startup. If we execute the SUL on a query $\bar{\sigma}$ then it should return some interesting *observation*. Without loss of generality, we shall assume that this observation is a string $\omega_0, \ldots, \omega_l \in \Omega^*$, of length $l + 1$. Then for each $0 \leq i \leq l$, we can assume that ω_i is the result of uniformly iterating a state transition function δ, i.e.

$$\omega_i = \lambda(\delta^*(\sigma_1, \ldots, \sigma_i)),$$

where $\delta^*(\varepsilon) = q_0$ and $\delta^*(\sigma_1, \ldots, \sigma_{i+1}) = \delta(\delta^*(\sigma_1, \ldots, \sigma_i), \sigma_{i+1})$.

We can now ask: *Given an SUL, is it possible to construct complete definitions of Q, q_0, δ and λ for a Moore automaton model from a finite set of queries*

$$Queries = \{\overline{\sigma_1}, \ldots, \overline{\sigma_m}\}$$

and the corresponding set of observations

$$Observations = \{\overline{\omega_1}, \ldots, \overline{\omega_m}\}.$$

This is the problem of *black-box learning a Moore automaton representation* of the SUL as illustrated in Fig. 6. It is clearly a supervised learning problem, in the sense of Sect. 2.1. Furthermore, this problem generalises to learning other, more complex representations of the SUL. Notice that the problem specifically relates to finding a *complete model* that models all possible behaviours of the SUL. For certain software analysis problems, e.g. bug-finding, it may already be sufficient to construct a *partial model* of the SUL, in which some SUL behaviours are missing. Notice also, that it is not *a-priori* clear whether a given SUL even *has* a complete finite state Moore machine model. For example, the behaviours of the SUL may correspond to a push-down automaton model using unbounded memory.

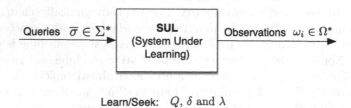

Fig. 6. Illustrating black-box learning a Moore automaton

If this learning problem can be solved, we can pose further questions.

- Can we characterise a minimally adequate set of queries?
- What algorithms can be used to efficiently construct Q, q_0, δ and λ from the query and observation sets?

Notice that for a behavioural analysis of the SUL, it is enough to reconstruct Q, δ and λ up to structural equivalence (i.e. isomorphism). The concrete name given to each state $q \in Q$ does not impact on the input/output behaviour of the learned model A.

3.1.1 Passive Versus Active Learning

At this point, an important distinction in black-box learning methods arises as follows. It may be that we are given fixed and finite sets of queries and observations for the SUL, and invited to produce our best guess about Q, q_0, δ and λ

that fits the known data. This could be because the SUL is offline, unavailable, or because we may monitor but not actively interfere with the activity of the SUL for safety reasons. This non-adaptive approach to learning is termed *passive learning*.

On the other hand, it may be possible for us to generate our own queries and observe the corresponding behaviour of the SUL directly. This might be because the SUL is constantly available online to answer our queries. In this more flexible situation, new queries could be constructed according to the response of the SUL to previous queries. This adaptive approach is termed *active learning*.

In the following, we will consider both of these important learning paradigms in turn.

3.1.2   Passive Automaton Learning

In passive automaton learning we are given a fixed and finite set of queries and observations for an SUL, and invited to produce our best guess about the automaton A (i.e. its components Q, q_0, δ and λ) that fits the known data. Passive automaton learning is a form of supervised learning, since we are given pairs of queries and observations, and asked to fit an optimal automaton structure to them[7]. Since more than one automaton A may fit the known data, the passive learning problem becomes an optimisation problem: how to choose the best model among a set of possible automata according to some criterion, e.g. size.

Passive learning is in some sense a simpler problem than active learning. However, the basic ideas of passive learning can be generalised to develop more interesting active learning algorithms, as we shall see later in this Section. The fundamental situation here is fairly positive. If an SUL has a representation as a finite state Moore automaton A, then the structure of A can be inferred in

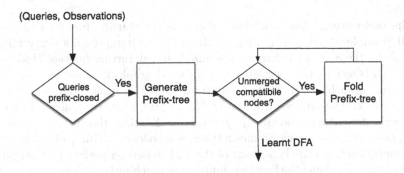

Fig. 7. Illustrating passive learning of Moore machines

---

[7] Here supervised learning is more obvious if we think in terms of regular languages rather than automata. Then we are inferring the language acceptance function L : $\Sigma^* \to \{0, 1\}$ from a finite set of instances. However, the two viewpoints are equivalent by Kleene's Theorem.

finite time from a finite number of queries. Figure 7 summarises the main steps for passive learning of Moore machines which we will explain in the following.

To see this, suppose that we start to systematically enumerate and execute a sequence of queries $\overline{\sigma_1}, \overline{\sigma_2}, \ldots$ on the SUL. For example, we could enumerate all possible input strings in Σ^* up to some maximum size l using the lexicographical ordering. This will produce a corresponding sequence of observations $\overline{\omega_1}, \overline{\omega_2}, \ldots$ from the SUL. Whatever query set is chosen, if it is *prefix closed*, i.e. every prefix of a query is also a query[8], then we can arrange the data set of all queries and responses into an efficient data storage structure termed a *prefix tree*.

Definition 2. *Let Queries $\subseteq \Sigma^*$ be a finite prefix closed set of queries and let Observations $\subseteq \Omega^*$ be the corresponding prefix closed set of observations for an SUL. The **prefix tree** $T(Queries, Observations)$ is the labelled rooted tree*

$$T(Queries, Observations) = (root, Queries, E \subseteq Queries^2, label : Queries \to \Omega)$$

where:

1. *$root = \varepsilon$,*
2. *for each $(\sigma_1, \ldots, \sigma_n) \in Queries$, where $n \geq 1$,*

$$((\sigma_1, \ldots, \sigma_{n-1}), (\sigma_1, \ldots, \sigma_n)) \in E,$$

3. *for each $(\sigma_1, \ldots, \sigma_n) \in Queries$*

$$label(\sigma_1, \ldots, \sigma_n) = \omega_{n+1}$$

where $\omega_1, \ldots, \omega_{n+1} \in Observations$ is the SUL output for $(\sigma_1, \ldots, \sigma_n)$.

Notice that this definition makes sense even if the set *Queries* is infinite, in which case $T(Queries, Observations)$ is a finitely branching infinite tree. In fact, if $|\Sigma| = k$ then $T(Queries, Observations)$ must have a branching degree of at most k.

The prefix tree $T(Queries, Observations)$ is the starting point for constructing all possible automaton models of the SUL, as it represents everything we know about the SUL, assuming we are unable to ask further queries. Notice that although $T(Queries, Observations)$ is a directed graph, it is not necessarily an automaton as such. In any finite prefix tree, if we start from the root and regard its edges as transitions, we eventually "jump off" when we reach a leaf node. However, interestingly enough, if $Queries = \Sigma^*$ then the infinite prefix tree $T(\Sigma^*, Observations)$ *is* an automaton (there are no leaves to jump off). This prefix tree exactly captures the behaviour of the SUL based on perfect (infinite) information about it[9]. Using the fact that finite state machine behaviour is always ultimately periodic, we could try to convert a prefix tree into a finite state machine model of the same data set.

---

[8] This assumption amounts to little more than retaining, i.e. not throwing away, any observational data.

[9] For algebraists, the important fact here is that $T(\Sigma^*, Observations)$ is the *initial object* in the appropriate category of automata and homorphisms, which is unique up to isomorphism. See [46] for details.

The most obvious way to bridge the gap between a prefix tree and an automaton model is to find a general method to *fold* any prefix tree (finite or infinite) into a finite automaton model[10]. The essential idea here is loop identification by searching for finitely or infinitely repeating subtrees in the prefix tree. For finite prefix trees an important *closed world assumption* is at work here. If a loop cannot be shown to not exist, i.e. the loop does not contradict the available data, then we could consistently assume that the loop does exist[11]. In fact, it is precisely this closed world assumption that lends inductive inference to automaton learning. A loop hypothesis is always an inductive inference, i.e. a hypothesis about infinitely many behaviours supported by just finite evidence.

Folding a prefix tree means merging nodes in the tree in such a way that we preserve the subtrees. Figure 8 gives an idea of this for $\Sigma = \{0, 1\}$ and $\Omega = \{a, b\}$. Fig (B) is obtained from the prefix tree in Fig (A) by merging the pair of nodes ε and 0 (giving a loop) and the pair 10 and 11 (giving a path join). Following this, in the second step Fig (C) is obtained from Fig (B) by merging the pair ε and 100 (giving a loop), as well as the pair ε and 101 (giving a loop).

Clearly, after we have merged two nodes $v_1, v_2 \in Queries$ they share all their entry and exit paths afterwards through the merged nodes[12]. Most importantly, if we merge two nodes $v_1, v_2 \in Queries$ which lie on the same path from the root[13], then this always introduces a *loop* or *cycle* into the resulting directed graph. For the result of merging to be well defined, the nodes v_1 and v_2 must be compatible in the following sense.

Definition 3. *Let*

$$T(Queries, Observations) = (root, Queries, E \subseteq Queries^2, label : Queries \rightarrow \Omega)$$

be a prefix tree. A pair of nodes $v_1, v_2 \in Queries$ is said to be **compatible** *if the sub-trees rooted at v_1 and v_2 are consistent with each other, i.e. for every suffix $\overline{s} \in \Sigma^*$, if $v_1.\overline{s} \in Queries$ and $v_2.\overline{s} \in Queries$ then*

$$label(v_1.\overline{s}) = label(v_2.\overline{s}).$$

We write $v_1 \simeq v_2$ if v_1 and v_2 are compatible.

The consistency condition in Definition 3 ensures that if we merge nodes v_1 and v_2 then they do not contradict each other in the resulting merged graph. This is summarised by the fact that for any $\sigma \in \Sigma$ we have[14]:

$$v_1 \simeq v_2 \implies v_1.\sigma \simeq v_2.\sigma \tag{1}$$

---

[10] The fundamental principle of initiality for $T(\Sigma^*, Observations)$ says that such folding is always possible.

[11] For active learning, counterfactual evidence may eventually emerge that destroys the loop hypothesis, but in passive learning this is not possible.

[12] Merging is a little complicated to define graph theoretically, so we leave it to the reader as an exercise!

[13] Then v_1 is a prefix of v_2 or vice versa.

[14] Assuming that $v_1.\sigma, v_2.\sigma \in Queries$.

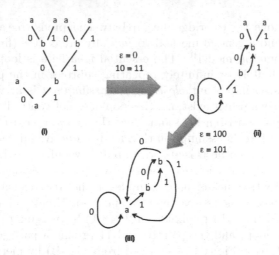

Fig. 8. A prefix tree folded in two steps with four node merges

Compatibility is a necessary condition for merging two nodes v_1 and v_2, since the merged graph must include the information carried in *both* subtrees. However, compatibility is not a sufficient condition to successfully derive an automaton from the prefix tree by folding.

To see this, consider that the compatibility relation $\simeq$, is clearly reflexive i.e. $v \simeq v$ and symmetric i.e. $v_1 \simeq v_2 \rightarrow v_2 \simeq v_1$. However, compatibility is not always transitive, i.e. in general $v_1 \simeq v_2$ and $v_2 \simeq v_3$ do not imply $v_1 \simeq v_3$. This is because in general v_1, v_2 and v_3 will have disjoint subtrees that need not be mutually consistent. Therefore: (i) the order in which we merge subtrees is important, (ii) different merge orders will lead to different (non-isomorphic) automaton models from the same data set, and (iii) some models may be preferable to others (e.g. in terms of size).

We can now express some necessary constraints on subtree folding for prefix trees in terms congruence properties.

Definition 4. *Let*

$$T(Queries, Observations) = (root, Queries, E \subseteq Queries^2, label : Queries \rightarrow \Omega)$$

be a prefix tree.

1. *By a **congruence** on $T(Queries, Observations)$ we mean an equivalence relation $\equiv$ on the set Queries such that for any $\overline{p}, \overline{q} \in$ Queries and any $\sigma \in \Sigma$, if $\overline{p}.\sigma \in$ Queries and $\overline{q}.\sigma \in$ Queries then*

$$\overline{p} \equiv \overline{q} \implies \overline{p}.\sigma \equiv \overline{q}.\sigma.$$

2. *A congruence $\equiv$ is **consistent** if, and only if, for any $\overline{p}, \overline{q} \in$ Queries, if $\overline{p} \equiv \overline{q}$ then $label(\overline{p}) = label(\overline{q})$.*

3. *A congruence $\equiv$ is **closed** if, and only if, for any query $\overline{p} \in$ Queries which is a leaf node in the prefix tree $T(Queries, Observations)$ there exists a non-leaf $\overline{q} \in$ Queries such that*

$$\overline{p} \equiv \overline{q}.$$

Based on the two first items, we can infer that congruence implies compatibility,

$$\overline{p} \equiv \overline{q} \implies \overline{p} \simeq \overline{q}.$$

However, a consistent congruence has stronger properties than compatibility as it is transitive. This means it consistently resolves conflicting node merges. Finally, the closure condition (the third item in Definition 4) rectifies the problem that the leaves of finite prefix trees are not closed under state transitions.

Now given a closed consistent congruence on a prefix tree we can construct a structure that is "almost" an automaton.

Definition 5. *Let*

$$T(Queries, Observations) = (root, Queries, E \subseteq Queries^2, Queries \to \Omega)$$

*be a prefix tree, and let $\equiv$ be a closed consistent congruence on $T(Queries, Observations)$. We define the **quotient structure***

$$T(Queries, Observations)/\equiv$$
$$= (Q, \Sigma, \Omega, q_0, \delta : Q \times \Sigma \twoheadrightarrow Q, \lambda : Q \to \Omega)$$

as follows[15].

1. *For the state set:*

$$Q = \{\overline{p}/\equiv \, : \overline{p}.\sigma \in Queries \text{ for some } \sigma \in \Sigma\}$$

   where $\overline{p}/\equiv$ is the equivalence class of $\overline{p}$ w.r.t. $\equiv$.
2. *For the initial state: $q_0 = \varepsilon/\equiv$,*
3. *For any $\overline{p} \in$ Queries and $\sigma \in \Sigma$, if $\overline{p}.\sigma \in$ Queries then*

$$\delta(\overline{p}/\equiv, \sigma) = \overline{p}.\sigma/\equiv,$$

   otherwise $\delta(\overline{p}/\equiv, \sigma)$ is undefined.
4. *For any $\overline{p}.\sigma \in$ Queries*

$$\lambda(\overline{p}/\equiv) = label(\overline{p}).$$

We meet the above construction many times in automaton learning. It appears again when we study active learning, and in modified forms when learning other types of automaton. The quotient structure defined above is *almost* an

---

[15] Notice here that $\delta : Q \times \Sigma \twoheadrightarrow Q$ is a partial function, i.e. δ is not necessarily defined on all arguments.

automaton, but for one small problem: the query set *Queries* may not contain enough information to define every transition. In this case, the state transition function δ is a partial function that is not defined on every state and input value. When we look into this problem more deeply, we realise that the query set may not even have enough information to define every state! So what kind of guarantee can we give about passive learning?

For the first time in this Chapter, but not the last, we must consider the *correctness problem* for a learning algorithm. Here we view passive learning as essentially a method for the construction of some closed consistent congruence from which we can concretely build an automaton as a quotient structure. Are there necessary and sufficient conditions on the underlying query set, such that passive learning is guaranteed to yield a quotient structure that: (i) is guaranteed to be a fully defined automaton, and (ii) is behaviourally equivalent to the SUL? Surprisingly (when compared with other paradigms of machine learning) complete and correct passive learning can be guaranteed when we have sufficient behavioural information about the SUL.

Definition 6. *Let*

$$A = (Q, \Sigma, \Omega, q_0, \delta : Q \times \Sigma \to Q, \lambda : Q \to \Omega),$$

be a deterministic Moore automaton.

1. *Let $q \in Q$ be any state. By an **access string** for q, we mean any string $\overline{\sigma} \in \Sigma^*$ such that $\delta^*(q_0, \overline{\sigma}) = q$.*
2. *Let $q, q' \in Q$ be any states. By a **distinguishing string** for q and q', we mean any string $\overline{\sigma} \in \Sigma^*$ such that $\lambda(\delta^*(q, \overline{\sigma})) \neq \lambda(\delta^*(q', \overline{\sigma}))$. We say that q and q' are **distinguishable** if there exists a distinguishing string for q and q'.*

For a pair of different states q and q' in A, a distinguishing string $\overline{\sigma}$ is not guaranteed to exist. But it must exist if there is no automaton that is both strictly smaller than A and behaviourally equivalent to A.

Theorem 1. *Correctness Theorem for Passive Learning.*
Suppose that the SUL behaviour can be precisely described by a deterministic Moore automaton,

$$A = (Q, \Sigma, \Omega, q_0, \delta : Q \times \Sigma \to Q, \lambda : Q \to \Omega).$$

Let Queries $\subseteq \Sigma^*$ be a set of queries such that:

1. *For every state $q \in Q$, Queries contains an access string $\overline{\sigma_q} \in \Sigma^*$ for q.*
2. *For every distinguishable pair $q, q' \in Q$ of states, Queries contains both $\overline{\sigma_q}.\overline{\delta}$ and $\overline{\sigma_{q'}}.\overline{\delta}$, where $\overline{\delta} \in \Sigma^*$ is a distinguishing string for q, q'.*
3. *For every state $q \in Q$, and for each input $\sigma \in \Sigma$, Queries contains the query $\overline{\sigma_q}.\sigma$.*

Then for any closed consistent congruence $\equiv$ on $T(Queries, Observations)$ the quotient structure $T(Queries, Observations)/\equiv$ is an automaton that is behaviourally equivalent to A.

Proof. Exercise.

To illustrate the Correctness Theorem 1 for Passive Learning, suppose that we take the final Fig. 8(iii) as the Moore automaton to be learned. Then the prefix tree of Fig. 8(i) satisfies the three properties of Theorem 1. Furthermore, there exists a closed consistent congruence $\equiv$ containing the equivalences (node identifications) $\varepsilon \equiv 0, 10 \equiv 11, \varepsilon \equiv 100$ and $\varepsilon \equiv 101$. Then the resulting quotient automaton derived from Fig. 8(i) using $\equiv$ is isomorphic with Fig. 8(iii). In other words, passive learning applied to Fig. 8(i) successfully gives Fig. 8(iii). It should be obvious that no larger prefix tree than Fig. 8(i) is necessary to learn Fig. 8(iii).

An important point to emphasise here is that in general there are many different congruences $\equiv$ on any specific prefix tree $T(Queries, Observations)$. Different congruences will lead to structurally different (i.e. non-isomorphic) quotient automata. Nevertheless, each quotient automaton $T(Queries, Observations)/\equiv$ will exhibit all of the behaviours observed in the original data set of *Queries* and *Observations*.

From this important observation, we are motivated to further refine model construction by choosing the "best" model according to some principle such as Occam's razor (the principle of parsimony). The best model might be considered to be a minimum state automaton. However [24] has shown that the problem of finding a minimum state DFA compatible with a given dataset is NP Hard. Thus all known algorithms for this problem require exponential time for some inputs.

Considering the fact that there is not usually a single maximum congruence, in general, there are several maximal[16] congruences and it is natural to choose from among these. Other criteria can be used to refine this choice.

One additional criterion is known as the *evidence driven approach*. Here we successively merge node pairs v_1, v_2 for which the compatibility evidence is greatest. This corresponds to choosing the largest possible subtrees, which have the greatest power to refute a merge. It also corresponds intuitively to making the least controversial hypotheses about the structure of the SUL. Algorithms based on this approach have performed well in benchmarking studies [38].

Obviously, passive automaton learning converges as a finite model construction from a fixed finite data set, when correctly implemented. Notice however, that in terms of query set size, Theorem 1 implies that passive automaton learning also converges in the limit. For once we have accumulated enough access strings, single input extensions to these, and distinguishing strings, then further querying cannot destroy any of these conditions.

Now the only question remains, short of exhaustive querying, how can we compile a set of queries that satisfies Conditions 1, 2 and 3 of Theorem 1, and how can we build the appropriate congruence $\equiv$? This question is best answered by the subject of active automaton learning, which we consider next.

---

[16] In a lattice, $(A, \leq)$ a maximum element exceeds all others while a maximal element is exceeded by none. Thus a maximum element must be unique, while a maximal element need not be.

3.1.3   Active Automaton Learning

In passive automaton learning we are given a dataset of queries and observations about the SUL and asked to construct an automaton model which best fits this dataset. The accuracy of any model will be limited by the number of queries in the dataset. Theorem 1 even suggests that we will obtain a behaviourally incomplete model of the SUL if key queries are missing from the dataset.

In active automaton learning, these problems can be circumvented since the training regime is more liberal. Active learning means that at any time in the learning process we can supplement the existing dataset by asking new queries which the SUL must answer. This also means we can focus on heuristics for active query generation that could speed up the learning process. From the study of active learning, it becomes clear that neither exhaustive nor random querying are good heuristics, since both methods generate many redundant queries.

Active automaton learning is again a form of supervised learning, since query and observation pairs are involved. Many active automaton learning algorithms have been published in the literature. Useful surveys include [9,28,68]. In this section, we will look at a well-known and widely used active learning algorithm L* originating[17] in [6]. This algorithm works quite well on small examples, though it can generate an excessive number of queries on larger case studies. Nevertheless, it is easy to understand and implement, while it involves similar principles to those used in more efficient algorithms. Under the assumption that we can efficiently detect differences between the learned automaton and the SUL, the L* algorithm can be mathematically proven to completely learn an automaton in polynomial time. One can even prove that L* constructs the unique minimum state automaton that is behaviourally equivalent to the SUL, which is in itself a useful property[18].

We begin by clarifying the experimental protocol for active learning. If there is a way to bring the SUL back to its initial state q_0 after each individual query $\overline{\sigma_i}$ then the SUL is said to satisfy the *reset assumption*. This assumption allows us to isolate the effects of each query from the next. Without the reset assumption, in black-box learning we have no way of knowing what state the SUL is left in after it processes query $\overline{\sigma_i}$. This unknown SUL state becomes the new initial state for processing the next query $\overline{\sigma_{i+1}}$. Thus, to query the SUL without the reset assumption is effectively to query it using one single long query. Learning algorithms exist (see the Chapter by Groz *et al.* [54]) that do not require the reset assumption. However, such algorithms tend to be complex. For applying L*, and many other active automaton learning algorithms, we assume that the reset assumption holds.

---

[17] We actually present a simple generalisation of L* to an arbitrary output alphabet Ω. This algorithm is termed L*Mealy and first appeared in [34] where it was applied to Mealy machines.

[18] Minimum state size seems to be a natural result of many active learning algorithms for Moore automata. This seems to be due to the difficulty of distinguishing pairs of states without any concrete evidence.

The basic idea of all active automaton learning algorithms is to find a way to identify *incompleteness* in a dataset. By an incomplete dataset, we mean a dataset of queries and observations that does not allow us to unambiguously infer a behaviourally equivalent SUL model. If a specific incompleteness can be identified in the dataset then this can be used to actively generate a new query. Executing this query on the SUL will then bring the entire dataset somewhat closer to completeness. By iterating this process of identifying and resolving dataset incompleteness (hopefully) eventually learning will be complete.

For many active automaton learning algorithms, a mathematical analysis can be used to show that learning will always eventually terminate yielding a behaviourally equivalent automaton model. Such a result is called a *convergence theorem* for the learning algorithm in question. Active automaton learning is rather rich both in algorithms and in convergence theorems. This can be contrasted with other branches of ML where convergence cannot always be guaranteed, e.g. deep learning. On the other hand, the datasets necessary to achieve complete learning may be infeasibly large. Good methods for approximate learning are an important open problem.

The L* algorithm has its own specific active querying heuristics. For L*, incompleteness is divided into two kinds: (i) incompleteness due to not being able to immediately generate a model, and (ii) incompleteness due to lacking a full set of queries (access and distinguishing strings) for the SUL. While type (ii) incompleteness is very intuitive, type (i) incompleteness is rather technical, and will be further broken down into more detailed requirements.

A good starting point for presenting L* is to define the underlying data structure used to identify type (i) incompleteness in the query set. This is more complex than the prefix tree (Definition 2) we saw earlier in passive learning. However, it is not unrelated in content.

Suppose that $Queries \subseteq \Sigma^*$ and $Observations \subseteq \Omega^*$ are the current dataset of queries and observations of the SUL. The main data structure for L* is a two dimensional table T. The table entries in T are output values from Ω. The table rows and columns are indexed by strings over Σ^*. However, the table T is allowed to expand dynamically over time, as we incrementally learn the SUL using new queries. One difficulty in presenting the L* algorithm is to explain this expansion process for T.

At any stage in the execution of L*, there are three distinguished table indexing sets:

- a set $Prefixes_{Red} \subseteq \Sigma^*$ of *red prefixes* which is a prefix-closed set of input strings,
- a set $Prefixes_{Blue} = Prefixes_{Red}.\Sigma$ of *blue prefixes* which is a prefix-closed set of input strings that extends each red prefix with one extra input symbol (chosen over all possible input symbols in Σ),
- a set $Suffixes \subseteq \Sigma^*$ which is a suffix-closed set of input strings.

We follow a common pedagogy here of distinguishing between *red* and *blue pre-fixes*[19]. The rows of T are indexed by red and blue prefixes from the set

$$Prefixes_{Red} \cup Prefixes_{Blue},$$

and the columns of T are indexed by suffixes from the set *Suffixes*.

How are SUL output values stored as table entries of T? Let us write $T[\overline{p}, \overline{s}]$ for the table entry of T in row $\overline{p}$ and column $\overline{s}$. We can concatenate prefix $\overline{p}$ with suffix $\overline{s}$ yielding the query string

$$\overline{p}.\overline{s} = p_1, \ldots, p_i, s_1, \ldots, s_j.$$

Now the behaviour of the SUL on $\overline{p}.\overline{s}$ will already be known if $\overline{p}.\overline{s}$ is a prefix of some $q \in Queries$. In this case we have a recorded SUL observation $\overline{\omega} = \omega_0, \ldots, \omega_{i+j}$ corresponding to $\overline{p}.\overline{s}$. In particular, we know the value of

$$\omega_{i+j} = \lambda(\delta^*(q_0, \overline{p}.\overline{s}))$$

(where δ^* is the iterated state transition function defined above) and this value ω_{i+j} is placed in the table entry $T[\overline{p}, \overline{s}]$.

Suppose on the other hand that $\overline{p}.\overline{s}$ is not currently a member of $Queries$. Then we can query the SUL using $\overline{p}.\overline{s}$ as an active query and observe the value of $\omega_{i+j} = \lambda(\delta^*(q_0, \overline{p}.\overline{s}))$. This value is placed in the table at $T[\overline{p}, \overline{s}]$. Thus, the most basic form of active querying in L* comes from filling in missing entries in the two dimensional table T. We call these *table-entry queries*.

The basic principle for inferring a Moore automaton from a completely filled-in two dimensional table T is as follows: if $T[\overline{p}, \overline{s}] \neq T[\overline{q}, \overline{s}]$, for some suffix $\overline{s}$ then the input strings $\overline{p}$ and $\overline{q}$ cannot possibly reach the same state in the SUL, provided that the SUL is deterministic[20]. In other words, the subtrees at $\overline{p}$ and $\overline{q}$ in the corresponding prefix tree (having the same query content as T) are incompatible.

It follows that if any two rows in T differ at all, say $T[\overline{p}] \neq T[\overline{q}]$ then $\overline{p}$ and $\overline{q}$ must access distinct states in the SUL. Therefore, we can partition the red prefix set $Prefixes_{Red}$ into equivalence classes of row-identical red prefixes using T. As a concrete representative of each equivalence class, typically the shortest access string is chosen as a state name.

Table-entry queries are the primary source of type (i) queries. But how is it that gaps ever arise in the table T? This is due to the already hinted expansion of T that takes place during the learning process. To be able to directly and unambiguously construct an automaton model from T, the structure of T must satisfy two very specific technical properties.

---

[19] In model construction, red prefixes are needed to represent states, while blue prefixes are needed for defining transitions. According to our definition, a prefix can be both red and blue, but this is not problematic.

[20] What to do when the SUL is non-deterministic will be discussed later.

Definition 7. *Let*

$$T : Prefixes_{Red} \cup Prefixes_{Blue} \times Suffixes \to \Omega$$

be a two dimensional table.

*(i) We say that T is **closed** if for each red prefix $\overline{p} \in Prefixes_{Red}$ and input $\sigma \in \Sigma$ there exists a red prefix $\overline{q} \in Prefixes_{Red}$ such that the rows $T[\overline{p}.\sigma]$ and $T[\overline{q}]$ in T are identical, i.e. $T[\overline{p}.\sigma] = T[\overline{q}]$.*

*(ii) We say that T is **consistent** if for any red prefixes $\overline{p}, \overline{q} \in Prefixes_{Red}$, if $T[\overline{p}] = T[\overline{q}]$ then for all inputs $\sigma \in \Sigma$ we have $T[\overline{p}.\sigma] = T[\overline{q}.\sigma]$[21].*

Notice that blue prefixes are necessary in both Definition 7(i) and (ii) since even if a prefix $\overline{p}$ is red, the prefix $\overline{p}.\sigma$ may be blue. This technical need for closure and consistency in T leads to two different sub-algorithms for generating active queries from T as follows.

ALGORITHM 1. makeConsistent()

```
1 find p̄,q̄ ∈ Prefixes_Red, σ ∈ Σ
2 and s̄ ∈ Suffixes such that
3 T(p̄) = T(q̄) and
4 T(p̄.σ, s̄) ≠ T(q̄.σ, s̄)
5 let Suffixes:= Suffixes ∪ {σ.s̄} // suffix set extension
6 extend T to Prefixes_Red ∪ Prefixes_Blue × Suffixes
7 using table-entry queries.
```

ALGORITHM 2. makeClosed()

```
1 find p̄ ∈ Prefixes_Red and σ ∈ Σ such that
2 T(p̄.σ) ≠ T(q̄) for all q̄ ∈ Prefixes_Red
3 let Prefixes_Red := Prefixes_Red ∪ {p̄.σ} // red prefix set extension
4 let Prefixes_Blue := Prefixes_Blue ∪ {p̄.σ} × Σ // blue prefix set extension
5 extend T to Prefixes_Red ∪ Prefixes_Blue × Suffixes
6 using table-entry queries
```

Using the concepts of closure and consistency, we can now make precise the basic iteration step in L* for learning a new automaton model M_{n+1}, given that we have previously learned M_n.

---

[21] For the reader familiar with algebra, condition (i) corresponds to an algebraic closure condition on the red prefix set under the operation of appending an input $\sigma \in \Sigma$ and modulo row equivalence. The closure condition (ii) corresponds to row equivalence being a congruence on the red prefix set with respect to the state transition function δ. Thus the red prefix set is able to provide a state set for a quotient automaton defined by the table T.

ALGORITHM 3. getNextHypothesis($equivalenceQuery \in \Sigma^*$)

---

1 $Prefixes_{Red} := Prefixes_{Red} \cup PrefixClosure(equivalenceQuery)$
2 $Prefixes_{Blue} := Prefixes_{Blue} \cup \{equivalenceQuery\} \times \Sigma$
3 $Suffixes := Suffixes \cup suffixClosure(equivalenceQuery)$
4 **extend** T to $Prefixes_{Red} \cup Prefixes_{Blue} \times Suffixes$
5 **using table-entry queries**
6
7 **while** T is not closed or T is not consistent **do**
8 **if** !consistent(T) makeConsistent()
9 **else if** !closed(T) makeClosed()

The routine `getNextHypothesis()` adds a single new query *equivalenceQuery* to the existing query set and extends the table T with the appropriate new red and blue prefixes and suffixes derived from *equivalenceQuery*. All new entries in the resulting expanded table T are filled in by table-entry queries. Following this, the structure of the newly expanded table T is analysed for failure of closure or consistency. The remedial measures `makeClosed()` and `makeConsistent()` may further expand the table T. Note that if the SUL is behaviourally equivalent to an automaton then the while loop in `getNextHypothesis()` will eventually terminate. Upon termination, i.e. when T is both closed and consistent, then the construction of model M_{n+1} can be carried out with the following routine.

ALGORITHM 4. mooreSynthesis()

---

1 // Choose state representatives as smallest red prefixes
2 $Q = \{\overline{p} \in Prefixes_{Red} : \forall \overline{q} \in Prefixes_{Red}, \overline{q} < \overline{p} \rightarrow T[\overline{p}] \neq T[\overline{q}]\}$
3 $q_0 = \varepsilon$
4 **foreach** $\overline{p} \in Q$, $\lambda(\overline{p}) = T[\overline{p}, \varepsilon]$
5 **foreach** $\overline{p} \in Q$ **do**
6 **foreach** $\sigma \in \Sigma$ **do**
7 $\delta(\overline{p}, \sigma) = \overline{q}$ if $\overline{q} \in Q$ and $T[\overline{p}.\sigma] = T[\overline{q}]$
8 **return** $A = (Q, \Sigma, q_0, \delta, \lambda)$

This algorithm may be compared with the quotient automaton construction of Definition 5 which it makes more concrete.

As already observed, red prefixes form the basis for the state set Q of M_{n+1}. In Algorithm 4, the first member $\overline{p}$ of each red prefix equivalence class under some linear ordering[22] $<$ is chosen to be the state representative. Note that the empty string ε will always be a red prefix, but needs to be the least member of its

---

[22] For example, the short-lex ordering $<$ on Σ^* is suitable. Here $\overline{\sigma} < \overline{\sigma}'$ if $|\overline{\sigma}| < |\overline{\sigma}'|$. If $|\overline{\sigma}| = |\overline{\sigma}'| = n$ then $\overline{\sigma} < \overline{\sigma}'$ if, and only if $\overline{\sigma} < \overline{\sigma}'$ in the lexicographical ordering on Σ^n.

equivalence class $[\varepsilon]$. Then ε is the appropriate access string for the initial state q_0 in M_{n+1}. It is easy to see that $\lambda : Q \to \Omega$ is mathematically well defined as a function. The reader should observe how the closure and consistency conditions on T ensure that the state transition map δ is also mathematically well defined.

- For each red prefix $\bar{p} \in Q$ and input $\sigma \in \Sigma$ there exists red prefix $\bar{q} \in Q$ that is row equivalent to the (possibly blue) prefix $\bar{p}.\sigma$ by closure of T. Thus the value of $\delta(\bar{p}, \sigma)$ is *defined*.
- By consistency of T, the row $T[\bar{p}.\sigma]$ and hence the value of $\delta(\bar{p}, \sigma)$ is *uniquely* defined.

We can construct the initial hypothesis automaton M_0, in the sequence of models $M_0, M_1, \ldots$, by calling `getNextHypothesis()` on the empty string as follows.

ALGORITHM 5. getInitialHypothesis()

---

1   $Prefixes_{Red} := \emptyset$ // emptyset
2   $Prefixes_{Blue} := \emptyset$
3   $Suffixes := \emptyset$
4   `return getNextHypothesis(` ε `)`

Finally, we can describe the complete L* algorithm. This algorithm combines `getInitialHypothesis()` with `getNextHypothesis()` and a stopping criterion for iterative model generation $M_0, M_1, \ldots$ based on *equivalence checking*. This equivalence checking of each learned model M_i with the SUL is the source of the active type (ii) queries mentioned previously.

The algorithm above assumes that L* has access to the SUL. This access is represented here as an algorithm parameter. The L* algorithm makes an initial call to `getInitialHypothesis()` to construct M_0 followed by a sequence of calls `getNextHypothesis`($equivalenceQuery_i$) in a `while` loop, for $i = 1, \ldots, n$. Together, these calls generate a sequence of hypothesis automata $M_0, M_1, \ldots M_n$.

The `while` loop is controlled by comparing each model M_i for behavioural equivalence with the SUL, returning the truth value *equivOracle().equivalent*. By definition, M_i and the SUL are behaviourally equivalent if, and only if, they give the same output sequence $\bar{\omega}$ on every input sequence $\bar{p}$. Thus if M_i and the SUL are *non-equivalent* then there must exist at least one input sequence $\bar{p}$ such that M_i and the SUL give different output sequences on $\bar{p}$. In that case *equivOracle().equivalenceQuery* returns such an input sequence, and this is taken as a new type (ii) query that drives the next iteration `getNextHypothesis`($equivalenceQuery_i$).

ALGORITHM 6. LStar(SUL)

```
1  var Prefixes_Red
2  var Prefixes_Blue
3  var Suffixes
4  var T : Prefixes_Red ∪ Prefixes_Blue × Suffixes → Ω  // table
5  var A
6  A := getInitialHypothesis()
7  while( !equivOracle(A, SUL).equivalent) do
8      A := getNextHypothesis(equivOracle(A, SUL).equivalenceQuery)
9  endwhile
10 return A
```

The desired behaviour of the equivalence oracle is specified as follows.

Definition 8. *Given two parameters consisting of a Moore automaton A and a system under learning SUL, an equivalence oracle on A and SUL returns two parameters: equivalent ∈ {true, false} and equivalenceQuery ∈ Σ*.*

1. *For the return parameter equivalent:*

$$equivalenceOracle(A, SUL).equivalent = \begin{cases} true & if \ \forall \overline{p} \in \Sigma^* \ A(\overline{p}) = SUL(\overline{p}) \\ false & otherwise \end{cases} \tag{2}$$

2. *For the return parameter equivalenceQuery:*

$$equivalenceOracle(A, SUL).equivalenceQuery = \begin{cases} \overline{p} & if \ A(\overline{p}) \neq SUL(\overline{p}) \\ null & otherwise \end{cases} \tag{3}$$

Designing an implementation of an equivalence oracle can be somewhat problematic. Firstly, the SUL is a black-box, so there is no direct way to compare its internal structure with the state transition structure of M_i. Black-box equivalence checking algorithms, that are independent of the internal structure of the SUL are for example the Vassilevsky-Chow algorithm [15,62]. Another approach is to use *stochastic equivalence checking*, (see e.g. [6]) based on a random sample of input sequences. Here the challenge is to identify an appropriate sample size and length bound for the random input string set. Stochastic equivalence checking might seem like machine learning using random queries, and in some sense this is true. However, the percentage of random queries in the overall query set will be very small, usually less than 1%. An advantage of stochastic equivalence checking is its connection to the PAC learning paradigm cited previously [61].

We conclude this section with a worked example of L* in action, to see how the various concepts fit together. Suppose that we wish to learn the simple DFA presented in Fig. 9. Now Table 1 depicts the very first table produced by L* through its single call to `getInitialHypothesis()`. We separate the red prefixes above from the blue prefixes below by inserting a horizontal space in between, e.g. in Table 1, ε is red while 0 and 1 are blue. Now Table 1 is consistent,

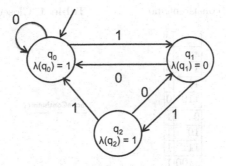

Fig. 9. Simple DFA for learning

Table 1. Closed: no, consistent: yes

Table 2. Closed: yes, consistent: yes

getInitialHypothesis( )
$\longrightarrow$

	ε
ε	1
0	1
1	0

makeClosed( )
$\longrightarrow$

	ε
ε	1
1	0
0	1
10	1
11	1

but not closed. A single call to `makeClosed()` produces Table 2 which is both closed and consistent. At this point, the initial model M_0 can be constructed by a call to `mooreSynthesis()`.

The initial model M_0 is depicted in Fig. 10. Clearly, this model replicates some but not all of the behaviour of the DFA in Fig. 9. A call to the equivalence oracle gives the following results:

$$equivalenceOracle(M_0, SUL).equivalent = false,$$

$$equivalenceOracle(M_0, SUL).equivalenceQuery = 110.$$

Adding the equivalence query 110 to Table 2 by calling `getNextHypothesis` (110) gives Table 3.

mooreSynthesis( )
$\longrightarrow$

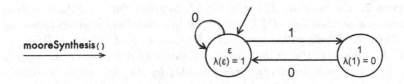

Fig. 10. M_0, the initial hypothesis model

Table 3. Closed: yes, consistent: no

	ε
ε	1
1	0
11	1
110	0
0	1
10	1
111	1
1100	1
1101	1

getNextHypothesis(110) $\longrightarrow$

makeConsistent() $\longrightarrow$

Table 4. Closed: yes, consistent: yes

	ε	0	1
ε	1	1	0
1	0	1	1
11	1	0	1
110	0	1	1
0	1	1	0
10	1	1	0
111	1	1	0
1100	1	1	0
1101	1	0	1

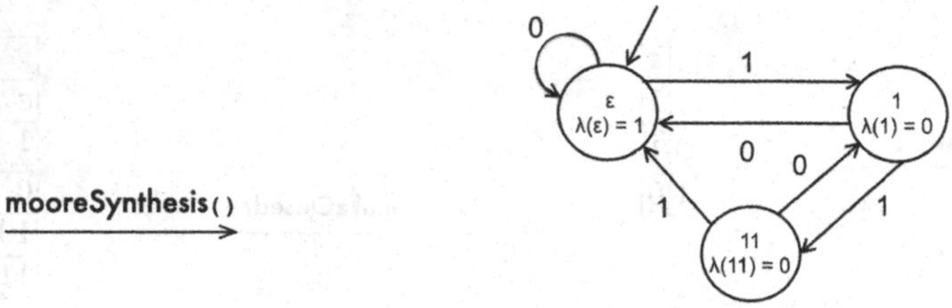

mooreSynthesis() $\longrightarrow$

Fig. 11. M_1, the second hypothesis model

Table 3 is closed, but there are two inconsistencies, since $T(\varepsilon) = T(11)$ but (1) $T(1) \neq T(111)$, and (2) $T(0) \neq T(110)$. So after two separate calls to makeConsistent(), we obtain Table 4.

Now Table 4 is closed and consistent, so the next model M_1 can be constructed by another call to mooreSynthesis() and is depicted in Fig. 11. Notice that in Table 4 there are four red prefixes, but two of these, 1 and 110, are row equivalent. Therefore, model M_1 has just three distinct states.

Now M_1 is structurally isomorphic with, and therefore behaviourally equivalent to, the SUL in Fig. 9. According to the theory of L*, structural isomorphism implies that Fig. 9 was a minimum state DFA to begin with.

A convergence result (i.e. a statement of both correctness and termination) for the L* learning algorithm is the following.

Theorem 2. *Convergence Theorem for L*. Suppose that the SUL behaviour can be precisely described by a DFA and let A be a minimal representation of this DFA. Then the L* algorithm eventually terminates and outputs a DFA isomorphic to A. Moreover, if n is the number of states of A and m is an upper bound on the length of any counterexample provided by the equivalence checker, then the total running time of L* is bounded by a polynomial in m and n.*

Proof. See [6].

We end this section with an important observation about both passive and active learning of deterministic finite state machines. Our theoretical exposition and the case study above both reveal the important fact that every feature of the final learned model M_i is *traceable* back to behaviours of the SUL. Therefore they can be reproduced and independently confirmed even after the learning session has terminated. This fact will be important in the future for software engineering applications, where traceability between conclusions and their evidence may be legally required, e.g. by certification processes such as ISO 26262 [1].

One reason for traceability in automaton learning is the absence (for better or worse) of any statistical learning methods, which smooth the dataset. Said simply: *what you get is what you see* (WYGIWYS). Another reason for traceability is the explicit state space structure and construction of the model M. There are other ML techniques which can also learn temporal behaviours, for example, recurrent and deep neural networks. However, for software engineering, such algorithms may be problematic in the sense that they lack traceability between the learned model and the original SUL.

3.2 Non-deterministic Finite State Machines

In the context of software engineering, given an arbitrary black-box SUL, it may be difficult to be certain that its behaviour is entirely deterministic. On the contrary, for many large-scale distributed systems that we would like to model, we can often be confident of extensive non-deterministic behaviour. The ML models and methods of Sect. 3.1 have a restricted value in this case. For example, L*, as we have described it, would record the first observed behaviour of a non-deterministic SUL in the table T and simply ignore later alternative behaviours. This yields a partial model that will lack any alternative behaviours. Clearly, it would be appropriate here to learn a more general non-deterministic automaton model.

Definition 9. *By a **non-deterministic Moore automaton** we mean a structure*

$$A = (Q, \Sigma, \Omega, q_0, \delta : Q \times \Sigma \times Q, \lambda : Q \to \Omega),$$

where: $Q = \{q_1, \ldots q_n\}$ *is a set of states,* $q_0 \in Q$ *is the initial state,* $\Sigma = \{\sigma_1, \ldots, \sigma_k\}$ *is a finite set of input values,* $\Omega = \{\omega_1, \ldots, \omega_{k'}\}$ *is a finite set of output values,* $\delta : Q \times \Sigma \times Q$ *is the state transition relation, and* $\lambda : Q \to \Omega$ *is the output function.*

The main difference in Definition 9 compared with Definition 1 of Sect. 3.1.3 is that the state transition *relation* δ allows us to capture each of the multiple states $q' \in Q$ to which A can transition from any given state $q \in Q$ under the same input $\sigma \in \Sigma$.

Non-deterministic automata models have been widely studied in the literature (see e.g. [30]), and have their own theory which is distinctively different from the deterministic case. For example, while every DFA has a unique minimum state representation, this property does not hold for NDFA.

There are advantages to learning non-deterministic automata. Obviously, they can give a more faithful representation of a non-deterministic SUL. However, even where the SUL is deterministic, an NDFA representation can be exponentially more succinct than a DFA representation [12].

There are also some difficulties associated with learning non-deterministic automata. It may be difficult to induce an SUL to exhibit every one of its alternative behaviours in practise. Some alternatives may be statistically very rare. This brings us to a more advanced modelling question: how can we model the probability of SUL behaviours? We discuss this question further in Sect. 3.3.

One simplistic approach to learning non-deterministic automata is to represent them as set-valued deterministic automata, where the non-deterministic choice of output is captured by a set-valued output function $\lambda : Q \to \wp(\Omega)$. In this case, we can generalise the L* algorithm (c.f. Algorithm 6) to allow the table entries to be set-valued. Then a table entry

$$T[\overline{p}, \overline{s}] = \{\omega_1, \ldots, \omega_i\}$$

gives the set of all known observations of the SUL for the input sequence $\overline{p}.\overline{s}$. This approach is easy to implement, and can suffice for some behavioural analyses of the SUL. However, it fails to completely capture the transition behaviour of the SUL. It also lacks the succinctness properties of NDFA representation.

There are several rather complex proposals in the literature for representing a non-deterministic SUL as true non-deterministic automaton. An important contribution was [16] which introduced the idea of residual finite state automata (RSFA) which are a subclass of NDFA having some similar properties to DFA. Subsequently [17] presented a passive learning algorithm for RSFA which can achieve exponential state space reduction without losing canonical minimum state models. In [12], the NL* algorithm was presented as an active automaton learning algorithm for RSFA that generalises the L* algorithm. A survey of learning for DFAs using representations as non-deterministic automata is [21].

3.3   Probabilistic Automata

We continue with the problem of modelling and learning non-deterministic SUL behaviour. A quantitative approach to non-determinism, via probabilities, is possible when the distributions involved are stationary, i.e. time invariant. In fact, even for a deterministic SUL, it may be interesting to apply probability values to model the frequency of different input patterns or user behaviours. There are a variety of state machine models that include probability values, including: *labelled Markov chains*, *labelled Markov decision processes* and *continuous-time Markov chains*.

One of the earliest contributions to learning probabilistic models of computation was the ALERGIA algorithm of [13]. This algorithm was designed to infer probabilistic finite automata having the following model structure.

Definition 10. *By a **probabilistic finite automaton** (PFA) we mean a structure*

$$A = (Q, \Sigma, I, F, \delta),$$

defined as follows.

1. $Q = \{q_1, \ldots q_n\}$ *is a finite set of states.*
2. $\Sigma = \{\sigma_1, \ldots, \sigma_k\}$ *is a finite set of input values.*
3. $I : Q \rightarrow [0, 1]$ *is the initial state probability distribution which satisfies* $\Sigma_{q \in Q} I(q) = 1$.
4. $F : Q \rightarrow [0, 1]$ *defines the termination probabilities.*
5. $\delta : Q \times \Sigma \times Q \rightarrow [0, 1]$ *is the transition probability function, which satisfies for each* $q \in Q$:

$$F(q) + \Sigma_{\sigma \in \Sigma, q' \in Q}\, \delta(q, \sigma, q') = 1.$$

One can determinise this PFA model as follows.

Definition 11. *A PFA is **deterministic** (a DPFA) if there exists a state $q \in Q$ such that $I(q) = 1$ and for each $q \in Q$ and $\sigma \in \Sigma$ there exists at most one $q' \in Q$ such that $\delta(q, \sigma, q') > 0$.*

*A **deterministic frequency finite automaton** (DFFA) is the same as a DPFA except that probabilities are replaced by frequencies, i.e. integer values.*

Clearly a DPFA can be derived from a DFFA by normalisation of the frequency values. PFA combine the non-deterministic automaton model of Sect. 3.2 with probability values. The transition probability function δ of a PFA encodes the probability of taking a non-deterministic transition (q, σ, q'). As a complementary concept to δ, termination probabilities are used to assign the probability that an input sequence will terminate at a particular state. DPFA combine the more restricted deterministic automaton model of Sect. 3.1 with probability values. The relative frequency interpretation of probability theory is appropriate in a machine learning context. For this reason, DFFA can provide a model that is closer to the original observation set, as we shall see below.

The ALERGIA algorithm is a passive automaton learning algorithm that works by merging compatible nodes in a frequency prefix tree acceptor (FPTA) (c.f. Definition 2 of Sect. 3.1.2) as follows. Let S be any multiset[23] of strings over Σ. Then $|S|$ denotes the size of S, $|S|_{\overline{\sigma}}$ denotes the number of instances of string $\overline{\sigma}$ in S, and $|S|_{pref(\overline{\sigma})}$ denotes the number of instances of strings in S with prefix $\overline{\sigma}$.

Definition 12. *Let S be a prefix-closed multiset of strings over Σ. The **deterministic FPTA representation** of S is the DFFA*

$$F(S) = (Q, \Sigma, I, F, \delta)$$

---

[23] Notice that it is necessary to use a multiset of observations, i.e. to repeat previous SUL experiments, in order to establish frequencies and probabilities. Thus the cost of learning a probabilistic automaton may be quite high in terms of the query count.

where:

$$Q = \{\overline{p} : \overline{p} \text{ is a prefix of some } \overline{q} \in S\}$$

$$I(\varepsilon) = |S|$$

$$F(\overline{\sigma}) = |S_{\overline{\sigma}}|$$

$$\delta(\overline{p}, \sigma, q_{\overline{p}}.\sigma) = |S_{pref(\overline{p}.\sigma)}|$$

In ALERGIA, starting from the FPTA $F(S)$ for a given multiset S of observations, we merge nodes to derive a DFFA. A perennial theme of Sect. 3.1 was that strings which are observationally indistinguishable belong in the same equivalence class. Each such class identifies a distinct state in the learned automaton. In ALERGIA, we relax the distinguishability test on strings somewhat to allow for an error bound on the observation set S. Thus in ALERGIA, different FPTA nodes may be merged to the same state provided they are *statistically compatible*. For two nodes v_1 and v_2 in the FPTA, statistical compatibility means all comparable features of these nodes satisfy a Hoeffding inequality on their relative frequencies f_1/n_1 and f_2/n_2 up to a specified error bound ϵ:

$$\left| \frac{f_1}{n_1} - \frac{f_2}{n_2} \right| < \left(\sqrt{\frac{1}{n_1}} + \sqrt{\frac{1}{n_2}} \right) \cdot \sqrt{\frac{1}{2} \ln \frac{2}{\epsilon}}$$

There are three types of comparable features in the subtrees of v_1 and v_2 that must satisfy the Hoeffding bound: (i) the termination frequencies $F(v_1)$ and $F(v_2)$ of v_1 and v_2, (ii) the transition frequencies $\delta(v_1, \sigma)$ and $\delta(v_2, \sigma)$ for v_1 and v_2 on each input value $\sigma \in \Sigma$ and (iii) the same comparable features for all corresponding states in the subtrees of $F(S)$ starting at v_1 and v_2, (a recursive check). The error bound ϵ can be decreased, leading to a larger learned model where more states are identified, or it can be increased, leading to a smaller model.

PFA, DPFA and DFFA are intended to model input-driven transitions only. The generalisation to include an output set Ω and output function λ is straightforward, but omitted here for reasons of space.

Theorem 3. *Convergence Theorem for ALERGIA. Algorithm ALERGIA identifies a DPFA in the limit with probability one and runs in time polynomial in $|S|$.*

Proof. See [28].

There exist a number of variants of ALERGIA such as [55,59]. An active automaton learning algorithm AALERGIA based on ALERGIA can be found in [40].

3.4   Other Types of Computational Model

Timed Automata. Timed automata [5] are a generalisation of deterministic finite automata that allow one to model time bounds on the transitions of an automaton by means of clocks. Such clocks can be set, reset and expire to model complex temporal behaviour. Timed automata are particularly useful in the analysis of real-time embedded systems. However, the problem of learning timed automata is in general significantly harder than the problem of learning a finite state automaton. Early results in [25] suggested that the problem of learning timed automata was an exponential time problem. However later attempts at efficient learning algorithms showed that polynomial time learning was possible, at least for certain restricted classes [63].

Hybrid Automata. Hybrid automata [4] are an approach to combine discrete and continuous state transitions into one automaton model. This is achieved by using differential equations to model continuous state transitions. Hybrid automata models have proven useful for modelling cyber-physical systems, including control algorithms. Since timed automata can be modeled as hybrid automata, the learning problem for hybrid automata is at least as difficult as the learning problem for timed automaton. There have been some attempts to define learning algorithms for restricted forms of hybrid automata for example: [26,51] and [42].

Register Automata. Register automata were introduced in [14] as a means of generalising finite automata to deal with simple forms of symbolic or abstract data types. This means allowing for an input alphabet that can include simple function calls or data expressions such as push(a,s) or pop(s).

A register automaton has a finite set of registers which can be assigned using such data expressions. A guard for a state transition is a Boolean expression built up from equations and inequations about register values. A state transition between two labelled states of a register automaton is enabled when its source state is occupied and its guard becomes true, at which point its associated register assignments are carried out, and its target state is reached.

Learning algorithms for register automata have been introduced in [32] that are capable of learning the behaviour of implementations of many abstract data types such as stacks, queues, bags etc. A survey of recent results on register automaton learning can be found in the Chapter by Howar and Steffen [19].

Learning Logic Formulas. At first sight, formulas in logical languages such as predicate and temporal logics seem to have little in common with models of computation. However, fragments of these logical languages are often executable by using efficient computational theorem proving techniques such as resolution. Such fragments are therefore capable of expressing algorithms. Accordingly, some ML researchers have looked at the problem of inferring logical formulas, for example Horn formulas [7,8], Prolog programs [57] and temporal logic formulas, see the Chapter by Alrajeh and Russo [3] of this Book.

Learning Term Rewriting Systems. Term rewriting systems (TRS) can be seen as a special case of logic formulas. They represent an efficient computational logic for first-order equations. Since arbitrary recursive functions can be encoded as term rewriting systems, the intractability results of [23] apply in the general case. However, for string rewriting systems as a special case there are some positive results, e.g. [18,46].

3.5 Summary

In this Section we have presented fundamental theoretical concepts, data structures, and basic algorithms for learning a variety of models of computation. These were mostly organised around the extended concept of a state machine model. We have shown how a sequence of increasingly structured and complex model classes, leads to learning problems which are increasingly more difficult. Indeed for the most general case of learning recursive functions, we again remind the reader of the intractability result [24].

Nevertheless, in the literature on applications of machine learning to software analysis there are already significant success stories. It is to such applications that we now turn.

4   Applications and Examples

4.1   Model Extraction

There is a prevalent need for models in software engineering, whether for verification, testing, component integration, or documentation. In the context of modern software engineering methods, we consider model construction to be a long-term task of continuously integrating new information, and identifying and discarding outdated information. This can come from a sequence of software revisions, or from a dynamic component-based software environment.

Traditionally, models were produced during the early design stages of a project. However, in modern development methods, product inception itself is a continuous and ongoing activity. In either case, traditional or modern, software projects rarely have models available in practice. Therefore, in software analysis, research has been initiated towards automatically creating or reverse engineering models from other available artefacts.

Models can play multiple roles in software engineering. They can be used for software documentation or to capture specific aspects of the behaviour of software, in order to be used for different types of software analysis. They are abstractions of a software system, and are therefore more amenable to exhaustive analysis techniques, which typically suffer from scalability issues.

Learning provides a promising approach for automatically documenting software as well as to extract models by observing the behaviour of a system as a black-box. It can also take advantage of additional knowledge when the source code is available. Learning is flexible in adapting models in the presence of changing external requirements as well as new or unanticipated environmental parameters.

Automata learning (aka. regular inference) has been the prevalent paradigm in this area of software engineering research. Angluin's classical L* learning algorithm for DFAs has been used and extended by researchers in a variety of contexts: formal verification of reactive systems [52], generating component abstractions for model checking, as well as assumptions for automating compositional verification through assume-guarantee reasoning [22]. Learning has also been compared to and combined with *counterexample guided abstraction refinement* (CEGAR) by some of these researchers.

Cassel et al. [14], Vaandrager [60], Cassel *et al.* [58], have contributed to research on learning register automata. As we saw in Sect. 3 this class of models is more expressive than finite automata. Steffen has developed the LearnLib[24] library that supports several learning algorithms and provides efficient approaches that increase the scalability of automata learning for realistic systems.

Challenging ML problems here are to build truly high-level models of code that capture design intentions such as decomposition, sharing and hierarchy. Furthermore, the underlying systems are usually infinite state, which raises the question of what level of abstraction to capture by learning, since machine learning of general infinite state systems is computationally intractable. Scalability is also a major challenge of automata learning, and recent ML research may have suggestions for improvement in that domain. One important observation is that the ML community has focussed on continuous mathematical models of learning (e.g., neural networks, support vector machines, kernel methods etc.) which are quite different from the discrete symbolic models of Sect. 3. However, such continuous approaches yield implicit model representations, with no explicit state space structure. It is not clear how to analyse such implicit models using a conventional theorem prover or symbolic model checker. Therefore an important challenge for the ML and SA communities is to combine powerful continuous methods for machine learning with discrete methods for model analysis. Particularly for software verification and testing, there is a need to consider learning for more diverse models of computation such as hybrid automata, term rewriting systems, logic programs etc. Inferring probabilistic and non-deterministic models of computation is important for autonomous or large-scale distributed systems, for which we may only ever have incomplete knowledge.

Statistical Learning for Inferring Semantics. Since a software system interface is typically described by textual documentation, e.g., XML documents, one can capitalise on the long tradition of research in *text categorisation*. Text categorisation enables the classification of a textual document into a predefined set of categories. One of the main techniques for text categorisation is the support vector machine (SVM) [35], which is a type of learning algorithm that has the ability to infer a *categorisation function* based on a set of *features*. For text categorisation, the standard representation of features is a *bag of words* [56].

---

[24] http://learnlib.de.

In this method, words are associated with dimensions of the vectors used by the SVM. For example, a textual document consisting of the string "get Weather, get Station" could be represented as the vector $(2, 1, 1, \ldots)$ where 2 in the first dimension is the frequency of the "get" token. The SVM algorithm is first given a training set that consists of textual documents, each of which is associated with the appropriate category. As a result it produces the categorisation function, which associates a textual document to a category according to its features. One can then use SVM to infer the categorisation function that relates an interface, which is considered as a textual document, to a semantic concept from the ontology of domains $\mathcal{D}$, which represents the set of possible categories. At runtime, the interface is analysed in order to infer the appropriate functionality, as illustrated in Fig. 12. Note that the type of the capability specifies whether it is required (*Req*) or provided (*Prov*) depending on whether the component is advertising its interface or looking for a component to interact with.

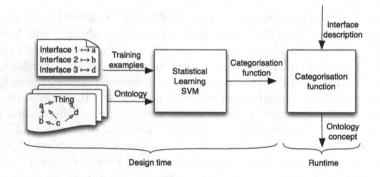

Fig. 12. Illustrating capability learning

Automata Learning For Inferring Component Behaviour. Learning techniques based on L^* algorithm have been used to extract the behaviour of a component when only its interface is known. This is based on an iterative process by which a hypothesis component's behaviour is incrementally refined by actively testing interactions with the corresponding component. Unlike passive learning algorithms [37,39] that only observe the interaction traces, L^* chooses the sequences of actions to execute in order to learn the behaviour in polynomial time. In the CONNECT project, the learning technique was provided by LearnLib [48], a framework for automata learning, which implements various improvements to the L^* algorithm such as abstraction/refinement or dealing with data values in order to be able to learn the behaviour of realistic components in minimal time.

Let us consider the simple example of learning the behaviour of a client for a weather service, called *C2*. The interface of *C2* defines three actions *req.login*, *req.logout*, and *req.getWeather*. The steps for learning the behaviour of *C2* are illustrated in Fig. 13. At time t_0, the learning algorithm begins by assuming that *C2* is able to perform any action in any order, that is its behaviour is represented using one single state where all the actions can be performed. However, when trying to interact with the system by performing, for example, *req.getWeather* and then *req.login*, an error (or exception) is raised. At time t_1, the model is updated so as to forbid this erroneous trace. Similarly, when performing *req.login, req.logout*, then *req.getWeather*, an error occurs, therefore the learning algorithm updates the model, which continues to be refined to obtain the model at time t_3. LearnLib verifies the data types of actions in order to refine the initial behaviour. Hence, it would directly start with the behaviour specified at t_1.

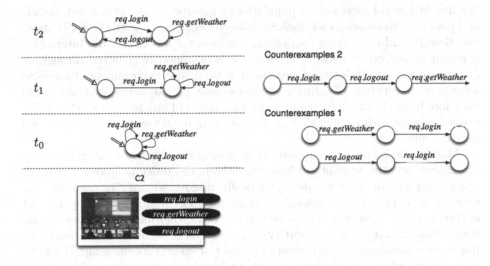

Fig. 13. Learning the behaviour of *C2*

4.2   Software Testing

Model-based testing has become well established, and can be traced back to Moore's 1956 "Gedanken experiments" [49] on finite state machines. Despite well documented productivity increases, model-based testing, faces a number of problems. Particularly in an agile environment it can be unrealistic to expect developers to maintain a detailed software model that is in synchronisation with a rapidly evolving code base.

To address this problem, new academic research has focused on techniques to automatically reverse engineer models directly from systems. The idea of combining the two areas (ML and testing) was enunciated as long ago as 1983 by Weyuker [67]. Early attempts to combine software testing with model inference include the work of Bergadano [11] and Zhu [69] in the 90s. However, it is only the fairly recent arrival of powerful automata-learning algorithms and model checkers that have made this approach practical for industrial scale problems. Since 2000, work in the groups of Grosz [54], Meinke [54], Steffen [19], and Walkinshaw [65] has begun to exploit modern techniques for automata learning. For example, the learning-based testing tool LBTest (Meinke) [43] has been successfully used to solve industrial testing problems up to 1 MLOC in the automotive [43], financial [47] and web sectors [20], within recent FP7 and ARTEMIS projects.

Challenging ML problems here include testing of distributed systems by distributed learning, also application of transferable learning to efficiently update legacy models of dynamically evolving systems.

4.3   Systems Integration

We live in a world increasingly populated by heterogeneous, networked, mobile and pervasive systems and services. Such heterogeneity may span the application, middleware, and underlying communication layers of infrastructure. Interaction between networked systems, where feasible, is customarily achieved through *ad hoc* means for specific pairs of systems in a particular environment. Principled automatic integration of multiple heterogeneous and dynamic systems would therefore bring about a labour-saving benefit. It would also provide the flexibility needed to cope with rapidly changing contexts, dynamic service availability and user mobility.

Machine learning can support such principled automatic integration by extracting essential semantic information about the different systems. Indeed, when network components are dynamically discovered, and interact spontaneously, as is the case in ubiquitous computing environments or the Internet of things, integration cannot even be planned but rather must take place at runtime. Semantic information about systems, such as capabilities and behaviours, has been acknowledged as an essential element of system specification. However, it is the exception rather than the rule to have such rich system descriptions available on the network. Given a description of a system's interface, learning techniques can be used to extract this missing semantic information. Initial evidence about the viability of such an approach was given by the European FP7 CONNECT project[25], that explored learning techniques for interoperability in systems of systems.

A major challenge is to understand the synergy between learning and system integration techniques. Indeed, the correctness of the integration is conditioned by the correctness of the models of the systems for which the related semantic information has been learned. While machine learning significantly improves automation by completing the model of the systems based on their interfaces, it also induces some inaccuracy that may lead the system to reach an erroneous state. This inaccuracy is inherent in learning techniques and cannot totally be removed. Hence, we can simply accept this imprecision and apply engineering techniques to increase precision over time, such as a control loop in which the

---

[25] See https://www.connect-forever.eu.

system is continuously monitored so as to evaluate the correspondence between the actual systems and their models.

4.4 Other Areas

Besides traditional software analysis, the learning techniques we have described in this Chapter are even being applied to non-traditional areas, such as bio-informatics and autonomous vehicles. For example, in the field of life sciences, the team of Grosu *et al.* [26] has recently applied model inference and model checking methods to analyse small 2-D and 3-D networks of heart-muscle excitable cells, starting from in-vitro observations. Similar methods of hybrid automata learning have been applied to analysis and verification of cyber-physical systems, control systems, bio-molecular and gene-regulatory networks.

Outside of software analysis, inference of probabilistic automata has long been used in the field of autonomous systems, such as self-driving cars and autonomous aircraft, for generating controllers or planners. These models have been learned from telemetry, flight, or other data, and their parameters can be tuned through reinforcement learning approaches. Challenging ML problems in these areas also involve the application of machine learning to infinite state and continuous systems.

5 A Roadmap for Future Research

In this Section we sketch a roadmap for future research in the field of machine learning methods for software analysis. This roadmap was compiled by members of the Dagstuhl Seminar 16172: *Machine Learning for Dynamic Software Analysis: Potentials and Limits* based on joint discussions [10].

Machine Learning for Model Extraction

– How can one learn truly high-level models of code that capture design intentions such as decomposition, sharing and hierarchy?
– What level of abstraction should be captured by learning and how can one combine powerful continuous and discrete methods for machine learning to support model analysis?
– How can one model and efficiently learn software systems that are not sufficiently documented, and are subject to constant change?
– How can one best model uncertainty and partial information arising from observing software systems that are too large to be completely learned? Can continuous learning methods be used interpolate missing information?
– Continuous mathematical models of learning are widely used in ML but largely unused in SA, since most analysis algorithms are not applicable. Is there a way to harness continuous learning without losing symbolic analysis methods?

Model-based Software Testing

- How can one learn distributed software systems, and efficiently construct globally non-deterministic system models that accurately integrate the results of local observations?
- What learning challenges do the extended and infinite state automata models coming from SA pose for ML? How can one model and quantify the complexity of different learning tasks going beyond finite state systems?
- What notions of convergence (i.e. progress) are appropriate for learning infinite state systems? How do measures of convergence relate to coverage and reliability models in software testing theory?
- How can one balance the necessary model size and accuracy needed by SA with efficiency of learning in ML?
- Can new and efficient SA techniques such as symbolic execution be exported back to ML, to speed up learning tasks such as glass-box equivalence checking?
- In SA, inferred models are the basis for later complex machine processing that needs to be scalable but accurate. How can such post-processing best be integrated with learning, e.g., correctness queries arising from model checking?

Machine Learning for Systems Integration

- How does the inaccuracy of learned models impact the correctness of software integration?
- Can one apply adaptive systems engineering techniques to increase the precision of learned models over time?

Applications of Machine Learning in Non-traditional Areas

- Can machine learning be used in the case of applications involving infinite state and continuous systems?

6   Conclusions

In this Chapter, we have presented an introduction to some of the major themes and results of machine learning, as these are being applied today to software analysis. Our target audience has been software engineers who wish to learn and apply machine learning as a tool, as well ML experts who wish to better understand the specific needs of software engineering. ML is a rapidly maturing branch of computer science, which has made great strides since its infancy in the 1950s. However, applications of ML to software analysis is an ongoing and emerging field, where much remains to be done.

6.1   Models, Methods and Applications: A Synthesis

We have developed a pedagogical approach to presenting ML for software analysis. This was based around first identifying appropriate types of *models* that could be used to perform different software engineering tasks such as functional testing, performance analysis, documentation, and interface, component and service identification.

For each model type, our goal was then to describe or reference different types of ML *methods*. The emphasis was on presenting basic algorithms that are pedagogically insightful while also being practically useful. However, these algorithms do not necessarily represent the state-of-the-art, which is covered elsewhere in this Book. Another pedagogical goal was to identify some fundamental principles used in ML methods that could be re-used in new situations. Such principles included abstract learning paradigms as well as concrete data structures and model construction methods.

Finally, we surveyed some *applications* applications of ML methods in software analysis and software engineering. This survey was not exhaustive, but aimed to provide an initial literature orientation that supports later more technical chapters in this Book.

6.2   Models

In Sect. 3, we focused on symbolic models of computation. Such models can represent software systems explicitly, and are thus directly applicable to many problems of software analysis. The discrete mathematical methods used in these models (such as graphs and congruences) can be contrasted with continuous models produced by learning techniques such as support vector machines and deep neural networks. The predominant class of computational models we focussed on were state machine models, though our survey also extended to logical models.

All the model types we considered (deterministic, non-deterministic, probabilistic, timed and hybrid automata) are currently well supported by a rich set of analytical techniques and tools for behaviour and performance. We saw that the difficulty of machine learning increases in line with increasing model complexity. Thus a principle of parsimony applies, i.e. use the simplest model type appropriate to an SE task.

The features of these model classes speak largely for themselves when representing real world systems. For example, deterministic models are appropriate and frequently successful for analysing simple monolithic software systems, and have the best scalability properties. The performance of state-of-the-art ML algorithms here are at least an order of magnitude better than the earliest ML algorithms from the 1980s. Non-deterministic and probabilistic models are more flexible for representing large scale distributed systems. They can model uncertainty in both behaviour and knowledge. For specialist applications, such as modelling real-time or cyber-physical systems, timed and hybrid automata are appropriate. Register automata are a promising approach to inferring both data and control properties of software systems. However for these more complex model types further fundamental research is needed to find general, efficient and scalable ML algorithms.

Finally a more declarative, and less operational approach to modelling can be achieved by using logical models. Such models are also well suited to available analytical techniques such as theorem proving and constraint solving.

6.3   Methods

Besides presenting or referencing basic ML methods for each of the above model types, we have also attempted to indicate what ML methods cannot do, by citing results from the complexity theory of ML. There is an extensive literature on the complexity theory of ML. The reader could begin with a basic introduction such as [36].

We gave a detailed and lengthy exposition of ML algorithms for deterministic automata, since these present a paradigm for learning other types computational models. This is because the discrete mathematical principles used, such as prefix trees, congruences, quotient automata, access and distinguishing strings, can be reused for more complex model types. Perhaps the concept of congruence could be pointed out as the single most important unifying theme. This concept is powerful precisely because it is so abstract[26]. However, we have also presented concrete ML algorithms and data structures as a counterbalance to such abstract theory. For the software engineer, practical and useful algorithms are necessary, while for the ML specialist, sound mathematical theory will be necessary for future progress.

6.4   Applications

Software is now evolving to encompass a world where the boundary between the machine and human disappears, merging wearable with the Internet of Things into 'a digital universe of people, places and things' [2]. Increasingly engineering these ubiquitous computing systems involves agile and adaptive software development where continual change and uncertainty are norms. In this context, machine learning is used to construct artefacts such as requirements specifications, models, and reports, as well as to analyse the large amount of data generated by those systems. Future system engineering will need more automation, adaptability and scalability and to integrate software engineering, adaptive systems, and machine learning techniques.

In this Chapter, we have focused on the application of machine learning techniques to software engineering problems, especially in the areas of model extraction, model-based software testing, and system integration. Yet, software engineering has also a lot to offer to machine learning. Software engineering has focused on capturing lessons, developing strategies and techniques, and building tools to assist with the creation of software systems. For example, machine

---

[26] In fact congruences and quotients are universal constructions throughout the whole of mathematics.

learning can be viewed as a tool for building a system inductively from a set of input-output examples, where specifications of such a system are given as training data sets [41]. In this context, requirements engineering can guide the selection of training data. Without having this selection inline with stakeholders' needs, the learnt system may diverge from their initial purpose, as it happened with Microsoft Tay chatbot [64]. Tay was a machine learning project designed for user engagement but which has learnt inappropriate language and commentary due to the data used in the learning process. In addition, eliciting transparency requirements [31] can also guide the selection of learning algorithm, which will ultimately play an important role in increasing users confidence in the system by explaining the decision made with the software system. A systematic way to clarify the synergies between the two discipline is an exciting area for future research.

6.5   Future Work

In Sect. 5, we presented a tentative roadmap for future research in this emerging field, based on surveying a group of currently active researchers.

Perhaps one of the major themes emerging in this survey was the tension between explicit symbolic models of computation such as state machine models, and implicit numerical models such as deep neural networks. For software engineering, needs such as efficient analysis and traceability between data and models are important, and at the current time it is difficult to see how these needs can be met by the neural network community. Nevertheless future research may change this or bring about a reconciliation.

A short chapter such as this is necessarily incomplete. The interested reader will find an exciting and constantly growing literature, starting from the references mentioned below. We hope that this Chapter will inspire other researchers to take up some of the challenging problems in this field.

Acknowledgments. We gratefully acknowledge financial support for this research from the following projects: EU ITEA 3 project 16032 Testomat, EU ECSEL project 692529-2 SafeCOP, Vinnova FFI project 2013-05608 VIRTUES, ERC Advanced Grant no. 291652 (ASAP), and the EPSRC EP/R013144/1 SAUSE project. We are also very thankful to the Schloss Dagstuhl for their support of the Dagstuhl Seminar 16172 and for the participant to this workshop for their insightful discussions.

References

1. Supporting Processes, Baseline 17. ISO 26262:(2011): Part 8 Road vehicles-functional safety. International Organization for Standardization (2011)
2. Abowd, G.D.: Beyond Weiser: from ubiquitous to collective computing. IEEE Comput. **49**(1), 17–23 (2016). https://doi.org/10.1109/MC.2016.22
3. Alrajeh, D., Russo, A.: Logic-based Learning: Theory and Application. In: Bennaceur, A., Hähnle, R., Meinke, K. (eds.) ML for Dynamic Software Analysis. LNCS, vol. 11026, pp. 219–256. Springer, Cham (2018)

4. Alur, R., Courcoubetis, C., Henzinger, T.A., Ho, P.-H.: Hybrid automata: an algorithmic approach to the specification and verification of hybrid systems. In: Grossman, R.L., Nerode, A., Ravn, A.P., Rischel, H. (eds.) HS 1991-1992. LNCS, vol. 736, pp. 209–229. Springer, Heidelberg (1993). https://doi.org/10.1007/3-540-57318-6_30
5. Alur, R., Dill, D.L.: A theory of timed automata. Theor. Comput. Sci. **126**(2), 183–235 (1994)
6. Angluin, D.: Learning regular sets from queries and counterexamples. Inf. Comput. **75**(2), 87–106 (1987)
7. Angluin, D., Frazier, M., Pitt, L.: Learning conjunctions of Horn clauses. Mach. Learn. **9**(2–3), 147–164 (1992)
8. Arias, M., Balcázar, J.L., Tirnăucă, C.: Learning definite Horn formulas from closure queries. Theor. Comput. Sci. **658**, 346–356 (2017)
9. Balcázar, J.L., Díaz, J., Gavaldà, R., Watanabe, O.: Algorithms for learning finite automata from queries: a unified view. In: Du, D.Z., Ko, K.I. (eds.) Advances in Algorithms, Languages, and Complexity- In Honor of Ronald V. Book, pp. 53–72. Springer, Boston (1997). https://doi.org/10.1007/978-1-4613-3394-4_2
10. Bennaceur, A., Giannakopoulou, D., Hähnle, R., Meinke, K.: Machine learning for dynamic software analysis: potentials and limits (Dagstuhl seminar 16172). Dagstuhl Rep. **6**(4), 161–173 (2016)
11. Bergadano, F., Gunetti, D.: Testing by means of inductive program learning. ACM Trans. Softw. Eng. Methodol. **5**(2), 119–145 (1996)
12. Bollig, B., Habermehl, P., Kern, C., Leucker, M.: Angluin-style learning of NFA. In: Proceedings of the 21st International Joint Conference on Artificial Intelligence, IJCAI 2009, Pasadena, California, USA, 11–17 July 2009, pp. 1004–1009 (2009)
13. Carrasco, R.C., Oncina, J.: Learning deterministic regular grammars from stochastic samples in polynomial time. ITA **33**(1), 1–20 (1999)
14. Cassel, S., Howar, F., Jonsson, B., Merten, M., Steffen, B.: A succinct canonical register automaton model. In: Bultan, T., Hsiung, P.-A. (eds.) ATVA 2011. LNCS, vol. 6996, pp. 366–380. Springer, Heidelberg (2011). https://doi.org/10.1007/978-3-642-24372-1_26
15. Chow, T.S.: Testing software design modeled by finite-state machines. IEEE Trans. Softw. Eng. **4**(3), 178–187 (1978)
16. Denis, F., Lemay, A., Terlutte, A.: Residual finite state automata. Fundam. Inform. **51**(4), 339–368 (2002)
17. Denis, F., Lemay, A., Terlutte, A.: Learning regular languages using RFSAs. Theor. Comput. Sci. **313**(2), 267–294 (2004)
18. Eyraud, R., de la Higuera, C., Janodet, J.: LARS: a learning algorithm for rewriting systems. Mach. Learn. **66**(1), 7–31 (2007)
19. Howar, F., Steffen, B.: Active automata learning in practice: an annotated bibliography of the years 2011 to 2016. In: Bennaceur, A., Hähnle, R., Meinke, K. (eds.) ML for Dynamic Software Analysis. LNCS, vol. 11026, pp. 123–148. Springer, Cham (2018)
20. Feng, L., Lundmark, S., Meinke, K., Niu, F., Sindhu, M.A., Wong, P.Y.H.: Case studies in learning-based testing. In: Yenigün, H., Yilmaz, C., Ulrich, A. (eds.) ICTSS 2013. LNCS, vol. 8254, pp. 164–179. Springer, Heidelberg (2013). https://doi.org/10.1007/978-3-642-41707-8_11
21. García, P., de Parga, M.V., Álvarez, G.I., Ruiz, J.: Learning regular languages using nondeterministic finite automata. In: Ibarra, O.H., Ravikumar, B. (eds.) CIAA 2008. LNCS, vol. 5148, pp. 92–101. Springer, Heidelberg (2008). https://doi.org/10.1007/978-3-540-70844-5_10

22. Giannakopoulou, D., Pasareanu, C.S.: Abstraction and learning for infinite-state compositional verification. In: Semantics, Abstract Interpretation, and Reasoning about Programs: Essays Dedicated to David A. Schmidt on the Occasion of his Sixtieth Birthday, Manhattan, Kansas, USA, 19–20th September 2013, pp. 211–228 (2013)

23. Gold, E.M.: Language identification in the limit. Inf. Control **10**, 447–474 (1967)

24. Gold, E.M.: Complexity of automaton identification from given data. Inf. Control **37**, 302–320 (1978)

25. Grinchtein, O., Jonsson, B., Leucker, M.: Inference of timed transition systems. Electr. Notes Theor. Comput. Sci. **138**(3), 87–99 (2005)

26. Grosu, R., Smolka, S.A., Corradini, F., Wasilewska, A., Entcheva, E., Bartocci, E.: Learning and detecting emergent behavior in networks of cardiac myocytes. Commun. ACM **52**(3), 97–105 (2009)

27. Harel, D., Politi, M.: Modeling Reactive Systems with Statecharts: The Statemate Approach, 1st edn. McGraw-Hill Inc., New York (1998)

28. de la Higuera, C.: Grammatical Inference: Learning Automata and Grammars. Cambridge University Press, New York (2010)

29. Holcombe, W.M.: Algebraic Automata Theory. Cambridge University Press, New York (1982)

30. Hopcroft, J.E., Motwani, R., Ullman, J.D.: Introduction to Automata Theory, Languages, and Computation, 3rd edn. Addison-Wesley Longman Publishing Co., Inc., Boston (2006)

31. Hosseini, M., Shahri, A., Phalp, K., Ali, R.: Four reference models for transparency requirements in information systems. Requir. Eng. **23**, 1–25 (2017)

32. Howar, F.: Active learning of interface programs. Ph.D. thesis, Dortmund University of Technology (2012)

33. Howar, F., Steffen, B., Jonsson, B., Cassel, S.: Inferring canonical register automata. In: Kuncak, V., Rybalchenko, A. (eds.) VMCAI 2012. LNCS, vol. 7148, pp. 251–266. Springer, Heidelberg (2012). https://doi.org/10.1007/978-3-642-27940-9_17

34. Hungar, H., Niese, O., Steffen, B.: Domain-specific optimization in automata learning. In: Hunt, W.A., Somenzi, F. (eds.) CAV 2003. LNCS, vol. 2725, pp. 315–327. Springer, Heidelberg (2003). https://doi.org/10.1007/978-3-540-45069-6_31

35. Joachims, T.: Text categorization with support vector machines: learning with many relevant features. In: Nédellec, C., Rouveirol, C. (eds.) ECML 1998. LNCS, vol. 1398, pp. 137–142. Springer, Heidelberg (1998). https://doi.org/10.1007/BFb0026683

36. Kearns, M.J., Vazirani, U.V.: An Introduction to Computational Learning Theory. MIT Press, Cambridge (1994)

37. Krka, I., Brun, Y., Popescu, D., Garcia, J., Medvidovic, N.: Using dynamic execution traces and program invariants to enhance behavioral model inference. In: ICSE, vol. 2, pp. 179–182 (2010)

38. Lang, K.J., Pearlmutter, B.A., Price, R.A.: Results of the Abbadingo one DFA learning competition and a new evidence-driven state merging algorithm. In: Honavar, V., Slutzki, G. (eds.) ICGI 1998. LNCS, vol. 1433, pp. 1–12. Springer, Heidelberg (1998). https://doi.org/10.1007/BFb0054059

39. Lorenzoli, D., Mariani, L., Pezzè, M.: Automatic generation of software behavioral models. In: Proceedings of the International Conference on Software Engineering, ICSE, pp. 501–510 (2008)

40. Mao, H., Chen, Y., Jaeger, M., Nielsen, T.D., Larsen, K.G., Nielsen, B.: Learning probabilistic automata for model checking. In: Eighth International Conference on Quantitative Evaluation of Systems, QEST 2011, Aachen, Germany, 5–8 September 2011, pp. 111–120 (2011)

41. Maruyama, H.: Machine learning as a programming paradigm and its implications to requirements engineering. In: Asia-Pacific Requirements Engineering Symposium, APRES (2016)

42. Meinke, K., Niu, F.: An incremental learning algorithm for hybrid automata. Techical report series, KTH Royal Institute of Technology, EECS School (2013)

43. Meinke, K., Sindhu, M.A.: LBTest: A learning-based testing tool for reactive systems. In: Sixth IEEE International Conference on Software Testing, Verification and Validation, ICST 2013, Luxembourg, Luxembourg, 18–22 March 2013, pp. 447–454 (2013)

44. Meinke, K., Tucker, J.V. (eds.): Many-Sorted Logic and Its Applications. Wiley, New York (1993)

45. Meinke, K., Tucker, J.: Universal algebra. In: Handbook of Logic in Computer Science (vol. 1): Background: Mathematical Structures (1993)

46. Meinke, K.: CGE: a sequential learning algorithm for mealy automata. In: Sempere, J.M., García, P. (eds.) ICGI 2010. LNCS (LNAI), vol. 6339, pp. 148–162. Springer, Heidelberg (2010). https://doi.org/10.1007/978-3-642-15488-1_13

47. Meinke, K., Nycander, P.: Learning-based testing of distributed microservice architectures: correctness and fault injection. In: Bianculli, D., Calinescu, R., Rumpe, B. (eds.) SEFM 2015. LNCS, vol. 9509, pp. 3–10. Springer, Heidelberg (2015). https://doi.org/10.1007/978-3-662-49224-6_1

48. Merten, M., Steffen, B., Howar, F., Margaria, T.: Next generation LearnLib. In: Abdulla, P.A., Leino, K.R.M. (eds.) TACAS 2011. LNCS, vol. 6605, pp. 220–223. Springer, Heidelberg (2011). https://doi.org/10.1007/978-3-642-19835-9_18

49. Moore, E.F.: Gedanken-experiments on sequential machines. In: Shannon, C., McCarthy, J. (eds.) Automata Studies, Princeton, NJ, pp. 129–153 (1956)

50. Moschitti, A.: Kernel-based machines for abstract and easy modeling of automatic learning. In: Bernardo, M., Issarny, V. (eds.) SFM 2011. LNCS, vol. 6659, pp. 458–503. Springer, Heidelberg (2011). https://doi.org/10.1007/978-3-642-21455-4_14

51. Niggemann, O., Stein, B., Vodencarevic, A., Maier, A., Kleine Büning, H.: Learning behavior models for hybrid timed systems. In: Proceedings of the Twenty-Sixth AAAI Conference on Artificial Intelligence, 22–26 July 2012, Toronto, Ontario, Canada (2012). http://www.aaai.org/ocs/index.php/AAAI/AAAI12/paper/view/4993

52. Peled, D., Vardi, M.Y., Yannakakis, M.: Black box checking. J. Autom. Lang. Comb. **7**(2), 225–246 (2001)

53. Reisig, W.: Understanding Petri Nets: Modeling Techniques, Analysis Methods, Case Studies. Springer, Heidelberg (2013). https://doi.org/10.1007/978-3-642-33278-4

54. Groz, R., Simao, A., Petrenko, A., Oriat, C.: Inferring FSM models of systems without reset. In: Bennaceur, A., Hähnle, R., Meinke, K. (eds.) ML for Dynamic Software Analysis. LNCS, vol. 11026, pp. 178–201. Springer, Cham (2018)

55. Ron, D., Singer, Y., Tishby, N.: On the learnability and usage of acyclic probabilistic finite automata. J. Comput. Syst. Sci. **56**(2), 133–152 (1998)

56. Salton, G., Yang, C.S., Yu, C.T.: Contribution to the theory of indexing. In: IFIP Congress, pp. 584–590 (1974)

57. Shinohara, T.: Inductive inference of monotonic formal systems from positive data. New Gener. Comput. **8**(4), 371–384 (1991)

58. Cassel, S., Howar, F., Jonsson, B., Steffen, B.: Extending automata learning to extended finite state machines. In: Bennaceur, A., Hähnle, R., Meinke, K. (eds.) ML for Dynamic Software Analysis. LNCS, vol. 11026, pp. 149–177. Springer, Cham (2018)
59. Thollard, F., Dupont, P., de la Higuera, C.: Probabilistic DFA inference using Kullback-Leibler divergence and minimality. In: Proceedings of the Seventeenth International Conference on Machine Learning (ICML 2000), Stanford University, Stanford, CA, USA, 29 June–2 July 2000, pp. 975–982 (2000)
60. Vaandrager, F.: Active learning of extended finite state machines. In: Nielsen, B., Weise, C. (eds.) ICTSS 2012. LNCS, vol. 7641, pp. 5–7. Springer, Heidelberg (2012). https://doi.org/10.1007/978-3-642-34691-0_2
61. Valiant, L.G.: A theory of the learnable. Commun. ACM **27**(11), 1134–1142 (1984)
62. Vasilevski, M.P.: Failure diagnosis of automata. Cybernetic **9**(4), 653–665 (1973)
63. Verwer, S.: Efficient identification of timed automata: theory and practice. Ph.D. thesis, Delft University of Technology, Netherlands (2010). http://resolver.tudelft.nl/uuid:61d9f199-7b01-45be-a6ed-04498113a212
64. Wakefield, J.: Microsoft chatbot is taught to swear on Twitter. Accessed 30 Mar 2017
65. Walkinshaw, N.: Testing functional black-box programs without a specification. In: Bennaceur, A., Hähnle, R., Meinke, K. (eds.) ML for Dynamic Software Analysis. LNCS, vol. 11026, pp. 101–120. Springer, Cham (2018)
66. Watkins, C.J.C.H.: Learning from delayed rewards. Ph.D. thesis, King's College, Cambridge (1989)
67. Weyuker, E.J.: Assessing test data adequacy through program inference. ACM Trans. Program. Lang. Syst. **5**(4), 641–655 (1983)
68. Wieczorek, W.: Grammatical Inference: Algorithms Routines and Applications, 1st edn. Springer, Cham (2016). https://doi.org/10.1007/978-3-319-46801-3
69. Zhu, H.: A formal interpretation of software testing as inductive inference. J. Softw. Test. Verif. Reliab. **6**(1), 3–31 (1996)

Testing and Learning

Learning-Based Testing: Recent Progress and Future Prospects

Karl Meinke[(✉)]

School of Electrical Engineering and Computer Science,
KTH Royal Institute of Technology, 100-44 Stockholm, Sweden
karlm@kth.se

Abstract. We present a survey of recent progress in the area of learning-based testing (LBT). The emphasis is primarily on fundamental concepts and theoretical principles, rather than applications and case studies. After surveying the basic principles and a concrete implementation of the approach, we describe recent directions in research such as: quantifying the hardness of learning problems, over-approximation methods for learning, and quantifying the power of model checker generated test cases. The common theme underlying these research directions is seen to be metrics for model convergence. Such metrics enable a precise, general and quantitative approach to both speed of learning and test coverage. Moreover, quantitative approaches to black-box test coverage serve to distinguish LBT from alternative approaches such as random and search-based testing. We conclude by outlining some prospects for future research.

1 Introduction

1.1 Overview

Learning-based testing [21,24,27,31,39,48] (LBT) is an emerging paradigm for fully automated black-box testing based on software model inference using machine learning (ML). Sometimes (but not always) this technique is combined with static analysis (e.g. model checking). In this case, formal requirements models are added to implement fully automated requirements testing.

The basic idea of LBT is to use *active machine learning* (see Chap. 1 of this Book) to dynamically generate (online) an efficient test suite for a *system under test* (SUT). This active learning process is used to infer, or reverse engineer, a sequence of increasingly accurate models $M_0, M_1, \ldots$ of the SUT. Because they are constructed by a process of *inductive inference*, these models M_i potentially offer the opportunity to predict unobserved errors in the SUT. To automatically generate reliable test verdicts from *requirements*, it is possible to statically analyse the reverse engineered models M_i. For example, we can analyse the functional correctness or performance characteristics of the learned model M_i to infer these properties for SUT.

© Springer International Publishing AG, part of Springer Nature 2018
A. Bennaceur et al. (Eds.): ML for Dynamic Software Analysis, LNCS 11026, pp. 53–73, 2018.
https://doi.org/10.1007/978-3-319-96562-8_2

As a software testing procedure, it is important in LBT to be able to measure the *progress* or *coverage* achieved by testing. One approach to this measurement task is to automate by means of equivalence checking algorithms. We can quantify test coverage as the degree of *convergence* of the learned model to a complete (i.e. behaviourally equivalent) model of the SUT. With appropriate machine learning algorithms and convergence measures, we indeed see model sequences $M_0, M_1, \ldots$ monotonically converging to a final complete model M_{final} of the SUT. Generally speaking, test coverage is a difficult property to define precisely for black-box testing techniques. So this *approximation model of coverage* is a novel contribution of LBT to the practise of black-box software testing.

The wide variety of model representations, active machine learning algorithms and static analysis tools that can be found in the literature support the claim that LBT constitutes a general paradigm of testing. Using state-of-the-art machine learning algorithms, the current generation of LBT tools can construct and execute anything between thousands and millions of test cases within a few hours. In fact, the main bottleneck to fast LBT seems to be the latency of the SUT itself. This latency can difficult to handle, although concurrent distributed LBT seems to be one approach (see e.g. [16,20,38]). Already with current technology and algorithms, LBT generated test suites are sufficient to infer complex models, e.g. state machines with tens of thousands of states and millions of transitions.

Our aim in this survey is to present a personal and selective account of some recent progress in learning-based testing. We focus on some technical questions that were identified during early research in our group, and where progress has recently been made. These questions include:

(i)   quantifying the hardness of testing and learning based on SUT structure,
(ii) fast learning using compact over-approximations, and
(iii) quantifying the learning power of static analysis generated test cases.

The unifying theme to tackle these questions has been quantitative measurement of the convergence of learning.

We will present the basic principles of LBT in a rather abstract and general way, in the hope that this stimulates new ideas and progress in algorithms and tool architectures. We mainly emphasize machine learning aspects of LBT, since this reflects our own research bias. However, it is certainly possible to conduct new research into static analysis methods appropriate for LBT. Some pertinent research questions will be mentioned in Sect. 8.

The organisation of this survey is as follows. In Sect. 2, we provide a more detailed account of the principles of learning-based testing. In Sect. 3, we describe how these abstract principles have been instantiated in a concrete learning-based test tool: LBTest. In Sect. 4, we consider the problem of quantifying the learning complexity of SUTs. In Sect. 5, we consider methods to accelerate learning using over-approximations based on non-deterministic finite automata. In Sect. 6 we consider the learning power of model checker generated queries. In Sect. 7 we survey some of the literature in the field of LBT. Finally in Sect. 8 we present some conclusions and pointers to significant future research problems.

2 General Principles of Learning-Based Testing

We begin with a presentation of some general principles for learning-based testing. Starting from these principles, a number of different design choices and architectures become apparent for constructing an LBT tool. It is therefore appropriate to discuss the fundamental principles first at a high level of abstraction.

2.1 Algorithms for Test Case Generation

Learning-based testing attempts to integrate several sources for automated test case generation (ATCG) such as machine-learning, static analysis, equivalence checking and even manually designed test suites. Experience has shown that no one method in isolation is adequate, although machine learning can be said to be the basis which leverages additional TCG techniques. A major theme of LBT research is *refining the individual TCG techniques, and investigating optimal architectures that integrate them.*

A basic philosophy of LBT is to generate, execute and judge test cases dynamically, i.e. we conduct *online testing.* The main advantage of this approach is that LBT tools can dynamically adapt each test session to changes in the underlying SUT such as refactoring, as well as changes in user requirements. So LBT is well adapted to modern *agile development methods* such as continuous integration. This philosophy is implemented by using active learning to rapidly explore the behaviour of the SUT during each new test session.

A second guiding principle of LBT in our own research has been the aim of supporting *fully automated verdict construction* (i.e. pass, fail, warning etc.). This is essential whenever a large volume of test cases must be executed, as manual verdict construction would be too slow and error prone. One approach is to generate test cases from user requirements simultaneously with their output predictions. Fortunately, formal requirements modeling languages and static analysis tools that can generate such predictions have existed for some time (e.g. temporal logic model checkers, SMT solvers etc.). As we have already seen in Sect. 1, such analysis tools can be applied either: (1) during active learning to the sequence of generated models $M_0, M_1, \ldots$, or (2) post-hoc to the final model M_{final} when the learning process has been terminated. The latter approach can be much more efficient in practise, as it can eliminate much redundant model analysis. When comparing these two approaches or architectures, an interesting question for machine learning emerges: *what is the power of static analysis generated test cases compared with active learning queries?* By power, we mean their potential to speed up model convergence. This is an interesting question that has consequences for architectural design, and we will take it up again in Sect. 6.

By introducing formal user requirements and static analysis into LBT we perhaps impose a significant hurdle for widespread take-up of LBT technology within the industrial testing community. It seems to be a widely held belief that precise requirements modeling is too difficult and/or time consuming outside the safety critical systems community. To this objection one can make several comments.

(1) Automated TCG seems a necessity in the near future for testing ever more complex systems. This will be difficult without formal requirements models that support precise fully-automated verdict construction.
(2) The advantages gained from formal requirements modeling, i.e. speed, volume, accuracy, and hence reduced time-to-market and lowered software quality assurance (SQA) costs, can outweigh the investment in education and effort.
(3) *Visual modeling languages* such as UML, and also natural language based *patterns*, can improve usability issues for testing tools that need formal requirements modeling. In fact the reverse engineered models M_i derived from LBT are themselves amenable to interesting forms of *post-test model visualisation*.

However, clearly this criticism has some validity, and further research into requirements modeling is needed. To this end, there are an increasing number of published case studies of LBT, e.g. [14,16,35,37], that aim to promote better understanding of domain-specific formal requirements modeling and its impact on testing.

As is well-known, high-volume test case generation can also be obtained by random testing [2] or search-based testing [26]. Therefore a deeper understanding of the novel contribution to testing made by machine learning and static analysis methods is necessary. In LBT, rather than discarding any test vectors after execution, these are always accumulated and integrated into a model of the SUT which becomes increasingly accurate over time. This model could be:

- a mathematical function such as a piecewise polynomial approximation [29],
- a finite state machine [31],
- a timed automaton [47],
- a term rewriting system [30],
- a logic program [5],
- or even an infinite state machine [33].

The choice of an appropriate computational model depends on both the behaviour of the SUT, as well as the availability of algorithms for subsequent static analysis.[1]

Semantically rich and complex learned models can support sophisticated analyses of functional behaviour and performance. For example, using temporal logic the liveness and fairness properties of an SUT can be analysed, even though counter-examples to such properties are infinite sequences that are not directly executable on the SUT.[2] Such analyses go beyond the usual domain of software

---

[1] For certain models of computation, such as neural networks, it seems that no static analysis techniques are currently known. So this paradigm of machine learning seems less useful in LBT at the present time.

[2] Infinite counter-examples can be approximated by finite truncations, and in this way warning verdicts can be generated.

testing, and begin to integrate the most powerful features of both software testing and static analysis, achieving some compensation of the weaknesses of each approach when used in isolation.

We conclude this section with an important observation: as long as the learning process is incomplete, then a test case found by static analysis of a model M_i may either be a *false negative* (a transient artifact of incomplete learning) or a *true negative* (a correct observation or prediction). Only by executing the counter-example on the SUT and observing the actual SUT behaviour can we distinguish between these two. For sufficiently complex SUTs we must accept the fact that learning must necessarily be terminated before completion. Therefore, models of test coverage are also important for interpreting the results of LBT tools.

2.2   Test Coverage, Test Termination and Model Convergence

After the construction of each intermediate model M_i, we need to consider whether it is worthwhile to continue the testing session. We address this well known *test termination problem* in terms of the degree of completeness of M_i as a model of the SUT. We call this degree of completeness of M_i its *convergence measure*. An important advantage of LBT over random and search-based testing is that we can address test termination precisely in terms of model convergence. This is a powerful side-effect of explicit model construction.

It is obvious that continued testing is worthwhile only if, there is something more to learn about the SUT behaviour, i.e. M_i and the SUT are not yet *behaviourally equivalent*. In other words, there exists at least one test vector on which M_i and the SUT behave differently. So the test termination problem can be reduced to the equivalence problem for M_i and the SUT. However, this equivalence problem is complicated by the fact that M_i and the SUT might not belong to the same class of models. For example M_i might be a finite state machine, while the SUT might be a piece of C code in which we cannot explicitly identify any states at all.[3] For this reason, we generally ignore glass box equivalence checking methods in LBT.

Instead, LBT makes use of black-box equivalence checking techniques. These may either be *deterministic* (e.g. for finite automata the Vasileskii-algorithm [10,46]) or *randomised* (stochastic equivalence checking). A randomised approach to equivalence checking not only provides a generic solution, it also supports a probabilistic approach to model convergence and coverage metrics, which seems to work reasonably well in practise. Furthermore, randomised equivalence checking allows us to introduce non-uniform probability distributions on the choice of test cases. This opens up the possibility to apply *risk-based testing*. It also connects LBT with the very extensive theory of PAC (probably approximately correct) learning theory (ref).

---

[3] The SUT may also be inherently more complex then the model, e.g. having the structure of a pushdown automaton that is not reducible to any finite automaton.

Stochastic equivalence metrics are fairly simple to describe. We empirically estimate the relative frequency (and/or the average length) of randomly chosen test cases where M_i and the SUT differ, using Monte Carlo methods. We then take this stochastic measure of divergence to be an estimate of the completeness of M_i (normalised in percentage terms) as a model of the SUT. It is important to ensure that the randomly chosen sample set used for convergence estimation contains an insignificant proportion of members from the training set (i.e. previous test cases) to avoid bias.

Stochastic equivalence checking is also easy to implement. However, an accurate estimation of convergence for a large model M_i can require an infeasibly large number of samples.[4] One solution is to compute a *moving average* of the convergence measure over k models $M_i, M_{i-1}, \ldots M_{i-k}$, for a suitable window size k. This can gives an estimate over a larger population of samples, and enhances monotonicity of the convergence measure, at the expense of some local accuracy.

In practical case studies we have observed that stochastic convergence measures do not always correlate in a linear way with the state space size of inferred models (see e.g. Figs. 3 and 4). However, as we shall see in Sect. 4, although state space size seems like an intuitive metric for coverage, it can be very misleading if the structural complexity of the SUT is not factored in. Further research on convergence and coverage concepts is still needed, especially in relation to PAC learning.

3 LBTest: An Architecture for Testing Embedded Systems

Within our research into LBT, commencing with [27], we have defined and investigated a number of different component algorithms and global architectures for learning-based testing. A survey of our early research is [32]. One long-term research direction has been to explore the scope of the LBT paradigm, especially the *semantic expressiveness* of models of computation for which convergent learning algorithms can be found [29,33]. However, expressive models usually come at a price, which includes slower learning and static analysis. Therefore, the opposite direction of research has also been important: to develop learning algorithms and architectures for simple models of computation that are *scalable* to large problem instances. This latter research programme has enabled us to conduct industrial research collaboration on real-world testing problems, such as [14].

This research into scalable testing has yielded the testing tool LBTest, which has been re-implemented and extended from the original published version [34]. Therefore, a review of the current architecture (LBTest 2.2) and its features is both timely and appropriate to concretely illustrate the abstract principles of LBT outlined in Sect. 2.

---

[4] This problem is most acute where the SUT *latency*, i.e. the time to execute one test case, is high.

LBTest makes use of *deterministic Moore automata*[5] over user-defined finite symbolic input and output alphabets as the class of learned models. However, to improve the efficiency of learning, to minimise model size, and also to speed up the convergence of learning, this class of models has been extended to include *non-deterministic Moore automata*. We will discuss this extension in more detail in Sect. 5.

Finite automata are an appropriate class of models for representing many types of embedded systems, occurring in industries such as automotive and avionics. In embedded applications, recursion and dynamic data structures are usually avoided for safety reasons. So a bounded memory model, such as a finite automaton, is usually applicable. As is well known, finite automata can be learned by so-called *regular inference algorithms*, of which many examples are known in the literature [3,19], including Angluin's L* algorithm [1]. What is unclear from traditional machine learning research is the efficiency and scalability of regular inference algorithms, particularly in the non-traditional context of software testing. This has called for empirical research to implement and benchmark existing and new learning algorithms. Furthermore, the frequency of model construction (i.e. the number of active learning queries needed per model M_i) has never been considered. As we have seen in Sect. 2, frequent construction of many models M_i is crucial if static analysis is to make an impact on the learning process.

For requirements testing, LBTest makes use of *linear temporal logic* (LTL) [15]. From many industrial case studies, we have found only a small number of real-world requirements on embedded systems that could not be directly modeled in this logic. The static analyser used by LBTest is of course a model checker. LBTest has a file interface so that it can be loosely integrated with a variety of different model checkers that are called externally from the tool. Since it is mature, stable and one of the most reliable model checkers available, we have mainly used NuSMV [11], and more recently nuXmv [6]. Both the BDD-based and BMC (SAT-based) model checkers of NuSMV have been evaluated. These two generally lead to different results in terms of performance and logical analysis, and recent benchmark results can be found in [53].

A significant issue with NuSMV, that seems common to all model checkers we are aware of, is the lack of efficient support for generating different counterexamples to the same formula within a model. From a testing perspective, it is important to generate the largest possible set of counter-examples (modulo some appropriate equivalence relationship) and not just one. This is an appropriate research topic for the model checker community.

The architecture of LBTest is illustrated in Fig. 1. This illustrates the main feedback loop that allows model checker queries and equivalence checker queries to be executed at regular intervals after the construction of each new model M_i. A manual test suite, if one exists, can be executed as an initial set of queries. Otherwise, testing usually commences from a single state automaton, that rep-

---

[5] Recall that a Moore automaton is a finite state machine which has an output value associated with each state.

resents a null hypothesis about the SUT. The length of the intervals between successive models M_i and M_{i+1} is dependent upon the choice of active learning algorithm. For example, for L* the intervals can grow cubically, so that this particular learning algorithm scales poorly, and much better algorithms exist.

LBTest has a modular structure so that new learning algorithms and model checkers can easily be integrated. New learning algorithms are added by sub-classing abstract learner classes such as `MooreAutomatonLearner` which involves implementing abstract methods such as
`MooreAutomaton getInitialHypothesis()` and
`MooreAutomaton getNextHypothesis(CounterExample newCounterExample)`
to support iterative model construction. The LBTest architecture is configured at run-time through a configuration file, which specifies run-time options, data type models, and LTL requirements.

Noteworthy in Fig. 1 is the *communication wrapper* (aka. test harness) around the SUT. This software component, which must be manually customised to the API of the SUT, is responsible for all communication and data transla-tion between the SUT and LBTest. Wrappers implement all test set-up and tear-down actions between the individual test case executions. These actions can be technically challenging for distributed systems testing, where complex network management and large scale reset actions for databases may be neces-sary [14,35]. Besides solving such pragmatic problems, wrappers also implement more fundamental semantic concepts, including the following.

(1) Wrappers support the *abstraction of infinite state systems* into finite state models, through data partitioning. This well-known technique of traditional testing allows simple but efficient learning and model checking algorithms to deal with complex real-world systems.
(2) Wrappers implement *communication protocols* between the SUT and the learning algorithm, which may be *synchronous* (clock driven) or *asyn-chronous* (event driven). Generally, synchronous protocols are necessary for testing hard real-time systems, while more data efficient asynchronous protocols are appropriate for soft real-time systems. Both synchronous and asynchronous protocols can be used to support *abstractions of real time*, by *undersampling* the SUT at fixed (synchronous) or variable (asynchronous) rates. Temporal abstraction is often necessary to handle high data rates between LBTest and the SUT.
(3) Wrappers can be used to define the semantics of *fault injection*, i.e. injection of values into the infrastructure surrounding the SUT which can simulate or induce some type of infrastructure failure (e.g. a communications failure). This opens the way to *robustness testing* using LBT [35].

The principles of wrapper construction are technically complex, and quickly become tool specific. Therefore we refer the reader to [36] for further discussion of this subject.

This concludes our discussion of the fundamental concepts of learning-based testing. In the following sections we turn our attention to some specific research problems and recent results.

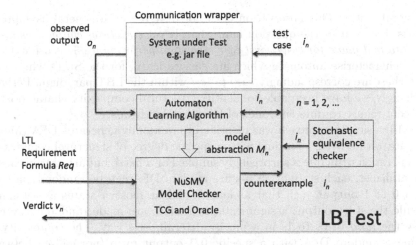

Fig. 1. LBTest architecture

4   Quantifying the Complexity of Testing and Learning

In this section we consider the problem of characterising the difficulty of testing an SUT as an intrinsic property of its structural complexity. This problem, which is perhaps generic to all software testing methods, is well suited to be addressed within the framework of learning-based testing.

Both intuition and practical experience suggest that among similar sized SUTs, some are harder to test than others. Why is this so, and what are the dominant factors? To discuss this concretely, based on empirical investigation with regular inference algorithms, we will assume some familiarity with the concepts of an *accessor string* and *distinguishing string*, widely used in the literature on regular inference.[6]

LBT is a black-box testing method, so the structure and complexity of the SUT is always something unknown. However, questions about the complexity of testing can be translated into questions about the complexity of learning. Specifically, we can study the complexity of learning as a function of the structural complexity of the learned model. The asymptotic complexity of specific regular inference algorithms has been extensively studied, since Angluin's observation that L* can infer DFA in polynomial time wrt. the number of states to be learned. Empirical analysis of the actual performance of different learning algorithms has also been conducted both as a research task [4], and by means of open competitions e.g. [23,44].

Within our own research, we have repeatedly observed that the time complexity of learning different automata with roughly the same state space size can

---

[6] An accessor string is an input sequence needed to reach a specific state in the SUT state space. A distinguishing string is suffix that can distinguish two SUT states in terms of their output behaviour. See e.g. [19].

vary significantly. This observation does not disagree with general asymptotic analysis, but focuses the question more sharply on *structural characteristics of automata that make for best/worst case algorithm performance*. It is useful to be able to characterise automata which are easy to learn, for the SUTs which give rise to these are correspondingly *easy to test* within the LBT paradigm. Perhaps surprisingly, we have been able to identify structural complexity characteristics that seem robust to different kinds of learning algorithms.

In [13] a simple approach was identified to randomly generate[7] DFA (Moore automata with only 0/1 output) with a specific degree of structural complexity. The generation principle is surprisingly simple. For a fixed, but arbitrarily chosen input alphabet, each state of an n-state random DFA can be randomly labeled with a 0 or 1 output such that at least 0 and at most n states are assigned 0. While the state output assignments themselves are made randomly, we can choose the *ratio* of 0s to 1s in a precise deterministic way. The complexity of learning a random DFA with a specific 0/1 output ratio (normalised between 0% and 100%) can then be measured in terms of the number of queries needed.

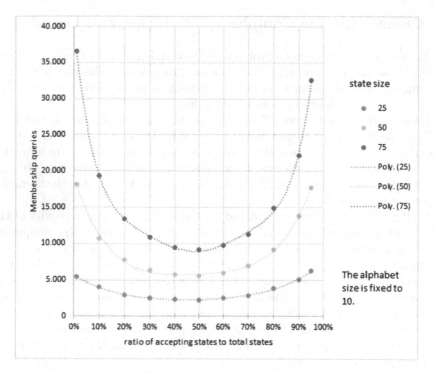

Fig. 2. Complexity of L* learning as a function of SUT complexity (acceptance ratio).

Fast random generation is important to measure average performance over large sample sizes.

Figure 2 shows results obtained when studying the performance of Angluin's L* algorithm using random DFA examples classified by output ratio.[8] The three curves, corresponding to different state space sizes, all show horizontal symmetry due to the symmetry of permuting 0s and 1s. More importantly, all three curves show that as the incidence of 0s (respectively 1s) becomes sparse, the complexity of learning increases sharply. Furthermore, the gap between the easiest and the hardest examples increases dramatically as the state space size increases. A similar study of Kearns algorithm [22] exhibits the same properties, and we conjecture that these results are robust to all types of regular inference algorithm.

How should we interpret these results? Clearly, when a DFA has an increasingly high percentage of 0s (or 1s) then when two states with accessor strings a_1, a_2 are not behaviourally equivalent, then a distinguishing suffix s such that $\lambda(a_1 s) \neq \lambda(a_2 s)$ becomes increasingly difficult to find. Thus when the complexity of finding accessor strings is uniformised by means of glass-box equivalence checking, then the complexity of finding distinguishing strings becomes dominant. These results cast doubt on the validity of benchmarking performance for regular inference algorithms in terms of state space size alone.

We can make some generalisations from these observations. Moore automata which satisfy the *Markov property*, i.e. a distinguishing string of length 0 always suffices to distinguish two non-equivalent states, constitute the most easily learned and hence easily tested systems. By contrast, Moore automata which are highly *history sensitive*, i.e. the next state is a function of the current state and the previous history to reach that state, can be arbitrarily harder learn. This is because the previous history of a state determines the difficulty to find an accessor string for it, while its future paths determine the difficulty to find distinguishing strings for non-equivalent states.

Another important generalisation from these observations concerns the data abstraction methods used to approximate infinite state systems by finite state automata (c.f. Sect. 3). It is sometimes possible to choose a data abstraction that yields a more Markov-like finite automaton after learning. This abstraction is clearly worthwhile since the SUT becomes easier to learn and hence to test. For example we can try to use a finer data partition on output values, yielding more output equivalence classes. We can also try to expose more SUT output variables to the learning algorithm. Practical experimentation seems to confirm that when they are possible, both these approaches can make systems easier to learn and test.

5   Inductive Inference, Regular Inference and Over-Approximation

In learning-based testing, it is the inductive inference principles inherent in machine learning algorithms that allow us to generalise from a finite set of

---

[8] These results where obtained using a glass-box equivalence checker, so that the complexity of finding equivalence counter-examples is constant.

observations (test cases results) to an infinite set of model behaviours. Inductive inference starting from a finite set of observations has two effects on the testing process:

(1) it can lead to the prediction of unseen SUT errors from previous observations, and
(2) it can increase the rate of convergence of learning.

The principle of inductive inference employed in regular inference algorithms is rather simple. Any finite set of SUT observations can be organised into a prefix tree.[9] Then an automaton model can be synthesized by merging prefix tree nodes n_i and n_j which are behaviourally consistent, i.e. common suffixes of n_i and n_j are identical in the prefix tree. When a merged pair of nodes n_i and n_j lie along the same path from the prefix tree root, this leads to a *loop* in the automaton model. Otherwise, merging simply leads to a *join* of their two paths from the root. This inductive inference principle is based on a *closed world assumption*. That is to say, in the absence of any conflicting evidence (a closed world) that two nodes are behaviourally inconsistent, we assume that they are consistent. This approach gives a *non-monotonic learning process*, because early hypotheses about node pair merges must be abandoned in the face of later conflicting evidence. Despite their non-monotonicity, regular inference algorithms are usually provably convergent. However, non-monotonicity does make convergence of learning difficult to formulate in terms of regular language inclusion.

Before learning has converged, there is always some degree of *under-approximation* of the SUT by the inferred model, since the full SUT structure has not yet been found. That is, paths exist in the SUT which do not exist in the model. On the other hand, because of the node merging process there is also some degree of *over-approximation* since paths may exist in the inferred model which do not actually exist in the SUT.

Recent results have shown that it is possible to greatly accelerate the testing process by increasing this degree of over-approximation within the inferred model. Intuitively, this corresponds to the learner making bolder hypotheses about the SUT behaviour (which may not be true!). One approach to over-approximation that we have studied results in the use of *non-deterministic automata to infer deterministic SUTs*.

A more mathematically precise statement of model construction for regular inference algorithms than the one sketched above can be expressed in terms of *quotient automata*. These are constructed from an *absolutely free* finite automaton (for specific input and output alphabets) which is unique up to isomorphism. This algebraic construction highlights the fact that it is essentially a *congruence relation* on the free automaton which has to be learned (e.g. as a 2-dimensional table). Further mathematical details can be found in [28].

Now for any Moore automaton

$$A = \langle Q, \Sigma, \Omega, \delta : Q \times \Sigma \to Q, \lambda : Q \to \Omega, q_0 \rangle$$

---

[9] The prefix tree consists of all input/output observations of the SUT stored as an n-ary tree, where n is the size of the input alphabet.

an equivalence relation $\equiv \subseteq Q \times Q$ on the state set Q of A is a *congruence* if, and only if, $\equiv$ satisfies two *substitutivity conditions*

$$q \equiv q' \;\rightarrow\; \delta(\,q,\,\sigma\,) \;\equiv\; \delta(\,q',\,\sigma\,), \tag{1}$$

$$q \equiv q' \;\rightarrow\; \lambda(\,q\,) \;=\; \lambda(\,q'\,), \tag{2}$$

for any states q, $q' \in Q$ and input symbol $\sigma \in \Sigma$. The motivation for this substitutivity condition is that it ensures that in the resulting quotient automaton, $A/\equiv$, both the state transition function $\delta_{A/\equiv}$ and output function $\lambda_{A/\equiv}$ are well defined as functions (i.e. unique valued). Hence the quotient automaton $A/\equiv$ will be deterministic.

To build a congruence that yields a deterministic model, each observed non-equivalence between two states must propagated through all prefixes of the prefix tree by inverting rule (1) to its contrapositive form

$$\delta(\,\overline{\sigma_1},\,\sigma\,) \;\not\equiv\; \delta(\,\overline{\sigma_2},\,\sigma\,) \;\rightarrow\; \overline{\sigma_1} \;\not\equiv\; \overline{\sigma_2} \tag{3}$$

for input strings $\overline{\sigma_1}, \overline{\sigma_2} \in \Sigma^*$.

What would happen if we simply omit propagation rule (3) in a regular inference algorithm? This omission has many interesting and useful consequences.

(1) The relation $\equiv$ would be an equivalence relation, but not a congruence.
(2) We would save the effort of propagation itself.
(3) The quotient automaton $A/\equiv$ would be a non-deterministic automaton in which the state transition relation $\delta_{A/\equiv}$, defined in the usual way for quotient relations by

$$\delta_{A/\equiv}(\overline{\sigma}/\equiv,\,\sigma) \;\leftrightarrow\; \delta_A(\overline{\sigma},\,\sigma) \in \overline{\sigma}.\sigma/\equiv.$$

is a relation, but not a function (i.e. not unique-valued).
(4) The quotient object $A/\equiv$ will be a non-deterministic automaton.
(5) The quotient automaton $A/\equiv$ will be more compact, since states distinguished under rule (3) are no longer separated.
(6) A more compact quotient automaton requires less storage and can be model checked faster.
(7) The quotient automaton $A/\equiv$ will contain many more paths than if we had used rule (3). This stronger over-approximation leads to faster discovery of SUT errors.

Does this approach work in practise? We have designed and implemented the regular inference algorithm *MinSplit* that relaxes the propagation rule (3), and does indeed achieve over-approximation. It has been integrated with the LBTest tool for evaluation. While the algorithm itself is too complex to more than sketch here[10] we can present some preliminary results. The graph in Fig. 3 illustrates the difference in rates of convergence between *MinSplit* and L* when learning a complex brake-by-wire automotive application [14]. We can see that while L* fails to converge on any reasonable time scale, *MinSplit* converges rather rapidly, but does so by over-approximation. In Fig. 4 we show the rate of growth of models over time using *MinSplit* and L*. Clearly the non-deterministic representation of *MinSplit* leads to significant compaction of the inferred model.

---

[10] In practise rule (3) is not completely relaxed.

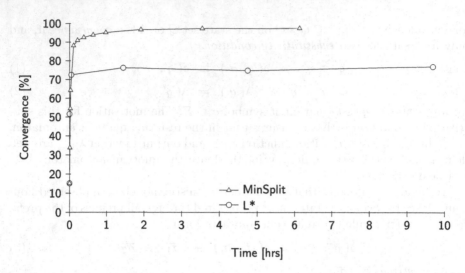

Fig. 3. Relative convergence of MinSplit and L* learning algorithms testing a brake-by-wire application [14].

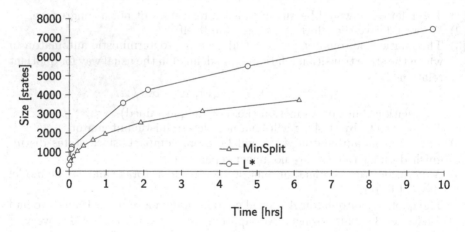

Fig. 4. Rate of growth of inferred models for MinSplit and L* testing a brake-by-wire application [14].

6   The Querying Power of Model Checkers

As we have seen, LBT uses counter-examples to correctness generated by static analysers (such as model checkers) as a source of queries to augment active learning. An interesting question is therefore whether these model checker queries accelerate the learning process at all. We have recently begun to investigate this question using the LBTest tool. However, in its full generality, the question is a complex one that is sensitive to more factors then have yet been examined.

To investigate this question using the LBTest tool we simply switch off the model checker during the learning process, by using a command in the tool configuration file. This does not entirely sever the feedback loop within the LBTest architecture (c.f. Fig. 1), since equivalence checker queries are still used after each new model.

By measuring the rate and final degree of convergence of learning both with and without model checking, we have been able to precisely quantify the power of model checker generated queries. We performed this benchmarking for one of our standard benchmark case studies, the brake-by-wire application of [14, 37]. The results were somewhat surprising. No decrease in the rate of model convergence could be seen at all after disabling the model checker. This observation held true across each of a set of ten different user requirements. Furthermore, the observation could not be influenced by the choice of different learning algorithms.

This rather surprising result suggests that the feedback loop architecture of Fig. 1 (which seems also to be the subject of the patent [25]) is actually highly sub-optimal. This is because empirically, we observe that model checking, when interleaved with machine learning, contributes significantly to the overall testing time by more than 50%. Furthermore, conventional off-the-shelf model checkers are forced to completely re-analyse each model M_i many times, without any re-use of previous results. This approach is highly inefficient. So from this perspective, the pipeline LBT architecture of Fig. 5 is superior, and can shorten test session times by 50% or more. However, further research remains to be done on this question in the context of different models, learning algorithms, static analysers and requirements modeling languages.

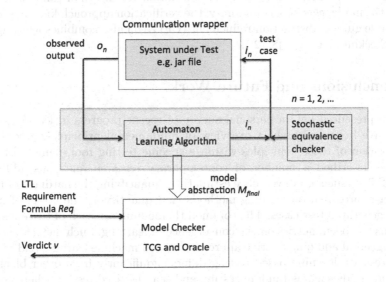

Fig. 5. A pipelined LBT architecture

7 Literature Survey

The connections between computational learning and software testing have been a fruitful line of research since Elaine Weyuker's PhD research, [49]. Early research includes [5] on inferring and testing Prolog programs and [51,52] on PAC-learning and testing of axiomatic models. Complexity theoretic results on testing derived from models of machine learning include [9,42,43].

A notable contribution historically is [39]. This paper introduced a testing architecture similar to that of Fig. 1 for learning-based testing of reactive systems using Angluin's L* algorithm for learning, the Vasileskii-Chow algorithm for black-box equivalence checking, and Buchi automata as specifications. This work seems to be the basis of the patent [25]. In [27], a somewhat similar LBT architecture for testing numerical analysis programs was presented. This approach was focused more on data correctness than control correctness. It used models based on piecewise polynomial approximation, machine learning based on finite differences, requirements modeling based on Hoare's logic and static analysis based on the CAD algorithm for satisfiability over real-closed fields. Taken together, these two early alternative approaches suggested that an underlying general paradigm existed.

Automaton learning, with or without model checking, was subsequently considered for testing by many other researchers e.g. [16,18,21,24,31,41]. The literature has grown too extensive to provide a full bibliography here, and many other references will be found elsewhere in this Book, e.g. Chap. 1. Interestingly, [48] has shown that even without model checking, model inference alone provides better functional coverage for black-box testing than random testing. Within the model checking community, the verification approach known as counterexample guided abstraction refinement (CEGAR) also combines learning and model checking, (see e.g. [8,12]).

8 Conclusions and Future Work

We have presented here a personal survey of recent progress in learning-based testing. We began with short overview of fundamental principles, followed by an exposition of these principles within a specific testing tool, namely LBTest. We have described a number of contemporary research questions addressed using LBTest, such as convergence estimation, quantifying the hardness of learning, over-approximation learning methods, and quantifying the power of model checker generated test cases. The common theme unifying each of these research questions has been metrics on the convergence of learning. Such metrics enable a precise, general and quantitative approach to both machine learning and testing. In this respect, learning-based testing differs significantly from other black-box testing methods such as random testing and search-based testing where convergence measures based on models are absent.

8.1 Future Prospects

What are the future prospects for learning-based testing? What are the major scientific challenges today and the ultimate theoretical limits in the future? Is it possible to adopt this technique industrially? It is difficult to definitively answer all of these important questions at this time. Many questions are the topic of ongoing research projects within a small but growing community. Further empirical study, theoretical research and practical algorithm and architecture design is needed. However, we can draw some conclusions based on academic and industrial research so far.

(1) The technical advantages of LBT have been shown to be:
    (a) flexibility derived from a black-box approach to testing and requirements;
    (b) extensibility to more complex testing scenarios such as fault injection, robustness testing and risk-based testing;
    (c) support for high-volume and hence high coverage testing derived from active learning;
    (d) a precise coverage model derived from stochastic equivalence checking;
    (e) a high degree of automation, once a test harness has been constructed and requirements gathered; and
    (f) the accuracy of test verdicts through the use of precise formal user requirements.

(2) Formal requirements models have been perceived as a bottleneck to industrial adoption. But this criticism is not specific to LBT, and can be leveled at any use of formal methods. At the same time, critics of formal methods have yet to come up with any widely applicable and viable alternative that is sufficiently precise. Indeed, there seems to be an element of denial that requirements testing is even important.

(3) Successful case studies of LBT often depend upon being able to execute large test suites that can infer complex models. The size of test suites generated by active machine learning tends to grow rapidly as model complexity and the number of parameters to be inferred increases. However, run times often scale linearly wrt. the input alphabet size. Many types of real-time system have sufficiently low test latency to execute large test suites. However, this does not seem to hold for distributed systems such as client-server architectures. More aggressive techniques for over-approximation, such as presented in Sect. 5, may be necessary to address this problem. Furthermore, refined techniques which re-use inferred models from unit testing at the levels of integration and systems testing may also be necessary [45].

(4) At the outset of our research, machine learning was the main bottleneck for LBT, in the sense that regular inference was more computationally expensive than model checking. Today, this situation has more or less reversed. The converse definitely holds if we take into account the additional complexity of generating a large number of distinct counter-examples, and not just one as is current practice with most model checking tools. For future progress it will be necessary to find machine learning and model checking techniques that support each other in a more efficient way.

Acknowledgements. We wish to acknowledge the financial support of several research grants and agencies that allowed us to reach this point in our research. These include: EU project FP7-231620 HATS, ARTEMIS project JU 269335 MBAT, VIN-NOVA project 2013-05608 VIRTUES, EU ECSEL project 692529 SafeCOP and ITEA 3 project 16032 TESTOMAT.

References

1. Angluin, D.: Learning regular sets from queries and counterexamples. Inf. Comput. **75**, 87–106 (1987)
2. Arcuri, A., Iqbal, M.Z., Briand, L.: Formal analysis of the effectiveness and predictability of random testing. In: ACM International Symposium on Software Testing and Analysis (ISSTA) (2010)
3. Balcázar, J.L., Dáaz, J., Gavaldà, R.: Algorithms for learning finite automata from queries: a unified view. In: Du, D.Z., Ko, K.I. (eds.) Advances in Algorithms, Languages, and Complexity, pp. 53–72. Springer, Boston (1997). https://doi.org/10.1007/978-1-4613-3394-4_2
4. Berg, T., Jonsson, B., Leucker, M., Saksena, M.: Insights to Angluin's learning. Electr. Notes Theor. Comput. Sci. **118**, 3–18 (2005)
5. Bergadano, F., Gunetti, D.: Testing by means of inductive program learning. ACM Trans. Softw. Eng. Methodol. **5**(2), 119–145 (1996)
6. Cavada, R., et al.: The NUXMV symbolic model checker. In: Biere, A., Bloem, R. (eds.) CAV 2014. LNCS, vol. 8559, pp. 334–342. Springer, Cham (2014). https://doi.org/10.1007/978-3-319-08867-9_22
7. Broy, M., Jonsson, B., Katoen, J.-P., Leucker, M., Pretschner, A. (eds.): Model-Based Testing of Reactive Systems. LNCS, vol. 3472. Springer, Heidelberg (2005). https://doi.org/10.1007/b137241
8. Chauhan, P., Clarke, E., Kukula, J., Sapra, S., Veith, H., Wang, D.: Automated abstraction refinement for model checking large state spaces using SAT based conflict analysis. In: Aagaard, M.D., O'Leary, J.W. (eds.) FMCAD 2002. LNCS, vol. 2517, pp. 33–51. Springer, Heidelberg (2002). https://doi.org/10.1007/3-540-36126-X_3
9. Cherniavsky, J.C., Smith, C.H.: A recursion theoretic approach to program testing. IEEE Trans. Softw. Eng. **SE–13**(7), 777–784 (1987)
10. Chow, T.S.: Testing software design model by finite state machines. IEEE Trans. Softw. Eng. **SE–4**(3), 178–187 (1978)
11. Cimatti, A., et al.: NuSMV 2: an OpenSource tool for symbolic model checking. In: Brinksma, E., Larsen, K.G. (eds.) CAV 2002. LNCS, vol. 2404, pp. 359–364. Springer, Heidelberg (2002). https://doi.org/10.1007/3-540-45657-0_29
12. Clarke, E., Gupta, A., Kukula, J., Strichman, O.: SAT based abstraction-refinement using ILP and machine learning techniques. In: Brinksma, E., Larsen, K.G. (eds.) CAV 2002. LNCS, vol. 2404, pp. 265–279. Springer, Heidelberg (2002). https://doi.org/10.1007/3-540-45657-0_20
13. Czerny, M.X.: Learning-based software testing: evaluation of Angluin's L* algorithm and adaptations in practice. Batchelors thesis, Karlsruhe Institute of Technology, Department of Informatics Institute for Theoretical Computer Science (2014)

14. Feng, L., Lundmark, S., Meinke, K., Niu, F., Sindhu, M.A., Wong, P.Y.H.: Case studies in learning-based testing. In: Yenigün, H., Yilmaz, C., Ulrich, A. (eds.) ICTSS 2013. LNCS, vol. 8254, pp. 164–179. Springer, Heidelberg (2013). https://doi.org/10.1007/978-3-642-41707-8_11

15. Fisher, M.: An Introduction to Practical Formal Methods Using Temporal Logic. Wiley, Chichester (2011)

16. Fiterău-Broştean, P., Howar, F.: Learning-based testing the sliding window behavior of TCP implementations. In: Petrucci, L., Seceleanu, C., Cavalcanti, A. (eds.) FMICS/AVoCS -2017. LNCS, vol. 10471, pp. 185–200. Springer, Cham (2017). https://doi.org/10.1007/978-3-319-67113-0_12

17. Fraser, G., Wotawa, F., Ammann, P.E.: Testing with model checkers: a survey. SNA Technical report, 2007-P2-04, TU Graz (2007)

18. Groce, A., Peled, D., Yannakakis, M.: Adaptive model checking. Log. J. IGPL 14(5), 729–744 (2006)

19. de la Higuera, C.: Grammatical Inference. Cambridge University Press, Cambridge (2010)

20. Howar, F., Bauer, O., Merten, M., Steffen, B., Margaria, T.: The teachers' crowd: the impact of distributed oracles on active automata learning. In: Hähnle, R., Knoop, J., Margaria, T., Schreiner, D., Steffen, B. (eds.) ISoLA 2011. CCIS, pp. 232–247. Springer, Heidelberg (2012). https://doi.org/10.1007/978-3-642-34781-8_18

21. Hungar, H., Margaria, T., Steffen, B.: Test-based model generation for legacy systems. In: Proceedings of the 2003 International Test Conference (ITC 2003), pp. 971–980 (2003)

22. Kearns, M.J., Vazirani, U.: An Introduction to Computational Learning Theory. MIT Press, Cambridge (1994)

23. Lang, K.J., Pearlmutter, B.A., Price, R.A.: Results of the Abbadingo one DFA learning competition and a new evidence-driven state merging algorithm. In: Honavar, V., Slutzki, G. (eds.) ICGI 1998. LNCS, vol. 1433, pp. 1–12. Springer, Heidelberg (1998). https://doi.org/10.1007/BFb0054059

24. Li, K., Groz, R., Shahbaz, M.: Integration testing of components guided by incremental state machine learning. In: TAIC PART, pp. 59–70 (2006)

25. Lucent Technologies Inc.: Directly verifying a black box system Patent, US Patent Number 6,526,544, September 1999

26. McMinn, P.: Search-based software test data generation: a survey. Softw. Test. Verif. Reliab. 14(2), 105–156 (2004)

27. Meinke, K.: Automated black-box testing of functional correctness using function approximation. In: Rothermel, G. (ed) Proceedings of the ACM SIGSOFT International Symposium on Software Testing and Analysis, ISSTA 2004, pp. 143–153. ACM Press (2004). Softw. Eng. Not. 29(4)

28. Meinke, K.: CGE: a sequential learning algorithm for Mealy automata. In: Sempere, J.M., García, P. (eds.) ICGI 2010. LNCS (LNAI), vol. 6339, pp. 148–162. Springer, Heidelberg (2010). https://doi.org/10.1007/978-3-642-15488-1_13

29. Meinke, K., Niu, F.: A learning-based approach to unit testing of numerical software. In: Petrenko, A., Simão, A., Maldonado, J.C. (eds.) ICTSS 2010. LNCS, vol. 6435, pp. 221–235. Springer, Heidelberg (2010). https://doi.org/10.1007/978-3-642-16573-3_16

30. Meinke, K., Niu, F.: Learning-based testing for reactive systems using term rewriting technology. In: Wolff, B., Zaïdi, F. (eds.) ICTSS 2011. LNCS, vol. 7019, pp. 97–114. Springer, Heidelberg (2011). https://doi.org/10.1007/978-3-642-24580-0_8

31. Meinke, K., Sindhu, M.A.: Incremental learning-based testing for reactive systems. In: Gogolla, M., Wolff, B. (eds.) TAP 2011. LNCS, vol. 6706, pp. 134–151. Springer, Heidelberg (2011). https://doi.org/10.1007/978-3-642-21768-5_11

32. Meinke, K., Niu, F., Sindhu, M.: Learning-based software testing: a tutorial. In: Hähnle, R., Knoop, J., Margaria, T., Schreiner, D., Steffen, B. (eds.) ISoLA 2011. CCIS, pp. 200–219. Springer, Heidelberg (2012). https://doi.org/10.1007/978-3-642-34781-8_16

33. Meinke, K., Niu, F.: An incremental learning algorithm for hybrid automata. Internal report, School of Computer Science and Communication, KTH Royal Institute of Technology (2013)

34. Meinke, K., Sindhu, M.: LBTest: a learning-based testing tool for reactive systems. In: Proceedings of the Sixth International IEEE Conference on Software Testing, Verification and Validation (ICST 2013), pp. 447–454 (2013)

35. Meinke, K., Nycander, P.: Learning-based testing of distributed microservice architectures: correctness and fault injection. In: Bianculli, D., Calinescu, R., Rumpe, B. (eds.) SEFM 2015. LNCS, vol. 9509, pp. 3–10. Springer, Heidelberg (2015). https://doi.org/10.1007/978-3-662-49224-6_1

36. Meinke, K.: LBTest user manual. Internal report, School of Computer Science and Communication, KTH Royal Institute of Technology (2016)

37. Khosrowjerdi, H., Meinke, K., Rasmusson, A.: Learning-based testing for safety critical automotive applications. In: Bozzano, M., Papadopoulos, Y. (eds.) IMBSA 2017. LNCS, vol. 10437, pp. 197–211. Springer, Cham (2017). https://doi.org/10.1007/978-3-319-64119-5_13

38. Meinke, K.: Learning-based testing of cyber-physical systems-of-systems: a platooning study. In: Reinecke, P., Di Marco, A. (eds.) EPEW 2017. LNCS, vol. 10497, pp. 135–151. Springer, Cham (2017). https://doi.org/10.1007/978-3-319-66583-2_9

39. Peled, D., Vardi, M.Y., Yannakakis, M.: Black-box checking. In: Wu, J., et al. (eds.) Formal Methods for Protocol Engineering and Distributed Systems. FORTE/PSTV, pp. 225–240. Kluwer, Beijing (1999)

40. Raffelt, H., Steffen, B., Margaria, T.: Dynamic testing via automata learning. In: Yorav, K. (ed.) HVC 2007. LNCS, vol. 4899, pp. 136–152. Springer, Heidelberg (2008). https://doi.org/10.1007/978-3-540-77966-7_13

41. Raffelt, H., Merten, M., Steffen, B., Margaria, T.: Dynamic testing via automata learning. STTT **11**(4), 307–324 (2009)

42. Romanik, K.: Approximate testing and its relationship to learning. Theor. Comp. Sci. **188**, 79–99 (1997)

43. Romanik, K., Vitter, J.S.: Using Vapnik-Chervonenkis dimension to analyze the testing complexity of program, segments. Inf. Comput. **128**(2), 87–108 (1996)

44. Dupont, P.: StaMiNa regular inference competition (2010). www.stamina.chefbe. net

45. Shahbaz, M., Groz, R.: Analysis and testing of black-box component-based systems by inferring partial models. Softw. Test. Verif. Reliab. **24**, 253–288 (2014)

46. Vasilewskii, M.P.: Failure diagnosis of automata. Kibertetika **9**(4), 98–108 (1973)

47. Verwer, S., de Weerdt, M., Witteveen, C.: A likelihood-ratio test for identifying probabilistic deterministic real-time automata from positive data. In: Sempere, J.M., García, P. (eds.) ICGI 2010. LNCS (LNAI), vol. 6339, pp. 203–216. Springer, Heidelberg (2010). https://doi.org/10.1007/978-3-642-15488-1_17

48. Walkinshaw, N., Bogdanov, K., Derrick, J., Paris, J.: Increasing functional coverage by inductive testing: a case study. In: Petrenko, A., Simão, A., Maldonado, J.C. (eds.) ICTSS 2010. LNCS, vol. 6435, pp. 126–141. Springer, Heidelberg (2010). https://doi.org/10.1007/978-3-642-16573-3_10
49. Weyuker, E.: Assessing test data adequacy through program inference. ACM Trans. Program. Lang. Syst. **5**(4), 641–655 (1983)
50. Whalen, M., Rajan, A., Heimdahl, M., Miller, S.: Coverage metrics for requirements-based testing. In: Proceedings of the International Symposium on Software Testing and Analysis, ISSTA 2006, pp. 25–35. ACM Press (2006)
51. Zhu, H., Hall, P., May, J.: Inductive inference and software testing. J. Softw. Test. Verif. Reliab. **2**(2), 3–31 (1992)
52. Zhu, H.: A formal interpretation of software testing as inductive inference. J. Softw. Test. Verif. Reliab. **6**(1), 3–31 (1996)
53. Khosrowjerdi, H., Meinke, K.: Learning-based testing for autonomous systems using spatial and temporal requirements. Technical report, School of Electrical Engineering and Computer Science, KTH Royal Institute of Technology (2018)

Model Learning and Model-Based Testing

Bernhard K. Aichernig[1], Wojciech Mostowski[2],
Mohammad Reza Mousavi[2,3(✉)], Martin Tappler[1], and Masoumeh Taromirad[2]

[1] Institute of Software Technology, Graz University of Technology, Graz, Austria
[2] Centre for Research on Embedded Systems, Halmstad University, Halmstad,
Sweden
[3] Department of Informatics, University of Leicester, Leicester, UK
mm789@le.ac.uk

Abstract. We present a survey of the recent research efforts in integrating model learning with model-based testing. We distinguished two strands of work in this domain, namely test-based learning (also called test-based modeling) and learning-based testing. We classify the results in terms of their underlying models, their test purpose and techniques, and their target domains.

1 Introduction

On one hand, learning (functional or behavioral) models of software and computer systems (e.g., hardware, communication protocols) has been studied extensively in the past two decades. Various machine learning techniques [Mit97, Alp14] have been adopted to this domain and new domain-specific techniques have been developed for model learning (cf. the chapters on (Extended) Finite Stat Machine learning in this volume).

On the other hand, testing has been the dominant verification and quality assurance technique in industrial practice. Traditionally, testing has been an unstructured and creative effort in which requirements and domain knowledge is turned into a set of test cases, also called a test suite, while trying to cover various artifacts (such as requirements, design, or implementation code). Model-based testing (MBT) [UPL12, UL07] is a structured approach to testing in which the testing process is driven by a model (e.g., defining the correct behavior of the system under test, or specifying the relevant interactions with the environment).

The focus of the present paper is precisely in the intersection of the above-mentioned two fields: learning (functional or behavioral) models and model-based testing. In this intersection fall two types of research:

1. *test-based learning*: various (active) learning techniques make queries to the to-be-learned system in order to verify a learning hypothesis. Such queries can be tests that are generated from a learned model. We refer to this strand of work as test-based learning or test-based modeling [MNRS04, Tre11].

© Springer International Publishing AG, part of Springer Nature 2018
A. Bennaceur et al. (Eds.): ML for Dynamic Software Analysis, LNCS 11026, pp. 74–100, 2018.
https://doi.org/10.1007/978-3-319-96562-8_3

2. *learning-based testing*: models are cornerstones of model-based testing; how-ever, complete and up-to-date models hardly ever exist. Learning can hence be used to create and complement models for model-based testing. We refer to this category of work as learning-based testing [MS11].

To structure our survey of the field we focus on the following classification criteria:

1. Types of models: different types of models have been learned and have been used for model-based testing. We distinguish the following categories of mod-els: predicates and functions, and logical structures (such as Kripke struc-tures, cf. the chapter on logic-based learning in this volume), finite state machines (including their variants and extensions, cf. the chapters on FSM and Extended FSM learning, as well as learning-based testing in this volume), and labeled transition systems. The distinction between variants of these mod-els is not always well-defined and there are several property-preserving trans-lations among them. However, this classification gives us a general overview and a measure of matching between different learning and testing techniques.
2. Types of testing: requirement-based and conformance testing are the most prominent uses of model-based testing. However, other types of model-based testing have also been considered in combination with learning; these include: integration testing, performance testing, and security testing.
3. Domain: test-based learning and model-based testing have been applied to various domains, such as embedded systems, network protocols, and web ser-vices. If a research result considers a particular application domain, we classify the result in terms of the domain, as well.

The rest of this paper is organized as follows. In Sect. 2, an overview of model-based testing is provided. In Sect. 3, the basic ideas behind model learning and their relation to testing are presented. In Sect. 4, we review the types of models that have been used in integrating learning and testing and survey the different pieces of research related to each type of model. In Sect. 5, we classify the test purposes and testing techniques that have been considered in combination with learning. In Sect. 6, we review the domains to which the combination of testing and learning has been applied. Finally, we conclude the survey in Sect. 7 by pointing out some of the open challenges in this domain.

2   Model-Based Testing

Model-based testing (MBT) is a structured testing technique in which models are used to guide the testing process. Specification test models can, for example, describe the input-output functionality of a unit (function, class, module, or component) [HRD07,MN10], specify the state-based behavior of a unit [UL07] or a system [VT14], or sequences of interactions with graphical user interface [YCM09]. Ideally such specification models have a mathematical underpinning, i.e., have a formal semantics; such formal models include algebraic properties, finite state machines, and labeled transition systems. Once specification test models are in place, much of the testing process can be mechanized thanks to various MBT techniques and algorithms.

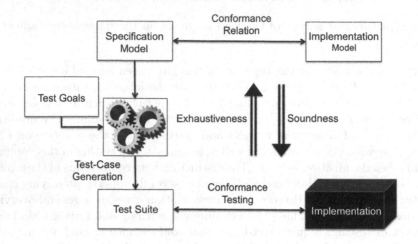

Fig. 1. An overview of model-based testing [ARM16, UPL12]

Figure 1 presents a general overview of MBT theory and practice. The underlying assumption of MBT is the existence of a formalization of the requirements in the form of a specification test model. This is a highly non-trivial assumption; models are often absent or incomplete in practice. Learning is a technique that can help reinstate the underlying assumption of MBT.

To put MBT on firm formal grounds, a common assumption is that the behavior of the implementation under test can be described by some (unknown) model with the same mathematical underpinning as the specification test model. This enables grounding the theory of MBT in a mathematical definition of a conformance relation between the specification model and the purported implementation model.

One of the most important ingredients of a practical MBT approach is a test-case generation algorithm that can automatically generate a test suite (a set of test cases) from the specification model (in an online or offline manner), taking into account the specified test goals. Then using a mechanized adapter the generated abstract test suite can be translated into concrete test cases that are executed on the system under test (which is traditionally considered to be a black box). The results of the test execution are then compared with the results prescribed by the specification test model.

The formal notion of conformance and the conformance testing algorithm are linked through soundness and completeness theorems. Soundness states that conformance testing never rejects a conforming implementation and exhaustiveness states that conformance testing is able to reject all non-conforming implementations. A sound and exhaustive conformance testing algorithm is called complete.

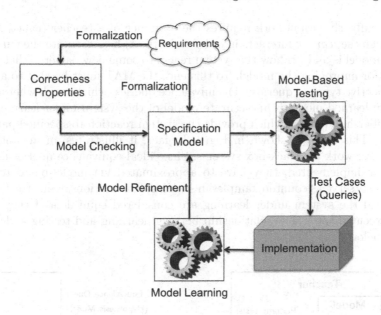

Fig. 2. Creating models for model-based testing

Specification test models can be learned from (reference) implementations and validated or verified by the domain experts, e.g., by manual inspection or model checking (as well as equivalence checking tools); Fig. 2 illustrates this process. Also incomplete or outdated models can be augmented or corrected (possibly with user feedback) using learning techniques.

Since the scope of this paper is the combination of model-based testing and learning, we only explore the part of the literature that serves at least one of the following two categories of purposes (cf. the chapter on testing stateless black-box programs in this volume for a complementary survey):

1. Model-based test-based learning, i.e., the use of model-based testing as a teaching mechanism in learning models, or
2. Learning-based model-based testing, i.e., the use of learning techniques to come up with models (of specification or implementation) in the model-based testing process.

3   Learning

In this section, we review the main ideas concerning model learning and their connections to (model-based) testing. We mainly consider active automata learning in the minimally adequate teacher (MAT) framework as introduced by Angluin [Ang87], since it shares clear common grounds with testing; for other machine learning techniques (some of which are also used in combination with model-based testing), we refer to [Mit97, Alp14].

Generally, this framework requires the existence of a teacher (called MAT) with which the *learner* interacts in order to learn (1) how accurate the currently learned model is and (2) how the system reacts to some new patterns that are of interest for improving the model. To this end, the MAT must be able to answer two respective types of queries: (1) equivalence queries, which check whether the currently learned model is an accurate model of the system under learning and (2) membership queries, which provide the system reaction to specified patterns of input. This setup is shown in Fig. 3. In fact, it illustrates an instantiation of this framework for black-box systems. Since ideal equivalence queries usually cannot be implemented, they have to approximated via model-based testing. Failing tests serve as counterexamples in such implementations, while the learned model and the system under learning are considered equivalent if they agree on all executed tests. The relationship between learning and testing is detailed further below.

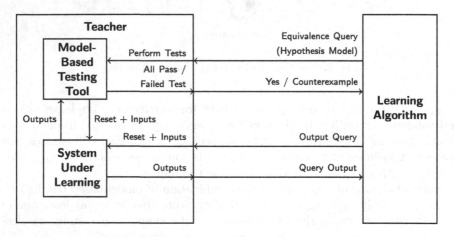

Fig. 3. Learning setup in the MAT framework. Figure adapted from a figure in [SMVJ15].

In the original L^* algorithm by Angluin, a deterministic finite automaton (DFA) representing an initially unknown regular language is learned. Membership queries correspond to the question whether some string is in the target language. In equivalence queries, the learner asks whether the language of a hypothesized DFA is equivalent to the target language.

These queries enable the learner to follow a two-step procedure in which it gains knowledge by posing membership queries. If there is sufficient information to create a hypothesis, an equivalence query is issued. The teacher either answers *yes*, signaling that learning is finished, or it responds with a counterexample to equivalence. Such a counterexample is then processed by the learner which eventually starts another round of learning.

Several variations of this general learning process have been proposed. All of them have in common that two types of queries are posed in an inter-leaved and iterative manner. As an example, consider learning of Mealy-machine models [Nie03, MNRS04, SG09]: instead of posing membership queries, the learner asks output queries [SG09], i.e., it asks for a sequence of outputs pro-duced in response to a sequence of inputs. Analogously to L^*, equivalence queries are issued whereby a counterexample is a string of inputs for which the system under learning (SUL) and the current hypothesis produce different outputs.

3.1 Relation Between Learning and Testing

Early work relating testing and program inference predates Angluin's L^* algorithm. Weyuker [Wey83] proposed a program-inference-based test-adequacy criterion. She points out the importance of distinguishing between test-selection criteria and test-adequacy criteria. The latter should be used to assess if a pass-ing test set contains sufficient data. For that she proposes to infer a program from a test set and deem it adequate if the inferred program is equivalent to both program and specification. Noting that checking equivalence is in general unde-cidable, she suggest that equivalence checks may be approximated by testing as is usually done for equivalence queries in active automata learning.

More recently, Berg et al. [BGJ+05] discussed the relationship between con-formance testing and active automata learning, referred to as regular inference. Basically, both techniques try to gain information about a black-box system based on a limited number of observations, but with different goals. One tech-nique solves a checking problem and the other a synthesis problem. They showed that a conformance test suite for a model m provides enough information to learn a model isomorphic to m. Conversely, observations made during learning a model m form a conformance test suite for m. This resembles the intuition behind Weyuker's work [Wey83]: a test set should contain information to infer a program equivalent to the original program.

Aside from the theoretical relationship, they referred to another connection between learning and testing. Since equivalence oracles do not exist in general, they can be approximated by conformance testing (as shown in Fig. 3). Hence, in practice a testing problem has to be solved each time an equivalence query is issued. Two examples of commonly used equivalence testing methods are the W-method [Vas73, Cho78] and partial W-method [FvBK+91], the latter aiming at improving efficiency. Both of these have for instance been implemented in the automata-learning library LearnLib [IHS15].

3.2 Test Case Selection vs. Query Minimization

Since exhaustive model-based testing is usually infeasible, it is necessary to select a subset of test cases based on some user-specified criterion [UPL12]. In other words, the number of tests has to be reduced. Because of the rela-tionship described above, it can be concluded that a reduction of queries is required for learning as well. There are several possibilities for implementing such measures. Most importantly, abstraction is essential for learning to be feasible. While abstraction is mostly done manually, techniques have been developed to derive abstraction automatically through counterexample-guided abstraction refinement [AHK+12, Aar14, HSM11]. In addition to that, we give three examples for ways to reduce the number of tests required for learning.

Algorithmic Adaptations. Following the work of Angluin [Ang87], shortcomings of the L^* algorithm have been identified and optimizations have been developed. A well-known example of such an optimization is the adapted counterexample processing proposed by Rivest and Schapire [RS93]. They extract a single suffix from a counterexample which distinguishes states in the current hypothesis. As a result, the observation table size and thereby the required membership queries are reduced.

Equivalence Testing Optimisations. Well-known methods for conformance testing are the W-method [Vas73, Cho78] and partial W-method [FvBK+91]. Thus, they may be used to check whether the current hypothesis is equivalent to the SUL. However, they suffer from two drawbacks. Firstly, they assume a known upper bound on the number of states of the SUL. Since we consider black-box systems, we cannot know such a bound. Furthermore, their complexity grows exponentially in the difference of the number of states of hypothesis and SUL. This makes the application in industrial scenarios impractical. Alternative ways of selecting tests should thus be considered. The ZULU challenge [CdlHJ09] called for solutions to this issue. Competing approaches were only allowed to pose a limited number of membership queries/tests. This resembles a setting in which the cost of test execution matters and equivalence has to be checked via testing.

Howar et al. [HSM10] describe that a different interpretation of equivalence queries is necessary in this case. Rather than testing for equivalence, it is necessary to find counterexamples fast. This is a reasonable approach, as learning is inherently incomplete anyway, because of its relation to black-box testing. Furthermore, they discuss their approaches to selecting test cases which are based on heuristics. They consider hypotheses to be evolving, i.e. testing is not started from scratch once a new hypothesis is constructed. Additionally, they base their test selection on the improved counterexample handling [RS93], combined with randomization.

Efficient equivalence testing has been addressed by Smeenk et al. [SMVJ15] as well. Since their SUL is too large for testing with the W-method, they developed a randomized conformance testing technique. It is based on a method for finding adaptive distinguishing sequences described by Lee and Yannakakis [LY94]. In addition to that, they selected a subset of the original alphabet which they tested more thoroughly. This is done to ensure that specific sequences relevant to the initialization of the considered application are covered although it would be unlikely to select them otherwise.

Another randomized conformance testing technique for automata learning has been presented in [AT17a]. It addresses coverage by mutation-based test-case selection whereby the applied mutations are tailored to the specifics of learning. Furthermore, stochastic equivalence checking has for instance been applied in learning-based testing to measure convergence [MN15].

Purely random testing, without taking heuristics into account, is a viable option as well. It has successively been used for experiments with the tool Tomte [AHK+12, AFBKV15]. However, Aarts et al. [AKT+14] also point out that while being effective in most cases, random testing may also fail if the probability of reaching some state is low. Still, quantitative analysis of learned models, e.g. giving some confidence for the correctness of the models, are mostly lacking. This is despite early work discussing such ideas [Ang87, RS93].

Domain-Specific Optimisations. Another important insight is that the inclusion of knowledge about the application domain can increase learning performance. This has for instance been shown by Hungar et al. [HNS03], who applied techniques such as partial-order reduction methods to reduce the number of queries. Another example of a domain-specific optimization is the modification of the W-method by de Ruiter and Poll [dRP15].

3.3 State Merging Techniques

A prominent alternative to learning in the MAT framework is learning via state merging. State merging techniques infer models from given samples, that is, sequences of symbols. This is usually done passively, i.e. without interaction with a teacher. Prominent examples are the RPNI algorithm [OG92] and ALERGIA [CO94]. In a first step, state merging techniques generally build a prefix tree acceptor (PTA) from the given samples. They then iteratively check nodes in the tree for compatibility and merge them if they are compatible. The tree is transformed into a finite automaton through this procedure. Depending on the actual algorithm, different techniques are used for the steps in this generic procedure and different types of models are created.

In the case of RPNI for instance, a deterministic finite automaton is inferred and samples are split into negative and positive samples. Furthermore, the PTA is built from positive samples while negative samples are used to check whether two nodes may be merged. ALERGIA requires only positive samples to learn a probabilistic finite automaton. Therefore, it augments the PTA with frequencies and bases its compatibility check on a statistical test.

The QSM algorithm is an interactive state-merging algorithm with membership queries [DLDvL08]. Hence, it is a query-driven State-Merging DFA induction technique. The induction process starts by constructing an initial DFA covering all positive scenarios only. The induced DFA is then successively generalized under the control of the available negative scenarios and newly generated scenarios classified by the end-user (membership queries). This generalization is carried out by successively merging well-selected state pairs of the initial automaton.

4   Models

In this section, we provide an overview of the kind of models that have been learned for testing. Most of the work concentrates on different types of finite state machines and labeled transition systems. Some researchers have considered other models, e.g. for stateless systems.

4.1   Finite State Machines

In [AKT+12, AKT+14], the authors use a combination of automata learning techniques to learn a model of the implementation, which is then compared to a reference specification model using equivalence checking techniques.

In [LGS06a], the authors use an approach based on L^* to learn Mealy machines, which is extended and more thoroughly described in [SG09]. Other work considers more expressive versions of Mealy machines [LGS06b, SLG07a], which include parameters for actions, predicates over input parameters and allow for observable non-determinism.

Margaria et al. [MNRS04] optimized the L* algorithm for generalized Mealy machines, i.e. Mealy machines that may produce a sequence of outputs rather than exactly one output in response to a single input. They report significant performance gains as compared to learning DFA models.

In [CHJS14, CHJS16], Cassel et al. consider generating models from test cases and present a framework for generating a class of EFSM models, called register automata, from black-box components using active automata learning. They introduce an extension to the L* algorithm called *SL** (for *Symbolic L**). However, they do not explicitly mention any particular testing technique. They only suggest using conformance testing in hypothesis validation (i.e., providing counterexamples). The SL* algorithm is available as an extension to Learn-Lib [IHS15], namely RaLib.

Ipate et al. [ISD15] propose an approach which, given a state-transition model of a system (EFSM), constructs an approximate automaton model and a test suite for the system. The approximate model construction relies on a variant of Angluin's automata learning algorithm, adapted to *finite cover automata* [CSY99]. In parallel with automata construction, they incrementally generate conformance test suites for the investigated models, using the W-method [Cho78] adapted to bounded sequences. These test suites are used to find counterexamples in the learning process. Their approach is presented and implemented in the context of the Event-B modeling language [DIMS12, DIS12].

Arts et al. [AT10] automatically extract finite state machines from sets of unit tests using an FSM inference technique, namely StateChum [WBHS07]. Then, the inferred FSMs are used to provide feedback on the adequacy of the set of tests and to develop properties for testing state-based systems. They use QuickCheck for testing and thus, consider generating QuickCheck properties. An FSM model is incrementally extracted from the test suite as it evolves.

In [RMSM09] a method for learning-based testing is presented, where the alphabet of the system under learning is progressively extended during the process based on previous interactions. This extension, and the knowledge gained about the system is used to further derive test cases. The method uses classic deterministic Mealy machines and the LearnLib for learning, and it is showcased with the Mantis Bug Tracker case study.

Relying on a heuristic approach to model inference, Schulze et al. [SLBW15] discussed an model-based testing supported by model generation. They propose to generate a model from manually created test cases in order to generate further tests from this model which possibly find undetected issues. In the case study, they report on manual effort for GUI testing a web-based system.

4.2 Labeled Transition Systems

Hagerer et al. [HHNS02] presented a technique called regular extrapolation for learning labeled transition systems (LTS) with inputs and outputs. For testing purposes, labels and states may have additional observations, i.e. parameters and attributes. Their technique starts with a set of abstract traces, either gathered passively via log-files or actively via testing. These traces are merged into a tree and then states with equivalent observations, i.e. equivalent attributes, are merged. Furthermore, a user may specify independence relations in order to simplify the model via partial order reduction. Model checking is used to verify if the learned model satisfies a set of Linear Temporal Logic (LTL) specifications.

Hungar et al. [HNS03] used the L* algorithm to learn LTS models with inputs and outputs that are input-enabled and input-deterministic. Several optimizations for reducing the number of membership queries are presented, most notably the application of partial-order reduction techniques that exploit domain-specific independence and symmetry properties.

Walkinshaw et al. [WDG09] introduce a reverse-engineering technique which infers state machines, in the form of LTS, from implementations. They use active state-merging techniques [DLDvL08] for learning a model based on program executions and model-based testing in refining the hypothesis model. The learning process starts with an initially small set of execution traces, based on which an initial hypothesis model is constructed. Then, iteratively, a given MBT framework automatically generates tests from the hypothesis model which are executed in the program. Any test conflicting the expected behavior by the model would restart the process to construct a refined hypothesis model. The process iterates until no more conflicts can be found by testing. For model inference, they use StateChum, developed by the authors [WBHS07], and use QuickCheck for MBT [AHJW06].

Walkinshaw et al. [WBDP10] use the technique introduced in [WDG09] and propose inductive testing to increase functional coverage in the absence of a complete specification.

Tretmans [Tre11] discusses both learning-based testing as well as testing-based learning. It is rightfully noted that intermixing the two directions is dangerous due to a risk of a circular dependency in the resulting testing process.

Most approaches by Tretmans, employ ioco-based conformance testing methods, and they treat both deterministic and non-deterministic models given as Mealy machines. The learning process is delegated to the LearnLib suite with custom extensions to facilitate better learning, Volpato and Tretmans [VT14] extend the Angluin's L* algorithm to work with non-determinism in input-output labeled transition systems. The ioco-based testing methodology is implemented in the TorXakis tool [TB03] and employs random model exploration to generate tests. The learning approach is further improved in subsequent work [VT15] which weakens assumptions related to the completeness of information obtained during learning. An important improvement is that the new approach does not require exhaustive equivalence checks.

Groz et al. [GLPS08] present inference of k-*quotients* of FSMs, but also of input output transition systems (IOTSs). They address the composition IOTSs and asynchronous communication between components. The latter is accounted for by introducing queues modeled by IOTSs.

4.3   Other Models

Meinke and Sindhu [MS11] apply the learning-based testing paradigm to reactive systems and present an incremental learning algorithm for Kripke structures.

For stateless behavior, predicates and functions provide a natural abstraction for the input-output functionality of programs. In [BG96], inductive program learning (and inductive logic programming) is used to learn the behavior of programs; the technique is used to generate adequate tests in order to distinguish the program under test from all other alternative programs that can be learned. In [HRD07], algebraic specifications of Java programs are learned. In [Mei04, MN10], functional models of numerical software are learned and the learned models are used for automatic generation of unit tests.

Walkinshaw and Fraser presented *Test by Committee*, test-case generation using *uncertainty sampling* [WF17]. The approach is independent of the type of model that is inferred and an adaption of *Query By Committee*, a technique commonly used in active learning. In their implementation, they infer several hypotheses at each stage via genetic programming, generate random tests and select those tests which lead to the most disagreement between the inferred hypotheses. In contrast to most other works considered, their implementation infers non-sequential programs. It infers functions mapping from numerical inputs to single outputs. Papadopoulos and Walkinshaw also considered similar types of programs, but in a more general learning-based testing setting [PW15]. Therefore, they presented the Model-Inference driven Testing (MINTEST) framework which they also instantiated and evaluated.

5   Test Purposes and Types of Testing

5.1   Behavioral Conformance Testing

Behavioral conformance testing is a common form of model-based testing, in which tests are generated in order to establish whether the behavior of the implementation under test is "equivalent" to that of the specification model, according to a well-defined notion of equivalence. Typically behavioral conformance testing is integrated with model-learning in that the specification test models are learned and are subsequently used for generating a conformance test suite [VT15, ASV10]. However, in [AKT+14], an alternative integration is also explored. Namely, model learning is used to learn both a model of a reference implementation and the implementation under test and then equivalence checking tools are used to check the equivalence between the two learned model. This way conformance checking is performed in an intensional manner by comparing models rather than by generating test cases from the specification model and executing test cases on the implementation.

A case study following a similar approach is presented in [TAB17]. However, instead of comparing to the model of a reference implementation, learned models of implementations are compared among each other. Detected differences are considered to point to possible bugs which should be analyzed manually. Experiments involving five implementations of the MQTT protocol revealed 18 errors in all but one of the implementations. The system HVLearn described by Sivakorn et al. [SAP+17] follows a similar approach. It learns DFA-models of SSL/TLS hostname verification implementations via the KV algorithm [KV94]. Given learned models, HVLearn is able to list unique differences between pairs models and additionally provides analysis capabilities for single models. The authors reported that they found eight previously unknown unique RFC violations by comparing inferred models. Another example using a similar technique in the security domain is SFADiff [ASJ+16]. In contrast to the other approaches, it learns symbolic finite automata (SFA) and is able to find differences between pairs of sets of programs, e.g., for fingerprinting or creating evasion attacks against security measures. It has been evaluated in case studies considering TCP state machines, web application firewalls and parsers in web browsers.

These approaches to conformance testing between implementations can in general not guarantee exhaustiveness. In other words, if models are found to be equivalent this does neither imply that the implementations are equivalent nor that the implementations are free of errors. In testing of complex systems, however, the reverse will often hold, i.e. there will be differences. These may either help to extend the learned models in case learning introduced the differences, or may point to actual differences between systems. The discussed case studies showed that such differences can be exploited in practice, e.g., to find bugs.

5.2   Requirements-Based Testing

With the introduction of black box checking, Peled et al. [PVY99] pioneered a line of research combining learning, black-box testing and formal verification. In order to check whether a black-box system satisfies some formally-defined property, a model is learned with Angluin's L^*-algorithm and the property is checked on this model. If a counterexample is found, it either shows that the property is violated or it is spurious and can be used to extend the model.

To avoid false positives, conformance testing as described by Vasilevskii [Vas73] and Chow [Cho78] is also used to extend the model, i.e., to implement equivalence queries.

Following that, several optimisations and variations have been proposed. Adaptive model checking [GPY02a, GPY02b] optimizes black box checking by using a model of the system which is assumed to be inaccurate but relevant. Another early developed variation is grey-box checking [EGPQ06], which considers a setting in which a system is composed of some completely-specified components and some black-box systems. With regard to testing, the VC-method [Vas73, Cho78] and other conformance testing approaches, taking the grey-box setting into account, are used and compared.

Adaptive model-checking combined with assume-guarantee verification has also been considered for the verification of composed systems [HK08]. Furthermore, another variation of adaptive model-checking has been described by Lai et al. [LCJ06]. They use genetic algorithms instead of L^* in order to learn a system model. Their results show promising performance for prefix-closed languages.

Meinke and Sindhu [MS11] applied the learning-based testing paradigm to reactive systems and present an incremental learning algorithm for Kripke structures. Here, an intermediate learned model is model checked against a temporal specification in order to produce a counter-example input stimulus. The SUT is then tested with this input. If the resulting output satisfies the specification, then this new input-output pair is integrated into the model. Otherwise, a fault has been found and the algorithm terminates.

Following ideas of black box checking, a testing approach for stochastic systems is presented in [AT17b]. It focuses on reachability properties and basically infers testing strategies which optimize the probability of observing certain outputs. This is done via iterated model-inference, strategy generation via probabilistic model-checking, and property-directed sampling, i.e. testing, of the SUT.

5.3   Security Testing

Based on black box checking [PVY99], Shu and Lee had described an approach to learning-based security testing [SL07]. Instead of checking more general properties, they try to find violations of security properties in the composition of learned models of components. In following work, they presented a combination of learning and model-based fuzz testing and considered both active and passive model inference [SHL08]. This approach is more extensively described in [HSL08] with a focus on passive model inference. For this purpose they detail their state-merging-based inference approach, discuss the type of fuzz functions and the coverage criteria they used. Additionally, they provide a more exhaustive evaluation.

The compositional approach is also taken in [ORT+07], where several methods are used to study the security of cryptographic protocols, where learning by testing black-box implementations is one of the techniques employed. The secrecy and authenticity properties are then checked on both the protocol specifications and the actual implementations through the learned model of the implementation.

Hossen et al. [HGOR14] presented an approach to model inference specifically tailored to security testing of web applications. The approach is based on the Z-quotient algorithm [PLG+14].

Cho et al. [CBP+11] developed a security testing tool called MACE. This tool combines the learning of a Mealy machine with concolic execution of the source code in order to explore the state space of protocol implementations more efficiently. Here, the learning algorithm guides the concolic execution in order to gain more control over the search process. When applied to four server applications, MACE could detect seven vulnerabilities.

5.4   Integration Testing

Tackling the issue that complex systems commonly integrate third-party components without specification, Li et al. [LGS06a] proposed a learning-based approach to integration testing. They follow an integrated approach in which they learn models of components from tests and based on the composition of these models, they generate integration tests. The execution of such tests may eventually lead to an update of the learned models if discrepancies are detected. Integration testing thus serves also as equivalence oracle. In following work, Li et al. [LGS06b, SLG07a, SLG07b] extended their learning-based integration testing approach to more expressive models. These models also account for data, through the introduction of parameters for actions and predicates over input parameters. Additionally, they also allow for observable non-determinism [SLG07a, SLG07b].

Groz et al. present an alternative approach to inference of component models [GLPS08]. Instead of learning each component model separately, they infer a k-quotient of the composed system and by projection they infer component models. With an initial model at hand, they perform a reachability analysis to detect compositional problems. If a detected problem can be confirmed, they warn that a problem exists, otherwise they refine the inferred models if the problem could not be confirmed. Testing is stopped when no potential compositional problem can be found.

In a similar setting as [LGS06a] and using the same algorithm, Shahbaz et al. [SPK07] described an approach to detect feature interaction in an integrated system. Basically, they infer models of components by testing, and execute the same tests of the composed system again. If the observations in the second phase do not conform to the inferred models, a feature interaction is detected.

Based on their previous works, Shahbaz and Groz [SG14] present an approach for analyzing and testing black-box components by combining model learning and MBT techniques. The procedure starts by learning each component's (partial) behavioral model and composing them as a product. The product is then fed to a model-based test case generator. The tests are then applied on the real system. Any discrepancies between the learned models and the system's real behavior counts as counterexample for the learned models, to be used to refine the models. For a more extensive discussion of learning-based integration testing, see also the corresponding chapter in the volume.

In [KMMV16] a test-based learning approach is devised, where an *already specified system* under test is executed to find and record deviations from that specification. Based on the collection of these deviations, a fault-model is learned, which is then used to perform model-based testing with QuickCheck [AHJW06] for the discovery of similar faults in other implementations. Being a preliminary work, it uses classic deterministic Mealy machines in the learning process with the LearnLib implementation. The models utilized in this approach are rich state-based models with full support for predicates. It falls into the integration testing category in that overall goal of the work is to test implementations composed of different versions of components, some of which may exhibit deviations from the reference model.

5.5   Regression Testing

Hagerer et al. [HHNS02] and Hungar et al. [HNS03] consider regression testing as a particularly fruitful application scenario for model learning. With the possibility of automatically maintaining models during the evolution of a system regression testing could be largely improved.

Regression testing and learning is also related in [LS14], however, in a slightly different fashion and not directly connected to model learning. Namely, machine-learning techniques are used to identify, select, and prioritize tests for regression testing based on test results from previous iterations and test meta-data.

Selection and extension of test cases, consequently leading to the refinement of the software model used for MBT, is also considered in [GS16]. Additional tests are recorded from the Exploratory Testing process [MSB11] and checked to be covered in the existing MBT model. If they are not, the model undergoes a refinement procedure to include the new execution traces. This can be classified as expert supported continuous learning process to build an MBT model.

5.6   Performance Testing

Adamis et al. proposed an approach to passively learn FSM models from conformance test logs to aid performance testing [AKR15]. Since the learned models may be inaccurate, manual postprocessing is required.

5.7   GUI Testing

Choi et al. described *Swifthand* a passive-learning-based testing tool for user interfaces of Android apps [CNS13]. They interleave learning and testing: (1) they use the learned model to steer testing to previously unexplored states and (2) refine the model based on test observations. Their test selection strategy aims at minimizing the number of restarts, the most time-consuming action in the considered domain, while maximizing (code) coverage. The evaluation shows that *Swifthand* outperforms L^*-based and random testing.

6 Domain

Model learning and model-based testing has been applied to many different domains with different characteristics. In this section, we provide an overview of such application domains.

6.1 Embedded Systems

Embedded systems are a very suitable application domain for model learning and model-based testing; they often have a confined interaction with the environment through an interface. One of the earliest application of such techniques to the embedded system domain has been the application of model learning to telephone systems with large legacy subsystems [HHNS02,HNS03]. Meinke and Sindhu [MS11] applied their learning algorithm to a cruise control and an elevator controller.

Test-based learning (based on a variant of the well-known FSM-based testing, called the W-method) has been applied in [SMVJ15] to learn an industrial embedded control software.

The combination of learning and testing has also been applied in the automotive domain. In [KMMV16], the basic ideas about learning faulty behavior of AUTOSAR components is explored in order to predict possible failures in component integration. In [KMR] learning-based testing is applied to testing ECU applications.

6.2 Network and Security Protocols

Another application area often explored in the context of learning and testing is that of security protocols and protocol implementations. Using the abstraction technology described in [AHK+12] and Mealy machines learned through Learn-Lib, [FBJV16] reports on learning different TCP stack implementations. Instead of for testing, the learned models are used for model checking to verify properties of these implementations in an off-line fashion. A similar case study carried out in a security setting focused on SSH implementations [FBLP+17]. Model checking the learned models of different implementations revealed minor violations of the standard but no security-critical issues. In [MCWKK09], the learned protocols are used as an input for fuzzing tools in order to reveal security vulnerabilities. Learning-based fuzz testing has also been applied for the Microsoft MSN instant messaging protocol [SHL08,HSL08]. Furthermore, learning-based testing of security protocols is addressed in [SL07] as well.

The authors of [MCWKK09] learned a number of malware, text-based and binary protocols using some domain-specific and heuristic-based learning techniques. Aarts et al. [AKT+12,AKT+14] combined various learning techniques to learn and test the bounded re-transmission protocol and Fiterau-Brostean et al. [FBJV14] extended this work to fragments of TCP. Walkinshaw et al. [WBDP10] applied their inductive testing approach to explore the behavior of the Linux TCP stack.

Test-based learning has been extensively used to learn models of different sorts of smart-card based applications. Being black-box systems and typically specified using imprecise language, test-based learning helped to devise more precise models of such applications. In particular, the models of a biometric passport and a bank card have been produced this way, see [ASV10, AdRP13], respectively. In both works, a suitable data abstraction between the learning alphabet and the actual system inputs and output had to be developed to facilitate the learning process. This led to the development of Tomte, a framework for automated data abstraction for the purpose of real system learning [AHK+12, Aar14]. The learned model produced [ASV10] was also compared to the manually developed model for the conformance testing of the Dutch biometric passport [MPS+09].

6.3 Web Services

Raffelt et al. applied dynamic testing on web applications [RMSM08]. More concretely, they described a test environment *Webtest*, combining traditional testing methods, like record-and-replay, and dynamic testing. The latter provides benefits such as systematic exploration and model extrapolation, while the former eases dynamic testing by defining possible input actions.

Bertolino et al. [BIPT09] used test-based learning (based on finite state machines) to learn the behavioral interfaces for web services.

6.4 Biological Systems

Biological systems have been recently studied as instances of reactive systems [BFFK09]. This provides the prospect of using models of reactive and hybrid systems to replace in vivo and in vitro experiments on living organisms and cells with in silico experiments (e.g., replacing the experiments with model checking or model-based testing) [BFFH14, Col14]. In [AL13], test-based learning is used to learn hybrid automata models of biological systems (cell models). In [MHR+06], automata learning technique is integrated with requirement-driven engineering to create and improve models of biological systems.

7   Conclusions

Learning-based testing is an active research area that has produced impressive results despite being a relatively young discipline. Different systems in various critical domains have been tested successfully including controllers, communication protocols, web applications, mobile apps and smart cards. Every year new algorithms, techniques and tools are proposed in order to learn and test increasingly complex systems.

The prevailing concern in the domain of model-learning (in the context of testing) is the scalability and applicability to real systems. For such applications, abstraction techniques for input and output data are needed to support the learning process. The researchers are actively looking into automating this process, which in many cases is still manual and requires either domain-specific knowledge, or apriori knowledge about the system under test. Several discussed papers either mention this as an issue, or provide some solution for it.

Another open issue surfacing in the described works is the treatment of richer models, both in the context of learning and testing. For example, stochastic models, or models that consider time or system dynamics. Such rich models bring new challenges in both research domains, moreover, they underline the scalability issues mentioned above.

Completeness (or a quantified approximation thereof) is another major concern in this domain. A property of algorithms in the MAT framework is "that a learned model is either complete and correct, or not correct at all" [VT15]. Note that in this context, correctness expresses that the learned model and the system under learning agree on all possible inputs. In [VT15], this property has been dropped by learning an over- and an underapproximation and preserving ioco-conformance during learning. In other words, there are two learned models which may not agree with the system under learning on all inputs but which are in a conformance relation with the system. However, such an adaptation may not be possible for all types of models. Steffen et al. [SHM11] also mention this property, stating that it must be accepted and that incompletely learned models may still provide benefits in certain scenarios, e.g., for test-case generation [HHNS02].

Scenarios like black-box checking [PVY99] on the other hand suffer from incompleteness[1]. They can guarantee that a verified property either holds or the number of states of the system is larger than an assumed upper bound. More quantitative measures of correctness would be useful for this type of verification such that, e.g., statistical guarantees could be given with a certain confidence. Although already early work discussed such matters, there has not been much research in this direction. In fact, Angluin considered learning without equivalence queries in a stochastic setting in her seminal paper [Ang87]. Furthermore, Rivest and Schapire also gave probabilities for learning the correct model [RS93]. Despite its practical usefulness, recent work usually does not assign probabilities or confidence levels to the learning result, also in case stochastic (testing) strategies are applied.

Testing has always been a challenge due to (1) its incompleteness by nature, (2) the lack of good specifications and (3) by its high demand for resources. With the growing complexity of the systems-under-tests this process is not going to be easier. Learning-based testing offers an opportunity to master this complexity with modern learning-based techniques. It represents a natural evolution of testing: with the trend of our environment becoming "smarter", e.g. smart homes, smart cars, smart production, smart energy, our testing process needs to be smart as well. We are seeing the advent of smart testing.

Acknowledgments. The insightful comments of Karl Meinke and Neil Walkinshaw on an earlier draft led to improvements and are gratefully acknowledged.

---

[1] The authors also briefly discuss stochastic properties of Mealy machines, though.

The work of B. K. Aichernig and M. Tappler was supported by the TU Graz LEAD project "Dependable Internet of Things in Adverse Environments". The work of M. R. Mousavi and M. Taromirad has been partially supported by the Swedish Research Council (Vetenskapsradet) award number: 621-2014-5057 (Effective Model-Based Testing of Concurrent Systems) and the Strategic Research Environment ELLIIT. The work of M. R. Mousavi has also been partially supported by the Swedish Knowledge Foundation (Stiftelsen for Kunskaps- och Kompetensutveckling) in the context of the AUTO-CAAS HöG project (number: 20140312).

References

[Aar14] Aarts, F.: Tomte: bridging the gap between active learning and real-world systems. Ph.D. thesis, Department of Computer Science (2014)

[AdRP13] Aarts, F., de Ruiter, J., Poll, E.: Formal models of bank cards for free. In: Proceedings of the 2013 IEEE Sixth International Conference on Software Testing, Verification and Validation Workshops, ICSTW 2013, pp. 461–468. IEEE Computer Society, Washington, DC (2013)

[AFBKV15] Aarts, F., Fiterau-Brostean, P., Kuppens, H., Vaandrager, F.: Learning register automata with fresh value generation. In: Leucker, M., Rueda, C., Valencia, F.D. (eds.) ICTAC 2015. LNCS, vol. 9399, pp. 165–183. Springer, Cham (2015). https://doi.org/10.1007/978-3-319-25150-9_11

[AHJW06] Arts, T., Hughes, J., Johansson, J., Wiger, U.T.: Testing telecoms software with QuviQ QuickCheck. In: Feeley, M., Trinder, P.W. (eds.) Proceedings of the 2006 ACM SIGPLAN Workshop on Erlang, Portland, Oregon, USA, 16 September 2006, pp. 2–10. ACM (2006)

[AHK+12] Aarts, F., Heidarian, F., Kuppens, H., Olsen, P., Vaandrager, F.: Automata learning through counterexample guided abstraction refinement. In: Giannakopoulou, D., Méry, D. (eds.) FM 2012. LNCS, vol. 7436, pp. 10–27. Springer, Heidelberg (2012). https://doi.org/10.1007/978-3-642-32759-9_4

[AKR15] Adamis, G., Kovács, G., Réthy, G.: Generating performance test model from conformance test logs. In: Fischer, J., Scheidgen, M., Schieferdecker, I., Reed, R. (eds.) SDL 2015. LNCS, vol. 9369, pp. 268–284. Springer, Cham (2015). https://doi.org/10.1007/978-3-319-24912-4_19

[AKT+12] Aarts, F., Kuppens, H., Tretmans, J., Vaandrager, F.W., Verwer, S.: Learning and testing the bounded retransmission protocol. In: Heinz, J., de la Higuera, C., Oates, T. (eds.) Proceedings of the Eleventh International Conference on Grammatical Inference, ICGI 2012, University of Maryland, College Park, USA, 5–8 September 2012, JMLR Proceedings, vol. 21, pp. 4–18. JMLR.org (2012)

[AKT+14] Aarts, F., Kuppens, H., Tretmans, J., Vaandrager, F.W., Verwer, S.: Improving active mealy machine learning for protocol conformance testing. Mach. Learn. 96(1–2), 189–224 (2014)

[AL13] Ansin, R., Lundberg, D.: Automated inference of excitable cell models as hybrid automata. Bachelor thesis. School of Computer Science and Communication, KTH Stockholm (2013)

[Alp14] Alpaydin, E.: Introduction to Machine Learning, 3rd edn. MIT Press, Cambridge (2014)

[Ang87] Angluin, D.: Learning regular sets from queries and counterexamples. Inf. Comput. **75**(2), 87–106 (1987)

[ARM16] Aerts, A., Reniers, M.A., Mousavi, M.R.: Model-based testing of cyber-physical systems. In: Song, H., Rawat, D.B., Jeschke, S., Brecher, C. (eds.) Cyber-Physical Systems Foundations, Principles and Applications, Chap. 19, pp. 287–304. Elsevier (2016)

[ASJ+16] Argyros, G., Stais, I., Jana, S., Keromytis, A.D., Kiayias, A.: SFADiff: automated evasion attacks and fingerprinting using black-box differential automata learning. In: Weippl, E.R., Katzenbeisser, S., Kruegel, C., Myers, A.C., Halevi, S. (eds.) Proceedings of the 2016 ACM SIGSAC Conference on Computer and Communications Security, Vienna, Austria, 24–28 October 2016, pp. 1690–1701. ACM (2016)

[ASV10] Aarts, F., Schmaltz, J., Vaandrager, F.W.: Inference and abstraction of the biometric passport. In: Margaria, T., Steffen, B. (eds.) ISoLA 2010. LNCS, vol. 6415, pp. 673–686. Springer, Heidelberg (2010). https://doi.org/10.1007/978-3-642-16558-0_54

[AT10] Arts, T., Thompson, S.: From test cases to FSMs: augmented test-driven development and property inference. In: Proceedings of the 9th ACM SIGPLAN Workshop on Erlang, Erlang 2010 (2010)

[AT17a] Aichernig, B.K., Tappler, M.: Learning from faults: mutation testing in active automata learning. In: Barrett, C., Davies, M., Kahsai, T. (eds.) NFM 2017. LNCS, vol. 10227, pp. 19–34. Springer, Cham (2017). https://doi.org/10.1007/978-3-319-57288-8_2

[AT17b] Aichernig, B.K., Tappler, M.: Probabilistic black-box reachability checking. In: Lahiri, S.K., Reger, G. (eds.) RV 2017. LNCS, vol. 10548, pp. 50–67. Springer, Cham (2017). https://doi.org/10.1007/978-3-319-67531-2_4

[BFFH14] Bonzanni, N., Feenstra, K.A., Fokkink, W., Heringa, J.: Petri nets are a biologist's best friend. In: Fages, F., Piazza, C. (eds.) FMMB 2014. LNCS, vol. 8738, pp. 102–116. Springer, Cham (2014). https://doi.org/10.1007/978-3-319-10398-3_8

[BFFK09] Bonzanni, N., Feenstra, K.A., Fokkink, W., Krepska, E.: What can formal methods bring to systems biology? In: Cavalcanti, A., Dams, D.R. (eds.) FM 2009. LNCS, vol. 5850, pp. 16–22. Springer, Heidelberg (2009). https://doi.org/10.1007/978-3-642-05089-3_2

[BG96] Bergadano, F., Gunetti, D.: Testing by means of inductive program learning. ACM Trans. Softw. Eng. Methodol. **5**(2), 119–145 (1996)

[BGJ+05] Berg, T., Grinchtein, O., Jonsson, B., Leucker, M., Raffelt, H., Steffen, B.: On the correspondence between conformance testing and regular inference. In: Cerioli, M. (ed.) FASE 2005. LNCS, vol. 3442, pp. 175–189. Springer, Heidelberg (2005). https://doi.org/10.1007/978-3-540-31984-9_14

[BIPT09] Bertolino, A., Inverardi, P., Pelliccione, P., Tivoli, M.: Automatic synthesis of behavior protocols for composable web-services. In: van Vliet, H., Issarny, V. (eds.) Proceedings of the 7th Joint Meeting of the European Software Engineering Conference and the ACM SIGSOFT International Symposium on Foundations of Software Engineering 2009, Amsterdam, The Netherlands, 24–28 August 2009, pp. 141–150. ACM (2009)

[CBP+11]   Cho, C.Y., Babić, D., Poosankam, P., Chen, K.Z., Wu, E.X., Song, D.: MACE: model-inference-assisted concolic exploration for protocol and vulnerability discovery. In: Proceedings of the 20th USENIX Conference on Security. USENIX Association (2011)

[CdlHJ09] Combe, D., de la Higuera, C., Janodet, J.-C.: Zulu: an interactive learning competition. In: Yli-Jyrä, A., Kornai, A., Sakarovitch, J., Watson, B.W. (eds.) FSMNLP 2009. LNCS (LNAI), vol. 6062, pp. 139–146. Springer, Heidelberg (2010). https://doi.org/10.1007/978-3-642-14684-8_15

[CHJS14]   Cassel, S., Howar, F., Jonsson, B., Steffen, B.: Learning extended finite state machines. In: Giannakopoulou, D., Salaün, G. (eds.) SEFM 2014. LNCS, vol. 8702, pp. 250–264. Springer, Cham (2014). https://doi.org/10.1007/978-3-319-10431-7_18

[CHJS16]   Cassel, S., Howar, F., Jonsson, B., Steffen, B.: Active learning for extended finite state machines. Formal Aspects Comput. **28**(2), 233–263 (2016)

[Cho78]   Chow, T.S.: Testing software design modeled by finite-state machines. IEEE Trans. Softw. Eng. **4**(3), 178–187 (1978)

[CNS13]   Choi, W., Necula, G.C., Sen, K.: Guided GUI testing of android apps with minimal restart and approximate learning. In: Hosking, A.L., Eugster, P.T., Lopes, C.V. (eds.) Proceedings of the 2013 ACM SIGPLAN International Conference on Object Oriented Programming Systems Languages & Applications, OOPSLA 2013, Part of SPLASH 2013, Indianapolis, IN, USA, 26–31 October 2013, pp. 623–640. ACM (2013)

[CO94]   Carrasco, R.C., Oncina, J.: Learning stochastic regular grammars by means of a state merging method. In: Carrasco, R.C., Oncina, J. (eds.) ICGI 1994. LNCS, vol. 862, pp. 139–152. Springer, Heidelberg (1994). https://doi.org/10.1007/3-540-58473-0_144

[Col14]   Collins, P.: Model-checking in systems biology - from micro to macro. In: Fages, F., Piazza, C. (eds.) FMMB 2014. LNCS, vol. 8738, pp. 1–22. Springer, Cham (2014). https://doi.org/10.1007/978-3-319-10398-3_1

[CSY99]   Câmpeanu, C., Sântean, N., Yu, S.: Minimal cover-automata for finite languages. In: Champarnaud, J.-M., Ziadi, D., Maurel, D. (eds.) WIA 1998. LNCS, vol. 1660, pp. 43–56. Springer, Heidelberg (1999). https://doi.org/10.1007/3-540-48057-9_4

[DIMS12]   Dinca, I., Ipate, F., Mierla, L., Stefanescu, A.: Learn and test for Event-B – a Rodin plugin. In: Derrick, J., et al. (eds.) ABZ 2012. LNCS, vol. 7316, pp. 361–364. Springer, Heidelberg (2012). https://doi.org/10.1007/978-3-642-30885-7_32

[DIS12]   Dinca, I., Ipate, F., Stefanescu, A.: Model learning and test generation for Event-B decomposition. In: Margaria, T., Steffen, B. (eds.) ISoLA 2012. LNCS, vol. 7609, pp. 539–553. Springer, Heidelberg (2012). https://doi.org/10.1007/978-3-642-34026-0_40

[DLDvL08] Dupont, P., Lambeau, B., Damas, C., van Lamsweerde, A.: The QSM algorithm and its application to software behavior model induction. Appl. Artif. Intell. **22**(1–2), 77–115 (2008)

[dRP15]   de Ruiter, J., Poll, E.: Protocol state fuzzing of TLS implementations. In: Jung, J., Holz, T. (eds.) 24th USENIX Security Symposium, USENIX Security 15, Washington, D.C., USA, 12–14 August 2015, pp. 193–206. USENIX Association (2015)

[EGPQ06] Elkind, E., Genest, B., Peled, D.A., Qu, H.: Grey-box checking. In: Najm, E., Pradat-Peyre, J.-F., Donzeau-Gouge, V.V. (eds.) FORTE 2006. LNCS, vol. 4229, pp. 420–435. Springer, Heidelberg (2006). https://doi.org/10.1007/11888116_30

[FBJV14] Fiterău-Broştean, P., Janssen, R., Vaandrager, F.W.: Learning fragments of the TCP network protocol. In: Lang, F., Flammini, F. (eds.) FMICS 2014. LNCS, vol. 8718, pp. 78–93. Springer, Cham (2014). https://doi.org/10.1007/978-3-319-10702-8_6

[FBJV16] Fiterău-Broştean, P., Janssen, R., Vaandrager, F.W.: Combining model learning and model checking to analyze TCP implementations. In: Chaudhuri, S., Farzan, A. (eds.) CAV 2016. LNCS, vol. 9780, pp. 454–471. Springer, Cham (2016). https://doi.org/10.1007/978-3-319-41540-6_25

[FBLP+17] Fiterău-Broştean, P., Lenaerts, T., Poll, E., de Ruiter, J., Vaandrager, F.W., Verleg, P.: Model learning and model checking of SSH implementations. In: Erdogmus, H., Havelund, K. (eds.) Proceedings of the 24th ACM SIGSOFT International SPIN Symposium on Model Checking of Software, Santa Barbara, CA, USA, 10–14 July 2017, pp. 142–151. ACM (2017)

[FvBK+91] Fujiwara, S., von Bochmann, G., Khendek, F., Amalou, M., Ghedamsi, A.: Test selection based on finite state models. IEEE Trans. Softw. Eng. **17**(6), 591–603 (1991)

[GLPS08] Groz, R., Li, K., Petrenko, A., Shahbaz, M.: Modular system verification by inference, testing and reachability analysis. In: Suzuki, K., Higashino, T., Ulrich, A., Hasegawa, T. (eds.) FATES/TestCom -2008. LNCS, vol. 5047, pp. 216–233. Springer, Heidelberg (2008). https://doi.org/10.1007/978-3-540-68524-1_16

[GPY02a] Groce, A., Peled, D.A., Yannakakis, M.: Adaptive model checking. In: Katoen, J.-P., Stevens, P. (eds.) TACAS 2002. LNCS, vol. 2280, pp. 357–370. Springer, Heidelberg (2002). https://doi.org/10.1007/3-540-46002-0_25

[GPY02b] Groce, A., Peled, D.A., Yannakakis, M.: AMC: an adaptive model checker. In: Brinksma, E., Larsen, K.G. (eds.) CAV 2002. LNCS, vol. 2404, pp. 521–525. Springer, Heidelberg (2002). https://doi.org/10.1007/3-540-45657-0_44

[GS16] Gebizli, C.Ş., Sözer, H.: Automated refinement of models for model-based testing using exploratory testing. Softw. Qual. J. **25**(3), 1–27 (2016)

[HGOR14] Hossen, K., Groz, R., Oriat, C., Richier, J.-L.: Automatic model inference of web applications for security testing. In: Seventh IEEE International Conference on Software Testing, Verification and Validation, ICST 2014 Workshops Proceedings, 31 March–4 April 2014, Cleveland, Ohio, USA, pp. 22–23. IEEE Computer Society (2014)

[HHNS02] Hagerer, A., Hungar, H., Niese, O., Steffen, B.: Model generation by moderated regular extrapolation. In: Kutsche, R.-D., Weber, H. (eds.) FASE 2002. LNCS, vol. 2306, pp. 80–95. Springer, Heidelberg (2002). https://doi.org/10.1007/3-540-45923-5_6

[HK08] Hung, P.N., Katayama, T.: Modular conformance testing and assume-guarantee verification for evolving component-based software. In: 15th Asia-Pacific Software Engineering Conference (APSEC 2008), 3–5 December 2008, Beijing, China, pp. 479–486. IEEE Computer Society (2008)

[HNS03] Hungar, H., Niese, O., Steffen, B.: Domain-specific optimization in automata learning. In: Hunt, W.A., Somenzi, F. (eds.) CAV 2003. LNCS, vol. 2725, pp. 315–327. Springer, Heidelberg (2003). https://doi.org/10.1007/978-3-540-45069-6_31

[HRD07] Henkel, J., Reichenbach, C., Diwan, A.: Discovering documentation for Java container classes. IEEE Trans. Softw. Eng. 33(8), 526–543 (2007)

[HSL08] Hsu, Y., Shu, G., Lee, D.: A model-based approach to security flaw detection of network protocol implementations. In: Proceedings of the 16th Annual IEEE International Conference on Network Protocols, ICNP 2008, Orlando, Florida, USA, 19–22 October 2008, pp. 114–123. IEEE Computer Society (2008)

[HSM10] Howar, F., Steffen, B., Merten, M.: From ZULU to RERS. In: Margaria, T., Steffen, B. (eds.) ISoLA 2010. LNCS, vol. 6415, pp. 687–704. Springer, Heidelberg (2010). https://doi.org/10.1007/978-3-642-16558-0_55

[HSM11] Howar, F., Steffen, B., Merten, M.: Automata learning with automated alphabet abstraction refinement. In: Jhala, R., Schmidt, D.A. (eds.) VMCAI 2011. LNCS, vol. 6538, pp. 263–277. Springer, Heidelberg (2011). https://doi.org/10.1007/978-3-642-18275-4_19

[IHS15] Isberner, M., Howar, F., Steffen, B.: The open-source LearnLib. In: Kroening, D., Păsăreanu, C.S. (eds.) CAV 2015. LNCS, vol. 9206, pp. 487–495. Springer, Cham (2015). https://doi.org/10.1007/978-3-319-21690-4_32

[ISD15] Ipate, F., Stefanescu, A., Dinca, I.: Model learning and test generation using cover automata. Comput. J. 58(5), 1140–1159 (2015)

[KMMV16] Kunze, S., Mostowski, W., Mousavi, M.R., Varshosaz, M.: Generation of failure models through automata learning. In: Workshop on Automotive Systems/Software Architectures (WASA 2016), pp. 22–25. IEEE Computer Society, April 2016

[KMR]   Khosrowjerdi, H., Meinke, K., Rasmusson, A.: Automated behavioral requirements testing for automotive ECU applications (2016, Submitted)

[KV94] Kearns, M.J., Vazirani, U.V.: An Introduction to Computational Learning Theory. MIT Press, Cambridge (1994)

[LCJ06] Lai, Z., Cheung, S.C., Jiang, Y.: Dynamic model learning using genetic algorithm under adaptive model checking framework. In: Sixth International Conference on Quality Software (QSIC 2006), 26–28 October 2006, Beijing, China, pp. 410–417. IEEE Computer Society (2006)

[LGS06a] Li, K., Groz, R., Shahbaz, M.: Integration testing of components guided by incremental state machine learning. In: McMinn, P. (ed.) Testing: Academia and Industry Conference - Practice and Research Techniques (TAIC PART 2006), 29–31 August 2006, Windsor, United Kingdom, pp. 59–70. IEEE Computer Society (2006)

[LGS06b] Li, K., Groz, R., Shahbaz, M.: Integration testing of distributed components based on learning parameterized I/O models. In: Najm, E., Pradat-Peyre, J.-F., Donzeau-Gouge, V.V. (eds.) FORTE 2006. LNCS, vol. 4229, pp. 436–450. Springer, Heidelberg (2006). https://doi.org/10.1007/11888116_31

[LS14] Lachmann, R., Schaefer, I.: Towards efficient and effective testing in automotive software development. In: Plödereder, E., Grunske, L., Schneider, E., Ull, D. (eds.) 44. Jahrestagung der Gesellschaft für Informatik, Informatik 2014, Big Data - Komplexität meistern, 22–26 September 2014, Stuttgart, Deutschland. LNI, vol. 232, pp. 2181–2192. GI (2014)

[LY94] Lee, D., Yannakakis, M.: Testing finite-state machines: state identification and verification. IEEE Trans. Comput. **43**(3), 306–320 (1994)

[MCWKK09] Comparetti, P.M., Wondracek, G., Krügel, C., Kirda, E.: Prospex: protocol specification extraction. In: 30th IEEE Symposium on Security and Privacy (S&P 2009), 17–20 May 2009, Oakland, California, USA, pp. 110–125. IEEE Computer Society (2009)

[Mei04] Meinke, K.: Automated black-box testing of functional correctness using function approximation. SIGSOFT Softw. Eng. Notes **29**(4), 143–153 (2004)

[MHR+06] Margaria, T., Hinchey, M.G., Raffelt, H., Rash, J.L., Rouff, C.A., Steffen, B.: Completing and adapting models of biological processes. In: Pan, Y., Rammig, F.J., Schmeck, H., Solar, M. (eds.) BICC 2006. IIFIP, vol. 216, pp. 43–54. Springer, Boston, MA (2006). https://doi.org/10.1007/978-0-387-34733-2_5

[Mit97] Mitchel, T.M.: Machine Learning. McGraw Hill, New York (1997)

[MN10] Meinke, K., Niu, F.: A learning-based approach to unit testing of numerical software. In: Petrenko, A., Simão, A., Maldonado, J.C. (eds.) ICTSS 2010. LNCS, vol. 6435, pp. 221–235. Springer, Heidelberg (2010). https://doi.org/10.1007/978-3-642-16573-3_16

[MN15] Meinke, K., Nycander, P.: Learning-based testing of distributed microservice architectures: correctness and fault injection. In: Bianculli, D., Calinescu, R., Rumpe, B. (eds.) SEFM 2015. LNCS, vol. 9509, pp. 3–10. Springer, Heidelberg (2015). https://doi.org/10.1007/978-3-662-49224-6_1

[MNRS04] Margaria, T., Niese, O., Raffelt, H., Steffen, B.: Efficient test-based model generation for legacy reactive systems. In: 2004 Ninth IEEE International High-Level Design Validation and Test Workshop, pp. 95–100. IEEE (2004)

[MPS+09] Mostowski, W., Poll, E., Schmaltz, J., Tretmans, J., Wichers Schreur, R.: Model-based testing of electronic passports. In: Alpuente, M., Cook, B., Joubert, C. (eds.) FMICS 2009. LNCS, vol. 5825, pp. 207–209. Springer, Heidelberg (2009). https://doi.org/10.1007/978-3-642-04570-7_19

[MS11] Meinke, K., Sindhu, M.A.: Incremental learning-based testing for reactive systems. In: Gogolla, M., Wolff, B. (eds.) TAP 2011. LNCS, vol. 6706, pp. 134–151. Springer, Heidelberg (2011). https://doi.org/10.1007/978-3-642-21768-5_11

[MSB11] Myers, G.J., Sandler, C., Badgett, T.: The Art of Software Testing, 3rd edn. Wiley Publishing, Hoboken (2011)

[Nie03] Niese, O.: An integrated approach to testing complex systems. Ph.D. thesis, Dortmund University of Technology (2003)

[OG92] Oncina, J., Garcia, P.: Identifying regular languages in polynomial time. In: Advances in Structural and Syntactic Pattern Recognition. Series in Machine Perception and Artificial Intelligence, vol. 5, pp. 99–108. World Scientific (1992)

[ORT+07] Oostdijk, M., Rusu, V., Tretmans, J., de Vries, R.G., Willemse, T.A.C.: Integrating verification, testing, and learning for cryptographic protocols. In: Davies, J., Gibbons, J. (eds.) IFM 2007. LNCS, vol. 4591, pp. 538–557. Springer, Heidelberg (2007). https://doi.org/10.1007/978-3-540-73210-5_28

[PLG+14] Petrenko, A., Li, K., Groz, R., Hossen, K., Oriat, C.: Inferring approximated models for systems engineering. In: 15th International IEEE Symposium on High-Assurance Systems Engineering, HASE 2014, Miami Beach, FL, USA, 9–11 January 2014, pp. 249–253. IEEE Computer Society (2014)

[PVY99] Peled, D., Vardi, M.Y., Yannakakis, M.: Black box checking. In: Wu, J., Chanson, S.T., Gao, Q. (eds.) PSTV 1999, FORTE 1999. IAICT, vol. 28, pp. 225–240. Springer, Boston, MA (1999). https://doi.org/10.1007/978-0-387-35578-8_13

[PW15] Papadopoulos, P., Walkinshaw, N.: Black-box test generation from inferred models. In: Harrison, R., Bener, A.B., Turhan, B. (eds.) 4th IEEE/ACM International Workshop on Realizing Artificial Intelligence Synergies in Software Engineering, RAISE 2015, Florence, Italy, 17 May 2015, pp. 19–24. IEEE Computer Society (2015)

[RMSM08] Raffelt, H., Margaria, T., Steffen, B., Merten, M.: Hybrid test of web applications with webtest. In: Bultan, T., Xie, T. (eds.) Proceedings of the 2008 Workshop on Testing, Analysis, and Verification of Web Services and Applications, Held in Conjunction with the ACM SIGSOFT International Symposium on Software Testing and Analysis (ISSTA 2008), TAV-WEB 2008, Seattle, Washington, USA, 21 July 2008, pp. 1–7. ACM (2008)

[RMSM09] Raffelt, H., Merten, M., Steffen, B., Margaria, T.: Dynamic testing via automata learning. STTT **11**(4), 307–324 (2009)

[RS93] Rivest, R.L., Schapire, R.E.: Inference of finite automata using homing sequences. Inf. Comput. **103**(2), 299–347 (1993)

[SAP+17] Sivakorn, S., Argyros, G., Pei, K., Keromytis, A.D., Jana, S.: HVLearn: automated black-box analysis of hostname verification in SSL/TLS implementations. In: 2017 IEEE Symposium on Security and Privacy, SP 2017, San Jose, CA, USA, 22–26 May 2017, pp. 521–538. IEEE Computer Society (2017)

[SG09] Shahbaz, M., Groz, R.: Inferring mealy machines. In: Cavalcanti, A., Dams, D.R. (eds.) FM 2009. LNCS, vol. 5850, pp. 207–222. Springer, Heidelberg (2009). https://doi.org/10.1007/978-3-642-05089-3_14

[SG14] Shahbaz, M., Groz, R.: Analysis and testing of black-box component-based systems by inferring partial models. Softw. Test. Verification Reliab. **24**(4), 253–288 (2014)

[SHL08] Shu, G., Hsu, Y., Lee, D.: Detecting communication protocol security flaws by formal fuzz testing and machine learning. In: Suzuki, K., Higashino, T., Yasumoto, K., El-Fakih, K. (eds.) FORTE 2008. LNCS, vol. 5048, pp. 299–304. Springer, Heidelberg (2008). https://doi.org/10.1007/978-3-540-68855-6_19

[SHM11] Steffen, B., Howar, F., Merten, M.: Introduction to active automata learning from a practical perspective. In: Bernardo, M., Issarny, V. (eds.) SFM 2011. LNCS, vol. 6659, pp. 256–296. Springer, Heidelberg (2011). https://doi.org/10.1007/978-3-642-21455-4_8

[SL07] Shu, G., Lee, D.: Testing security properties of protocol implementations - a machine learning based approach. In: 27th IEEE International Conference on Distributed Computing Systems (ICDCS 2007), 25–29 June 2007, Toronto, Ontario, Canada, p. 25. IEEE Computer Society (2007)

[SLBW15] Schulze, C., Lindvall, M., Bjorgvinsson, S., Wiegand, R.: Model generation to support model-based testing applied on the NASA DAT web-application - an experience report. In: 26th IEEE International Symposium on Software Reliability Engineering, ISSRE 2015, Gaithersbury, MD, USA, 2–5 November 2015, pp. 77–87. IEEE Computer Society (2015)

[SLG07a] Shahbaz, M., Li, K., Groz, R.: Learning and integration of parameterized components through testing. In: Petrenko, A., Veanes, M., Tretmans, J., Grieskamp, W. (eds.) FATES/TestCom - 2007. LNCS, vol. 4581, pp. 319–334. Springer, Heidelberg (2007). https://doi.org/10.1007/978-3-540-73066-8_22

[SLG07b] Shahbaz, M., Li, K., Groz, R.: Learning parameterized state machine model for integration testing. In: 31st Annual International Computer Software and Applications Conference, COMPSAC 2007, Beijing, China, 24–27 July 2007, vol. 2, pp. 755–760. IEEE Computer Society (2007)

[SMVJ15] Smeenk, W., Moerman, J., Vaandrager, F.W., Jansen, D.N.: Applying automata learning to embedded control software. In: Butler, M., Conchon, S., Zaïdi, F. (eds.) ICFEM 2015. LNCS, vol. 9407, pp. 67–83. Springer, Cham (2015). https://doi.org/10.1007/978-3-319-25423-4_5

[SPK07] Shahbaz, M., Parreaux, B., Klay, F.: Model inference approach for detecting feature interactions in integrated systems. In: du Bousquet, L., Richier, J.-L. (eds.) Feature Interactions in Software and Communication Systems IX, International Conference on Feature Interactions in Software and Communication Systems, ICFI 2007, 3–5 September 2007, Grenoble, France, pp. 161–171. IOS Press (2007)

[TAB17] Tappler, M., Aichernig, B.K., Bloem, R.: Model-based testing IoT communication via active automata learning. In: 2017 IEEE International Conference on Software Testing, Verification and Validation, ICST 2017, Tokyo, Japan, 13–17 March 2017, pp. 276–287 (2017)

[TB03] Tretmans, J., Brinksma, E.: TorX: automated model-based testing. In: Hartman, A., Dussa-Ziegler, K. (eds.) First European Conference on Model-Driven Software Engineering, pp. 31–43, December 2003

[Tre11] Tretmans, J.: Model-based testing and some steps towards test-based modelling. In: Bernardo, M., Issarny, V. (eds.) SFM 2011. LNCS, vol. 6659, pp. 297–326. Springer, Heidelberg (2011). https://doi.org/10.1007/978-3-642-21455-4_9

[UL07] Utting, M., Legeard, B.: Practical Model-Based Testing - A Tools Approach. Morgan Kaufmann, Burlington (2007)

[UPL12] Utting, M., Pretschner, A., Legeard, B.: A taxonomy of model-based testing approaches. Softw. Test. Verification Reliab. 22(5), 297–312 (2012)

[Vas73] Vasilevskii, M.P.: Failure diagnosis of automata. Cybernetics 9(4), 653–665 (1973)

[VT14] Volpato, M., Tretmans, J.: Active learning of nondeterministic systems from an ioco perspective. In: Margaria, T., Steffen, B. (eds.) ISoLA 2014. LNCS, vol. 8802, pp. 220–235. Springer, Heidelberg (2014). https://doi.org/10.1007/978-3-662-45234-9_16

[VT15] Volpato, M., Tretmans, J.: Approximate active learning of nondeterministic input output transition systems. ECEASST 72 (2015)

[WBDP10] Walkinshaw, N., Bogdanov, K., Derrick, J., Paris, J.: Increasing functional coverage by inductive testing: a case study. In: Petrenko, A., Simão, A., Maldonado, J.C. (eds.) ICTSS 2010. LNCS, vol. 6435, pp. 126–141. Springer, Heidelberg (2010). https://doi.org/10.1007/978-3-642-16573-3_10

[WBHS07] Walkinshaw, N., Bogdanov, K., Holcombe, M., Salahuddin, S.: Reverse engineering state machines by interactive grammar inference. In: 14th Working Conference on Reverse Engineering (WCRE 2007), 28–31 October 2007, Vancouver, BC, Canada, pp. 209–218. IEEE Computer Society (2007)

[WDG09] Walkinshaw, N., Derrick, J., Guo, Q.: Iterative refinement of reverse-engineered models by model-based testing. In: Cavalcanti, A., Dams, D.R. (eds.) FM 2009. LNCS, vol. 5850, pp. 305–320. Springer, Heidelberg (2009). https://doi.org/10.1007/978-3-642-05089-3_20

[Wey83] Weyuker, E.J.: Assessing test data adequacy through program inference. ACM Trans. Program. Lang. Syst. 5(4), 641–655 (1983)

[WF17] Walkinshaw, N., Fraser, G.: Uncertainty-driven black-box test data generation. In: 2017 IEEE International Conference on Software Testing, Verification and Validation, ICST 2017, Tokyo, Japan, 13–17 March 2017, pp. 253–263 (2017)

[YCM09] Yeh, T., Chang, T.-H., Miller, R.C.: Sikuli: using GUI screenshots for search and automation. In: Proceedings of the 22nd Annual ACM Symposium on User Interface Software and Technology, pp. 183–192. ACM (2009)

Testing Functional Black-Box Programs
Without a Specification

Neil Walkinshaw[✉]

University of Leicester, Leicester, UK
nw91@le.ac.uk

Abstract. In this chapter we examine the problem of testing functional black-box programs that do not require sequential inputs. We specifically focus on the case where there is no existing specification from which to derive tests. Research into this problem dates back over three decades, and has produced a variety of techniques, all of which employ various types of data mining and machine learning algorithms to examine test executions and to inform the selection of new tests. Here we provide an overview of these techniques and examine their limitations and opportunities for future research.

1   Introduction

This chapter is concerned with the challenge of devising test sets for *functional, black box* components. By 'functional', we mean that the component does not store its data in such a way that the internal state could affect its behaviour with respect to subsequent inputs. By 'black-box' we mean that the internal workings of the system are hidden; we cannot inspect the source code, or obtain execution traces of internal variables; we can only monitor the inputs given to the system, and the outputs returned in response. Finally, we assume that we do not have a useful model of the system that could be used to guide our selection of inputs, which prevents us from resorting to traditional model-based testing techniques.

Functional programs (or portions of programs) are highly prevalent[1]. There are the obvious functions, such as the various mathematical functions that are built into most programming languages. Functions that might appear non-functional (such as the Stack.push(o) operation in Java) can be recharacterised in functional terms by simply making the state of the stack part of the input and output.

There are many occasions in which a system might have to be treated as a 'black boxes'. In some cases it might be because we genuinely have no access to the internals of the system; for example we are dealing with a COTS component procured from a developer who has not given us access to the source code, or the system under test involves web-services that are hosted on a remote

---

[1] Note that the use of 'functional' in this chapter refers to the external behaviour of the program, not the programming paradigm used to implement it.

© Springer International Publishing AG, part of Springer Nature 2018
A. Bennaceur et al. (Eds.): ML for Dynamic Software Analysis, LNCS 11026, pp. 101–120, 2018.
https://doi.org/10.1007/978-3-319-96562-8_4

machine. In others, it might be because we do not wish to base our testing on established white-box notions such as code-coverage alone, because these have been repeatedly shown to be unreliable as a basis for test-adequacy, or we simply do not have the wherewithal to identify a test set that obtains a reasonable degree of coverage in the first place.

Section 2 starts by examining the essential challenge of constructing test sets in this scenario. It shows how the baseline approach of simply executing arbitrary random inputs is not an effective, scalable approach. We also consider some properties that an ideal, hypothetical testing technique should possess. It is then followed by Sect. 3, which describes a feedback-driven approach to random testing known as Adaptive Random Testing. In Sect. 4 we then provide an overview of a family of techniques that are based on the idea of using feedback from test executions to infer models, which can in turn drive test generation. In Sect. 5 we cast a critical eye over the various techniques covered, pick out some general weaknesses, and highlight several open questions. This is finally followed by the conclusions in Sect. 6.

2   The Challenge of Testing Unspecified Functional Black-Box Systems

The essential challenge of testing black-box systems without a reference model is that there is no obvious guidance from which to drive test efforts. Once a test has been executed, all that can be observed is the output. There is no source code or control flow graph that can be used to elicit additional test cases that could perhaps expose new aspects of program behaviour.

2.1   State-Based and Functional Systems

The problem of devising test cases in this scenario has been studied for several decades. Numerous techniques have been devised that use a variety of heuristics and reasoning mechanisms to experiment with and test such systems. These techniques can be, in broad terms, split into two families of approaches: (1) Approaches that target systems that react to sequences of inputs, and (2) approaches that target systems that react to individual inputs.

Most of the chapters in this book that consider black-box testing are concerned with the state-based family of systems. These approaches characterise the system under test as a state machine. The test cases are sequences of events that can be fed to the system, and a "state" in the system amounts to the future set of inputs that the system can be expected to respond to at a given point in its execution.

In this chapter we focus upon the functional family of systems. For such systems, inputs are not sequential. Inputs and outputs tend to be data values as opposed to events or signals. They can often be referred to as "stateless" because a truly functional software component does not incorporate any datastate that could persist across and affect future executions. Whereas sequential systems are overwhelmingly represented as automata, functional programs can be represented and reasoned about in a variety of ways.

2.2   The Challenge

In order to test any system it is first necessary to establish the 'interface' of the System Under Test (SUT). In other words, what are the types of parameters that are expected? As a concrete example we might consider the scenario where we are testing an implementation of the Bessel function (e.g. as can be found in Apache Commons Math). For this we would need to now that a Bessel function expects two parameters (*order* and *x*).

The de-facto test-generation approach is to provide random combinations of values for *order* and *x*. In order to apply random testing in the proper sense, it is first necessary to define an appropriate probability distribution over the inputs, representing the anticipated "operational profile" of how the SUT is to be used once deployed. Testing then amounts to sampling inputs according to these distributions. If this is done for a sufficiently large sample of tests, it becomes possible to apply probability theory to reason about notions such as reliability [15].

Unfortunately, random testing is problematic in our scenario. Firstly, it is unlikely that we are fully aware of the "operational profile" of our system, which hampers the selection of useful parameters. If we then resort to a default distribution (e.g. the uniform distribution), it is liable to either generate an overwhelmingly large number of trivially invalid inputs, or will fail to adequately probe the full range of software behaviour.

The essential weaknesses of conventional random testing are thus: (1) it requires knowledge about the SUT that goes beyond its interface, and (2) it is inefficient; it can take an infeasibly large number of test executions to expose a fault. Accordingly, this sets out the goals for any techniques that seek to offer an improvement. They should not depend upon knowledge that is difficult to obtain about the SUT (such as its operational profile), and should (2) seek to be efficient – to minimise the number of tests required, whilst maximising the range of software behaviour covered.

3   Adaptive Random Testing (ART)

Adaptive Random Testing (ART) [8] was developed to address the weakness of inefficiency with respect to purely random testing mentioned above. The key idea is, instead of blindly attempting inputs, to keep track of previously attempted inputs, and to use these in the process of selecting more effective new ones. The ultimate goal of ART is to select inputs that are as "different" as possible from those that have been selected previously.

The approach is captured in Algorithm 1. It starts from an existing set of test cases (*TestInputs*). The algorithm operates over a given number of *iterations* - where each iteration yields an additional test case to add to *TestInputs*. The core loop starts by generating a pool of size *poolSize* of random test inputs

Input: *TestInputs,poolSize*
Uses: *generateRandom,minDistance,terminate*

```
 1  i ← 0 ;
 2  while (¬terminate(i, TestInputs)) do
 3      i ← i + 1;
 4      Candidates ← generateRandom(poolSize);
 5      maxDistance ← 0;
 6      Furthest ← ε;
 7      for c ∈ Candidates do
 8          minDist ← minDistance(c, TestInputs);
 9          if (Furthest = ε) ∨ (minDist > maxDistance) then
10              Furthest ← c;
11              maxDistance ← minDist;
12          end
13      end
14  end
15  return TestInputs;
```

Algorithm 1. Adaptive Random Testing

(without executing them). Each candidate input c is then compared against the existing inputs, by measuring the distance between c and the other inputs. The final distance with the test set is recorded as the shortest distance to any member of *TestInputs*. Once this is done for all candidates, the candidate with the largest distance is added to the test set, and the process continues for the given number of iterations.

At the heart of ART lies the use of a "distance" metric. The default approach, if the inputs are numerical, is to compute the Euclidean distance. However, this can be problematic. For example, if parameters are on different scales, it can become easy for a distance calculation to ignore small-scale inputs. This problem of 'test distance' has recently been the focus of an increasing amount of attention. Recently, several 'test diversity' metrics have been devised that use information theory, such as Feldt *et al.*'s Test Set Diameter [11].

Recent efforts have been made to extend ART to non-numerical inputs too. For example, ARTOO [10] considers input objects in an Object-Oriented programming context. To enable this, they devised a custom object-oriented distance function, which incorporates object types and values to form a composite value.

Strengths:	Weaknesses:
• Test sets can be created without needing to execute the program.	
• Experimental evidence indicates that ART is effective for programs with numerical input, and that ARTOO is effective for Eiffel programs.	• Effectiveness is sensitive to parameters, including distance functions, sampling ranges, and the choice of *poolSize*. • Clustering and sampling invariably impose a time-penalty.

4   Inference-Driven Techniques

The success of ART is founded on the principle that it is possible to memorise which inputs have been attempted, so that successive new inputs can be selected in such a way that they avoid re-executing previously executed program features. The weakness is that inputs alone do not necessarily capture the actual behaviour of a system. Inputs might be superficially diverse, yet still end up covering a relatively homogeneous set of program executions.

Inference driven test generation techniques are based on a similar premise – of memorising test executions. However, instead of merely focussing on program inputs, inference-driven techniques aim to capture executions in a more comprehensive sense, by inferring a model that relates test inputs to their corresponding outputs. Instead of periodically clustering input data as in ART, inference-driven test generation techniques periodically infer a model of the input/output behaviour of the system under test, with the aim of using this model as a basis for test generation.

> **Input**: *TestInputs*
> 1 *Executions* ← ∅;
> 2 **for** *(input ← TestInputs)* **do**
> 3 | *Executions* ← *Executions* ∪ *execute(input)*;
> 4 **end**
> 5 *hyp* ← *inferModel(Executions)*;
> 6 **while** *(¬terminate(hyp))* **do**
> 7 | *NewInputs* ← *selectInputs(hyp)*;
> 8 | **for** *(input ← NewInputs)* **do**
> 9 | | *Executions* ← *Executions* ∪ *execute(input)*;
> 10 | **end**
> 11 | *hyp* ← *inferModel(Executions)*;
> 12 | *TestInputs* ← *TestInputs* ∪ *NewInputs*;
> 13 **end**
> 14 **return** *TestInputs*;

Algorithm 2. A generic inference-driven testing procedure.

The basic iterative procedure is illustrated in Algorithm 2. For every test execution (stored in *Executions*) it captures both the input(s) and output. Similarly to the ART algorithm, it then operates on an iterative basis: A model is inferred, the model is used to select new inputs, these are executed, and the resulting execution data is used to infer a refined model. The process an either continue for a fixed number of iterations or until some termination condition is satisfied (e.g. the model stabilises and further test executions fail to result in changes to the model).

The essential idea for inferring a model from test executions dates back to Moore's work on "Gedanken Experiments with Sequential Machines" [20] from 1956. In this early work, Moore envisaged a situation whereby the "component" under test could be potentially modelled as a finite state machine. He went on to enliven the situation somewhat by conjecturing that the mechanism being experimented on *"may explode, particularly if it is a bomb, a mine, or some other infernal machine. Since the experimenter is presumably intelligent enough to have anticipated this possibility, he may be assumed to have conducted his experimentation by remote control from a safe distance".*

Moore's line of state machine inference and testing has become a highly active area of research (spurred by the combined availability of an extensive array of state machine inference and testing algorithms). Given that this is the subject of extensive treatment elsewhere in this book, this chapter will instead focus on the family of inference-based testing techniques that are not specifically targeted towards sequential (state-machine based) systems.

As a family of techniques, inference-driven testing techniques share certain strengths and weaknesses. Whereas the following apply across all techniques, the specific strengths and weaknesses that pertain to individual techniques will be listed individually. In the remainder of this section we examine some of the key contributions in this area. We put them in an approximately chronological order.

Strengths:

- Test generation can adapt to observed behaviour (software outputs are taken into account as well as inputs).
- Produces explicit models that have an intrinsic value (e.g. for validating tested behaviour).

Weaknesses:

- Efficiency is tied to execution-speed of system under test, as well as amount of time taken for inference.
- Dependent on identifying a suitable match between the system being tested, the inference algorithm, and the test generation approach.

4.1 Theoretical Links Between Machine Learning and Test Adequacy

Throughout the 80s and early 90s, most of the work linking Machine Learning with testing was focussed on the conceptual links between the two areas. Both Budd and Angluin [7] and Weyuker [32] independently investigated the idea in 1982-3. Their work was subsequently developed by Cherniavsky and Smith in 1987 [9]. They all set out broad theoretical frameworks within which to discuss the relationships between the two areas.

These early pieces of research were particularly interested in the question of *adequacy* [13]. Specifically they focussed on the question of whether Machine Learning concepts could be used to characterise when a test set can be deemed to be complete - something that had traditionally been (and still is) measured via crude, imperfect proxy measures such as code coverage. In terms of Algorithm 2, the focus was on whether a *terminate* function could exist and how it might work.

Although the bulk of the work was theoretical, Weyuker's work did include a proof-of-concept implementation. In it she used a simple inference engine by Summers [27] to infer programs (comprised from a subset of LISP) from program executions. Weyuker's work highlighted the limitation that an inferred model cannot be shown to be equivalent to the code of the underlying program or a given specification. To work around this she proposed that the *terminate* function might instead resort to a weaker interpretation of equivalence, using a pool of random executions of the program to gauge whether or not the behaviour of the inferred model was sufficiently close (either to the program or the given specification).

This line of work was subsequently carried on in the early 90s by Zhu *et al.* [35,36], and by Romanik and Vitter [24,25]. Both investigated how testability could be linked to (what had by then become) more established Machine Learning concepts. Zhu *et al.* showed how test adequacy could be linked to Valiant's Probably Approximately Correct framework [29]. Romanik and Vitter, in a similar vein, proposed a link between test adequacy and the Vapnik Chervonenkis Dimension [30] (which underpins Structured Vector Machine learning).

4.2   Combining Testing with Inductive Logic Programming

Although Weyuker's work had focussed on the *terminate* function in Algorithm 2, her proof of concept implementation also provided an implementation of the *inferModel* function in the form of Summers' LISP program inference engine [27].

Summers' engine was an example of what is known as Inductive Logic Programming (ILP) [19]. ILP operates by encoding all of the knowledge about the target subject (in our case this would be the SUT) into logical facts that can be represented in a programming language such as LISP or Prolog. This may include observed examples (in our case set *Executions* in Algorithm 2), as well as any ancillary knowledge. This is then used as a database from which a generalised hypothesis is inferred.

In the mid-90s, Bergadano and Gunnetti [4] used IPL in the first concerted effort (since Weyuker's work) to implement Algorithm 2. For their work they used their own IPL system [3]. Their proof of concept demonstrated the generation of an adequate test set for a Prolog implementation of a merge function.

Approximately a decade later, in 2004, ILP was again used to drive the inference-test loop. However, this time the system 'under test' was not a conventional software system, but a genetic pathway. In their work on the "robot scientist" King *et al.* [17] set up a physical version of the inference loop. This time, test executions amounted to physical experiments on the gene function of yeast, which were devised to test a hypothesis model that was inferred by ILP.

Strengths:	Weaknesses:
• Suited to inferring models of programs that suit declarative languages such as Prolog. • Recent growth in the popularity of such languages, such as Elixir/Erlang (particularly in telecoms and web-apps).	• Unclear what range of behaviours can be accurately inferred by ILP. • The ILP setup has to be tailored to the inferred program, and the extent to which this can be automated is uncertain. • There is limited empirical evidence to corroborate the efficacy of the resulting test sets.

4.3 Test-Driven Algebraic Specification Inference

In 2003 Henkel and Diwan [16] proposed an approach to discover algebraic specifications from Java programs[2]. The approach was not primarily intended as a software testing approach, but as a generic specification mining tool. We nevertheless cover the approach here because their approach marries model inference with test generation (even if the tests are ultimately considered a mere by-product).

> **Input**: *SUT*
> 1 *Algebra* ← *obtainAlgebra(SUT)*;
> 2 *Tests* ← *generateTests(Algebra)*;
> 3 *Executions* ← *execute(Tests)*;
> 4 *Equations* ← *generateEquations(Tests, Executions)*;
> 5 *Spec* ← *generateAxioms(Equations)*;
> 6 **return** *Spec*;

Algorithm 3. Henkel and Diwan's algorithm for inferring algebraic specifications.

Although it marries Machine Learning with software testing, Henkel and Diwan's approach is a departure from the iterative approach in Algorithm 2. Their approach is shown in Algorithm 3. It starts off by generating the basic terms in the algebra by extracting the signatures of the methods in the SUT (since they focus on Java programs, they achieve this by using Java's reflection API). These terms are subsequently combined into sequences. From these sequences, it is necessary to generate a set of test cases by supplying suitable input parameters (the sequences can be seen as Parameterised Unit Tests [28]). Once tests are executed, the sequences of corresponding terms can be formulated into equations, indicating which sequences result in an equivalent state, so

---

[2] The idea of combining algebraic specification inference with test generation was proposed in the same year by Xie and Notkin [34], though this was not accompanied by an implementation.

that they can be generalised into the resulting specification. This equivalence is established by identifying a set of "observer" methods in the target class that do not mutate the object, but can provide some feedback on its state.

It is difficult to evaluate the efficacy of Henkel and Diwan's approach from a test-generation perspective, because tests are more of a by-product in their approach. They do not prescribe a particular test generation strategy or procedure for generating the tests. They do not link their test-generation to some adequacy criterion; instead they specify a number of tests to be generated for each sequence (e.g. in their experiments this was set to 4). The value of these tests will clearly depend on the accuracy of the model, coupled with the choice of test-data generation strategy.

However, this lack of focus upon testing is not an essential limitation of their approach. It would be relatively straightforward to re-purpose Henkel and Diwan's approach towards testing, in line with the iterative test-inference cycle in Algorithm 2. Lines 4 and 5 in Algorithm 3 would amount to inferring the model from tests (*inferModel* in Algorithm 2), and lines 2–3 would amount to selecting and executing tests from the inferred model (lines 8–10 in Algorithm 2).

Strengths:	Weaknesses:
• Particularly suited to testing data types. As such, especially suited to unit testing. • Empirical evidence to suggest that their approach is applicable to collection data types in the Java API.	• There has been no evidence wrt. the effectiveness of the test sets that are produced in the inference process – all of the emphasis has been placed on the accuracy of the inferred models. • Appropriate observer methods are not necessarily available, or even obviously identifiable. • Can involve the execution of large numbers of tests to establish object equality. • No evidence to corroborate the efficacy of the generated test sets.

4.4   Decision-Tree Based Approaches

Decision tree models are interesting from a testing perspective, because they provide a concise means by which to link constraints (i.e. on input variables) to functional program outcomes. When modelling the behaviour of a software system, a decision tree in essence presents a hierarchy of decisions on the input space, where each leaf node in the tree amounts to a conjunction of decisions that lead to a specific outcome. In the context of inference-based testing, there are two approaches that specifically revolve around decision trees: Briand *et al.*'s MELBA approach, and Papadopoulos and Walkinshaw's MINTEST framework.

4.4.1 MELBA

Briand *et al.* [6] proposed MELBA - a semi-automated variant of the inference-test loop. They considered the typical situation where the developer is given a partial, inadequate set of test cases, and needs to decide how to augment it. The process of testing, informed by the inferred model, is carried out according to the Category Partition method [21]. The approach is distinguished from others considered so far for two reasons: (1) it explicitly incorporates input from a human developer, and (2) it is linked with a systematic test selection strategy.

In terms of Algorithm 2 the *inferModel* function is carried out by an off-the-shelf decision tree learner (they opt for the C4.5 algorithm [23]). However *terminate* and *selectInputs* are carried out by the developer. For *terminate* it is left to the developer to scrutinise the inferred model to determine whether the behaviour that has been tested is sufficiently representative of the expected behaviour (or whether the model indicates any obvious faults). For *generateTests*, Briand *et al.* leave the developer with two options. They can either update the test specification that is used to generate test cases (the categories and partitions [21]), or can add individual test cases themselves.

Briand *et al.* argue that it is necessary to keep the developer in the loop, because it is otherwise impossible to validate the inferred model and to identify potentially faulty behaviour. This highlights a key assumption that is made by most other approaches: that there is some oracle (perhaps in the form of runtime assertions) that is able to flag up any faulty behaviour should it occur.

MELBA was demonstrated on two case studies – the typical Triangle program was used to illustrate the approach. The larger PackHexChar program (a Java adaptation of a GhostScript function used to compress hexadecimal characters into bit strings) was used as a case study. They illustrated (via a study on students) that their combination of decision tree inference with the category partition method could lead to an improvement in test sets (as assessed by seeded faults).

Strengths:	Weaknesses:
• Empirical evidence indicating that the test sets are effective.	• Evidence only collected for a single subject program.
• Reliance upon a human oracle enables stronger conclusions to be made about the absence of faults in the system once testing is complete.	• Reliance upon a human oracle increases expense, especially when required to visually inspect inferred decision trees.
	• Tied to programs that have categorical outputs. This rules out a large range of programs.

4.4.2 MINTEST

Papadopoulos and Walkinshaw presented an automated variant of Briand *et al.*'s MELBA approach [22]. It was automated in the sense that the *generateTests* part was amended to automatically generate sets of tests that satisfied the various combinations of constraints set out by the decision tree. The test sets are generated by, for each leaf-node in the tree, identifying all of the constraints that lead to it, and feeding the conjunction of the various constraint to a constraint solver (Z3 in their case). This is then used to identify a set of test inputs that satisfy the various constraints and cumulatively span the range of behaviours set out in the tree.

Their MINTEST framework includes a proof of concept implementation that can, in principle, automatically test any program that can be executed from the command line (if a suitable descriptor file of the interface is provided). The limitation, as with MELBA, is that the program in question must be capable of being modelled as a decision tree: it must take as input either numerical or categorical inputs, and produce a single output variable (that is also numerical or categorical).

To illustrate the effectiveness, the authors include a small experiment on three small Java programs, which indicates that the approach is better able to identify test sets that expose (seeded) faults than equivalent random approaches.

Strengths:	Weaknesses:
• Some limited empirical evidence indicating that the test sets are effective. • Automated - framework enables approach to be applied to arbitrary programs that can be launched from the command line.	• Tied to programs that have categorical outputs. This rules out a large range of programs. • Only demonstrated on small number of small Java programs.

4.5   Model-Agnostic Techniques

One of the limitations of most of the approaches mentioned previously is the fact that they are tied to a specific family of Machine Learning algorithms. As such, these approaches can only be practically applied to programs where the underlying behaviour is a suitable fit to the type of model inferred by that approach. ILP-driven approaches are a good fit for approaches that operate on arrays, but less appropriate for systems with sequential behaviour. The converse applies to approaches that are based upon algebraic specifications or state machines. Decision-tree based approaches such as MELBA are particularly good for systems that produce categorical outputs, but are again unsuitable for systems that operate on complex data structures such as lists, or are sequential in nature.

4.5.1   Coevolutionary Inference of Models and Tests

Bongard and Lipson applied a version of the test-and-infer loop in the context of nonlinear dynamical systems [5]. Such systems tend to involve multiple interacting components. There is no assumption that the systems under test are necessarily software systems; they demonstrate their approach on a variety of problems, including the inference of gene networks, grammars, and robot behaviours. In practice they are often simulations of physical systems – as is the case with the gene networks. In practice this distinction between software and non-software is not significant, and the work is reminiscent of the ILP-driven gene pathway identification work by King *et al.* [17], which appeared a year earlier.

Bongard and Lipson's approach is particularly interesting because they do not tie themselves to a specific model inference algorithm. They are interested in the broader process by which one can, with the help of tests, infer a demonstrably accurate model of an arbitrary (potentially non-linear) dynamic system. At the heart of their approach lies a "coevolutionary" algorithm – an evolutionary algorithm that evolves a population of models and corresponding test cases in tandem with each other.

This coevolutionary approach is an embodiment of the familiar loop in Algorithm 2. Bongard and Lipson refer to this as the *Estimation-Exploration Algorithm*. They start from a random set of tests. The *inferModel* function is assumed to be based on a genetic algorithm that encourages diversity within its population. The fitness function is presumed to be based on the ability of the inferred model to explain the test case executions. The *selectInputs* function is called the *Exploration* phase. This is again assumed to be under the control of a genetic algorithm, where fitness is measured by the capacity of the tests to disagree with the inferred model. They also have the ability to flexibly define the *terminate* function, to stop the inference once both model inference fails to achieve an improved model, and test inference fails to identify tests that disagree with the model.

Strengths:	Weaknesses:
• Empirically evaluated on a range of systems (grammars, robots, gene pathway models). • Can be linked to arbitrary model inference techniques.	• Efficacy of tests has not been evaluated in a software testing context. • Lack of documented implementation detail, specifically with respect to choice of learners and testing strategies.

4.5.2   The BESTEST Framework

Recent work by Fraser and Walkinshaw [12] has adopted a similar approach to Bongard and Lipson's, but with more of a focus on software systems. Their BESTEST framework provides 'stubs' for *inferModel*, for which it is possible to supply arbitrary Machine Learning algorithms (for example it is possible to specify any Machine Learning algorithm implemented within the WEKA framework [14]).

The test case generation (*selectInputs*) also applies a Genetic Algorithm. However, in their case the fitness function aims to identify test cases that maximise the extent to which they cover the source code of the system under test[3], whilst also maximising disagreement with the inferred model. This disagreement is measured according the ability to diminish the assessment that it is 'Probably Approximately Correct' [29].

The approach was evaluated on 18 Java units. Given the restriction to off-the-shelf WEKA learners, these all had to have relatively straightforward interfaces (with numerical or categorical inputs, and a single numerical or categorical output), and were accordingly relatively simple (all apart from one were under 100 SLOC). They showed that BESTEST outperforms standard code-coverage driven and random test generation approaches, but only if the approach is configured appropriately (which relies to an extent upon human judgement).

Strengths:	Weaknesses:
• Can be linked to arbitrary model inference techniques. • Evidence suggests that generated test sets are more effective and efficient (on a per-test basis) than random testing.	• Reliant upon generating large numbers of quasi-random tests (albeit optionally guided by code coverage if code is accessible). • Use of WEKA means currently restricted to programs with simple interfaces (primitive types, single-output values). • Only demonstrated on small Java units.

4.5.3   Uncertainty-Based Sampling

The process of generating tests to refine inferred models (*selectInputs*) is commonly either random, or is driven by the model in some way. The disadvantage of random or quasi-random testing is that these tests tend to struggle to properly explore and probe the behaviour as represented by the inferred models. This is especially the case if the behaviour is difficult to trigger (e.g. is governed by highly specific pre-conditions on the data state).

However, when it comes to generating tests from an inferred model, the specific implementation of *selectInputs* is invariably tied to the specific type of model. This means that approaches that are model-agnostic such as Bongard and Lipson's approach, or BESTEST ultimately rely on quasi-random test generation for *selectInputs*. Both approaches ultimately rely on generating random tests with the help of a genetic algorithm which aims to maximise disagreement between the tests and the model.

This approach has the weakness that it is possible, in principle, to generate lots of tests that trivially disagree with the model, without actually probing the more subtle 'deeper' behaviour of what has been executed so far. In a scenario

---

[3] This requirement for access to source code coverage can be waived if it is not available, in which case the coverage becomes entirely driven by the inferred model.

where we have co-evolution (in our case between the inferred model and the generated test set), this is referred to by Bongard and Lipson as the "Red Queen Effect". Although they assert that this effect diminishes over time with their coevolutionary approach, this ultimately depends on the genetic algorithm finding more probing test-cases, which is not necessarily realistic in the domain of software systems where specific behaviour trajectories can have complex preconditions.

Walkinshaw and Fraser [31] recently proposed an alternative test generation approach, designed to provide more probing test cases. Their approach is based on a technique from Active Machine Learning [26] known as *uncertainty sampling*. This approach is based on the assumption that, for a given input, the inferred model is capable not only of giving a predicted output, but also of associating that output with a level of confidence or probability. The rationale is that, by identifying those test cases that elicit the greatest uncertainty from the inferred model, a subsequent training set that contains the ground-truth behaviour for these inputs will be of most 'utility' for model inference, and will lead to the greatest improvements in model accuracy.

Although some inferred models have an in-built means by which to assess probability (e.g. C4.5 decision trees [23]), this is not necessarily always the case. One way by which to obtain confidence measures from arbitrary types of models is to use *inferModel* to produce populations of multiple models, instead of a single model. For example, Walkinshaw and Fraser use Genetic Programming, which intrinsically produces a population of models (individual chromosomes), but it is similarly possible to adopt the Ensemble Learning approach of inferring diverse models from different sub-samples of the training set [18]. Once there are multiple models, a confidence value for a given input can be ascertained by measuring the level of agreement or disagreement amongst the models.

Strengths:	Weaknesses:
• Empirical evidence indicates that the approach is more effective on a per-test basis than random testing and ART. • Can be linked to arbitrary model inference techniques. • Only selects few tests per iteration (as opposed to a large set) and thus relies on fewer test executions than BESTEST and Bongard and Lipsons co-evolutionary approach.	• Only applied on a Genetic Programming inference system, which leads to similar interface restrictions to BESTEST. • Only demonstrated on small Java units.

5 Limitations of the State of the Art

Despite being the subject of several decades worth of research, none of the techniques to have emerged has transferred into widespread use. In part, this is because off-the-shelf Machine Learning and clustering implementations have only become widely available relatively recently.

Nevertheless, there are several other, potentially more fundamental problems that need to be overcome before such techniques become readily applicable. This section presents a brief survey of some of these key problems.

5.1 Time Penalties Imposed by Inference

In their critique of ART, Arcuri and Briand [1] observed that empirical evaluations of ART had tended to focus on its relative effectiveness in terms of the number of test cases executed, whilst ignoring the time taken. They observed that as soon as this was taken into account, ART is shown to be impractical. They point to an example of the notorious Triangle classification program, where random testing required merely 10 ms to find the first failure, whereas ART required 47 min.

This criticism is not merely restricted to ART, but potentially also applies to all of the other techniques that revolve around model inference. All iteratively involve a repeated inference step. For the most part, the time-penalty of this step also increases for each iteration, as it needs to take an ever increasing number of test executions into account.

The extent to which this criticism applies to model-inference based techniques depends on a variety of factors. Arcuri's research focussed on subject systems that had a trivially small execution time. For systems where software execution takes longer, the relative efficacy of random testing would probably rapidly diminish. Examples of such systems obviously include the (non-software) robot scientist system [17], where an execution amounted to a robot carrying out a physical experiment, or the robotic simulations considered by Bongard and Lipson [5].

One factor that was not explicitly considered by Arcuri and Briand was the question of where the oracle fits in to the testing loop. Depending on the development context, for example if test executions have to be inspected manually, the prospect of randomly producing tens of thousands of test executions might not be tenable. In this case, investing more care in selecting test cases might be a preferable option.

It is clear that, regardless of the context, there is a need to evaluate inference-driven techniques in terms of their time-efficiency in comparison to baseline techniques. In cases where time is of the essence, this could also indicate the need to focus on more efficient Machine Learning techniques that are capable of handling large streams of data (e.g. on-line algorithms).

5.2 Selection of Appropriate Model Inference Algorithms

Most of the techniques in this chapter make the strong assumption that the inference technique in question is capable of inferring a model that approximates the behaviour of the system under test. In the papers, the case study systems tend to be chosen to reflect the learner; Bergadano and Gunetti's ILP-based technique was demonstrated on a Prolog function, Henkel and Diwan's approach was demonstrated on implementations of collections data types, and the decision tree-based approaches by Briand *et al.* and Papadopoulos and Walkinshaw were illustrated on small Java units with simple interfaces.

Although the approach can be (and has been) applied to larger, complex software systems, there is always the presumption that the resulting behaviour can ultimately be summarised and captured with the chosen inference algorithm. This assumption can however readily be confounded. For example, it is common for data processing implementations (e.g. data compression or sequence alignment frameworks) to switch between different algorithms depending on particular characteristics of the dataset.

The problem is that the question of whether a given phenomenon is 'learnable' is often far from clear. In the Machine Learning domain this problem has been studied under the term "computational learning theory", and have particularly focussed on the question of whether it is possible to even approximately learn a model of a given phenomenon [29]. Even then, answers tend to only be forthcoming for well understood subjects, such as regular grammars. However, the question of whether a vaguely understood black box program can be inferred by a given learner is inevitably subject to a high degree of supposition and doubt.

Even once a given learning algorithm is chosen, there is the challenge of selecting appropriate configurations of parameters. It is a corollary of the 'No Free Lunch' theorem [33] that, although there may be certain configurations that excel for certain inference problems, there are no configurations that perform better than others in the general case. Ultimately, identifying a suitable Machine Learning configuration requires, again, an understanding of the behaviour of the subject being inferred which, in our use case, is not necessarily available.

This limitation is partly founded on the presumption that the subject system really is a 'black box'. It is however possible that the limitation could be at least partially addressed by gaining access to particular implementation details or aspects of domain knowledge.

5.3   The Oracle Problem

With the notable exception of Briand *et al.*'s MELBA approach, none of the testing approaches covered here involve any validation of what is being tested. The emphasis tends to be placed upon automation. The general presumption is that the checking of the outputs can be left to some existing set of assertions.

Of course, this presumption is usually fanciful. Often the only reliable oracle available is to detect obvious failures such as crashes or uncaught exceptions. However, such oracles will not highlight more subtle faulty behaviour. This is the essence of the "oracle problem", which is omnipresent in testing; the value of a highly rigorous set of test inputs is undermined if there is no means by which to check its outputs.

The availability of inferred models does offer the potential to facilitate verification by a human [2]. This step is not by necessity restricted to MELBA, but could in principle be applied with any of the other model inference based techniques as well. The question of whether to do so depends on the following factors:

- **Model readability:** Inferred models can become highly complex. They tend to be the product of a large number of test execution traces, and are often large, requiring a lot of effort to read and understand.
- **Domain knowledge:** In order to identify faults in the model, the developer has to have a sufficiently in-depth understanding of the idealised behaviour of the system, and be able to relate this to the inferred model.
- **Ability to debug or verify faults:** If the developer detects a discrepancy with the inferred model, the problem could either lie with the model inference (the inference algorithm made a mistake and the inferred model is not a true reflection of the SUT), or with the system itself (the inference algorithm was correct and the SUT is indeed buggy). Either way, this requires developer effort. If there is no bug in the SUT, then the developer also has to identify the necessary test executions to elicit the behaviour that will prevent the inference from making the mistake in subsequent iterations.
- **Time and expertise:** Reading, validating the model, and debugging any problems require a lot of time and expertise, which is generally at a premium in routine software development environments.

6   Conclusions

In this chapter we have focussed specifically on the challenge of testing 'stateless' black box programs. By 'stateless', we mean programs are not sequential in nature. This has been the subject of a substantial amount of research over the past three to four decades, and we have attempted to provide a concise overview of these efforts here.

The chapter started from a description of the testing challenge. This was followed up by a brief overview or Adaptive Random Testing (which works by identifying clusters of inputs, to support the identification of more distinctive inputs). Most of the chapter, however, was devoted to a myriad of techniques to have emerged that revolve around model inference, where models are inferred that are then used to feed back into test generation.

At first glance, the model inference approaches appear to be quite diverse. Some were devised primarily for model inference, with tests as a by-product. Others were devised entirely for testing. Some were intended solely for software testing, others had a broader remit (e.g. to infer models of robot behaviour or models of genetic pathways). However, all of the approaches are underpinned by the same sequence of steps - executing test cases, inferring a model from the execution traces, using the model to identify new inputs, and repeating the loop.

There are of course major differences between the techniques. These mainly reside in the types of models that they infer. These have included logic programs, algebraic specifications, decision trees, and fully fledged programs (inferred by

Genetic Programming). The best choice invariably depends on the nature of the behaviour of the software system that is being tested.

The relative merits of the different approaches are difficult to compare. Although most approaches have been subject to some form of applied case study or even an empirical study, these vary substantially in nature. Techniques that were mainly intended for reverse-engineering tend to assess the models, whereas test-centric approaches tend to assess the test sets. Nevertheless, in this chapter we have attempted to take whatever evidence is available, and to use this to highlight any apparent strengths and weaknesses for each approach.

The chapter has set out some of the limitations with the state of the art. It remains the case that choosing an appropriate inference algorithm, and setting up an interface between the system under test and the algorithm, can be challenging. The inference step can incur time penalties that can, under certain circumstances, render the approach too expensive in comparison with random testing. There is also the enduring oracle problem; even if useful tests are generated, there is no straightforward automated approach by which to check them. These all remain challenges that must be addressed in future research.

References

1. Arcuri, A., Briand, L.: Adaptive random testing: an illusion of effectiveness? In: Proceedings of the 2011 International Symposium on Software Testing and Analysis, pp. 265–275. ACM (2011)
2. Barr, E.T., Harman, M., McMinn, P., Shahbaz, M., Yoo, S.: The Oracle problem in software testing: a survey. IEEE Trans. Softw. Eng. **41**(5), 507–525 (2015)
3. Bergadano, F., Gunetti, D.: An interactive system to learn functional logic programs. In: IJCAI, pp. 1044–1049 (1993)
4. Bergadano, F., Gunetti, D.: Testing by means of inductive program learning. ACM Trans. Softw. Eng. Methodol. (TOSEM) **5**(2), 119–145 (1996)
5. Bongard, J.C., Lipson, H.: Nonlinear system identification using coevolution of models and tests. IEEE Trans. Evol. Comput. **9**(4), 361–384 (2005)
6. Briand, L.C., Labiche, Y., Bawar, Z., Spido, N.T.: Using machine learning to refine category-partition test specifications and test suites. Inf. Softw. Technol. **51**(11), 1551–1564 (2009)
7. Budd, T.A., Angluin, D.: Two notions of correctness and their relation to testing. Acta Informatica **18**(1), 31–45 (1982)
8. Chen, T.Y., Leung, H., Mak, I.K.: Adaptive random testing. In: Maher, M.J. (ed.) ASIAN 2004. LNCS, vol. 3321, pp. 320–329. Springer, Heidelberg (2004). https://doi.org/10.1007/978-3-540-30502-6_23
9. Cherniavsky, J., Smith, C.: A recursion theoretic approach to program testing. IEEE Trans. Softw. Eng. **13**, 777–784 (1987)
10. Ciupa, I., Leitner, A., Oriol, M., Meyer, B.: ARTOO: adaptive random testing for object-oriented software. In: Proceedings of the 30th International Conference on Software Engineering, pp. 71–80. ACM (2008)
11. Feldt, R., Poulding, S., Clark, D., Yoo, S.: Test set diameter: quantifying the diversity of sets of test cases. In: 2016 IEEE International Conference on Software Testing, Verification and Validation (ICST), pp. 223–233. IEEE (2016)

12. Fraser, G., Walkinshaw, N.: Assessing and generating test sets in terms of behavioural adequacy. Softw. Test. Verif. Reliab. **25**(8), 749–780 (2015)
13. Goodenough, J.B., Gerhart, S.L.: Toward a theory of test data selection. IEEE Trans. Softw. Eng. **2**, 156–173 (1975)
14. Hall, M., Frank, E., Holmes, G., Pfahringer, B., Reutemann, P., Witten, I.H.: The WEKA data mining software: an update. SIGKDD Explor. Newsl. **11**, 10–18 (2009). ISSN 1931-0145
15. Hamlet,R.: Random testing. In: Encyclopedia of Software Engineering (1994)
16. Henkel, J., Diwan, A.: Discovering algebraic specifications from Java classes. In: Cardelli, L. (ed.) ECOOP 2003. LNCS, vol. 2743, pp. 431–456. Springer, Heidelberg (2003). https://doi.org/10.1007/978-3-540-45070-2_19
17. King, R.D., Whelan, K.E., Jones, F.M., Reiser, P.G.K., Bryant, C.H., Muggleton, S.H., Kell, D.B., Oliver, S.G.: Functional genomic hypothesis generation and experimentation by a robot scientist. Nature **427**(6971), 247–252 (2004)
18. Kuncheva, L.I., Whitaker, C.J.: Measures of diversity in classifier ensembles and their relationship with the ensemble accuracy. Mach. Learn. **51**(2), 181–207 (2003)
19. Lavrac,N., Dzeroski, S.: Inductive logic programming. In: WLP, pp. 146–160. Springer, Heidelberg (1994)
20. Moore, E.F.: Gedanken-experiments on sequential machines. Automata Stud. **34**, 129–153 (1956)
21. Ostrand, T.J., Balcer, M.J.: The category-partition method for specifying and generating fuctional tests. Commun. ACM **31**(6), 676–686 (1988)
22. Papadopoulos, P., Walkinshaw, N.: Black-box test generation from inferred models. In: Proceedings of the Fourth International Workshop on Realizing Artificial Intelligence Synergies in Software Engineering, pp. 19–24. IEEE Press (2015)
23. Quinlan, J.R.: C4.5 Programs for Machine Learning. MK, San Mateo (1993)
24. Romanik, K., Vitter, J.S.: Using computational learning theory to analyze the testing complexity of program segments. In: Proceedings Seventeenth Annual International Computer Software and Applications Conference. COMPSAC 1993, pp. 367–373. IEEE (1993)
25. Romanik, K., Vitter, J.S.: Using Vapnik-Chervonenkis dimension to analyze the testing complexity of program segments. Inf. Comput. **128**(2), 87–108 (1996)
26. Settles, B.: Active learning literature survey, vol. 52, no. 55–66, p. 11. University of Wisconsin, Madison (2010)
27. Summers, P.D.: A methodology for LISP program construction from examples. J. ACM (JACM) **24**(1), 161–175 (1977)
28. Tillmann, N., Schulte, W.: Parameterized unit tests. In: ACM SIGSOFT Software Engineering Notes, vol. 30, pp. 253–262. ACM (2005)
29. Valiant, L.G.: A theory of the learnable. Commun. ACM **27**(11), 1134–1142 (1984)
30. Vapnik, V.N., Chervonenkis, A.Y.: On the uniform convergence of relative frequencies of events to their probabilities. In: Vovk, V., Papadopoulos, H., Gammerman, A. (eds.) Measures of Complexity, pp. 11–30. Springer, Cham (2015). https://doi.org/10.1007/978-3-319-21852-6_3
31. Walkinshaw, N., Fraser, G.: Uncertainty-driven black-box test data generation. In: International Conference on Software Testing (ICST) (2017)
32. Weyuker, E.J.: Assessing test data adequacy through program inference. ACM Trans. Program. Lang. Syst. (TOPLAS) **5**(4), 641–655 (1983)
33. Wolpert, D.H., Macready, W.G.: No free lunch theorems for optimization. IEEE Trans. Evol. Comput. **1**(1), 67–82 (1997)

34. Xie, T., Notkin, D.: Mutually enhancing test generation and specification inference. In: Petrenko, A., Ulrich, A. (eds.) FATES 2003. LNCS, vol. 2931, pp. 60–69. Springer, Heidelberg (2004). https://doi.org/10.1007/978-3-540-24617-6_5
35. Zhu, H.: A formal interpretation of software testing as inductive inference. Softw. Test. Verif. Reliab. **6**(1), 3–31 (1996)
36. Zhu, H., Hall, P., May, J.: Inductive inference and software testing. Softw. Test. Verif. Reliab. **2**(2), 69–81 (1992)

Extensions of Automata Learning

Active Automata Learning in Practice
An Annotated Bibliography of the Years 2011 to 2016

Falk Howar[1]($\boxtimes$) and Bernhard Steffen[2]

[1] Dortmund University of Technology and Fraunhofer ISST, Dortmund, Germany
falk.howar@tu-dortmund.de
[2] Dortmund University of Technology, Dortmund, Germany
steffen@cs.tu-dortmund.de

Abstract. Active automata learning is slowly becoming a standard tool in the toolbox of the software engineer. As systems become ever more complex and development becomes more distributed, inferred models of system behavior become an increasingly valuable asset for understanding and analyzing a system's behavior. Five years ago (in 2011) we have surveyed the then current state of active automata learning research and applications of active automata learning in practice. We predicted four major topics to be addressed in the then near future: efficiency, expressivity of models, bridging the semantic gap between formal languages and analyzed components, and solutions to the inherent problem of incompleteness of active learning in black-box scenarios. In this paper we review the progress that has been made over the past five years, assess the status of active automata learning techniques with respect to applications in the field of software engineering, and present an updated agenda for future research.

1 Introduction

Active automata learning [13] infers models from observations. Alternating between deriving conjectures from experiments and observations and then trying to corroborate or disprove conjectures, active automata learning can be seen as one instance of the fundamental method in science described by Popper [126], who postulates that models (of the world) cannot be verified or reliably generalized, not even probabilistically. Rather, models (of the world) can only be falsified and repaired.

In a world of evermore complex man-made systems that consist of many components, developed by large groups of engineers, and use independently developed libraries or basic software, referring to Popper's scientific method seems appropriate for analyzing, understanding, and validating the behavior of (software) systems whose complexity is beyond the reach of deductive methods.

When learning the behavior of software systems, an observation can be a simple execution of some target component, or a sequence of packages exchanged with a networked system, but also an instance of model checking the feasibility

© Springer International Publishing AG, part of Springer Nature 2018
A. Bennaceur et al. (Eds.): ML for Dynamic Software Analysis, LNCS 11026, pp. 123–148, 2018.
https://doi.org/10.1007/978-3-319-96562-8_5

of a sequence of steps on a system. Learned models enable the application of (formal) analysis and verification techniques or testing approaches, e.g., of model checking [42] or model-based testing [27].

This has first been demonstrated in the concrete scenario of testing computer telephony integrated (CTI) systems [12,69,71], where a finite automaton model was inferred from experiments and used as a basis for regression testing. When analyzing bigger systems, however, it became clear quickly that the success of automata learning in practice would hinge on practical optimizations like efficient implementation of existing learning algorithms, strategies for selecting experiments, and the development of new and more efficient learning algorithms that infer more expressive models. An example of early practical optimizations is the exploitation of the prefix-closedness of a system's set of traces for generating observations to many experiments performed by a learning algorithm without executing actual tests on a system [72,86,107,140].

In 2011, we wrote a report and published a book chapter on the practical challenges in applying active automata learning in software engineering and surveyed the then current state of active automata learning research and applications [81]. We predicted four major topics to be addressed in the then near future: efficiency, expressivity of models, bridging the semantic gap between formal languages and analyzed components, and solutions to the inherent problem of incompleteness of active learning in black-box scenarios. In this paper, we survey the literature on active automata and provide a brief overview of the progress that has been made in the years 2011 to 2016 towards these challenges.

Organization. We give a very brief introduction to active automata learning in Sect. 2 and revisit the challenges that we identified in 2011 in Sect. 3. Section 4 surveys work that focuses on active automata learning in software engineering in the past six years (i.e., from 2011 to 2016). Finally, we asses the progress that has been made and update the list of challenges, taking into account the results of the survey, in Sect. 5.

2   Active Automata Learning

Active automata learning [13] is concerned with the problem of inferring an automaton model for an unknown formal language L over some alphabet Σ.

MAT Model. Active learning is often formulated as a cooperative game between a learner and a teacher, as is sketched in Fig. 1. The task of the learner is to learn a model of some unknown formal language L. The teacher can assist the learner by answering two kinds of queries:

Membership queries ask for a single word $w \in \Sigma^*$ if it is in the unknown language L. The teacher answers these queries with "yes" or "no".

Equivalence queries ask for a candidate language L_H if L_H equals L. In case a conjectured language L_H does not equal L, the teacher will provide a counterexample: a word from the symmetric difference of L_H and L.

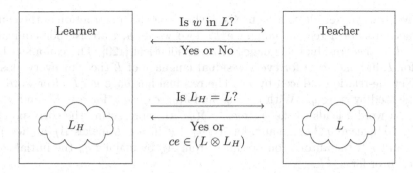

Fig. 1. Active automata learning in the MAT model.

The teacher in this model is called a *minimally adequate teacher* (MAT) and the learning model is hence often referred to as MAT learning.

Dana Angluin's original contribution (in hindsight) is twofold: with the MAT learning model, she introduced an abstraction that allowed for the separation of concerns (constructing stable preliminary models and checking the correctness of these models). This enabled an algorithmic pattern or framework of reasoning that allowed the formulation and optimization of learning algorithms. The second contribution is the original L^* learning algorithm for regular languages and a sequence of lemmas on the status of preliminary models, e.g., showing that for L^* all conjectured models are consistent with all previous observations. The learning algorithm and the sequence of lemmas have served as a basis for proving corresponding properties for many learning algorithms for more complex classes of concepts.

Languages and Automata. A conjectured language L_H is represented by its canonical deterministic acceptor and identified using its residual languages. Intuitively, a residual language [48] of a language is the language after some prefix. Formally, for some language L and a word $u \in \Sigma^*$, the residual language $u^{-1}L$ is the set $\{w \in \Sigma^* \mid uw \in L\}$. A regular language L can be characterized by a finite set of residual languages and every state of the language's canonical acceptor corresponds to one of these languages.

Definition 1. *A Deterministic Finite Automaton (DFA) is a tuple* $A = \langle Q, q_0, \Sigma, \delta, F \rangle$ *where:*

- *Q is a finite nonempty set of states,*
- *$q_0 \in Q$ is the initial state,*
- *Σ is a finite alphabet,*
- *$\delta : Q \times \Sigma \to Q$ is the transition function, and*
- *$F \subseteq Q$ is the set of accepting states.*

We extend δ to words in the natural way by defining $\delta(q, \epsilon) = q$ for the empty word ϵ and $\delta(q, ua) = \delta(\delta(q, u), a)$ for $u \in \Sigma^*$ and $a \in \Sigma$. A word w is accepted by A if $d(q_0, w) \in F$.

The well-known Nerode congruence is the basis for the construction of the canonical acceptor for a regular language L: Two words u, v are Nerode-equivalent w.r.t. L if their residual languages in L are identical [120]. The canonical DFA A_L for L has one state for every residual language of L (i.e., for every class of the Nerode-relation induced by L). The residual language $u^{-1}L$ after word u is represented by state q_u. With $q_\epsilon = q_0$ and $\delta(q_u, a) = q_{ua}$ for $u \in \Sigma^*$ and $a \in \Sigma$ in A_L, a word u leads to the state $q_u = \delta(q_0, u)$, representing the corresponding residual language $u^{-1}L$. Finally, letting $q_u \in F$ iff $u \in L$ makes A_L an acceptor for L and A_L^u, the automaton obtained from A_L by making q_u the initial state, an acceptor for $u^{-1}L$.

The L* Algorithm. Active learning algorithms are based on the dual characterization of states in the canonical acceptor A_L, by words leading to states and their residual languages. The key observation is that words u and u' cannot lead to the same state if for some $v \in \Sigma^*$ the word uv is in L while $u'v$ is not in L (or vice versa). Thus, a finite nonempty set U of *prefixes* can be used to identify states and a finite nonempty set V of *suffixes* can be used to distinguish states.

The L^* algorithm[1] for regular languages uses an observation table $Obs :$ $(U \cup U \cdot \Sigma) \times V \mapsto \{1, 0\}$ for organizing results of membership queries, letting $Obs(u, v) = 1$ iff $uv \in L$ and 0 otherwise. Sets U and V are initialized as $\{\epsilon\}$, i.e., with a prefix for the initial state and a suffix that distinguishes final states from non-final states, and are extended incrementally. An automaton A_{Obs} can be generated from Obs with states q_u for $u \in U$, initial state q_ϵ, transitions $\delta(q_u, a) = q_{u'}$ for $u, u' \in U$ and $a \in \Sigma$ where $Obs(ua) = Obs(u')$ and $q_u \in F$ iff $Obs(u, \epsilon) = 1$. This automaton is only well-defined if δ is total. The algorithm ensures this when extending the table (and hence refining the corresponding automaton) on the basis of query results, iterating the two main steps (1) establishing *closedness* via membership queries, and (2) *testing for equivalence* via equivalence queries.

Local exploration. The first phase checks whether the knowledge, gathered from membership queries and accumulated in the observation table, suffices to construct a hypothesis automaton with a total transition function. This requires that the table is *closed*, meaning that for every word $w \in U \cdot \Sigma$ there is a prefix $u \in U$ with $Obs(u) = Obs(w)$. The set U of prefixes is extended by words from $U \cdot \Sigma$ until the table is closed and a hypothesis automaton A_{Obs} (accepting L_H in Fig. 1) can be generated.

Checking Equivalence. An equivalence query checks whether A_{Obs} is the canonic acceptor of the target language L. Once this is true, the learning procedure terminates successfully. Otherwise, the equivalence query returns a counterexample from the symmetric difference of L and L_H. As was shown by Rivest and

---

[1] We only provide a very brief sketch of the improved version of L^* due to Rivest and Schapire here [130]. A more detailed presentation can be found in Angluin's original paper [13].

Schapire [130], a counterexample w indicates that the set V of suffixes, approximating the characterization of states by residual languages, can be refined by adding one of the suffixes of w to V: The word $w = a_1 \cdots a_m$ traverses states $q_0, q_1, \ldots, q_m$ in A_{Obs}. For index $0 \le i \le m$, let $\tilde{u}_i$ be the prefix for q_i in U with $\delta(q_0, \tilde{u}_i) = q_i$ and for $1 \le j \le m$ let v_j be the suffix $a_j \cdots a_m$ of w. There is a pair $\tilde{u}_{i-1}$ and $\tilde{u}_i$ of prefixes in U with $Obs(\tilde{u}_{i-1}a_i) = Obs(\tilde{u}_i)$ while $\tilde{u}_{i-1}a_i \cdot v_{i+1} \in L$ and $\tilde{u}_i \cdot v_{i+1} \notin L$ (or vice versa).[2] Adding v_{i+1} to the set V of suffixes will lead to unclosedness of the observation table, which in turn will lead to adding prefixes to U, and result in a refined conjecture.

Correctness and Termination. The correctness argument for this approach follows a straightforward pattern, which does not only hold for L^*, but also for all of the derivatives [96, 107, 123, 130, 132] presented so far.

Partial correctness [75] is obvious, because learning only terminates after the equivalence oracle guaranteed the correctness of the inferred model. What remains to be shown is termination. The following four steps suffice to prove that the learning procedure always terminates after at most n equivalence queries, where n is the number of states of the desired minimal acceptor for L:

1. The state construction, using distinguishing suffixes in lieu of residual languages, guarantees that the number of states of the hypothesis automaton can never exceed the number of states of the smallest deterministic automaton accepting the considered language.
2. The closedness procedure guarantees that each transition of the hypothesis automaton is represented by a prefix during learning. This means in particular that a hypothesis automaton of the size (in terms of number of states) of the smallest deterministic automaton for the considered language must already be isomorphic to this (canonic) automaton.
3. The analysis of counterexamples guarantees that at least one additional state is added to the hypothesis automaton for each counterexample. Thus, due to (1) and (2), such treatments can happen only n times.
4. The equivalence checking mechanism, often called equivalence oracle, provides new counterexamples as long as the language of the hypothesis automaton does not match the desired result.

Using the underlying concept of query learning a number of optimizations and akin algorithms have been proposed in the 1990s [96, 130], Balcázar et al. give a unifying overview [17].

Application in Model Learning. To meet the requirements in practical scenarios, Margaria et al. transferred automata learning to Mealy machines [107].

---

[2] While the word $w = \tilde{u}_0 \cdot v_1$ is a counterexample, $\tilde{u}_m$ cannot be a counterexample (by construction of A_{Obs}), and all words $\tilde{u}_i \cdot v_{i+1}$ with $0 \le i \le m-1$ lead to the same state as $\tilde{u}_m$ in A_{Obs}. As a consequence, at one index $\tilde{u}_{i-1}a_i \cdot v_{i+1} \in L$ and $\tilde{u}_i \cdot v_{i+1} \notin L$ (or vice versa).

Mealy machines are widely used models of deterministic reactive systems and multiple optimized algorithms have been proposed [72,129,132]. Examples of applications in the years before 2011 are the learning of behavioral models for Web Services [127], communication protocol entities [139], or software components [86,117,128].

Extensions to inference methods focus on modeling phenomena that occur in real systems. On the basis of inference algorithms for Mealy machines, inference algorithms for I/O-automata [8], timed automata [124], Petri Nets [52], and Message Sequence Charts [22,23] have been developed. With the I/O-automata model, a wide range of systems that comprise quiescence is made accessible for query learning. Timed automata model explicitly time dependent behavior. With Petri Nets, systems with explicit parallel state are addressed.

3   A Short Review of Challenges in Applications

In this section, we discuss the challenges we identified in 2011 for the practical application of active automata learning. Automata learning can be considered as a key technology for dealing with *black-box systems*, i.e., systems that can be observed, but for which no or little knowledge about the internal structure is available. *Active* automata learning is characterized by its specific means of observation, i.e., its proactive way of posing membership queries and equivalence queries. It requires some way to realize this query-based interaction for the considered application contexts. Whereas membership queries may often be realized via testing in practice, equivalence queries are typically unrealistic.

3.1   Interacting with Real Systems

The interaction with a realistic target system comes with a number of challenges. A merely technical problem is establishing an adequate interface that allows one to realize membership queries. This can be rather simple for systems designed for connectivity (e.g., Web-services or libraries) which have a native concept of being invoked from the outside and come with documentation on how to accomplish this (cf. the work on so-called dynamic Web testing [128]). It may be more difficult for other systems, e.g., embedded systems that work on streams of data.

Establishing an adequate abstraction for learning is a second challenge: An abstraction has to produce a useful and finite model while at the same time allowing for an automatic back and forth translation between the abstract model and the concrete target system. At the time, there was some work focusing explicitly on the use of abstraction in learning [4,6] and even first steps in the direction of automatic abstraction refinement [84,89].

Another challenge is that active learning requires membership queries to be independent. Solutions range here from reset mechanisms via homing sequences [130] or snapshots of the system state to the generation of observably equivalent initial conditions. E.g., for session-based protocols, it may be sufficient to perform every membership query with a fresh session identifier [81].

3.2   Efficiency

Whereas small learning experiments typically require only a few hundred membership queries, learning realistic systems may easily require several orders of magnitude more. In some scenarios, each membership query may need multiple seconds or sometime even minutes to compute. In such a case minimizing the number of required membership queries is the key to success.

In [83,132] optimizations are discussed to classic learning algorithms that aim at saving membership queries in practical scenarios. Additionally, the use of filters (exploiting domain specific expert knowledge) has been proven as a practical solution to the problem [72,140]. Finally, the choice of a concrete learning algorithm may have a huge influence on the number of membership queries that are used to infer a model of a target system [77].

3.3   Expressivity of Models

Active learning classically is based on abstract communication alphabets. Parameters and interpreted values are only treated to an extend expressible within the abstract alphabet. In practice, this typically is not sufficient, not even for systems as simple as communication protocols, where, e.g., increasing sequence numbers must be handled, or where authentication requires matching user/password combinations.

First attempts to deal with parameters in models range from case studies with manual solutions [117] to extensions of learning algorithms that can deal with Boolean parameters [137,138]. One big future challenge at the time was extending learning to models with state variables and arbitrary data parameters in a more generic way, as explored by [10].

3.4   Equivalence Queries

Equivalence queries compare a learned hypothesis model with the target system for language equivalence and, in case of failure, return a counterexample exposing a difference. Their realization is rather simple in white-box scenarios: equivalence can be checked. In black-box scenarios, however, equivalence queries have to be approximated using membership queries. Without the introduction of additional assumptions, such equivalence tests are not decidable: the possibility of having not tested extensively enough always remains.

Conformance testing has been used to simulate equivalence queries. If, e.g., an upper bound on the number of states the target system can have is known, the W-method [41] or the Wp-method [57] can be applied. Both methods have an exponential complexity (in the size of the target system and measured in the number of membership queries needed). The relationship between regular extrapolation and conformance testing methods is discussed in [19].

Without introducing any additional assumptions, only approximate solutions exploiting membership queries exist. Here, conformance testing methods may not always be a wise choice. It has turned out that changing the view from "trying to proof equivalence", e.g., by using conformance testing techniques, to "finding counter examples fast" has a strong positive impact. An attempt to intensify research in this direction was the 2010 Zulu challenge [44]. The winning solution is discussed in [83]. The main contribution of this solution is a strategy for sharing information on test coverage for the evolving model between individual equivalence queries.

4   Recent Advances in Active Automata Learning

In order to assess the advances in practical application of active automata learning in the domain of Software engineering, we survey the literature on active automata learning in the years 2011 to 2016. Basis for the survey are the ACM's digital library and the proceedings of several big software engineering conferences (i.e., ICSE, CAV, ETAPS). The survey is not exhaustive since the number of candidate publications is in the thousands. We have used different heuristics for filtering out relevant publications: cited foundational papers, used keywords, and authors known to work in the field.

We sort publications into categories based on their main focus and differentiate between advances that have been made by application of automata learning and those that have been made to the methodology of active automata learning itself. Finally we discuss advances in lines of work that are closely related (i.e., learning from examples or active learning of other classes of concepts).

4.1   Advances in Applications

There have been impressive advances in the application of automata learning in diverse scenarios over the past years. Applications are found in black-box contexts as well as in white-box scenarios. The broad range of application areas documents that active (automata) learning is becoming one of the well-established tools in the toolbox of the formal methods trained software engineer.

Specification Generation. The most obvious application of active automata learning is the *a posteriori* generation of specifications from prototypes or from running (legacy) systems. Esparza et al. present a learning algorithm for Workflow Petri Nets [52] using log data and a teacher that answers executability of conjectured workflows. Sun et al. use active automata learning in combination with automated abstraction refinement and random testing for finding abstract behavioral models of Java classes [136]. Aarts et al. demonstrate how a combination of active automata learning with manually crafted abstraction mappers can be used to infer models of the SIP and TCP protocols [7]. Gu and Roychowdhury present a variant of L^* for inferring finite state abstractions of continuous circuits defined by differential equations [67]. Aadithya and Roychowdhury go on and extend the approach from learning regular abstractions to models with arbitrary I/O alphabets [1].

Model-based Testing without Models. One of the earliest practical applications of active automata learning was testing of telecommunication systems [12,69]. The idea of model-based testing without (a priori) models was later elaborated and, e.g., applied to Web-based systems [128]. In recent years this line of application has been continued for several different types of systems. Dinca et al. develop an approach for generating test-suites for Event-B models through active automata learning [49,50]. Choi et al. use active automata learning for testing the behavior of the graphical user interfaces of Android applications [39,40]. Shahbaz and Groz use automata learning for integration testing [133]. They infer models of embedded components and use these models as a basis for test case generation. Meinke and Sindhu present LBTest, a tool for learning-based testing for reactive systems, integrating model checking, active automata learning, and random testing [111]. In this volume, the relation between learning and testing is discussed in [11] and an overview of learning-based testing is presented in [109].

Software Re-engineering. Inferred models cannot only be used for testing but also for comparing different versions or implementations of a system. This can, e.g., be useful for searching (accidental) differences in the behavior of subsequent version of a software system. Neubauer et al. develop 'active continuous quality control': they use active automata learning on subsequent versions of a Web-application (during development) and analyze models for unintended behavioral changes between versions [121,122,145]. The approach integrates active automata learning, model checking, regression testing, and risk-based testing. Schuts et al. use model learning and equivalence checking to assist re-engineering of legacy software in an industrial context at Philips [131]. Howar et al. validate a model-to-code translator. They use active automata learning to extract behavioral models from generated implementations and compare these models to specification models [80]. Bainczyk et al. presented an easy to use tool for mixed-mode learning, which, in particular, allows one to compare back-end and front-end functionality of web applications [16].

Verification and Validation. Inferred models can be used in (formal) verification and system analysis as well, as sketched below.

Security. Behavioral models of systems can be used for identifying vulnerabilities. Active learning in these scenarios is often used to automate the work of a prospective attacker, exploring state of a systems in a structured way. Over the past years, a number of real vulnerabilities have been identified in this manner.

Cho et al. present MACE an approach for concolic exploration of protocol behavior. The approach uses active automata learning for discovering so-called deep states in the protocol behavior. From these states, concolic execution is employed in order to discover vulnerabilities [38]. Chalupar et al. use active automata learning and a LEGO robot to physically interact with smart cards and reverse engineer their protocols [34]. De Ruiter and Poll use active automata learning for inferring models of TLS implementations and discover previously unknown security flaws in the inferred models [46].

Botinčan and Babić present a learning algorithm for inferring models of stream transducers that integrates active automata learning with symbolic execution and counterexample-guided abstraction refinement [26]. They show how the models can be used to verify properties of input sanitizers in Web-applications. Xue et al. use active automata learning for inferring models of JavaScript malware [146].

Argyros et al. present SFADiff, a tool based on active automata learning for inferring symbolic automata that characterize the difference between similar programs [15]. The work is motivated by the security challenge of fingerprinting programs based on their behavior.

Safety/Correctness. Active learning can be used to generate (abstract) models at interfaces of systems. The behavior at such interfaces is often an issue when integrating systems into environments (virtual or physical). Inferred models can be used for analyzing safety in such situations. Combéfis et al. use active learning to generate abstract models of systems as a basis for analyzing potential mode confusion, a well-known problem in human machine interaction [45], while Howar et al. use the register automaton model [32] for inferring precise semantic interfaces of data structures [79]. Giannakopoulou et al. develop an active learning algorithm that infers safe interfaces of software components with guarded actions. In their model, the teacher is implemented using concolic execution [62,78]. Khalili et al. [97] use active automata learning to obtain behavioral models of the middleware of a robotic platform. The models are used during verification of control software for this platform. Fiterău-Broştean et al. use learning and model checking to analyze the behavior of different implementations of the TCP protocol stack and document several instances of implementations violating RFC specifications [56].

Assume-Guarantee Reasoning.

Assume-guarantee reasoning has been a big area of application of active automata learning algorithms for much longer than the past couple of years (cf. [43,101,125]). The moderate style of exploration that is achieved by learning is used to reduce the problem of state space explosion. Recent advances have been made by finding active automata learning to many classes of systems. Learning algorithms are usually based quite directly on the classic L^* algorithm. The required extensions in expressivity of models are usually realized through powerful teachers.

Chaki and Gurfinkel infer assumptions for ω-regular systems [33]. He et al. present a framework automated symbolic assume-guarantee reasoning that incorporates a MAT learning algorithm for BDDs [74]. He and some of the same and some other co-authors also present a compositional reasoning framework for concurrent probabilistic systems using an active learning algorithm for multi-terminal binary decision diagrams [73]. Feng et al. present an algorithm for inferring assumptions for probabilistic assume/guarantee reasoning [53,54]. Komuravelli et al. develop automata learning of non-deterministic probabilistic models that then serve as assumptions during automated assume/guarantee reasoning [99]. Meller et al. develop learning-based assume-guarantee reasoning for behavioral UML systems, using the L^* algorithm "off the shelf" [112].

Synthesis. The latest area of application of active automata learning that could be identified is synthesis. In synthesis, active learning is used for exploring and constructing formal models of safe (emerging) behavior that can be used as a basis for synthesizing safe mediators or controllers. Lin and Hsiung use learning-based assume-guarantee reasoning to build a compositional synthesis algorithm [104]. Cheng et al. synthesize safe and deadlock-free component-based systems using priorities and automated assumption learning [37]. Neider and Topcu use active automata learning to solve safety games [118,119].

4.2   Tools and Libraries

There are many tools presented in the work surveyed that integrate active learning algorithms. For this category we focus on tools and libraries that provide active automata learning algorithms to applications.

Since 2004, Bernhard Steffen's group develops LearnLib[3], a library for active automata learning that comprises infrastructure (e.g., filters and abstractions) for learning models of real-world systems [116,129]. Merten et al. present an extension of LearnLib for inferring data-aware models of Web-Services [115] fully automatically using only WSDL interface descriptions to bootstrap the learning process. The maturity of today's version of the LearnLib, which is now open source, is witnessed by the CAV 2015 artifact award [91].

There exist at least two other open-source automata learning libraries that provide implementations of textbook algorithms, complemented by own developments: libalf[4], the *Automata Learning Framework* [24], was developed primarily at the RWTH Aachen. Its active development seems to have ceased; the last version was released in April 2011. AIDE[5] [98], the *Automata-Identification Engine*, developed by a group at University of Genoa. It is not clear from the web-page if the library is still maintained.

Several tools and libraries for learning more expressive automata models have been developed over the past couple of years. The *Tomte*[6] [3] tool is developed at Radboud University. The tool fully automatically constructs abstractions (i.e., mappers) for automata learning and uses LearnLib for inferring models. Drews and D'Antoni develop a library for symbolic automata and symbolic visibly pushdown automata[7] [51]. The library provides learning algorithms for symbolic automata. Cassel et al. develop *RaLib*[8] [134], an extension to LearnLib for

---

[3] https://learnlib.de/.
[4] http://libalf.informatik.rwth-aachen.de/.
[5] http://aide.codeplex.com/.
[6] http://tomte.cs.ru.nl/.
[7] https://github.com/lorisdanto/symbolicautomata.
[8] https://bitbucket.org/learnlib/ralib/.

learning algorithms that infer extended finite state machine models. All three tools seem to be actively maintained.

4.3 Algorithmic Advances

While active automata learning has gained a lot of traction as a tool in software engineering applications, there is another group of work aiming at improving the foundations of active automata learning by extending it to semantically richer models, by developing more efficient learning algorithms, by exploring new learning models, and by working on techniques for approximating equivalence queries in black-box scenarios that yield quantifiable correctness guarantees for inferred models.

Expressivity. Meinke and Sindhu present IKL, a learning algorithm in the MAT model that infers Kripke structures [110]. Lin et al. develop a mixed active and passive learning algorithm that infers a subclass of timed automata, so-called event-recording automata [103].

Howar et al. extend active automata learning in the MAT model to register automata, which model control-flow as well as data-flow between data parameters of inputs, outputs, and a set of registers [82,114]. Registers and data parameters can be compared for equality. The authors demonstrate the effectiveness of their approach by inferring models of data structures [79] and extent the expressivity to allow for arbitrary data relations that meet certain learnability criteria [31,134]. A summary of this work can be found in this volume [30]. Aarts et al. develop a slightly different approach for inferring register automata models that can compare registers and data parameter for equality [2,3]. The two approaches are compared in [5].

Garg et al. develop an active learning algorithm for so-called quantified data automata over words that can model quantified invariants over linear data structures [59]. Volpato and Tretmans investigate the necessary assumptions under which models of nondeterministic systems can be inferred [141]. Kasprzik shows how residual finite-state tree automata can be inferred from membership queries and positive examples [95]. Isberner presents an active learning algorithm that infers visibly push-down automata [88].

Learning Models. Abel and Reinecke address the problem of inferring a model of a component that can only be addressed through a given and known intermediate component [9]. Decker et al. present active learning of networks of automata that consist of one base automaton and a number of identical components [47].

Groz et al. present a learning algorithm of scenarios in which the system cannot be reset into a well-defined initial state [66] (an extended version can be found in this volume [65]). Leucker and Neider present an active learning algorithm that learns models from an 'inexperienced' teacher, i.e., a teacher that fails to answer some membership queries [102].

A separate line of work focuses on learning regular languages from so-called automatic classes in different learning models [28,29,92,93].

Efficiency. For the case of finite regular languages, Ipate presents an active learning algorithm that infers deterministic finite cover automata and in some cases leads to substantial savings compared to more generic active learning algorithms [87]. Groz et al. develop optimizations of the L^* algorithm targeting large input sets, parameterized inputs, and processing counterexamples [64]. Björklund et al. develop a MAT-model learning algorithm that infers universal automata as a representation of regular languages [21]. Angluin et al. develop learning algorithms for universal automata, and alternating automata [14] and evaluate the performance trade offs for inferring these automata models—compared to deterministic finite state automata.

Means and Maler present a variant of L^* that learns concise models for systems with big sets of inputs by inferring symbolic characterizations of equivalent sets of inputs [113], an approach reminiscent of [89].

Finally, Isberner et al. develop the TTT algorithm [90], a space-optimal active learning algorithm that computes minimal distinguishing suffixes from counterexamples. The TTT algorithms is particularly well-suited when aiming at lifelong learning [20], where equivalence queries are essentially replaced by continuous monitoring of the running system.

Quality of Models. Van den Bos et al. develop a quality metric for inferred models and introduce a so-called 'Comparator' that can be used to enforce that the quality of intermediate models obtained during learning always increases (w.r.t. to the introduced metric) [25]. Chen et al. use the PAC result presented in Angluin's original paper on L^* for implementing a learning-based framework for program verification [35]. Using a PAC result allows them to quantify the confidence in the verification result in the absence of a perfect equivalence oracle.

4.4 Related Lines of Work

Learning in general is gaining traction in software engineering. This includes active learning of different concepts, as well learning from examples, which is the method of choice when inferring models from logs and traces.

Active Learning of Loop Invariants. One line of work aims at synthesizing invariants for loops in programs using combinations of active learning of logic formulas, predicate abstraction, and counterexample-guided abstraction refinement (e.g., [94]). Konev et al. present an algorithm for learning logic TBoxes from a teacher that answers entailment queries and equivalence queries [100]. Chen and Wang present an active learning algorithm for Boolean functions and use it for inferring loop invariants [36].

Garg et al. develop several learning algorithms for invariants in different learning models. In [60], they present algorithms for inferring Boolean combinations of numerical invariants for scalar variables and for quantified invariants of arrays and dynamic lists. In [61], they infer inductive invariants in a model where the teacher instructs a learner through positive, negative, and implication examples [61].

Learning from Examples. Passive automata learning infers automata models from positive or from positive and negative examples - the learning model is referred to as "in the limit" [63]. Learning from examples has an equally big recent impact in software engineering as active learning. The application scenarios and advances resemble closely the ones of active learning, as the following examples show.

Applications. Walkinshaw uses passively inferred models as a basis for deciding the adequacy of test suites for black-box systems [142]. Adamis et al. mine for sequential patterns (i.e., frequently observed transitions) in conformance test logs and use these to generate a finite state machine model. The finite state model is then used for performance testing [10].

Medhat et al. present an approach for mining hybrid automata specifications from input/output traces using several machine learning techniques [108]. Mao et al. extend the Alergia algorithm that learns probabilistic models from positive examples to more expressive reactive and timed models [106]. They then investigate how these models can be used for model checking and demonstrate the feasibility in a comparison to statistical model checking. Statistical model checking samples the system directly for a property, while in their approach first a model is inferred and then a property is checked on this model.

Another line of work focuses on designing domain-specific languages for Object processing and formatting, e.g., in Excel, and then learning models in the respective DSL from examples [68,85,144]. Barowy et al. learn formatting rules for spread sheet data from examples [18].

Algorithmic Advances. One recent theoretic results is shown by García et al.: the authors prove the existence of polynomial characteristic samples for every order in which states are merged during learning, i.e., sets of examples that allow correct identification of unknown regular languages [58].

Staworko and Wieczorek present learning algorithms that learn XML path queries from positive and negative examples [135]. Walkinshaw et al. develop a passive learning algorithm that infers extended finite state machines that model control-flow and data-flow from [143]. Högberg presents an algorithm for inferring regular tree languages from positive and negative examples [76].

5   Discussion and Open Challenges

The survey of the literature documents progress concerning all challenges that we identified in our earlier work. A careful analysis shows that progress in some directions has been stronger than in other directions. This yields some potential directions for further research.

Interacting with Real Systems. There is, by now, a considerable number of case studies that show how active learning can be beneficial in different scenarios: In our survey, the number of publications that present applications exceeds the number of publications that focus primarily on algorithmic or theoretic contributions. It can be observed that in black-box scenarios, membership queries are typically realized through tests, and equivalence queries are approximated by tests. In white-box scenarios, both types of queries are often implemented using model-checking or program analysis.

While interaction with real systems is reported in many publications their corresponding conceptual progress is typically small. Specifically, the proposed methods for establishing appropriate abstractions underlying the learning alphabet or for guaranteeing equivalent initial conditions for membership queries are still mostly a case-specific manual effort.

Efficiency and Tools. In the past ten years, many improved active automata learning algorithms have been developed. Some rely on the observation table, the basic data structure introduced by Angluin, and differ from the original L^* algorithm mostly in the way counterexamples are analyzed. Others use decision trees as data structures. Observations clearly indicate the superiority of tree-based algorithms, combined with efficient counter example analysis. It is striking that despite this algorithmic progress, many applications still use the original L^* algorithm or one of the optimized versions that have been developed in the early 1990s. Sometimes heuristics to overcome well-known weaknesses of L^* are even proposed as general achievements.

One future challenge is therefore the systematic transfer of the existing algorithmic improvements into tools. As of today, there seem to exist only very few tools and libraries that are actively maintained and publicly available (compared to, e.g., the tools in the areas of satisfiability modulo theories or automated theorem proving). In these other domains, competitions have been used to encourage development of new methods and implementation of tools. Maybe model learning needs a similar vehicle for driving the transfer of theoretic results into tools.

Expressivity. Over the years, active learning has been extended to produce more expressive models, like register automata, extended finite state machines, visibly push-down automata, event recording automata, or symbolic automata. It appears that most of the corresponding active learning approaches use the L^* algorithm (or one of its variants) as a reference and often adapt correctness proofs (e.g., [51,105]). This does not only result in inefficient solutions, but often also in quite indirect correctness arguments. The more efficient algorithms are typically technically more involved than the original L^* algorithm making their adaptation to new domains harder. On the other hand, e.g., the TTT algorithm reveals very much of the information-theoretic essence of active automata learning which promotes a better understanding and provides significant performance gains.

One direction for future work is therefore leveraging this potential and providing modular conceptual frameworks that support the adaptation of learning algorithms to new domains and classes of models. Conceptual frameworks have to be complemented by implementations enabling the systematic profiling of various learning algorithms in order to identify the best fitting algorithm for a given application domain. The LearnLib Studio [116] was a first step into this direction and the authors are currently working on transferring this idea to the open-sourced version of LearnLib.

Equivalence Queries. Equivalence queries are mostly addressed on a per-case-study basis. They are usually implemented as conformance tests or through random testing in black-box scenarios. The concrete strategy for generating test cases varies, but there has hardly been progress on efficient and effective methods for approximating equivalence queries. In order to further develop active automata learning to a point where it can be used by verification techniques or for documentation even in industrial (black-box) contexts, equivalence queries will have to provide a quantifiable measure for the likelihood or precision of inferred models.

One way of obtaining such results is the PAC (probably approximately correct) framework. Angluin obtained a PAC result for the original L^* algorithm by implementing equivalence queries using sequences of membership queries [13]. Recently, this result (which had been largely ignored for 20 years) was picked up and extended [55,105]. In some application scenarios "lifelong learning" seems to be an adequate answer, i.e., monitoring running systems relative the current hypothesis model, identifying behavioral discrepancies, and correcting either the model or, if required, the systems. One major obstacle to this approach are the resulting excessively long counterexamples. The TTT algorithm has been specifically designed to address this challenge [90].

6 Conclusions

In the last 15 years, active automata learning, an originally merely theoretical enterprise, has received attention as a method for dealing with black-box or third-party systems in software engineering. Especially, in the past six years (2011 to 2016) active automata learning has found many applications, ranging from security analysis, to testing, to verification, and even synthesis. At the same time, algorithmic and theoretic advances have led to more efficient learning algorithms that can infer more expressive models (e.g. [30], in this volume) Scalability of active automata learning is still a major challenge. Hybrid approaches that complement the power of black box analysis with white box analysis methods seem to emerge as one possible technique for addressing this challenge (cf. [70], in this volume). Summarizing, active automata learning has developed far beyond what could have been anticipated 15 years ago. However, with every solved problem, news questions arise - making active automata learning a very fruitful area of research with increasingly high practical impact.

References

1. Aadithya, K.V., Roychowdhury, J.: DAE2FSM: automatic generation of accurate discrete-time logical abstractions for continuous-time circuit dynamics. In: Proceedings of the 49th Annual Design Automation Conference, DAC 2012, pp. 311–316. ACM, New York (2012)
2. Aarts, F., Fiterau-Brostean, P., Kuppens, H., Vaandrager, F.: Learning register automata with fresh value generation. In: Leucker, M., Rueda, C., Valencia, F.D. (eds.) ICTAC 2015. LNCS, vol. 9399, pp. 165–183. Springer, Cham (2015). https://doi.org/10.1007/978-3-319-25150-9_11
3. Aarts, F., Heidarian, F., Kuppens, H., Olsen, P., Vaandrager, F.: Automata learning through counterexample guided abstraction refinement. In: Giannakopoulou, D., Méry, D. (eds.) FM 2012. LNCS, vol. 7436, pp. 10–27. Springer, Heidelberg (2012). https://doi.org/10.1007/978-3-642-32759-9_4
4. Aarts, F., Heidarian, F., Vaandrager, F.: A theory of history dependent abstractions for learning interface automata. In: Koutny, M., Ulidowski, I. (eds.) CONCUR 2012. LNCS, vol. 7454, pp. 240–255. Springer, Heidelberg (2012). https://doi.org/10.1007/978-3-642-32940-1_18
5. Aarts, F., Howar, F., Kuppens, H., Vaandrager, F.: Algorithms for inferring register automata. In: Margaria, T., Steffen, B. (eds.) ISoLA 2014. LNCS, vol. 8802, pp. 202–219. Springer, Heidelberg (2014). https://doi.org/10.1007/978-3-662-45234-9_15
6. Aarts, F., Jonsson, B., Uijen, J.: Generating models of infinite-state communication protocols using regular inference with abstraction. In: Petrenko, A., Simão, A., Maldonado, J.C. (eds.) ICTSS 2010. LNCS, vol. 6435, pp. 188–204. Springer, Heidelberg (2010). https://doi.org/10.1007/978-3-642-16573-3_14
7. Aarts, F., Jonsson, B., Uijen, J., Vaandrager, F.: Generating models of infinite-state communication protocols using regular inference with abstraction. Formal Methods Syst. Des. **46**(1), 1–41 (2015)
8. Aarts, F., Vaandrager, F.: Learning I/O automata. In: Gastin, P., Laroussinie, F. (eds.) CONCUR 2010. LNCS, vol. 6269, pp. 71–85. Springer, Heidelberg (2010). https://doi.org/10.1007/978-3-642-15375-4_6
9. Abel, A., Reineke, J.: Gray-box learning of serial compositions of mealy machines. In: Rayadurgam, S., Tkachuk, O. (eds.) NFM 2016. LNCS, vol. 9690, pp. 272–287. Springer, Cham (2016). https://doi.org/10.1007/978-3-319-40648-0_21
10. Adamis, G., Kovács, G., Réthy, G.: Generating performance test model from conformance test logs. In: Fischer, J., Scheidgen, M., Schieferdecker, I., Reed, R. (eds.) SDL 2015. LNCS, vol. 9369, pp. 268–284. Springer, Cham (2015). https://doi.org/10.1007/978-3-319-24912-4_19
11. Aichernig, B.K., Mostowski, W., Mousavi, M.R., Tappler, M., Taromirad, M.: Model learning and model-based testing. In: Bennaceur, A., Hähnle, R., Meinke, K. (eds.) ML for Dynamic Software Analysis. LNCS, vol. 11026, pp. 74–100. Springer, Cham (2018)
12. Hagerer, A., Hungar, H., Niese, O., Steffen, B.: Model generation by moderated regular extrapolation. In: Kutsche, R.-D., Weber, H. (eds.) FASE 2002. LNCS, vol. 2306, pp. 80–95. Springer, Heidelberg (2002). https://doi.org/10.1007/3-540-45923-5_6
13. Angluin, D.: Learning regular sets from queries and counterexamples. Inf. Comput. **75**(2), 87–106 (1987)

14. Angluin, D., Eisenstat, S., Fisman, D.: Learning regular languages via alternating automata. In: Proceedings of the 24th International Conference on Artificial Intelligence, IJCAI 2015, pp. 3308–3314. AAAI Press (2015)
15. Argyros, G., Stais, I., Jana, S., Keromytis, A.D., Kiayias, A.: SFADiff: automated evasion attacks and fingerprinting using black-box differential automata learning. In: Proceedings of the 2016 ACM SIGSAC Conference on Computer and Communications Security, CCS 2016, pp. 1690–1701. ACM, New York (2016)
16. Bainczyk, A., Schieweck, A., Isberner, M., Margaria, T., Neubauer, J., Steffen, B.: ALEX: mixed-mode learning of web applications at ease. In: Margaria, T., Steffen, B. (eds.) ISoLA 2016. LNCS, vol. 9953, pp. 655–671. Springer, Cham (2016). https://doi.org/10.1007/978-3-319-47169-3_51
17. Balcázar, J.L., Díaz, J., Gavaldà, R., Watanabe, O.: Algorithms for learning finite automata from queries: a unified view. In: Du, D.Z., Ko, K.I. (eds.) Advances in Algorithms, Languages, and Complexity, pp. 53–72. Springer, Boston (1997). https://doi.org/10.1007/978-1-4613-3394-4_2
18. Barowy, D.W., Gulwani, S., Hart, T., Zorn, B.: FlashRelate: extracting relational data from semi-structured spreadsheets using examples. SIGPLAN Not. **50**(6), 218–228 (2015)
19. Berg, T., Grinchtein, O., Jonsson, B., Leucker, M., Raffelt, H., Steffen, B.: On the correspondence between conformance testing and regular inference. In: Cerioli, M. (ed.) FASE 2005. LNCS, vol. 3442, pp. 175–189. Springer, Heidelberg (2005). https://doi.org/10.1007/978-3-540-31984-9_14
20. Bertolino, A., Calabrò, A., Merten, M., Steffen, B.: Never-stop learning: continuous validation of learned models for evolving systems through monitoring. ERCIM News **2012**(88), 28–29 (2012)
21. Björklund, J., Fernau, H., Kasprzik, A.: Polynomial inference of universal automata from membership and equivalence queries. Inf. Comput. **246**(C), 3–19 (2016)
22. Bollig, B., Katoen, J.-P., Kern, C., Leucker, M.: Replaying play in and play out: synthesis of design models from scenarios by learning. In: Grumberg, O., Huth, M. (eds.) TACAS 2007. LNCS, vol. 4424, pp. 435–450. Springer, Heidelberg (2007). https://doi.org/10.1007/978-3-540-71209-1_33
23. Bollig, B., Katoen, J.-P., Kern, C., Leucker, M.: *Smyle*: a tool for synthesizing distributed models from scenarios by learning. In: van Breugel, F., Chechik, M. (eds.) CONCUR 2008. LNCS, vol. 5201, pp. 162–166. Springer, Heidelberg (2008). https://doi.org/10.1007/978-3-540-85361-9_15
24. Bollig, B., Katoen, J.-P., Kern, C., Leucker, M., Neider, D., Piegdon, D.R.: Libalf: the automata learning framework. In: Touili, T., Cook, B., Jackson, P. (eds.) CAV 2010. LNCS, vol. 6174, pp. 360–364. Springer, Heidelberg (2010). https://doi.org/10.1007/978-3-642-14295-6_32
25. van den Bos, P., Smetsers, R., Vaandrager, F.: Enhancing automata learning by log-based metrics. In: Ábrahám, E., Huisman, M. (eds.) IFM 2016. LNCS, vol. 9681, pp. 295–310. Springer, Cham (2016). https://doi.org/10.1007/978-3-319-33693-0_19
26. Botinčan, M., Babić, D.: Sigma*: symbolic learning of input-output specifications. In: Proceedings of the 40th Annual ACM SIGPLAN-SIGACT Symposium on Principles of Programming Languages, POPL 2013, pp. 443–456. ACM, New York (2013)
27. Broy, M., Jonsson, B., Katoen, J.-P., Leucker, M., Pretschner, A. (eds.): Model-Based Testing of Reactive Systems. LNCS, vol. 3472. Springer, Heidelberg (2005). https://doi.org/10.1007/b137241

28. Case, J., Jain, S., Le, T.D., Ong, Y.S., Semukhin, P., Stephan, F.: Automatic learning of subclasses of pattern languages. In: Dediu, A.-H., Inenaga, S., Martín-Vide, C. (eds.) LATA 2011. LNCS, vol. 6638, pp. 192–203. Springer, Heidelberg (2011). https://doi.org/10.1007/978-3-642-21254-3_14

29. Case, J., Jain, S., Ong, Y.S., Semukhin, P., Stephan, F.: Automatic learners with feedback queries. In: Löwe, B., Normann, D., Soskov, I., Soskova, A. (eds.) CiE 2011. LNCS, vol. 6735, pp. 31–40. Springer, Heidelberg (2011). https://doi.org/10.1007/978-3-642-21875-0_4

30. Cassel, S., Howar, F., Jonsson, B., Steffen, B.: Extending automata learning to extended finite state machines. In: Bennaceur, A., Hahnle, R., Meinke, K. (eds.) ML for Dynamic Software Analysis. LNCS, vol. 11026, pp. 149–177. Springer, Cham (2018)

31. Cassel, S., Howar, F., Jonsson, B., Steffen, B.: Active learning for extended finite state machines. Formal Asp. Comput. **28**(2), 233–263 (2016)

32. Cassel, S., Jonsson, B., Howar, F., Steffen, B.: A succinct canonical register automaton model for data domains with binary relations. In: Chakraborty, S., Mukund, M. (eds.) ATVA 2012. LNCS, pp. 57–71. Springer, Heidelberg (2012). https://doi.org/10.1007/978-3-642-33386-6_6

33. Chaki, S., Gurfinkel, A.: Automated assume-guarantee reasoning for omega-regular systems and specifications. Innov. Syst. Softw. Eng. **7**(2), 131–139 (2011)

34. Chalupar, G., Peherstorfer, S., Poll, E., De Ruiter, J.: Automated reverse engineering using lego®. In: Proceedings of the 8th USENIX Conference on Offensive Technologies, WOOT 2014, p. 9. USENIX Association, Berkeley (2014)

35. Chen, Y.F., Hsieh, C., Lengál, O., Lii, T.J., Tsai, M.H., Wang, B.Y., Wang, F.: PAC learning-based verification and model synthesis. In: Proceedings of the 38th International Conference on Software Engineering, ICSE 2016, pp. 714–724. ACM, New York (2016)

36. Chen, Y.-F., Wang, B.-Y.: Learning Boolean functions incrementally. In: Madhusudan, P., Seshia, S.A. (eds.) CAV 2012. LNCS, vol. 7358, pp. 55–70. Springer, Heidelberg (2012). https://doi.org/10.1007/978-3-642-31424-7_10

37. Cheng, C.-H., et al.: Algorithms for synthesizing priorities in component-based systems. In: Bultan, T., Hsiung, P.-A. (eds.) ATVA 2011. LNCS, vol. 6996, pp. 150–167. Springer, Heidelberg (2011). https://doi.org/10.1007/978-3-642-24372-1_12

38. Cho, C.Y., Babić, D., Poosankam, P., Chen, K.Z., Wu, E.X., Song, D.: MACE: model-inference-assisted concolic exploration for protocol and vulnerability discovery. In: Proceedings of the 20th USENIX Conference on Security, SEC 2011, p. 10. USENIX Association, Berkeley (2011)

39. Choi, W.: Automated testing of graphical user interfaces: a new algorithm and challenges. In: Proceedings of the 2013 ACM Workshop on Mobile Development Lifecycle, MobileDeLi 2013, pp. 27–28. ACM, New York (2013)

40. Choi, W., Necula, G., Sen, K.: Guided GUI testing of android apps with minimal restart and approximate learning. SIGPLAN Not. **48**(10), 623–640 (2013)

41. Chow, T.S.: Testing software design modeled by finite-state machines. IEEE Trans. Softw. Eng. **4**(3), 178–187 (1978)

42. Clarke, E.M., Grumberg, O., Peled, D.A.: Model Checking. The MIT Press, Cambridge (1999)

43. Cobleigh, J.M., Giannakopoulou, D., PĂsĂreanu, C.S.: Learning assumptions for compositional verification. In: Garavel, H., Hatcliff, J. (eds.) TACAS 2003. LNCS, vol. 2619, pp. 331–346. Springer, Heidelberg (2003). https://doi.org/10.1007/3-540-36577-X_24

44. Combe, D., de la Higuera, C., Janodet, J.-C.: Zulu: an interactive learning competition. In: Yli-Jyrä, A., Kornai, A., Sakarovitch, J., Watson, B. (eds.) FSMNLP 2009. LNCS (LNAI), vol. 6062, pp. 139–146. Springer, Heidelberg (2010). https://doi.org/10.1007/978-3-642-14684-8_15

45. Combéfis, S., Giannakopoulou, D., Pecheur, C., Feary, M.: Learning system abstractions for human operators. In: Proceedings of the International Workshop on Machine Learning Technologies in Software Engineering, MALETS 2011, pp. 3–10. ACM, New York (2011)

46. De Ruiter, J., Poll, E.: Protocol state fuzzing of TLS implementations. In: Proceedings of the 24th USENIX Conference on Security Symposium, SEC 2015, pp. 193–206. USENIX Association, Berkeley (2015)

47. Decker, N., Habermehl, P., Leucker, M., Thoma, D.: Learning transparent data automata. In: Ciardo, G., Kindler, E. (eds.) PETRI NETS 2014. LNCS, vol. 8489, pp. 130–149. Springer, Cham (2014). https://doi.org/10.1007/978-3-319-07734-5_8

48. Denis, F., Lemay, A., Terlutte, A.: Residual finite state automata. Fundam. Informaticae **51**(4), 339–368 (2002)

49. Dinca, I., Ipate, F., Mierla, L., Stefanescu, A.: Learn and test for event-B – A rodin plugin. In: Derrick, J., et al. (eds.) ABZ 2012. LNCS, vol. 7316, pp. 361–364. Springer, Heidelberg (2012). https://doi.org/10.1007/978-3-642-30885-7_32

50. Dinca, I., Ipate, F., Stefanescu, A.: Model learning and test generation for event-B decomposition. In: Margaria, T., Steffen, B. (eds.) ISoLA 2012. LNCS, vol. 7609, pp. 539–553. Springer, Heidelberg (2012). https://doi.org/10.1007/978-3-642-34026-0_40

51. Drews, S., D'Antoni, L.: Learning symbolic automata. In: Legay, A., Margaria, T. (eds.) TACAS 2017. LNCS, vol. 10205, pp. 173–189. Springer, Heidelberg (2017). https://doi.org/10.1007/978-3-662-54577-5_10

52. Esparza, J., Leucker, M., Schlund, M.: Learning workflow petri nets. Fundam. Informaticae **113**(3-4), 205–228 (2011)

53. Feng, L., Han, T., Kwiatkowska, M., Parker, D.: Learning-based compositional verification for synchronous probabilistic systems. In: Bultan, T., Hsiung, P.-A. (eds.) ATVA 2011. LNCS, vol. 6996, pp. 511–521. Springer, Heidelberg (2011). https://doi.org/10.1007/978-3-642-24372-1_40

54. Feng, L., Kwiatkowska, M., Parker, D.: Automated learning of probabilistic assumptions for compositional reasoning. In: Giannakopoulou, D., Orejas, F. (eds.) FASE 2011. LNCS, vol. 6603, pp. 2–17. Springer, Heidelberg (2011). https://doi.org/10.1007/978-3-642-19811-3_2

55. Fiterău-Broştean, P., Howar, F.: Learning-based testing the sliding window behavior of TCP implementations. In: Petrucci, L., Seceleanu, C., Cavalcanti, A. (eds.) FMICS/AVoCS -2017. LNCS, vol. 10471, pp. 185–200. Springer, Cham (2017). https://doi.org/10.1007/978-3-319-67113-0_12

56. Fiterău-Broştean, P., Janssen, R., Vaandrager, F.: Combining model learning and model checking to analyze TCP implementations. In: Chaudhuri, S., Farzan, A. (eds.) CAV 2016. LNCS, vol. 9780, pp. 454–471. Springer, Cham (2016). https://doi.org/10.1007/978-3-319-41540-6_25

57. Fujiwara, S., von Bochmann, G., Khendek, F., Amalou, M., Ghedamsi, A.: Test selection based on finite state models. IEEE Trans. Softw. Eng. **17**(6), 591–603 (1991)

58. García, P., López, D., De Parga, M.V.: Polynomial characteristic sets for DFA identification. Theor. Comput. Sci. **448**, 41–46 (2012)

59. Garg, P., Löding, C., Madhusudan, P., Neider, D.: Learning universally quantified invariants of linear data structures. In: Sharygina, N., Veith, H. (eds.) CAV
2013. LNCS, vol. 8044, pp. 813–829. Springer, Heidelberg (2013). https://doi.org/
10.1007/978-3-642-39799-8_57
60. Garg, P., Löding, C., Madhusudan, P., Neider, D.: ICE: a robust framework for learning invariants. In: Biere, A., Bloem, R. (eds.) CAV 2014. LNCS,
vol. 8559, pp. 69–87. Springer, Cham (2014). https://doi.org/10.1007/978-3-319-
08867-9_5
61. Garg, P., Neider, D., Madhusudan, P., Roth, D.: Learning invariants using decision
trees and implication counterexamples. In: Proceedings of the 43rd Annual ACM
SIGPLAN-SIGACT Symposium on Principles of Programming Languages, POPL
2016, pp. 499–512. ACM, New York (2016)
62. Giannakopoulou, D., Rakamarić, Z., Raman, V.: Symbolic learning of component
interfaces. In: Miné, A., Schmidt, D. (eds.) SAS 2012. LNCS, vol. 7460, pp. 248–
264. Springer, Heidelberg (2012). https://doi.org/10.1007/978-3-642-33125-1_18
63. Gold, E.M.: Language identification in the limit. Inf. Control 10(5), 447–474
(1967)
64. Groz, R., Irfan, M.-N., Oriat, C.: Algorithmic improvements on regular inference
of software models and perspectives for security testing. In: Margaria, T., Steffen,
B. (eds.) ISoLA 2012. LNCS, vol. 7609, pp. 444–457. Springer, Heidelberg (2012).
https://doi.org/10.1007/978-3-642-34026-0_33
65. Groz, R., Simao, A., Petrenko, A., Oriat, C.: Inferring FSM models of systems
without reset. In: Bennaceur, A., Hahnle, R., Meinke, K. (eds.) ML for Dynamic
Software Analysis. LNCS, vol. 11026, pp. 178–201. Springer, Cham (2018)
66. Groz, R., Simao, A., Petrenko, A., Oriat, C.: Inferring finite state machines without reset using state identification sequences. In: El-Fakih, K., Barlas, G., Yevtushenko, N. (eds.) ICTSS 2015. LNCS, vol. 9447, pp. 161–177. Springer, Cham
(2015). https://doi.org/10.1007/978-3-319-25945-1_10
67. Gu, C., Roychowdhury, J.: FSM model abstraction for analog/mixed-signal circuits by learning from I/O trajectories. In: Proceedings of the 16th Asia and
South Pacific Design Automation Conference, ASPDAC 2011, pp. 7–12. IEEE
Press, Piscataway (2011)
68. Gulwani, S.: Automating string processing in spreadsheets using input-output
examples. In: Proceedings of the 38th Annual ACM SIGPLAN-SIGACT Symposium on Principles of Programming Languages, POPL 2011, pp. 317–330. ACM,
New York (2011)
69. Hagerer, A., Margaria, T., Niese, O., Steffen, B., Brune, G., Ide, H.D.: Efficient
regression testing of CTI-systems: testing a complex call-center solution. Ann.
Rev. Commun. 55, 1033–1040 (2001)
70. Hähnle, R., Steffen, B.: Constraint-based behavioral consistency of evolving software systems. In: Bennaceur, A., Hahnle, R., Meinke, K. (eds.) ML for Dynamic
Software Analysis. LNCS, vol. 11026, pp. 205–218. Springer, Cham (2018)
71. Hungar, H., Steffen, B.: Behavior-based model construction. Int. J. Softw. Tools
Technol. Transf. 6(1), 4–14 (2004)
72. Hungar, H., Niese, O., Steffen, B.: Domain-specific optimization in automata
learning. In: Hunt, W.A., Somenzi, F. (eds.) CAV 2003. LNCS, vol. 2725, pp.
315–327. Springer, Heidelberg (2003). https://doi.org/10.1007/978-3-540-45069-
6_31
73. He, F., Gao, X., Wang, M., Wang, B.Y., Zhang, L.: Learning weighted assumptions for compositional verification of Markov decision processes. ACM Trans.
Softw. Eng. Methodol. 25(3), 21:1–21:39 (2016)

74. He, F., Wang, B.Y., Yin, L., Zhu, L.: Symbolic assume-guarantee reasoning through BDD learning. In: Proceedings of the 36th International Conference on Software Engineering, ICSE 2014, pp. 1071–1082. ACM, New York (2014)

75. Hoare, C.A.R.: An axiomatic basis for computer programming. Commun. ACM **12**(10), 576–580 (1969)

76. Högberg, J.: A randomised inference algorithm for regular tree languages. Nat. Lang. Eng. **17**(2), 203–219 (2011)

77. Howar, F., Bauer, O., Merten, M., Steffen, B., Margaria, T.: The teachers' crowd: the impact of distributed oracles on active automata learning. In: Hähnle, R., Knoop, J., Margaria, T., Schreiner, D., Steffen, B. (eds.) ISoLA 2011. CCIS, pp. 232–247. Springer, Heidelberg (2012). https://doi.org/10.1007/978-3-642-34781-8_18

78. Howar, F., Giannakopoulou, D., Rakamarić, Z.: Hybrid learning: interface generation through static, dynamic, and symbolic analysis. In: Proceedings of the 2013 International Symposium on Software Testing and Analysis, ISSTA 2013, pp. 268–279. ACM, New York (2013)

79. Howar, F., Isberner, M., Steffen, B., Bauer, O., Jonsson, B.: Inferring semantic interfaces of data structures. In: Margaria, T., Steffen, B. (eds.) ISoLA 2012. LNCS, vol. 7609, pp. 554–571. Springer, Heidelberg (2012). https://doi.org/10.1007/978-3-642-34026-0_41

80. Howar, F., Margaria, T., Wagner, C.: Simplifying translation validation via model extrapolation. J. Integr. Des. Process Sci. **17**(3), 71–91 (2013)

81. Howar, F., Merten, M., Steffen, B., Margaria, T.: Practical aspects of active automata learning, pp. 235–267. John Wiley and Sons, Inc. (2012)

82. Howar, F., Steffen, B., Jonsson, B., Cassel, S.: Inferring canonical register automata. In: Kuncak, V., Rybalchenko, A. (eds.) VMCAI 2012. LNCS, vol. 7148, pp. 251–266. Springer, Heidelberg (2012). https://doi.org/10.1007/978-3-642-27940-9_17

83. Howar, F., Steffen, B., Merten, M.: From ZULU to RERS. In: Margaria, T., Steffen, B. (eds.) ISoLA 2010. LNCS, vol. 6415, pp. 687–704. Springer, Heidelberg (2010). https://doi.org/10.1007/978-3-642-16558-0_55

84. Howar, F., Steffen, B., Merten, M.: Automata learning with automated alphabet abstraction refinement. In: Jhala, R., Schmidt, D. (eds.) VMCAI 2011. LNCS, vol. 6538, pp. 263–277. Springer, Heidelberg (2011). https://doi.org/10.1007/978-3-642-18275-4_19

85. Hrnčič, D., Mernik, M., Bryant, B.R., Javed, F.: A memetic grammar inference algorithm for language learning. Appl. Soft Comput. **12**(3), 1006–1020 (2012)

86. Hungar, H., Margaria, T., Steffen, B.: Test-based model generation for legacy systems. In: 2003 Proceedings of the International Test Conference, ITC 2003, vol. 1, pp. 971–980, 30 September–2 October 2003

87. Ipate, F.: Learning finite cover automata from queries. J. Comput. Syst. Sci. **78**(1), 221–244 (2012)

88. Isberner, M.: Foundations of active automata learning: an algorithmic perspective. Ph.D. thesis (2015)

89. Isberner, M., Howar, F., Steffen, B.: Inferring automata with state-local alphabet abstractions. In: Brat, G., Rungta, N., Venet, A. (eds.) NFM 2013. LNCS, vol. 7871, pp. 124–138. Springer, Heidelberg (2013). https://doi.org/10.1007/978-3-642-38088-4_9

90. Isberner, M., Howar, F., Steffen, B.: The TTT algorithm: a redundancy-free approach to active automata learning. In: Bonakdarpour, B., Smolka, S.A. (eds.) RV

2014. LNCS, vol. 8734, pp. 307–322. Springer, Cham (2014). https://doi.org/10.1007/978-3-319-11164-3_26

91. Isberner, M., Howar, F., Steffen, B.: The open-source LearnLib. In: Kroening, D., Păsăreanu, C.S. (eds.) CAV 2015. LNCS, vol. 9206, pp. 487–495. Springer, Cham (2015). https://doi.org/10.1007/978-3-319-21690-4_32

92. Jain, S., Luo, Q., Stephan, F.: Learnability of automatic classes. J. Comput. Syst. Sci. **78**(6), 1910–1927 (2012)

93. Jain, S., Martin, E., Stephan, F.: Robust learning of automatic classes of languages. In: Kivinen, J., Szepesvári, C., Ukkonen, E., Zeugmann, T. (eds.) ALT 2011. LNCS (LNAI), vol. 6925, pp. 55–69. Springer, Heidelberg (2011). https://doi.org/10.1007/978-3-642-24412-4_8

94. Jung, Y., Lee, W., Wang, B.-Y., Yi, K.: Predicate generation for learning-based quantifier-free loop invariant inference. In: Abdulla, P.A., Leino, K.R.M. (eds.) TACAS 2011. LNCS, vol. 6605, pp. 205–219. Springer, Heidelberg (2011). https://doi.org/10.1007/978-3-642-19835-9_17

95. Kasprzik, A.: Inference of residual finite-state tree automata from membership queries and finite positive data. In: Mauri, G., Leporati, A. (eds.) DLT 2011. LNCS, vol. 6795, pp. 476–477. Springer, Heidelberg (2011). https://doi.org/10.1007/978-3-642-22321-1_45

96. Kearns, M.J., Vazirani, U.V.: An Introduction to Computational Learning Theory. MIT Press, Cambridge (1994)

97. Khalili, A., Natale, L., Tacchella, A.: Reverse engineering of middleware for verification of robot control architectures. In: Brugali, D., Broenink, J.F., Kroeger, T., MacDonald, B.A. (eds.) SIMPAR 2014. LNCS (LNAI), vol. 8810, pp. 315–326. Springer, Cham (2014). https://doi.org/10.1007/978-3-319-11900-7_27

98. Khalili, A., Tacchella, A.: Learning nondeterministic mealy machines. In: Proceedings of the 12th International Conference on Grammatical Inference, ICGI 2014, Kyoto, Japan, 17–19 September 2014, pp. 109–123 (2014)

99. Komuravelli, A., Pasareanu, C.S., Clarke, E.M.: Learning probabilistic systems from tree samples. In: Proceedings of the 2012 27th Annual IEEE/ACM Symposium on Logic in Computer Science, LICS 2012, pp. 441–450. IEEE Computer Society, Washington, DC (2012)

100. Konev, B., Lutz, C., Ozaki, A., Wolter, F.: Exact learning of lightweight description logic ontologies. In: Proceedings of the Fourteenth International Conference on Principles of Knowledge Representation and Reasoning, KR 2014, pp. 298–307. AAAI Press (2014)

101. Kwiatkowska, M., Norman, G., Parker, D., Qu, H.: Assume-guarantee verification for probabilistic systems. In: Esparza, J., Majumdar, R. (eds.) TACAS 2010. LNCS, vol. 6015, pp. 23–37. Springer, Heidelberg (2010). https://doi.org/10.1007/978-3-642-12002-2_3

102. Leucker, M., Neider, D.: Learning minimal deterministic automata from inexperienced teachers. In: Margaria, T., Steffen, B. (eds.) ISoLA 2012. LNCS, vol. 7609, pp. 524–538. Springer, Heidelberg (2012). https://doi.org/10.1007/978-3-642-34026-0_39

103. Lin, S.-W., André, É., Dong, J.S., Sun, J., Liu, Y.: An efficient algorithm for learning event-recording automata. In: Bultan, T., Hsiung, P.-A. (eds.) ATVA 2011. LNCS, vol. 6996, pp. 463–472. Springer, Heidelberg (2011). https://doi.org/10.1007/978-3-642-24372-1_35

104. Lin, S.-W., Hsiung, P.-A.: Compositional synthesis of concurrent systems through causal model checking and learning. In: Jones, C., Pihlajasaari, P., Sun, J. (eds.)

FM 2014. LNCS, vol. 8442, pp. 416–431. Springer, Cham (2014). https://doi.org/10.1007/978-3-319-06410-9_29

105. Maler, O., Mens, I.-E.: A generic algorithm for learning symbolic automata from membership queries. In: Aceto, L., Bacci, G., Bacci, G., Ingólfsdóttir, A., Legay, A., Mardare, R. (eds.) Models, Algorithms, Logics and Tools. LNCS, vol. 10460, pp. 146–169. Springer, Cham (2017). https://doi.org/10.1007/978-3-319-63121-9_8

106. Mao, H., Chen, Y., Jaeger, M., Nielsen, T.D., Larsen, K.G., Nielsen, B.: Learning deterministic probabilistic automata from a model checking perspective. Mach. Learn. **105**(2), 255–299 (2016)

107. Margaria, T., Niese, O., Raffelt, H., Steffen, B.: Efficient test-based model generation for legacy reactive systems. In: 2004 Ninth IEEE International Proceedings of the High-Level Design Validation and Test Workshop, HLDVT 2004, pp. 95–100. IEEE Computer Society, Washington, DC (2004)

108. Medhat, R., Ramesh, S., Bonakdarpour, B., Fischmeister, S.: A framework for mining hybrid automata from input/output traces. In: Proceedings of the 12th International Conference on Embedded Software, EMSOFT 2015, pp. 177–186. IEEE Press, Piscataway (2015)

109. Meinke, K.: Learning-based testing: recent progress and future prospects. In: Bennaceur, A., Hahnle, R., Meinke, K. (eds.) ML for Dynamic Software Analysis. LNCS, vol. 11026, pp. 53–73. Springer, Cham (2018)

110. Meinke, K., Sindhu, M.A.: Incremental learning-based testing for reactive systems. In: Gogolla, M., Wolff, B. (eds.) TAP 2011. LNCS, vol. 6706, pp. 134–151. Springer, Heidelberg (2011). https://doi.org/10.1007/978-3-642-21768-5_11

111. Meinke, K., Sindhu, M.A.: LBTest: a learning-based testing tool for reactive systems. In: Sixth IEEE International Conference on Software Testing, Verification and Validation, ICST 2013, Luxembourg, 18–22 March 2013, pp. 447–454 (2013)

112. Meller, Y., Grumberg, O., Yorav, K.: Learning-based compositional model checking of behavioral UML systems. In: Braga, C., Ölveczky, P.C. (eds.) FACS 2015. LNCS, vol. 9539, pp. 275–293. Springer, Cham (2016). https://doi.org/10.1007/978-3-319-28934-2_15

113. Mens, I., Maler, O.: Learning regular languages over large ordered alphabets. Log. Methods Comput. Sci. **11**(3), 1–22 (2015)

114. Merten, M., Howar, F., Steffen, B., Cassel, S., Jonsson, B.: Demonstrating learning of register automata. In: Flanagan, C., König, B. (eds.) TACAS 2012. LNCS, vol. 7214, pp. 466–471. Springer, Heidelberg (2012). https://doi.org/10.1007/978-3-642-28756-5_32

115. Merten, M., Howar, F., Steffen, B., Pellicione, P., Tivoli, M.: Automated inference of models for black box systems based on interface descriptions. In: Margaria, T., Steffen, B. (eds.) ISoLA 2012. LNCS, vol. 7609, pp. 79–96. Springer, Heidelberg (2012). https://doi.org/10.1007/978-3-642-34026-0_7

116. Merten, M., Steffen, B., Howar, F., Margaria, T.: Next generation LearnLib. In: Abdulla, P.A., Leino, K.R.M. (eds.) TACAS 2011. LNCS, vol. 6605, pp. 220–223. Springer, Heidelberg (2011). https://doi.org/10.1007/978-3-642-19835-9_18

117. Shahbaz, M., Li, K., Groz, R.: Learning and integration of parameterized components through testing. In: Petrenko, A., Veanes, M., Tretmans, J., Grieskamp, W. (eds.) FATES/TestCom -2007. LNCS, vol. 4581, pp. 319–334. Springer, Heidelberg (2007). https://doi.org/10.1007/978-3-540-73066-8_22

118. Neider, D.: Small strategies for safety games. In: Bultan, T., Hsiung, P.-A. (eds.) ATVA 2011. LNCS, vol. 6996, pp. 306–320. Springer, Heidelberg (2011). https://doi.org/10.1007/978-3-642-24372-1_22

119. Neider, D., Topcu, U.: An automaton learning approach to solving safety games over infinite graphs. In: Chechik, M., Raskin, J.-F. (eds.) TACAS 2016. LNCS, vol. 9636, pp. 204–221. Springer, Heidelberg (2016). https://doi.org/10.1007/978-3-662-49674-9_12

120. Nerode, A.: Linear automaton transformations. Proc. Am. Math. Soc. 9(4), 541–544 (1958)

121. Neubauer, J., Steffen, B., Bauer, O., Windmüller, S., Merten, M., Margaria, T., Howar, F.: Automated continuous quality assurance. In: Proceedings of the First International Workshop on Formal Methods in Software Engineering: Rigorous and Agile Approaches, FormSERA 2012, pp. 37–43. IEEE Press, Piscataway (2012)

122. Neubauer, J., Windmüller, S., Steffen, B.: Risk-based testing via active continuous quality control. Int. J. Softw. Tools Technol. Transf. 16(5), 569–591 (2014)

123. Maler, O., Pnueli, A.: On the learnability of infinitary regular sets. Inf. Comput. 118(2), 316–326 (1995)

124. Grinchtein, O., Jonsson, B., Pettersson, P.: Inference of event-recording automata using timed decision trees. In: Baier, C., Hermanns, H. (eds.) CONCUR 2006. LNCS, vol. 4137, pp. 435–449. Springer, Heidelberg (2006). https://doi.org/10.1007/11817949_29

125. Pasareanu, C.S., Giannakopoulou, D., Bobaru, M.G., Cobleigh, J.M., Barringer, H.: Learning to divide and conquer: applying the L* algorithm to automate assume-guarantee reasoning. Formal Methods Syst. Des. 32(3), 175–205 (2008)

126. Popper, K.: The Logic of Scientific Discovery. Classics Series. Routledge, Abingdon (2002)

127. Raffelt, H., Margaria, T., Steffen, B., Merten, M.: Hybrid test of web applications with webtest. In: Proceedings of the 2008 Workshop on Testing, Analysis, and Verification of Web Services and Applications, TAV-WEB 2008, pp. 1–7. ACM, New York (2008)

128. Raffelt, H., Merten, M., Steffen, B., Margaria, T.: Dynamic testing via automata learning. Int. J. Softw. Tools Technol. Transf. 11(4), 307–324 (2009)

129. Raffelt, H., Steffen, B., Berg, T., Margaria, T.: LearnLib: a framework for extrapolating behavioral models. Int. J. Softw. Tools Technol. Transf. 11(5), 393–407 (2009)

130. Rivest, R.L., Schapire, R.E.: Inference of finite automata using homing sequences. Inf. Comput. 103(2), 299–347 (1993)

131. Schuts, M., Hooman, J., Vaandrager, F.: Refactoring of legacy software using model learning and equivalence checking: an industrial experience report. In: Ábrahám, E., Huisman, M. (eds.) IFM 2016. LNCS, vol. 9681, pp. 311–325. Springer, Cham (2016). https://doi.org/10.1007/978-3-319-33693-0_20

132. Shahbaz, M., Groz, R.: Inferring mealy machines. In: Cavalcanti, A., Dams, D.R. (eds.) FM 2009. LNCS, vol. 5850, pp. 207–222. Springer, Heidelberg (2009). https://doi.org/10.1007/978-3-642-05089-3_14

133. Shahbaz, M., Groz, R.: Analysis and testing of black-box component-based systems by inferring partial models. Softw. Test. Verif. Reliab. 24(4), 253–288 (2014)

134. Cassel, S., Howar, F., Jonsson, B.: RALib: a LearnLib extension for inferring EFSMs. In: DIFTS 2015 at FMCAD 2015 (2015)

135. Staworko, S., Wieczorek, P.: Learning twig and path queries. In: Proceedings of the 15th International Conference on Database Theory, ICDT 2012, pp. 140–154. ACM, New York (2012)

136. Sun, J., Xiao, H., Liu, Y., Lin, S.W., Qin, S.: TLV: abstraction through testing, learning, and validation. In: Proceedings of the 2015 10th Joint Meeting on Foundations of Software Engineering, ESEC/FSE 2015, pp. 698–709. ACM, New York (2015)

137. Berg, T., Jonsson, B., Raffelt, H.: Regular inference for state machines with parameters. In: Baresi, L., Heckel, R. (eds.) FASE 2006. LNCS, vol. 3922, pp. 107–121. Springer, Heidelberg (2006). https://doi.org/10.1007/11693017_10

138. Berg, T., Jonsson, B., Raffelt, H.: Regular inference for state machines using domains with equality tests. In: Fiadeiro, J.L., Inverardi, P. (eds.) FASE 2008. LNCS, vol. 4961, pp. 317–331. Springer, Heidelberg (2008). https://doi.org/10.1007/978-3-540-78743-3_24

139. Bohlin, T., Jonsson, B.: Regular inference for communication protocol entities. Technical report. Department of Information Technology, Uppsala University, Schweden (2009)

140. Margaria, T., Raffelt, H., Steffen, B.: Knowledge-based relevance filtering for efficient system-level test-based model generation. Innov. Syst. Softw. Eng. 1(2), 147–156 (2005)

141. Volpato, M., Tretmans, J.: Active learning of nondeterministic systems from an ioco perspective. In: Margaria, T., Steffen, B. (eds.) ISoLA 2014. LNCS, vol. 8802, pp. 220–235. Springer, Heidelberg (2014). https://doi.org/10.1007/978-3-662-45234-9_16

142. Walkinshaw, N.: Assessing test adequacy for black-box systems without specifications. In: Wolff, B., Zaïdi, F. (eds.) ICTSS 2011. LNCS, vol. 7019, pp. 209–224. Springer, Heidelberg (2011). https://doi.org/10.1007/978-3-642-24580-0_15

143. Walkinshaw, N., Taylor, R., Derrick, J.: Inferring extended finite state machine models from software executions. Empirical Softw. Engg. 21(3), 811–853 (2016)

144. Wang, X., Gulwani, S., Singh, R.: FIDEX: filtering spreadsheet data using examples. In: Proceedings of the 2016 ACM SIGPLAN International Conference on Object-Oriented Programming, Systems, Languages, and Applications, OOPSLA 2016, pp. 195–213. ACM, New York (2016)

145. Windmüller, S., Neubauer, J., Steffen, B., Howar, F., Bauer, O.: Active continuous quality control. In: Proceedings of the 16th International ACM Sigsoft Symposium on Component-Based Software Engineering, CBSE 2013, pp. 111–120. ACM, New York (2013)

146. Xue, Y., Wang, J., Liu, Y., Xiao, H., Sun, J., Chandramohan, M.: Detection and classification of malicious JavaScript via attack behavior modelling. In: Proceedings of the 2015 International Symposium on Software Testing and Analysis, ISSTA 2015, pp. 48–59. ACM, New York (2015)

Extending Automata Learning
to Extended Finite State Machines

Sofia Cassel[1], Falk Howar[2], Bengt Jonsson[3(✉)], and Bernhard Steffen[4]

[1] Scania CV AB, Södertälje, Sweden
sofia.cassel@scania.com
[2] Dortmund University of Technology and Fraunhofer ISST, Dortmund, Germany
falk.howar@tu-dortmund.de
[3] Department of Information Technology, Uppsala University, Uppsala, Sweden
bengt@it.uu.se
[4] Chair for Programming Systems, TU Dortmund, Dortmund, Germany
steffen@cs.tu-dortmund.de

Abstract. Automata learning is an established class of techniques for inferring automata models by observing how they respond to a sample of input words. Recently, approaches have been presented that extend these techniques to infer extended finite state machines (EFSMs) by dynamic black-box analysis. EFSMs model both data flow and control behavior, and their mutual interaction. Different dialects of EFSMs are widely used in tools for model-based software development, verification, and testing.

This survey paper presents general principles behind some of these recent extensions. The goal is to elucidate how the principles behind classic automata learning can be maintained and guide extensions to more general automata models, and to situate some extensions with respect to these principles.

1 Introduction

Behavioral models of components and interfaces are the basis for many powerful software development and verification techniques, such as model checking, model based test generation, controller synthesis, and service composition. Ideally, such models should be part of documentation (e.g., of a component library), but in practice they rarely exist, or become outdated as the implementations evolve.

One approach to overcome the problem of nonexisting or outdated models is to develop techniques for automatically generating models of component behavior are being developed. In this paper, we are interested in a particular such technique, *active automata learning* [Ang87,RS93], using which we can infer automata models that represent the dynamic behavior of a software or hardware component. Mature techniques, based on active automata learning, are available for generating finite-state models that describe *control flow*, i.e., possible orderings of interactions between a component and its environment [HHNS02, HNS93, ABL02, SL07]. These techniques suppress data values, but have nevertheless been demonstrated to be useful for, e.g., mining APIs [ABL02], supporting

© Springer International Publishing AG, part of Springer Nature 2018
A. Bennaceur et al. (Eds.): ML for Dynamic Software Analysis, LNCS 11026, pp. 149–177, 2018.
https://doi.org/10.1007/978-3-319-96562-8_6

model-based testing [HHNS02,WBDP10] and conformance testing [AKT+12], and for analyzing security protocols [SL07,GIO12]. Perhaps the most well-known algorithm for inferring finite automata is L^* [Ang87], which has been implemented in the LearnLib framework [IHS15]. However, in many situations it is crucial for models to also be able to describe *data flow*, i.e., constraints on data parameters that are passed when the component interacts with its environment, as well as the mutual influence between control flow and data flow. For instance, models of protocol components must describe how different parameter values in sequence numbers, identifiers, etc. influence the control flow, and vice versa.

In order to capture both control flow and data flow aspects of component behavior (as well as their mutual influence), finite state machines can be, and commonly are, equipped with variables. Variables can store the values of data parameters; they can influence control flow by means of guards, and the control flow can cause variable updates. Finite state machines with variables are often called *extended finite state machines* (EFSMs). Different dialects of EFSMs are successfully used in tools for model-based testing (such as ConformiQ Qtronic [Hui07], which produces high-quality test suites), web service composition [BPT10], model-based development [GHP02], and by software model checkers to formally verify properties of all program behaviors [JM09].

Recently, various techniques have been employed to extend automata learning to EFSM models, which combine control flow with guards and assignments to data variables [CHJS16,AJUV15,BHLM13].

In this paper, we provide a condensed account of one way in which AAL can be generalized from the learning of DFAs to the learning of EFSM-like models. Our aim is to show how such a generalization can be obtained while keeping as much as possible of the structure that underpins mainstream AAL algorithms for DFAs. In particular, we will emphasize how such a generalization can preserve AAL as a gradual refinement process, which exploits central concepts from automata theory to converge monotonically to a correct target automaton. This view allows AAL to be seen as a partition refinement process, which generates successively more refined approximations to the Nerode congruence, and allows to give rather strong convergence guarantees.

The described generalization is very close to that presented in [CHJS16]. However, whereas [CHJS16] aims to describe a complete implementation of an AAL algorithm for EFSM-like models, here the aim is to focus on how central principles of AAL are generalized to the EFSM case. We have therefore tried to simplify the notation and concept machinery to a bare minimum; we describe only the main mechanisms of the AAL algorithm. In order to try to make the paper accessible, we have structured it into four parts:

- The next section summarizes main concepts underlying AAL for DFAs.
- Section 3 introduces register automata, a simple formalism for expresing EFSMs.

- Section 4 introduces the main concepts in the AAL generalization by means of an example.
- Section 5 formally defines the generalized concepts, and establishes key theorems of correctness and convergence.

Related Work. The problem of inferring behavioral models from implementations has been addressed in a number of different ways. Dynamic analysis approaches that combine automata learning techniques with methods for inferring constraints on data are the most closely related to our work. The pattern they follow is typically similar to CEGAR (counterexample-guided abstraction refinement): a sequence of models is refined in a process that is usually monotonic and converges to a fixpoint. All the approaches, however, suffer from limitations with respect to capturing the mutual influence of data flow and control flow on each other, and/or in what relations can be expressed between data parameters.

In white-box scenarios, access to the source code is presumed, so domain knowledge, manual abstractions, and/or symbolic execution can be used. White-box inference based on active automata learning (AAL) has been explored in several works. AAL has been combined with predicate abstraction [ACMN05] to infer interface specifications of Java classes, and with CEGAR [HJM05] to infer interface specifications as finite-state automata without data parameters. In [XSL+13], AAL is combined with support vector machines to infer constraints on data parameters; in [GRR12], AAL is combined with symbolic execution to recover guards from the analyzed system, producing DFA models where labels are guards over parameters of alphabet symbols.

In black-box scenarios, an early method for inferring EFSM-like models is [LMP08], where models are generated from execution traces by combining passive automata learning with the Daikon tool [EPG+07]. Since constraints on data parameters are only created for individual traces, there is no way to model the influence of data values on subsequent control flow. A more recent approach is that of [WTD16] which uses a different EFSM model than in this paper, and provides no statements about correctness or convergence.

Other approaches use AAL to infer data constraints from tests: In [AJUV15], a manually supplied abstraction on the data domain makes it possible to apply finite-state active automata learning techniques to the test cases. The approach has been successfully used in practical applications [ASV10, AdRP13], but a drawback is that a priori insight into the target component's behavior is required, making it not quite black-box. In [HSM11], automated (alphabet) refinement is used. Since the presented approach works at the level of concrete representative inputs, the resulting models have no symbolic interpretation but are rather minimal concrete representative systems. In [MM14, DD17], AAL is used to learn symbolic automata, and counterexamples used to refine transitions (representing equivalence classes in the language of the symbolic automata). The goal is to handle very large alphabets without having to store values in registers. The authors of [BHLM13] infer EFSMs that they claim to be incomparable with register automata, and that can represent components where data parameters are 'globally fresh', i.e., never before seen or stored since the last reset of the component.

The approach of this paper can be specialized to learning register automata where the only operation on data is comparison for equality. Descriptions of such approaches have appeared in [HSJC12], and we have successfully applied it to generate models of container-like interfaces (such as sets, stacks, queues, etc.) [HIS+12]. [IHS14] provides a then up-to-date overview of the extension of active automata, including [AHK+12,BHLM13,HSJC12]. This model was also considered in our earlier work [BJR08], which however is less suitable for implementation.

2   Background: Active Learning of DFAs

In this section, we review the main ideas underlying active automata learning (AAL) of DFAs. The exposition is intended to highlight the principles on which extensions, as outlined in Sects. 4 and 5, are based. Essentially, our intention is to show how AAL can be seen as a partition refinement procedure, which is based on the Nerode congruence, to which an exploration process is added. We first recall standard notions from the theory of finite automata.

Languages. Let A be a finite set of *symbols*. A *word* over A is a finite sequence of symbols in A. A *language* over A is a set of words over A. Let A^* denote the set of all words over A, and let ww' denote the concatenation of words w and w'.

Automata. A *deterministic finite automaton* (*DFA*) over A is a structure $\mathcal{M} = (Q, \delta, q_0, F)$ where Q is a non-empty finite set of *states*, $q_0 \in Q$ is the *initial state*, $\delta : Q \times A \to Q$ is the *transition function*, and $F \subseteq Q$ is the set of *accepting states*. The transition function is extended from input symbols to words of input symbols in the standard way, by defining $\delta(q, \epsilon) = q$ and $\delta(q, ua) = \delta(\delta(q, u), a)$. An input word u is *accepted* iff $\delta(q_0, u) \in F$. The *language* accepted by $\mathcal{M}$, denoted by $\mathcal{L}(\mathcal{M})$, is the set of accepted input words.

Nerode Congruence. Let $\mathcal{L}$ be a language over A. Two words w, w' over A are *Nerode equivalent*, denoted $w \equiv_{\mathcal{L}} w'$ if $wv \in \mathcal{L} \Leftrightarrow w'v \in \mathcal{L}$ for all words $v \in A^*$. It follows that $\equiv_{\mathcal{L}}$ is an equivalence relation, and also a (right) congruence (i.e., $w \equiv_{\mathcal{L}} w'$ implies $wv \equiv_{\mathcal{L}} w'v$ for any w, w', v). Given two words u and u', a *distinguishing suffix* for u and u' is a word v such that either uv or $u'v$ is in $\mathcal{L}$, but not both. Thus, two words are Nerode equivalent if there is no distinguishing suffix for them.

Regular Languages. The *index* of an equivalence relation is the number of equivalence classes. The language $\mathcal{L}$ is *regular* if $\equiv_{\mathcal{L}}$ has finite index. A main result in classical automata theory is that a language is regular if and only if it can be recognized by a DFA. The proof that a regular language $\mathcal{L}$ can be recognized by a DFA constructs the DFA $\mathcal{M} = (Q, \delta, q_0, F)$ where Q is the set of equivalence classes of $\equiv_{\mathcal{L}}$, where q_0 is $[\epsilon]_{\equiv_{\mathcal{L}}}$, where δ is defined by $\delta([w]_{\equiv_{\mathcal{L}}}, a) = [wa]_{\equiv_{\mathcal{L}}}$, and where F is defined by $[w]_{\equiv_{\mathcal{L}}} \in F \iff w \in \mathcal{L}$, and then demonstrates that $\mathcal{L}(\mathcal{M}) = \mathcal{L}$.

Active Automata Learning. Active Automata Learning (AAL) is most often formulated in the so-called MAT (for *minimally adequate teacher*) model of learning [Ang87]. In this model, learning proceeds by asking two kinds of queries.

- A *membership query* consists in asking whether a word w is in $\mathcal{L}$.
- An *equivalence query* consists in asking whether a hypothesized DFA $\mathcal{H}$ is correct, i.e., whether $\mathcal{L}(\mathcal{H}) = \mathcal{L}$. The query is answered by *yes* if $\mathcal{H}$ is correct, otherwise by a *counterexample*, which is a word from the symmetric difference of $\mathcal{L}$ and $\mathcal{L}(\mathcal{H})$.

The basic problem in any inductive learning is to generalize from the classification of a finite set to a classification of an infinite set. In AAL, this problem is to infer a language (i.e., a classification of an infinite set of words) from the classification of the finite set of words for which membership queries have been performed, or which have been returned by unsuccessful equivalence queries.

If we look at the construction of a DFA from a regular language, it shows that in order to construct a DFA we need

(i) at least one representative word in each Nerode equivalence class, and
(ii) a criterion which determines whether two words are in Nerode equivalent.

A learning algorithm starts with a small sample, which may not contain sufficiently many words for this need. In this case, these two concepts can only be approximated.

(i) The set of representative words is approximated from below, since we can only know about equivalence classes which have representative words in the sample.
(ii) The Nerode equivalence is overapproximated based on suffixes that are available in the sample. That is, two words are considered equivalent if the sample contains no concatenations of these words with a distinguishing suffix.

These considerations lead to the structuring of AAL algorithms as maintaining two finite sets of words:

- a non-empty prefix-closed set U of *short prefixes* (sometimes called *access strings*), which contains representatives of Nerode equivalence classes, and
- a set V of *suffixes*, which is used to define an overapproximation to the Nerode equivalence.

The set V represents an overapproximation of the Nerode equivalence, here denoted $\equiv_{\mathcal{L},V}$, defined by $w \equiv_{\mathcal{L},V} w'$ if $wv \in \mathcal{L} \iff w'v \in \mathcal{L}$ for all words $v \in V$. It is easy to see that $\equiv_{\mathcal{L},V}$ is an equivalence relation, which overapproximates $\equiv_{\mathcal{L}}$. If $\mathcal{L}$ is has finite index, then in fact $\equiv_{\mathcal{L},V}$ coincides with $\equiv_{\mathcal{L}}$ for sufficiently large finite V (it is sufficient that V contains a distinguishing suffix for each pair of inequivalent words).

Several AAL algorithms (of which [RS93] was maybe the first) maintain the property that the words in U are pairwise inequivalent wrt. $\equiv_{\mathcal{L},V}$. We will follow this approach here.

We say that the set U is *closed* wrt. V if for each $u \in U$ and $a \in A$ there is a $u' \in U$ such that $ua \equiv_{\mathcal{L},V} u'$. Whenever U is closed wrt. V, we can construct a DFA $\mathcal{H}(U,V) = (U, \delta, \epsilon, F)$ where $\delta(ua)$ is the u' such that $ua \equiv_{\mathcal{L},V} u'$ and where F is defined by $u \in F \iff u \in \mathcal{L}$.

It can be shown [Ang87, Lemma 3] that if U is prefix-closed and V is suffix-closed, then $\mathcal{H}(U,V)$ correctly classifies all words in UV.

AAL iterates two phases: hypothesis construction and hypothesis validation.

- During hypothesis construction, membership queries are performed for all words in $UV \cup UAV$. The purpose of this is to compute the relation $\equiv_{\mathcal{L},V}$ on $U \cup UA$. Whenever the set U is not closed wrt. V, then it is extended: if there is some ua with $u \in U$ such that $ua \not\equiv_{\mathcal{L},V} u'$ for all $u' \in U$, then ua is added to U, triggering new membership queries. The extension of U is continued in this way until U is closed wrt. V.
- When U is closed wrt. V, then the hypothesis $\mathcal{H}(U,V)$ is validated by submitting it in an equivalence query. If the query returns "yes", then the learning is completed, and $\mathcal{H}(U,V)$ accepts $\mathcal{L}$. If the query returns a counterexample word w, this is used to extend V as follows. By the fact that w is a counterexample, there is a suffix av of w such that $ua \equiv_{\mathcal{L},V} u'$ but $uav \in \mathcal{L} \iff u'v \in \mathcal{L}$ for some $u, u' \in U$. (To se this, let $w = a_1 \cdots a_n$, and define the sequence $u_0, u_1, \ldots, u_n$ of short prefixes in U by $u_0 = \epsilon$ and $u_{i-1}a_i \equiv_{\mathcal{L},V} u_i$ for $i = 1, \ldots n$, i.e., $u_0 \ldots u_n$ is the sequence of states visited when $\mathcal{H}(U,V)$ processes w. Let v_i be the suffix $a_{i+1} \cdots a_n$ of w length $n - i$. By the fact that w is a counterexample, we have $u_0 v_0 \in \mathcal{L} \iff u_n \in \mathcal{L}$, which implies that $u_{i-1}v_{i-1} \in \mathcal{L} \iff u_i v_i \in \mathcal{L}$ for some i; we can then take u_{i-1} as u and u_i as u'.) This means that v is a new separating suffix that should be added to V. After adding v to V, U is no longer closed wrt. V, so the algorithm can resume a next round of hypothesis construction, which will eventually generate a new hypothesis, etc.

Starting from some initial approximations (e.g., the singleton set consisting of the empty word), the sets U and V are successively extended, until U contains one element of each equivalence class of $\equiv_{\mathcal{L}}$, and $\equiv_{\mathcal{L},V}$ coincides with $\equiv_{\mathcal{L}}$. At termination the hypothesis is correct, by definition of equivalence query.

Since each round of hypothesis construction and validation adds at least one word to U, there can be at most n equivalence queries, where n is the index of $\mathcal{L}$. Since each equivalence query adds only one word to V, this means that $|V| \leq n$ when the algorithm finishes, implying that in total, at most $n^2|A|$ membership queries will be performed during hypothesis construction. During hypothesis validation, at most $2\log(m)$ membership queries need be performed (in addition to the equivalence query), where m is the length of the largest counterexample word returned.

3   Basic Definitions for Register Automata

In this and the following section, we introduce the principles for our generalization to data languages and register automata. In this section, we generalize the concepts of languages and automata by defining data languages and register automata. These are parameterized on a vocabulary that determines how data can be examined, which in our setting is called a *theory*.

Definition 1 (Theories). *A* theory *is a pair* $\langle \mathcal{D}, \mathcal{R} \rangle$ *where* $\mathcal{D}$ *is an infinite* domain *of data values, and* $\mathcal{R}$ *is a set of* relations *on* $\mathcal{D}$.

The relations in $\mathcal{R}$ can have arbitrary arity. Known constants can be represented by unary relations. The assumption that the domain $\mathcal{D}$ be infinite allows to avoid some technical complexities. Some examples of theories are

- $\langle \mathbb{N}, \{=\} \rangle$, the theory of natural numbers with equality; instead of the set of natural numbers, we could consider any other infinite domain, e.g., the set of strings (representing passwords or usernames),
- $\langle \mathbb{R}, \{<\} \rangle$, the theory of real numbers with inequality; this theory also allows to express equality between elements.

The above theories can all be extended with constants (allowing, e.g., theories of sums with predefined concrete constants). Technically, such an extension is achieved by defining new relations for every constant that can be added to a data values. As an example, $\langle \mathbb{N}, \{=\} \rangle$ could be extended to a theory that also allows modeling sums of data values with the constant 5 by adding relation $=_5$ with $a =_5 b$ for $a, b \in \mathbb{N}$ iff $a + 5 = b$. In the following, we assume that some theory has been fixed.

Data Languages. We assume a set Σ of *actions*, each with an arity that determines how many parameters it takes from the domain $\mathcal{D}$. For simplicity, we assume that all actions have arity 1; it is straightforward to extend the techniques to handle actions with arbitrary arities.

A *data symbol* is a term of form $\alpha(d)$, where α is an action and $d \in \mathcal{D}$ is a data value. A *data word* is a sequence of data symbols. The concatenation of two data words w and w' is denoted ww'. In this context, we often refer to w as a *prefix* and w' as a *suffix*. For a data word $w = \alpha_1(d_1) \ldots \alpha_n(d_n)$, let $Acts(w)$ denote its sequence of actions $\alpha_1 \ldots \alpha_n$, and $Vals(w)$ its sequence of data values $d_1 \ldots d_n$. Let $|w|$ denote the number of data symbols in w.

Two data words $w = \alpha_1(d_1) \ldots \alpha_n(d_n)$ and $w' = \alpha_1(d'_1) \ldots \alpha_n(d'_n)$ are $\mathcal{R}$-*indistinguishable*, denoted $w \approx_{\mathcal{R}} w'$, if

- $Acts(w) = Acts(w')$, and
- $R(d_{i_1}, \ldots, d_{i_j}) \Leftrightarrow R(d'_{i_1}, \ldots, d'_{i_j})$ whenever R is a j-ary relation in $\mathcal{R}$ and $i_1, \cdots, i_j$ are indices among $1 \ldots n$.

Intuitively, w and w' are $\mathcal{R}$-indistinguishable if they have the same sequences of actions and cannot be distinguished by any of the relations in $\mathcal{R}$.

A *data language* $\mathcal{L}$ is a set of data words that respects $\mathcal{R}$ in the sense that $w \approx_{\mathcal{R}} w'$ implies $w \in \mathcal{L} \leftrightarrow w' \in \mathcal{L}$. We will often represent data languages as mappings from the set of data words to $\{+, -\}$, where $+$ stands for *accept* and $-$ for *reject*.

Example 1. As a running example, we will use a simple version of a priority queue with bounded capacity. A priority queue stores a set of keys from some totally ordered set. We will use the set of rational numbers as the set of keys. An actual priority queue may store values along with keys, but here we only model the keys. The interface of the priority queue supports two operations: - *offer* inserts a given key into the priority queue. It succeeds if the queue is not full; - *poll* asks for the smallest key in the queue; the operation returns that key and removes it; if the queue contains several copies of the smallest key only one is removed; if the queue is empty, the operation does not succeed. The interface consists of operations with input parameters and return values. In order to represent it as a data language, we let data symbols represent successul operations: a successful *offer* is represented by the data symbol *offer*(d), where d is the inserted key, a successful *poll* operation is represented by the data symbol *poll*(d), where d is the returned key. We represent the interface as the data language consisting of sequences of data symbols that correspond to possible sequences of successful operations.

Register Automata. We assume a set of *registers* $x_1, x_2, \ldots$. A *parameterized symbol* is a term of form $\alpha(p)$, where α is an action and p a *formal parameter*. A *guard* is a conjunction of negated and unnegated relations (from $\mathcal{R}$) over the formal parameter p and registers. An *assignment* is a simple parallel update of registers with values from registers or the formal parameter p. We represent an assignment which updates the registers $x_{i_1}, \ldots, x_{i_m}$ with values from the registers $x_{j_1}, \ldots, x_{j_n}$ or p as a mapping π from $\{x_{i_1}, \ldots, x_{i_m}\}$ to $\{x_{j_1}, \ldots, x_{j_n}\} \cup \{p\}$, meaning that the value of the register or formal parameter $\pi(x_{i_k})$ is assigned to the register x_{i_k}, for $k = 1, \ldots, m$. Using multiple-assignment notation, this would be written as $x_{i_1}, \ldots, x_{i_m} := \pi(x_{i_1}), \ldots, \pi(x_{i_m})$.

Definition 2 (Register automaton). *A* register automaton *(RA) is a tuple* $\mathcal{A} = (L, l_0, \mathcal{X}, \Gamma, \lambda)$, *where*

- *L is a finite set of* locations, *with $l_0 \in L$ as the* initial location,
- *$\mathcal{X}$ maps each location $l \in L$ to a finite set $\mathcal{X}(l)$ of registers, and*
- *Γ is a finite set of* transitions, *each of form $\langle l, \alpha(p), g, \pi, l' \rangle$, where*
  - *$l \in L$ is a source location,*
  - *$l' \in L$ is a target location,*
  - *$\alpha(p)$ is a parameterized symbol,*
  - *g is a guard over p and $\mathcal{X}(l)$, and*
  - *π (the assignment) is a mapping from $\mathcal{X}(l')$ to $\mathcal{X}(l) \cup \{p\}$, and*
- *λ maps each $l \in L$ to $\{+, -\}$.*   □

We require register automata to be *determinate* and *non-blocking*; these concepts are defined after the definition of runs.

A restriction of register automata, as defined by Definition 2, is that transitions do not allow to assign arbitrary expressions to registers, only the value of a formal parameter or a register. A main reason for this restriction is to limit the number of possibilities for inferring guards and assignments that match the results of membership queries, thereby making learning more tractable. As an example, suppose that a SUL accepts sequences with increasing parameter values, e.g., *offer*(1) *offer*(2) *offer*(3) *offer*(4). We could then learn a RA if the theory includes, e.g., the relation *issucc*, defined by $issucc(x, y)$ iff $x + 1 = y$. If assignments to registers would allow expressions that include e.g., the $+1$ operator, or even arbitrary addition, then the learning algorithm would have to choose between a potentially large number of different guards and assignments on each transition, This would complicate the design of a learning algorithm. On the other hand, we do not foresee any conceptual difficulty in extending the theory for learning RAs in order to produce more expressive classes of RAs; this could possibly be done by making the implementation of tree queries more advanced and extending the Nerode equivalence (cf. Sect. 4). However, in order to focus on the conceptual extensions needed to learn RAs, we have so far excluded expressions in assignments of RAs.

Let us formalize the semantics of RAs. A *state* of an RA $\mathcal{A} = (L, l_0, \mathcal{X}, \Gamma, \lambda)$ is a pair $\langle l, \mu \rangle$ where $l \in L$ and μ is a valuation over $\mathcal{X}(l)$, i.e., a mapping from $\mathcal{X}(l)$ to $\mathcal{D}$. A *step* of $\mathcal{A}$, denoted $\langle l, \mu \rangle \xrightarrow{\alpha(d)} \langle l', \mu' \rangle$, transfers $\mathcal{A}$ from $\langle l, \mu \rangle$ to $\langle l', \mu' \rangle$ on input of the data symbol $\alpha(d)$ if there is a transition $\langle l, \alpha(p), g, \pi, l' \rangle \in \Gamma$ with

- $\mu \models g[d/p]$, i.e., d satisfies the guard g under the valuation μ, and
- μ' is the updated valuation $\mu' = \mu \circ [p \mapsto d] \circ \pi$ (i.e., $\mu'(x_i) = \mu(x_j)$ if $\pi(x_i) = x_j$, and $\mu'(x_i) = d$ if $\pi(x_i) = p$).

Here, and in the following, we use $[p \mapsto d]$ to denote a mapping, with suitable domain and range determined by context, which maps p to d and leaves all other elements in its domain unchanged.

A *run* of $\mathcal{A}$ over a data word $w = \alpha_1(d_1) \ldots \alpha_n(d_n)$ is a sequence of steps of $\mathcal{A}$

$$\langle l'_0, \mu_0 \rangle \xrightarrow{\alpha_1(d_1)} \langle l'_1, \mu_1 \rangle \quad \ldots \quad \langle l'_{n-1}, \mu_{n-1} \rangle \xrightarrow{\alpha_n(d_n)} \langle l'_n, \mu_n \rangle.$$

The run is *initialized* if l'_0 is the initial location and μ_0 is the initial (empty) valuation. An initialized run is *accepting* if $\lambda(l'_n) = +$ and *rejecting* if $\lambda(l'_n) = -$. The word w is *accepted (rejected) by $\mathcal{A}$ under μ_0* if $\mathcal{A}$ has an accepting (rejecting) initialized run over w.

An RA is *non-blocking* if for any initialized run ending in $\langle l, \mu \rangle$ and any data symbol $\alpha(d)$ there is a step of form $\langle l, \mu \rangle \xrightarrow{\alpha(d)} \langle l', \mu' \rangle$. An RA is *determinate* if there is no data word over which it has both accepting and rejecting initialized runs. We require RAs to be non-blocking and determinate. We have chosen to work with determinate, rather than deterministic, RAs. This distinction is not important, since a determinate RA can be easily transformed into a deterministic

RA by strengthening its guards, and a deterministic RA, by definition, is also determinate. Our construction of RAs in Sect. 5 will generate determinate RAs which are not necessarily deterministic.

We use RAs as acceptors for data languages. The language accepted by $\mathcal{A}$, denoted $\mathcal{L}(\mathcal{A})$, is the set of data words that it accepts.

Example. We illustrate by an RA that accepts the language modeling a priority queue with bounded capacity. We choose to represent a priority queue with capacity 2. Figure 1 shows a RA that accepts the corresponding data language. For conciseness, we have omitted nonaccepting locations. Thus the RA in Fig. 1 should be extended with a terminal non-accepting location; from each location, there should be transitions to the non-accepting location for data symbols that do not satisfy any of the existing guards. For instance, from l_1 there is a transition to the non-accepting location for $poll(p)$ symbols where $p \neq x_1$.

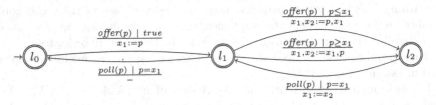

Fig. 1. Register automaton modeling a priority queue with capacity 2.

4 Generalizing Active Learning to EFSM Models

In this section, we discuss how the principles on which AAL for DFAs was based can be generalized to the learning of register automata. The challenge that faces AAL for register automata is to infer all the features of an RA, including locations, registers, guards, and assignments, using only membership queries and counterexamples returned by equivalence queries. The only *a priori* information available is the set Σ of actions that appear in data symbolc, and a theory which is expressive enough, in the sense that the language accepted by the RA respects the relations of the theory. For instance, in the case of the priority queue of our running example, the theory could be the theory of rational numbers with inequality. We will here try to illustrate how this challenge can be solved by suitable generalizations of the concepts underlying AAL for DFAs.

Recall from Sect. 2 that the essence of AAL for regular languages is to maintain a set U of short prefixes, which represent states in the DFA to be constructed, and an overapproximation of the Nerode equivalence, represented by a set V of suffixes. During hypothesis construction, the approximation of the Nerode equivalence triggers the expansion of U until it is closed, so that a hypothesis automaton can be formed. During hypothesis validation, returned counterexamples are used to refine the Nerode equivalence by expanding V.

In our generalization to learning register automata, we still let the algorithm maintain a set U of short prefixes. In contrast to the DFA case we will *not* let the short prefixes in U represent states of the RA: this would be highly impractical since an RA in general has an infinite number of states. Instead, we let short prefixes represent locations in the RA to be constructed; this seems like a natural way to obtain a suitable number of equivalence classes.

4.1 Symbolic Decision Trees and Approximated Nerode Equivalence

Let us now consider how to generalize the approximated Nerode equivalence. We first note that in the literature there is no standard generalization of Nerode equivalence for register automata, which we can just adapt and approximate.[1] We must therefore first define such an equivalence. It appears most convenient to first define an approximated Nerode equivalence, parameterized on a set of suffixes (which is what is actually needed for automata learning), from which a proper Nerode equivalence can be derived as the limit of increasingly precise approximations (as shown in Sect. 6).

Symbolic Suffixes. Let us consider how to define our approximated Nerode equivalence, parameterized on a set of suffixes. Recall that in the DFA case, the parameter is simply a finite set V of suffixes. In the RA case, sets of suffixes are typically infinite, due to the infinite data domain. A natural way to characterize such sets is by sets of sequences of actions. To this end, define a *symbolic suffix* to be a sequence of actions. A set $\mathcal{V}$ of symbolic suffixes represents the set of suffixes v with $Acts(v) \in \mathcal{V}$. Let $[\![\mathcal{V}]\!]$ denote the set of suffixes represented by $\mathcal{V}$.

We must now define an approximated Nerode equivalence, parameterized by a set $\mathcal{V}$ of symbolic suffixes. We first note that we cannot directly copy the definition of Nerode equivalence from the DFA case, i.e., to let two words be equivalent if their composition with an arbitrary suffix in $[\![\mathcal{V}]\!]$ result in words that are either both inside or outside the language. Let us illustrate this for the priority queue example: letting $\mathcal{V} = \{poll\}$ would make any two words of form $offer(d)$ with different data values d inequivalent, since after $offer(d)$, the continuation $poll(d')$ is accepted if and only if $d' = d$. Thus, $\mathcal{V} = \{poll\}$ would induce an infinite number of equivalence classes, which can not be used for constructing RAs.

Symbolic Decision Trees. A better idea is to let the equivalence reflect the idea that prefixes represent RA locations. A location l remembers data values from the already processed sequence of data symbols in its registers. The processing of future sequences of data symbols from a location involves to evaluate their data values using guards on relevant transitions. This future processing can be represented by an RA, in which l is an initial location with registers that store the remembered data values. If the future sequences of interest are restricted to

---

[1] The Nerode equivalence defined in [CHJ+15b] is defined only for the theory of equalities over an infinite domain, and can be obtained as a special case of the approach described in Sect. 6.

the suffixes in a set $[\![\mathcal{V}]\!]$ where $\mathcal{V}$ is finite, then such an RA can be tree-shaped with l as its root. Thus, the processing of a set of suffixes in $[\![\mathcal{V}]\!]$ after a given prefix u can be represented by a tree-shaped "RA-fragment", whose initial location may therefore have registers that store data values from u. And which only has branches that correspond to the symbolic suffixes in $\mathcal{V}$. Following [CHJS16], we use the term *symbolic decision tree* (SDT) for such an RA-fragment.

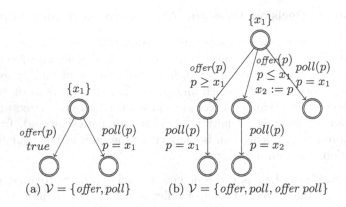

Fig. 2. SDTs for $u = offer(5)$ for various $\mathcal{V}$ in the priority queue example.

Let us illustrate this on the priority queue example for the prefix $u = offer(5)$ and the set $\mathcal{V} = \{offer, poll\}$ of symbolic suffixes. The acceptance/rejection of suffixes in $[\![\mathcal{V}]\!]$ after the prefix $offer(5)$ can be represented by the SDT in Fig. 2(a). We require that an SDT refers to data values in the prefix u only via registers in its initial location. Thus, in the initial location, the value 5 from $offer(5)$ is stored in a register. We annotate the root location by the set of its registers. In other words, the SDT generalizes from specific data values in prefixes (in this case 5) by using the guard $p = x_1$ instead of the more specific $p = 5$. In this way, the same SDTs can hopefully be used to represent the effect of suffixes in $[\![\mathcal{V}]\!]$ for many different prefixes. In order to know which values from the prefix are stored in which registers, we use the convention that register x_i stores the ith data value from the prefix. Thereafter, suffixes of form $poll(d)$ are accepted if the data value d equals the value stored in the register, whereas suffixes of form $offer(d)$ are always accepted. In the same way as for the RA in Fig. 1, we omit rejecting locations, and transitions leading to them.

Note that the initial location of an SDT only has registers for the data values of the prefix that are actually used in the SDT. Thus, even if the prefix u is very long, the SDT may use only a few of its data values, and equally many registers. Also note that the SDT in Fig. 2(a) is different from the corresponding fragment of the RA in Fig. 1, which starts in location l_1: the latter makes finer distinctions for parameters of *offer* actions, since it must also care about suffixes of length 2 or more. To move closer to the corresponding fragment in the RA of Fig. 1, we can extend the set $\mathcal{V}$ of symbolic suffixes to $\{\textit{offer}, \textit{poll}, \textit{offer poll}\}$. We can then obtain the SDT in Fig. 2(b), in which the outgoing *offer*-transitions are split by guards that compare the received data value to that stored in the register.

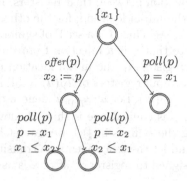

Fig. 3. Alternative SDT for $u = \textit{offer}(5)$ and $\mathcal{V} = \{\textit{offer}, \textit{poll}, \textit{offer poll}\}$ in the priority queue example.

The construction of SDTs that accept and reject suffixes in $[\![\mathcal{V}]\!]$ after some prefix u can in principle be done in different ways. For instance, for the prefix $u = \textit{offer}(5)$ and the set of symbolic suffixes $\mathcal{V} = \{\textit{offer}, \textit{poll}, \textit{offer poll}\}$, we could instead of the SDT in Fig. 2(b) produce the SDT in Fig. 3. Following our previous work, we prefer the SDT in Fig. 2(b) to that in Fig. 3, since it obeys the principle to perform comparisons between data values as early as possible to avoid direct comparisons between registers, and since such a principle makes it easier to define a canonical form for RAs.

In order to learn uniquely defined RAs, wee need to determine the form for SDTs. We do this by postulating the existence of a *tree oracle* $\mathcal{T}$, which for each data word u and set of symbolic suffixes $\mathcal{V}$ produces an SDT, denoted $\mathcal{T}_{\mathcal{V}}(u)$. In our running example the tree oracle will, for the prefix $\textit{offer}(5)$ and suffixes $\{\textit{offer}, \textit{poll}\}$ produce the SDT in Fig. 2(a). Tree oracles should satisfy a number of criteria, listed in Definition 4.

The tree oracle introduced here can be realized by a procedure which constructs SDTs by performing a bounded set of membership queries. For simple theories, such as $\langle \mathbb{N}, \{=\} \rangle$ and $\langle \mathbb{R}, \{<\} \rangle$, introduced in the beginning of Sect. 3, it is not difficult to devise techniuqes for SDT construction (see, e.g., [CHJS16]). An extension to sequence numbers is reported in [FH17]. For theories with a large number of relations, tree oracles may have to perform choices between a number of possible ways combine them for classifying suffixes. Different tree oracles may induce different approximations of the Nerode equivalence, and consequently generate different RAs.

Approximated Nerode Equivalence. Having introduced the notation $\mathcal{T}_{\mathcal{V}}(u)$ for the SDT for u and $\mathcal{V}$, we can use the constructed SDTs to define an approximated Nerode equivalence. A natural first idea is to let two prefixes, u and u', be equivalent wrt. $\mathcal{V}$ if $\mathcal{T}_\mathcal{V}(u)$ and $\mathcal{T}_\mathcal{V}(u')$ are the same. However, since RAs can perform arbitrary assignments between registers, it is sufficient that the registers in the root location of $\mathcal{T}_\mathcal{V}(u)$ can be renamed so that $\mathcal{T}_\mathcal{V}(u)$ and $\mathcal{T}_\mathcal{V}(u')$ become the same. The approximated Nerode equivalence between two SDTs will therefore be parameterized on a bijection between their registers. It suffices to specify the bijection for registers of the initial location; for the others it can be determined from the structure of the trees. Thus, for a set $\mathcal{V}$ of symbolic suffixes and prefixes u, u', let $u \simeq^\gamma_{\mathcal{T},\mathcal{V}} u'$ denote that γ is a bijection from the registers of the initial location of $\mathcal{T}_\mathcal{V}(u)$ to the registers of the initial location of $\mathcal{T}_\mathcal{V}(u')$ which can be extended to a bijection from all registers of $\mathcal{T}_\mathcal{V}(u)$ to all registers of $\mathcal{T}_\mathcal{V}(u')$, and which converts $\mathcal{T}_\mathcal{V}(u)$ into $\mathcal{T}_\mathcal{V}(u')$. Let $u \simeq_{\mathcal{T},\mathcal{V}} u'$ denote that $u \simeq^\gamma_{\mathcal{T},\mathcal{V}} u'$ for some bijection γ. The point of this equivalence is that whenever $u \simeq^\gamma_{\mathcal{T},\mathcal{V}} u'$, then for the purpose of classifying the suffixes in $[\![\mathcal{V}]\!]$, we can let let the prefix u' lead to the same location as u, and let the assignments on transitions be defined so that the data value that is assigned to register x_i after u is assigned to register $\gamma(x_i)$ after u'.

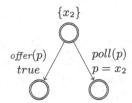

Fig. 4. $\mathcal{T}_\mathcal{V}(u')$ for $u' = \mathit{offer}(5)\mathit{offer}(7)\mathit{poll}(5)$ and $\mathcal{V} = \{\mathit{offer}, \mathit{poll}\}$

To illustrate the approximated Nerode equivalence, Fig. 4 shows $\mathcal{T}_\mathcal{V}(u')$ for $u' = \mathit{offer}(5)\mathit{offer}(7)\mathit{poll}(5)$ and $\mathcal{V} = \{\mathit{offer}, \mathit{poll}\}$. We see that $\mathit{offer}(5) \simeq^\gamma_{\mathcal{T},\mathcal{V}} \mathit{offer}(5)\mathit{offer}(7)\mathit{poll}(5)$, where γ maps x_1 to x_2.

4.2 Towards a Learning Algorithm

We have now developed sufficient machinery to illustrate our generalized AAL learning on the priority queue.

Suppose we start our learning algorithms with $U = \{\epsilon, \mathit{offer}(5), \mathit{offer}(5)$ $\mathit{offer}(7)\}$ and $\mathcal{V} = \{\mathit{offer}, \mathit{poll}\}$. We construct the RA-fragments $\mathcal{T}_\mathcal{V}(u)$ for $u \in U$, as shown in Fig. 5.

Since the SDTs are different, the corresponding prefixes are inequivalent, and should therefore lead to three different locations. The recepy for AAL prescribes to expand U until it is closed. In the DFA case, "closed" means that each one-symbol continuation of some prefix in U is equivalent to some prefix which is already in U. The naive generalization of this condition would be expensive to check, since each prefix has an unbounded number of one-symbol continuations, and often cause unnecessary work. Therefore, our generalization of "closed" performs this check only for one "representative" symbol for each transition from the

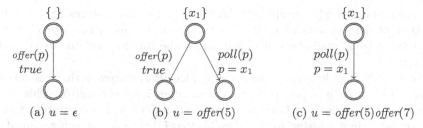

Fig. 5. SDTs $T_V(u)$ for $V = \{offer, poll\}$ in the priority queue example.

initial location of the corresponding RA-fragment. Our framework thus requires to define, for each prefix u and each guard g, a *representative data value*, denoted $\mathbf{d}_u^g$. We say that U is closed wrt. V if for each $u \in U$ and each transition from the initial location of $T_V(u)$ labeled by parameterized symbol $\alpha(p)$ and guard g, the extension $u\alpha(\mathbf{d}_u^g)$ is equivalent to a prefix in U. It is not crucial how the representative data value $\mathbf{d}_u^g$ is chosen, but it is advisable to avoid corner cases, such as unnecessarily letting $\mathbf{d}_u^g$ be equal to a data value in u. For the following, let us assume that representative data values are chosen as follows.

- The representative data value for the guard *true* is 5 after ϵ and 7 after *offer*(5) (avoiding the corner case 5).
- For a guard of form $p = x_i$, there is obviously only one possible representative data value, viz. the value of x_i.

In our example, let us check whether our set U is closed wrt. V.

- $u = \epsilon$: the extension *offer*(5) is also in U.
- $u = offer(5)$: here there are two outgoing transitions.
  - *offer*(p): the extension *offer*(5)*offer*(7) is also in U.
  - *poll*(p): for the guard $p = x_1$, the extension *offer*(5)*poll*(5) has the same SDT as ϵ.

  Recall that for the presentation we have omitted transitions leading to rejecting locations. E.g., after *offer*(5), we have thus omitted the *poll*-transition with guard $p \neq x_1$; the treatment of these cases is trivial in this example.
- $u = offer(5)offer(7)$: the only continuation is $u = offer(5)offer(7)poll(5)$, which has the SDT of Fig. 4, equivalent to that of *offer*(5).

Thus the set U is indeed closed wrt. V. In the DFA case, we should be able to construct a hypothesis automaton. However, in our setting there is still one problem remaining, which is that we cannot construct a transition from the location represented by *offer*(5)*offer*(7) to that represented by *offer*(5)*offer*(7)*poll*(5). The reason is that the SDT after *offer*(5)*offer*(7)*poll*(5) has a register containing data value 7 in its initial location, whereas the SDT after *offer*(5)*offer*(7) has a register which contains 5. Thus, we can not construct the assignment for the transition, since there is no register of $T_V(offer(5)offer(7))$ whose contents can be assigned to the register of $T_V(offer(5)offer(7)poll(5))$. Following [CHJS16], we solve this issue by requiring U and V to be *register-consistent*, meaning that the registers of $u\alpha(\mathsf{d}_u^g)$, except possibly the register which stores d_u^g, should be a subset of the registers of u. If U and $\mathcal{V}$ are not register consistent, then $\mathcal{V}$ is extended by a symbolic suffix that forces the missing register to be added to $\mathcal{T}_\mathcal{V}(u)$.

To remedy this deficiency, the learning algorithm discovers that the missing register x_2 is used in a *poll* transition after $offer(5)offer(7)poll(5)$. This corresponds to a suffix in $[\![\{poll\ poll\}]\!]$ after $offer(5)offer(7)$. Thus, in order to add the corresponding register to $\mathcal{T}_\mathcal{V}(offer(5)offer(7))$, the set of suffixes must be extended with *poll poll*. Resuming hypothesis construction, we construct $\mathcal{T}_\mathcal{V}(u)$ for u in U and $\mathcal{V} = \{offer, poll, poll\ poll\}$. The resulting SDTs are in Fig. 6.

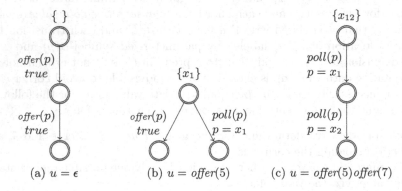

Fig. 6. SDTs $\mathcal{T}_\mathcal{V}(u)$ for $\mathcal{V} = \{offer, poll, poll\ poll\}$ in the priority queue example.

The new set of symbolic suffixes achieves both closedness and register consistency. We can thus proceed to constructing a hypothesis. The main principles for this construction are as follows.

- Each prefix u in U induces a location. Its registers are the registers of the initial location of $\mathcal{T}_\mathcal{V}(u)$.
- Each initial transition of $\mathcal{T}_\mathcal{V}(u)$ induces a transition from the location induced by u, with the same guard, to the prefix that is equivalent to its representative one-symbol extension. Its assignment is derived from the parameter γ of this equivalence.

Using these principles, we construct the hypothesis shown in Fig. 7.

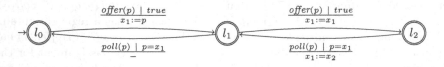

Fig. 7. Hypothesis RA for $\mathcal{V} = \{offer, poll\}$ in priority queue example.

We then move to the hypothesis validation phase. The hypothesis RA in Fig. 7 is supplied in an equivalence query. Since it is not equivalent to the one in Fig. 1, the equivalence query will return a counterexample. Suppose that this counterexample is the word $w = offer(5)\,offer(3)\,poll(3)$, which is rejected by the hypothesis but is in the language. Let us now illustrate how we generalize counterexample processing to the RA setting. The word w suggests that something is wrong with the symbolic path induced by w, i.e., the sequence of transitions that goes through the sequence of locations $l_0 l_1 l_2 l_1$. In the DFA case, a counterexample indicates that a one-symbol extension of some prefix in U, which has incorrectly been assumed to be equivalent to another prefix in U, should be added to U; it describes how to extend V to achieve this effect. In the RA case, a counterexample can point to additional deficiencies in the hypothesis:

– a guard may need to be refined, since it is satisfied by different data values that induce inequivalent subsequent behavior, but V must be extended to expose this difference,
– a representative one-symbol extension of a prefix in U may indeed be equivalent to another prefix in U, but an incorrect bijection has been used to check this.

These cases are also resolved by extending V and resuming hypothesis construction.

In our case, investigating the symbolic path induced by w reveals that the sequence of transitions $l_1 l_2 l_1$ treats the two suffixes $offer(7)\,poll(5)$ and $offer(3)\,poll(5)$ in the same way, although the first is in the language and the second is not. This discrepancy is visible after the location induced by the prefix $offer(5)$, and therefore its outgoing $offer$-transition must be refined. The remedy is to extend V by the symbolic suffix $offer\,poll$. Then the tree oracle will construct and SDT for $offer(5)$ with two outgoing $offer$-transitions. Resuming hypothesis construction, we construct $\mathcal{T}_V(u)$ for u in U and $V = \{offer, poll, poll\,poll, offer\,poll\}$. The resulting SDTs are in Fig. 8.

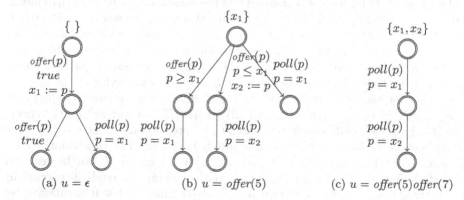

Fig. 8. SDTs $\mathcal{T}_V(u)$ for $V = \{offer, poll, offer\,poll, poll\,poll\}$ in the priority queue example.

Constructing an automaton based on these fragments yields the desired RA in Fig. 1.

5   Learning Register Automata: Formal Development

Let us now define the generalization more formally. We continue the line of definitions from Sect. 3.

5.1   Symbolic Decision Trees

A *symbolic suffix* is a sequence of actions. An *abstract suffix* is a set of symbolic suffixes. For an abstract suffix $\mathcal{V}$, let $[\![\mathcal{V}]\!]$ denote the set of data words v with $Acts(v) \in \mathcal{V}$, let $\alpha^{-1}\mathcal{V}$ denote the set of symbolic suffixes $\alpha_1 \ldots \alpha_n$ with $\alpha\alpha_1 \ldots \alpha_n \in \mathcal{V}$, and let $Initacts(\mathcal{V})$ be the set of actions α with $\alpha^{-1}\mathcal{V} \neq \emptyset$.

Assume a data word u with $Vals(u) = d_1 \ldots d_k$. Let μ_u be the valuation with domain $\{x_1, \ldots, x_k\}$ such that $\mu_u(x_i) = d_i$ for $i = 1, \ldots, k$. A u-*guard* is a predicate g over $x_1, \ldots, x_k$ and the formal parameter p. We require that to each u-guard g is assigned a unique *representative data value*, denoted d_u^g, which satisfies $\mu_u \models g[\mathsf{d}_u^g/p]$ (thus, each u-guard must have at least one satisfying instantiation of the formal parameter p); moreoever, if some other u-guard g' satisfies $\mu_u \models (g' \Rightarrow g)$ and $\mu_u \models g'[\mathsf{d}_u^{g'}/p]$, then $\mathsf{d}_u^{g'} = \mathsf{d}_u^g$.

We extend the definitions of u-guards to sequences, as follows. A sequence $\tau = (\alpha_{k+1}, g_{k+1}) \cdots (\alpha_{k+m}, g_{k+m})$ of action-guard pairs is a u-*path* if either (i) $m = 0$, or (ii) g_{k+1} is a u-guard and $(\alpha_{k+2}, g_{k+2}) \cdots (\alpha_{k+m}, g_{k+m})$ is a $u\alpha_{k+1}(\mathsf{d}_u^{g_{k+1}})$-path. We define $\mathcal{G}_\tau$ as $g_{k+1}[x_{k+1}/p] \wedge g_{k+m}[x_{k+m}/p]$. For a suffix v of form $\alpha_{k+1}(d_{k+1}) \cdots \alpha_{k+m}(d_{k+m})$, we say that v *satisfies* τ *after* u if $\mu_{uv} \models \mathcal{G}_\tau$. Intuitively, $\mathcal{G}_\tau$ is the condition on $d_{k+1}, \ldots, d_{k+m}$ under which v satisfies the sequence of guards $g_{k+1}, \ldots, g_{k+m}$, given some valuation of $\{x_1, \ldots, x_k\}$, and letting x_{k+i} represent d_{k+i} for $i \geq 1$.

For a set Π of u-paths and action α, let $Initgs_\Pi(\alpha)$ denote the set of guards g with $(\alpha, g)\tau \in \Pi$ for some τ. Let $\phi_\Pi(\alpha)$ be the constraint $\forall p. [\bigvee Initgs_\Pi(\alpha)]$. For an abstract suffix $\mathcal{V}$, let $\phi_\Pi(\mathcal{V})$ be the conjunction of $\phi_\Pi(\alpha)$ over $\alpha \in Initacts(\mathcal{V})$. Intuitively, $\phi_\Pi(\mathcal{V})$ is the constraint over $\{x_1, \ldots, x_k\}$ under which a data symbol $\alpha(d)$ with $\alpha \in Initacts(\mathcal{V})$ is guaranteed to find a satisfying initial guard in Π.

For $g \in Initgs_\Pi(\alpha)$ define $(\alpha, g)^{-1}\Pi$ as the set of $u\alpha(\mathsf{d}_u^g)$-paths τ' with $(\alpha, g)\tau' \in \Pi$. Define a $(u, \mathcal{V})$-*cover* as a set Π of u-paths satisfying $\mu_u \models \phi_\Pi(\mathcal{V})$, such that for each $\alpha \in Initacts(\mathcal{V})$ and $g \in Initgs_\Pi(\alpha)$ we have (i) $(\phi_\Pi(\mathcal{V}) \wedge g[x_{|u|+1}/p]) \Rightarrow \phi_{(\alpha,g)^{-1}\Pi}(\alpha^{-1}\mathcal{V})$, and (ii) $(\alpha, g)^{-1}\Pi$ is a $(u\alpha(\mathsf{d}_u^g), \alpha^{-1}\mathcal{V})$-cover. Intuitively, these conditions imply that Π can process any suffix $v \in [\![\mathcal{V}]\!]$ after u without being blocked by lack of a satisfying guard. The constraint $\phi_\Pi(\mathcal{V})$ characterizes those valuations of $\{x_1, \ldots, x_k\}$ from which Π can be used to classify suffixes in $[\![\mathcal{V}]\!]$. It is analogous to a path constraint in symbolic execution; to see this, note that the condition $\mu_u \models \phi_\Pi(\mathcal{V})$ means that it is satisfied by the prefix u, and that condition (i) is a natural condition for propagating path constraints.

Definition 3. *A $(u, \mathcal{V})$-tree T is a mapping from a $(u, \mathcal{V})$-cover to $\{+, -\}$.*

We write $Initgs_T(\alpha)$ for $Initgs_{Dom(T)}(\alpha)$ and ϕ_T for $\phi_{Dom(T)}(\mathcal{V})$. If T is a $(u, \mathcal{V})$-tree and $g \in Initgs_T(\alpha)$, then define $(\alpha, g)^{-1}T$ as the $(u\alpha(\mathsf{d}_u^g), \alpha^{-1}\mathcal{V})$-tree T' defined by $Dom(T') = (\alpha, g)^{-1}Dom(T)$ and $T'(\tau) = T((\alpha, g)\tau)$. Intuitively, $(\alpha, g)^{-1}T$ is the subtree of T reached after the action-guard pair (α, g). We will sometimes use the term *symbolic decision trees (SDTs)* for $(u, \mathcal{V})$-trees.

Definition 4. *A tree oracle $\mathcal{T}$ is a function which maps each data word u and abstract suffix $\mathcal{V}$ to a $(u, \mathcal{V})$-tree $\mathcal{T}_\mathcal{V}(u)$, subject to the consistency conditions that*

1. *whenever $g \in Initgs_{\mathcal{T}_\mathcal{V}(u)}(\alpha)$ then $\mathcal{T}_{\alpha^{-1}\mathcal{V}}(u\alpha(\mathsf{d}_u^g))$ is $(\alpha, g)^{-1}\mathcal{T}_\mathcal{V}(u)$, and*
2. *for any u, $\mathcal{V}$ and $\mathcal{V}'$, we have $(\phi_{\mathcal{T}_\mathcal{V}(u)} \wedge \phi_{\mathcal{T}_{\mathcal{V}'}(u)}) \Rightarrow \phi_{\mathcal{T}_{(\mathcal{V}\cup\mathcal{V}')}(u)}$.*

Intuitively, Condition 1 states that the SDT produced by $\mathcal{T}_{\alpha^{-1}\mathcal{V}}(u\alpha(\mathsf{d}_u^g))$ must be the same as the correponding subtree of $\mathcal{T}_\mathcal{V}(u)$, reached after the action-guard pair (α, g). This implies that the tree oracle can construct SDTs recursively bottom-up from the leaves of a tree. Condition 2 is a natural technical condition, used only in our subsequent discussion on counterexample processing. Intuitively, it states that if a prefix satisfies both the path constraint for processing suffixes in $[\![\mathcal{V}]\!]$ and the path constraint for processing suffixes in $[\![\mathcal{V}']\!]$, then that prefix should satisfy the path constraint for processing suffixes in $[\![\mathcal{V} \cup \mathcal{V}']\!]$.

We say that $\mathcal{T}$ *respects* the language $\mathcal{L}$ if for each u, $\mathcal{V}$, and $\tau \in Dom(\mathcal{T}_\mathcal{V}(u))$, it holds that $(\mathcal{T}_\mathcal{V}(u)(\tau) = + \Leftrightarrow uv \in \mathcal{L})$ whenever v satisfies τ after u. Let $mem_{\mathcal{T},\mathcal{V}}(u)$, also called the set of *memorable parameters*, denote the set of registers among $\{x_1, \ldots, x_k\}$ that occur on some u-path in $Dom(\mathcal{T}_\mathcal{V}(u))$.

The above definitions are illustrated by the SDTs in Sect. 4. Each SDT is labeled by the corresponding set $mem_{\mathcal{T},\mathcal{V}}(u)$ of memorable parameters. Consider, e.g., the $(u, \mathcal{V})$-tree in Fig. 8(b). Here, the middle branch corresponds to the u-path $\tau = (offer, p \leq x_1)(poll, p = x_2)$. The corresponding constraint $\mathcal{G}_\tau$ becomes $x_2 \leq x_1 \wedge x_3 = x_2$). In the examples, all constraints $\phi_{\mathcal{T}_\mathcal{V}(u)}$ are *true*. However, if we would consider a priority queue of capacity three, then after $u = offer(5)offer(7)$, a natural tree oracle would for suitable $\mathcal{V}$ result in $\phi_{\mathcal{T}_\mathcal{V}(u)}$ being $x_1 \leq x_2$, since guards for subsequent *offer*-symbols make sense only under this condition.

5.2   Approximated Nerode Equivalence

We can now define the generalization of the approximated Nerode equivalence. The generalization of the approximated Nerode equivalence is parameterized by a tree oracle and an abstract suffix.

Two $(u, \mathcal{V})$-trees, T and T', are said to be equivalent, denoted $T \equiv T'$, if $Dom(T) = Dom(T')$, and $T(\tau) = T'(\tau)$ for each $\tau \in Dom(T)$. For a mapping γ on registers, we define its extension to u-guards and u-paths in the natural way. For a $(u, \mathcal{V})$-tree T, we define $\gamma(T)$ by $Dom(\gamma(T)) = \{\gamma(\tau) : \tau \in Dom(T)\}$ and $\gamma(T)(\gamma(\tau)) = T(\tau)$.

Definition 5 (Approximated Nerode Equivalence). *Let $\mathcal{T}$ be a tree oracle which respects $\mathcal{L}$. Let u, u' be data words and $\mathcal{V}$ be an abstract suffix. Then $u \simeq_{\mathcal{T},\mathcal{V}}^{\gamma} u'$ denotes that $\gamma : mem_{\mathcal{T},\mathcal{V}}(u) \rightarrow mem_{\mathcal{T},\mathcal{V}}(u')$ is a bijection from $mem_{\mathcal{T},\mathcal{V}}(u)$ to $mem_{\mathcal{T},\mathcal{V}}(u')$ such that $\hat{\gamma}(\mathcal{T}_{\mathcal{V}}(u)) \equiv \mathcal{T}_{\mathcal{V}}(u')$, where $\hat{\gamma}$ extends γ by mapping $x_{|u|+i}$ to $x_{|u'|+i}$ for $i \geq 1$.*

Let $u \simeq_{\mathcal{T},\mathcal{V}} u'$ denote that $u \simeq_{\mathcal{T},\mathcal{V}}^{\gamma} u'$ for some bijection γ.

Intuitively, two words u and u' are equivalent if the bijection γ transforms the SDT for processing suffixes in $[\![\mathcal{V}]\!]$ after u to the SDT for processing suffixes in $[\![\mathcal{V}]\!]$ after u'. Note that in general, when $u \simeq_{\mathcal{T},\mathcal{V}} u'$, there can be several bijections γ such that $u \simeq_{\mathcal{T},\mathcal{V}}^{\gamma} u'$.

5.3   Register Automata Construction

To generalize automata construction and AAL to RAs, we must impose some technical requirements on tree oracles, to ensure that generated hypothesis automata converge monotonically towards an acceptor for the language.

Definition 6 (Monotone tree oracle). *A tree oracle $\mathcal{T}$ which respects the language $\mathcal{L}$ is monotone if whenever $\mathcal{V} \subseteq \mathcal{V}'$, then for any u, u' and action $\alpha \in Initacts(\mathcal{V})$,*

1. *for each $g \in Initgs_{\mathcal{T}_{\mathcal{V}}(u)}(\alpha)$ there is a $g' \in Initgs_{\mathcal{T}_{\mathcal{V}'}(u)}(\alpha)$ such that $\phi_{\mathcal{T}_{\mathcal{V}}(u)} \Rightarrow (g' \Rightarrow g)$ and $\mu_u \models g'[d_u^g/p]$,*
2. *$mem_{\mathcal{T},\mathcal{V}}(u) \subseteq mem_{\mathcal{T},\mathcal{V}'}(u)$,*
3. *whenever there are two u-paths $\tau \in Dom(\mathcal{T}_{\mathcal{V}}(u))$ and $\tau' \in Dom(\mathcal{T}_{\mathcal{V}'}(u))$ with the same sequences of actions, such that $\phi_{\mathcal{T}_{\mathcal{V}'}(u)} \wedge \mathcal{G}_{\tau} \wedge \mathcal{G}_{\tau'}$ is satisfiable, then $\mathcal{T}_{\mathcal{V}}(u)(\tau) = \mathcal{T}_{\mathcal{V}'}(u)(\tau')$.*
4. *$u \simeq_{\mathcal{T},\mathcal{V}'}^{\gamma} u'$ implies $u \simeq_{\mathcal{T},\mathcal{V}}^{\gamma} u'$.*

Intuitively, if $\mathcal{V} \subseteq \mathcal{V}'$, then the first condition states that the initial guards make more distinctions between data values when $\mathcal{V}$ increases. More precisely, each guard in $Initgs_{\mathcal{T}_{\mathcal{V}}(u)}(\alpha)$ is refined into a guard that is stronger under the associated path condition, and also includes its representative data value; more guards may have to be added in order to fill the induced gaps. The second condition states that more registers are needed to make these distinctions. The third condition states that a refinement must preserve the classification of all suffixes in $[\![\mathcal{V}]\!]$. An alternative statement of this condition is that if some suffix v satisfies both τ and τ' after u, where u satisfies $\phi_{\mathcal{T}_{\mathcal{V}'}(u)}$, then v must be classified in the same way by $\mathcal{T}_{\mathcal{V}}(u)$ and $\mathcal{T}_{\mathcal{V}'}(u)$. The fourth condition states that increasing $\mathcal{V}$ will induce a refinement of the approximated Nerode equivalence.

We now have sufficient machinery to generalize the construction of DFAs to construction of RAs. Let U be a set of data words, and let $\mathcal{V}$ be an abstract suffix with $\Sigma \subseteq Initacts(\mathcal{V})$.

– U is *closed* wrt. $\mathcal{V}$ if for each $u \in U$ and each $g \in Initgs_{\mathcal{T}_{\mathcal{V}}(u)}(\alpha)$ there is a $u' \in U$ such that $u\alpha(d_u^g) \simeq_{\mathcal{T},\mathcal{V}} u'$.

- U is *register-consistent* wrt. $\mathcal{V}$ if for each $u \in U$, each $\alpha \in \Sigma$, and each $g \in Initgs_{T_{\mathcal{V}}(u)}(\alpha)$ we have $mem_{T,\mathcal{V}}(u\alpha(\mathsf{d}_u^g)) \subseteq (mem_{T,\mathcal{V}}(u) \cup \{x_{|u|+1}\})$.
- U is *constraint-consistent* wrt. $\mathcal{V}$ if for each $u \in U$, each $\alpha \in \Sigma$, and each $g \in Initgs_{T_{\mathcal{V}}(u)}(\alpha)$ we have $(\phi_{T_{\mathcal{V}}(u)} \wedge g[x_{|u|+1}/p]) \implies \phi_{T_{\mathcal{V}}(u\alpha(\mathsf{d}_u^g))}$

Closedness ensures that each transition in the automaton to be constructed has a target location. Register-consistency states that the memorable parameters of $u\alpha(\mathsf{d}_u^g)$, possibly except $x_{|u|+1}$, are also memorable parameters of u. In the automaton to be constructed, it ensures that any data value from u that must be remembered after $u\alpha(\mathsf{d}_u^g)$ is also remembered after u. Constraint-consistency intuitively states that the initial guards of SDTs have stabilized, in the sense that the path constraints of form $\phi_{T_{\mathcal{V}}(u)}$ are kept invariant by each transition.

Definition 7 (Hypothesis automaton). *Let U be a set of words, which contains ϵ, and $\mathcal{V}$ an abstract suffix, with $\Sigma \subseteq Initacts(\mathcal{V})$, such that U is closed, register-, and constraint-consistent wrt. $\mathcal{V}$. Then the hypothesis automaton $\mathcal{H}(U,\mathcal{V})$ is the RA $\mathcal{H}(U,\mathcal{V}) = (L, l_0, \mathcal{X}, \Gamma, \lambda)$, where*

- *$L = U$ and $l_0 = \epsilon$,*
- *$\mathcal{X}$ maps each location $u \in U$ to $mem_{T,\mathcal{V}}(u)$ (thus $\mathcal{X}(l_0)$ is the empty set),*
- *$\lambda(u) = +$ if $u \in \mathcal{L}$, otherwise $\lambda(u) = -$, and*
- *for each $g \in Initgs_{T_{\mathcal{V}}(u)}(\alpha)$ there is a transition $\langle u, \alpha(p), g, \pi, u' \rangle$ in Γ, where*
  - *u' is the unique short prefix in U such that $u\alpha(\mathsf{d}_u^g) \simeq_{T,\mathcal{V}} u'$*
  - *$\pi : mem_{T,\mathcal{V}}(u') \to (mem_{T,\mathcal{V}}(u) \cup \{p\})$ is defined as $[x_{|u|+1} \mapsto p] \circ \gamma^{-1}$ for some γ with $u\alpha(\mathsf{d}_u^g) \simeq_{T,\mathcal{V}}^{\gamma} u'$*

Remark. In order to remove some arbitrariness in the last part of the construction, e.g., in order to construct canonical automata, we could let the set Γ contain a transition of form $\langle u, \alpha(p), g, \gamma^{-1}, u' \rangle$ for each γ such that $u\alpha(\mathsf{d}_u^g) \simeq_{T,\mathcal{V}}^{\gamma} u'$ (and not just for one of them).

We will now prove a theorem, which states that $\mathcal{H}(U,\mathcal{V})$ is consistent with the observations used to construct it, i.e., the set of words uv with $u \in U$ and $v \in [\![\mathcal{V}]\!]$. This will generalize the corresponding property for DFAs (e.g., [Ang87, Lemma 3]), stating that if U is prefix-closed and V is suffix closed, then $\mathcal{H}(U,V)$ correctly classifies all words in UV. The property of prefix-closedness is generalized as follows. We say that a set U of data words is $\mathcal{V}$-*induced* if whenever $u\alpha(d) \in U$ then $u \in U$ and $d = \mathsf{d}_u^g$ for some $g \in Initgs_{T_{\mathcal{V}}(u)}(\alpha)$.

Theorem 1. *Let T be a monotone tree oracle which respects $\mathcal{L}$. Let $\mathcal{V}$ be a suffix-closed abstract suffix with $\alpha^{-1}\mathcal{V} \neq \emptyset$ for each $\alpha \in \Sigma$, and U be a $\mathcal{V}$-induced set of words. Then $\mathcal{H}(U,\mathcal{V})$ correctly classifies all words uv with $u \in U$ and $v \in [\![\mathcal{V}]\!]$.*

Proof. The proof follows a similar pattern as the corresponding proof for the DFA case (see, e.g., [Ang87, Lemma 3]).

We first prove that for all $u \in U$, the hypothesis $\mathcal{H}(U,\mathcal{V})$ can process u to reach the state $\langle u, \mu_u|_{\mathcal{X}(u)} \rangle$, using induction on u (we let $\mu|_{\mathcal{X}}$ denote the

restriction of valuation μ to the set $\mathcal{X}$ of registers). For $u = \epsilon$, this follows from
$\mathcal{H}(U, \mathcal{V})(\epsilon) = l_0 = \epsilon$, and $\mathcal{X}(\epsilon) = \emptyset$. For the inductive step, assume $u\alpha(d) \in U$.
Since U is $\mathcal{V}$-induced we have $u \in U$ and $d = \mathsf{d}_u^g$ for some $g \in Initgs_{\mathcal{T}_\mathcal{V}(u)}(\alpha)$. By
the inductive hypothesis, $\mathcal{H}(U, \mathcal{V})$ can process u to reach the state $\langle u, \mu_u|_{\mathcal{X}(u)} \rangle$.
By the construction of $\mathcal{H}(U, \mathcal{V})$, there is a transition $\langle u, \alpha(p), g, \pi, u\alpha(d) \rangle$ in Γ,
where $\pi = [x_{|u|+1} \mapsto p]$. This implies that the transition $\langle u, \alpha(p), g, \pi, u\alpha(d) \rangle$
takes $\mathcal{H}(U, \mathcal{V})$ from the state $\langle u, \mu_u|_{\mathcal{X}(u)} \rangle$ to the state $\langle u, \mu_{u\alpha(d)}|_{\mathcal{X}(u\alpha(d))} \rangle$. It also
follows that $\mathcal{H}(U, \mathcal{V})$ accepts u iff $u \in \mathcal{L}$.

We next prove that $\mathcal{H}(U, \mathcal{V})$ correctly classifies all words uv with $u \in U$ and
$v \in \llbracket \mathcal{V} \rrbracket$. Assume wlog. that $uv \in \mathcal{L}$. Let $m = |v|$, let v_i be the suffix of v of
length $m - i$, and let t_i be the prefix of v of length i (i.e., v can be written as
$t_i v_i$ for $i = 0, \ldots, m$). Assume that $\mathcal{H}(U, \mathcal{V})$ processes v in a run

$$\langle u_0, \mu_0 \rangle \xrightarrow{\alpha_1(d_1)} \langle u_1, \mu_1 \rangle \quad \cdots \quad \langle u_{m-1}, \mu_{m-1} \rangle \xrightarrow{\alpha_m(d_m)} \langle u_m, \mu_m \rangle$$

where $\langle u_0, \mu_0 \rangle = \langle u, \mu_u|_{\mathcal{X}(u)} \rangle$. By the construction of $\mathcal{H}(U, \mathcal{V})$ and the semantics
of register automata, this means that for $i = 1, \ldots, m$ there is a transition
$\langle u_{i-1}, \alpha_i(p), g_i, \pi_i, u_i \rangle$ such that $\mu_{i-1} \models g_i[d_i/p]$ and $\pi_i = [x_{|u_{i-1}|+1} \mapsto p] \circ \gamma^{-1}$
for some γ with $u_{i-1}\alpha_i(\mathsf{d}_{u_{i-1}}^{g_i}) \simeq_{\mathcal{T},\mathcal{V}}^\gamma u_i$, and that $\mu_i = (\mu_{i-1} \circ [p \mapsto d_i]) \circ$
$[x_{|u_{i-1}|+1} \mapsto p] \circ \gamma^{-1} = \mu_{i-1} \circ [x_{|u_{i-1}|+1} \mapsto d_i] \circ \gamma^{-1}$.

We will now prove (by induction over i) that for $i = 0, \ldots, m$ we have (i)
$\mu_i \models \phi_{\mathcal{T}_\mathcal{V}(u_i)}$, and (ii) $\mathcal{T}_\mathcal{V}(u_i)(\tau) = +$ for each $\tau \in Dom(\mathcal{T}_\mathcal{V}(u_i))$, such that
v_i satisfies τ after ut_i. The base case is trivially true, since by construction,
$\mu_u \models \phi_{\mathcal{T}_\mathcal{V}(u)}$, and since $\mathcal{T}$ respects $\mathcal{L}$. For the inductive step, we assume as
inductive hypothesis that $\mu_{i-1} \models \phi_{\mathcal{T}_\mathcal{V}(u_{i-1})}$, and that $\mathcal{T}_\mathcal{V}(u_{i-1})(\tau) = +$ for
each $\tau \in Dom(\mathcal{T}_\mathcal{V}(u_{i-1}))$ that is satisfied by v_{i-1} after ut_{i-1}. We must prove
properties (i) and (ii) for i. For (i), from $\mu_{i-1} \models \phi_{\mathcal{T}_\mathcal{V}(u_{i-1})}$ (the inductive
hypothesis) and $\mu_{i-1} \models g_i[d_i/p]$, it follows by constraint consistency that
$(\mu_{i-1} \circ [x_{|u_{i-1}|+1} \mapsto d_i]) \models \phi_{\mathcal{T}_\mathcal{V}(u_{i-1}\alpha_i(\mathsf{d}_{u_{i-1}}^{g_i}))}$. From $u_{i-1}\alpha_i(\mathsf{d}_{u_{i-1}}^{g_i}) \simeq_{\mathcal{T},\mathcal{V}}^\gamma u_i$,
we then infer that $(\mu_{i-1} \circ [x_{|u_{i-1}|+1} \mapsto d_i] \circ \gamma^{-1}) \models \phi_{\mathcal{T}_\mathcal{V}(u_i)}$, i.e., that $\mu_i \models$
$\phi_{\mathcal{T}_\mathcal{V}(u_i)}$. For (ii), assume that $\tau' \in Dom(\mathcal{T}_\mathcal{V}(u_i))$ is satisfied by v_i after ut_i. We
first note that $\alpha_i \cdots \alpha_m \in \mathcal{V}$ since $\mathcal{V}$ is suffix-closed. Hence, by the assumption
that $\mathcal{T}_\mathcal{V}(u_{i-1})(\tau) = +$ for each $\tau \in Dom(\mathcal{T}_\mathcal{V}(u_{i-1}))$ that is satisfied by v_{i-1}
after ut_{i-1}, using Condition 1 on tree oracles (in Definition 4), we have that
$\mathcal{T}_{\alpha_i^{-1}\mathcal{V}}(u_i)(\tau'') = +$ for each $\tau'' \in Dom(\mathcal{T}_{\alpha_i^{-1}\mathcal{V}}(u_i))$ that is satisfied by v_i after
ut_i. Since $\alpha_i^{-1}\mathcal{V} \subseteq \mathcal{V}$ and since v_i satisfies both τ' and τ'' after ut_i, it means that
$\phi_{\mathcal{T}_\mathcal{V}(u_i)} \wedge \mathcal{G}_{\tau'} \wedge \mathcal{G}_{\tau''}$ is satisfiable. Hence, by Condition 3 in Definition 6 we have
$\mathcal{T}_\mathcal{V}(u_i)(\tau') = +$. This establishes the inductive step.

Letting i be m, it follows that $\mathcal{T}_\mathcal{V}(u_m)(\epsilon) = +$. Since u_m is the final location
in the run of $\mathcal{H}(U, \mathcal{V})$ over uv, this means that $\mathcal{H}(U, \mathcal{V})$ accepts uv. $\square$

5.4   Generalizing Active Automata Learning

The generalization of AAL for RAs will follow the same pattern of alternation
between hypothesis construction and hypothesis validation as for DFAs, during
which the sets U and $\mathcal{V}$ are increased.

During **hypothesis construction**, the tree oracle is used to construct SDTs of form $\mathcal{T}_{\mathcal{T},\mathcal{V}}(u)$, from which the approximated Nerode equivalence $\simeq_{\mathcal{T},\mathcal{V}}$ is constructed.

- Whenever the set U is not closed wrt. $\mathcal{V}$, then U is extended: if there is some $u \in U$, $\alpha \in \Sigma$, and $g \in Initgs_{\mathcal{T}_{\mathcal{V}}(u)}(\alpha)$, for which there is no u' with $u\alpha(\mathsf{d}_u^g) \simeq_{\mathcal{T},\mathcal{V}} u'$, then $u\alpha(\mathsf{d}_u^g)$ is added to U, triggering new membership queries.
- Whenever the set U is not register-consistent wrt. $\mathcal{V}$, then $\mathcal{V}$ is extended: if there is some $u \in U$, $\alpha \in \Sigma$, and $g \in Initgs_{\mathcal{T}_{\mathcal{V}}(u)}(\alpha)$, such that there is a x_i with $1 \le i \le |u|$ which is in $mem_{\mathcal{T},\mathcal{V}}(u\alpha(\mathsf{d}_u^g))$ but not in $mem_{\mathcal{T},\mathcal{V}}(u)$, then extend $\mathcal{V}$ with a symbolic suffix of form $\alpha\alpha_1 \ldots \alpha_m$ such that x_i occurs on some path of form $(\alpha_1, g_1) \cdots (\alpha_m, g_m)$ in $Dom(\mathcal{T}_{\mathcal{V}}(u\alpha(\mathsf{d}_u^g)))$.
- Whenever the set U is not constraint-consistent wrt. $\mathcal{V}$, then $\mathcal{V}$ is extended: if there is some $u \in U$ and $\alpha \in \Sigma$, such that there is a $g \in Initgs_{\mathcal{T}_{\mathcal{V}}(u)}(\alpha)$ with $(\phi_{\mathcal{T}_{\mathcal{V}}(u)} \wedge g[x_{|u|+1}/p]) \not\Rightarrow \phi_{\mathcal{T}_{\mathcal{V}}(u\alpha(\mathsf{d}_u^g))}$, then extend $\mathcal{V}$ with the set of symbolic suffixes of form $\alpha\alpha_1 \ldots \alpha_n$ with $\alpha_1 \ldots \alpha_n \in \mathcal{V}$.

This process of extending U and $\mathcal{V}$ is continued until U is closed, register consistent, and constraint consistent wrt. $\mathcal{V}$.

When U is closed, register consistent, and constraint consistent wrt. $\mathcal{V}$, **hypothesis validation** submits the hypothesis $\mathcal{H}(U, \mathcal{V})$ in an equivalence query. If the query returns "yes", then the learning is completed, implying that $\mathcal{H}(U, \mathcal{V})$ accepts $\mathcal{L}$. If the query returns a counterexample word w, this is used to extend $\mathcal{V}$, as follows. Let $w = \alpha_1(d_1) \cdots \alpha_n(d_n)$. Assume wlog. that $\mathcal{H}(U, \mathcal{V})$ accepts w but $w \notin \mathcal{L}$. Thus there is an initialized run of $\mathcal{H}(U, \mathcal{V})$ over w

$$\langle u_0, \mu_0 \rangle \xrightarrow{\alpha_1(d_1)} \langle u_1, \mu_1 \rangle \quad \cdots \quad \langle u_{n-1}, \mu_{n-1} \rangle \xrightarrow{\alpha_n(d_n)} \langle u_n, \mu_n \rangle$$

where $\langle u_0, \mu_0 \rangle$ is the initial state and $\lambda(u_n) = +$. For each $i = 1, \ldots, n$, the step $\langle u_{i-1}, \mu_{i-1} \rangle \xrightarrow{\alpha_i(d_i)} \langle u_i, \mu_i \rangle$ is derived from a transition $\langle u_{i-1}, \alpha_i(p), g_i, \pi_i, u_i \rangle$ with $\mu_{i-1} \models g_i[d_i/p]$, which is added to $\mathcal{H}(U, \mathcal{V})$ based on the properties that $u_{i-1}\alpha_i(\mathsf{d}_{u_{i-1}}^{g_i}) \simeq_{\mathcal{T},\mathcal{V}}^{\gamma} u_i$ for some γ, and where $\pi_i = [x_{|u|+1} \mapsto p] \circ \gamma^{-1}$ and $\mu_i = \mu_{i-1} \circ [x_{|u|+1} \mapsto d_i] \circ \gamma^{-1}$. For $i = 1, \ldots, n$, let $\mathcal{V}_i$ be the suffix-closure of $\mathcal{V} \cup \{\alpha_{i+1} \cdots \alpha_n\}$. By generalizing from the DFA case, we claim that if w is a counterexample then there must be an i among $0, \ldots, n$ such that either

1. $u_{i-1}\alpha_i(\mathsf{d}_{u_{i-1}}^{g_i}) \not\simeq_{\mathcal{T},\mathcal{V}_i}^{\gamma_i} u_i$, or
2. case 1 does not apply, but the guard in $Initgs_{\mathcal{T}_{\mathcal{V}_{i-1}}(u_{i-1})}(\alpha_i)$ which has $\mathsf{d}_{u_{i-1}}^{g_i}$ as representative value is not implied by g_i; in this case, the symbolic suffix $\mathcal{V}_{i-1}$ shows that the guard g_i can be strengthened.

These two cases are illustrated in Fig. 9. To prove that the existence of such an i is guaranteed, we assume (to get a contradiction) that $u_{i-1}\alpha_i(\mathsf{d}_{u_{i-1}}^{g_i}) \simeq_{\mathcal{T},\mathcal{V}_i}^{\gamma} u_i$, and that g_i is also a guard in $Initgs_{\mathcal{T}_{\mathcal{V}_i}(u_{i-1})}(\alpha_i)$ for $i = 1, \ldots, n$. We can then show that w would not be a counterexample, using a similar technique as in

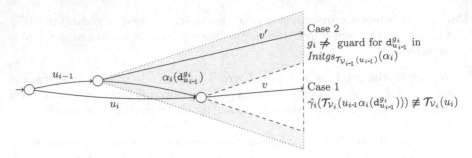

Fig. 9. Counterexamples for discussion

the proof of Theorem 1. Let v_i be the suffix of length $n - i$ of w, and let w_i be the prefix of w of length i. We shall establish, by induction over i, that for $i = 0, \ldots, n$ we have (i) $\mu_i \models \phi_{\mathcal{T}_{\mathcal{V}_i}(u_i)}$, and (ii) $\mathcal{T}_{\mathcal{V}_i}(u_i)(\tau) = -$ for each $\tau \in Dom(\mathcal{T}_{\mathcal{V}_i}(u_i))$, such that v_i satisfies τ after w_i. The base case is trivially true, since by construction, $\phi_{\mathcal{T}_{\mathcal{V}_0}(\epsilon)}$ is *true*, and since $\mathcal{T}$ respects $\mathcal{L}$. For the inductive step, we assume as inductive hypothesis that $\mu_{i-1} \models \phi_{\mathcal{T}_{\mathcal{V}_{i-1}}(u_{i-1})}$, and that $\mathcal{T}_{\mathcal{V}_{i-i}}(u_{i-1})(\tau) = -$ for each $\tau \in Dom(\mathcal{T}_{\mathcal{V}_{i-1}}(u_{i-1}))$ that is satisfied by v_{i-1} after w_{i-1}. We must prove properties (i) and (ii) for i. For (i), it follows by constraint consistency that $\mu_i \models \phi_{\mathcal{T}_{\mathcal{V}}(u_i)}$. It also follows by Condition 1 in Definition 4 on tree oracles that $\mu_i \models \phi_{\mathcal{T}_{\{\alpha_{i+1}\cdots\alpha_n\}}(u_i)}$. By Condition 2 of Definition 4, it follows that $\mu_i \models \phi_{\mathcal{T}_{\mathcal{V}_i}(u_i)}$. For (ii), assume that $\tau' \in Dom(\mathcal{T}_{\mathcal{V}_i}(u_i))$ is satisfied by v_i after w_i. We note that $\alpha_{i+1}\cdots\alpha_n \in \mathcal{V}_i$. Hence, by Condition 1 on tree oracles (in Definition 4), we have that $\mathcal{T}_{\alpha_i^{-1}(\mathcal{V}_{i-1})}(u_i)(\tau') = -$ for each $\tau'' \in Dom(\mathcal{T}_{\alpha_i^{-1}(\mathcal{V}_{i-1})}(u_i))$ that is satisfied by v_i after w_i. Since v_i satisfies both τ' and τ'' after w_i, it means that $\phi_{\mathcal{T}_{\mathcal{V}_i}(u_i)} \wedge \mathcal{G}_{\tau'} \wedge \mathcal{G}_{\tau''}$ is satisfiable. Hence, by Condition 3 in Definition 6 we have $\mathcal{T}_{\mathcal{V}_i}(u_i)(\tau') = -$. This establishes the inductive step. By specializing to $i = n$, we establish that w is rejected by $\mathcal{H}(U, \mathcal{V})$, which contradicts the assumption that w is a counterexample.

Thus, a value of i can be obtained by invoking the tree oracle for abstract suffixes of form $\mathcal{V}_i$. We should let i be as large as possible, since adding a shorter symbolic suffix to $\mathcal{V}$ induces fewer membership queries. The subsequently generated hypothesis automaton is guaranteed to refine the current one. In Case 1, some equivalence between prefixes is refuted, inducing either a new location or a removed transition (in case there are several transitions differing only in the remapping between two locations) In Case 2, some guard will be refined.

Starting from some initial approximations, e.g., $U = \{\epsilon\}$ and $\mathcal{V} = \Sigma$, the sets U and $\mathcal{V}$ are successively extended, until an equivalence query returns "yes". In the next section, we will give conditions, corresponding to regularity in the DFA case, under which termination is guaranteed.

6   Canonical Automata Construction

Nerode Equivalence. If our tree oracle is monotone, then the equivalence $\simeq$ can be used to define a Nerode Equivalence. Let $u \equiv_T^\gamma u'$ denote that $u \simeq_{T,\mathcal{V}}^\gamma u'$ for all abstract suffixes $\mathcal{V}$. Let $u \equiv_T u'$ denote that $u \equiv_T^\gamma u'$ for some γ.

Define a data language $\mathcal{L}$ to be *regular* with respect to T if $\equiv_T$ has finite index. Note that the regularity of $\mathcal{L}$ is relative to the particular tree oracle T that is used. Of course, it is assumed that T respects $\mathcal{L}$. We can now state and prove an analogue of the classical Myhill-Nerode theorem.

Theorem 2 (Myhill-Nerode).   *Let $\mathcal{L}$ be a data language, and let T be a monotone tree oracle which respects $\mathcal{L}$. If $\mathcal{L}$ is regular wrt. T, then there is a RA that accepts $\mathcal{L}$.*

Proof. Choose a $\mathcal{V}$ such that $\simeq_{T,\mathcal{V}}$ is maximally refined, such that $mem_{T,\mathcal{V}}(u)$, and such that $T_\mathcal{V}(u)$ is maximally refined for all u. Such a $\mathcal{V}$ must exist by standard finiteness arguments.

In the proof, we will first construct an RA $\mathcal{A}$, and thereafter establish that $\mathcal{A}$ accepts $\mathcal{L}$. First, we define the set L of locations with transitions between them, using the following spanning tree construction. The spanning tree construction incrementally constructs a set L of locations, each of which can be either marked or unmarked. Initially, L contains only the single unmarked location l_ϵ, which is also the initial location. The set L is then extended and modified as follows: As long as L contains unmarked locations, select an unmarked $l_u \in L$ and do:

1. for each $\alpha \in \Sigma$ and each $g \in Initgs_{T_{(\alpha^{-1}\mathcal{V})}(u)}(\alpha)$:
   - if there is already some $l_{u'}$ in L with $u\alpha(\mathrm{d}_u^g) \simeq_{T,\mathcal{V}}^\gamma u'$ for some γ, then add $\langle l_u, \alpha(p), g, \pi, l_{u'} \rangle$ to Γ, where $\pi : mem_{T,\mathcal{V}}(u') \to (mem_{T,\mathcal{V}}(u) \cup \{p\})$ is defined as $\pi = [x_{|u|+1} \mapsto p] \circ \gamma^{-1}$,
   - otherwise add $l_{u\alpha(\mathrm{d}_u^g)}$ (unmarked) to L, and add $\langle l_u, \alpha(p), g, \pi, l_{u\alpha(\mathrm{d}_u^g)} \rangle$ to Γ, where $\pi = [x_{|u|+1} \mapsto p] \circ Id$,
2. mark l_u;

When this procedure has finished, and L contains only marked locations, it is taken as the set of locations of $\mathcal{A}$. The procedure is guaranteed to terminate since there is a finite number of equivalence classes of $\simeq_{T,\mathcal{V}}$. Note that in general, L may contain fewer locations than there are equivalence classes of $\simeq_{T,\mathcal{V}}$, since not all equivalence classes need to have their own location. This can happen if some equivalence classes are "subsumed" by other ones. For instance, in the theory of equality, assume that $\mathcal{L}$ accepts only words of form $\alpha(d_1)\alpha(d_2)\alpha(d_3)\alpha(d_4)$ with $d_1 = d_3$ and $d_2 = d_4$. Then the equivalence class $u = \alpha(1)\alpha(2)$ is sufficient to cover the behavior for all prefixes of length 2. In particular, u subsumes the behavior of the prefix $u(1)u(1)$, which is not equivalent to u.

We now construct $\mathcal{A}$ as $\mathcal{H}(L, \mathcal{V})$. We must only check that $\mathcal{A}$ indeed accepts $\mathcal{L}$. This follows from Theorem 1, and the argument given when describing the hypothesis validation phase above: if there is a word w which is incorrectly classified by $\mathcal{A}$, then we can add a suffix of $Acts(w)$ to $\mathcal{V}$ and refine the equivalence or some guard, which contradicts that $\simeq_{\mathcal{T},\mathcal{V}}$ is maximally refined and that guards are maximally refined.   □

By similar arguments as in the proof of the preceding theorem, we can also prove an analogous theorem for the AAL procedure.

Theorem 3 (Termination of AAL). *Let $\mathcal{L}$ be a data language, and let $\mathcal{T}$ be a monotone tree oracle which respects $\mathcal{L}$. If $\mathcal{L}$ is regular wrt. $\mathcal{T}$, then the active automata learning algorithm of Sect. 5.4 will terminate and return a RA that accepts $\mathcal{L}$.*

Proof. The proof relies on using the RA constructed by Theorem 3 as bound on the monotonically increasing sets of locations, guards, and registers.   □

7   Conclusions

We have presented a condensed illustration and account of a symbolic active learning algorithm for generating EFSM models of black-box components using dynamic analysis. The algorithm, outlined in Sect. 5.4, shows the basic principles of the SL^* algorithm of our previous work [CHJS16].

We have implemented this approach in the tool RA-lib [CHJ15a]. Our preliminary implementation demonstrates that the approach can infer protocols comprising sequence numbers, time stamps, and variables that are manipulated using simple arithmetic operations or compared for inequality even in a black-box scenario.

We hope that the presentation of principles of SL^* in this paper can inspire further techniques for model learning.

Acknowledgment. This work was supported in part by the European FP7 project CONNECT (IST 231167), and by the Swedish Research Council as part of the UPMARC centre of excellence.

References

[ABL02]   Ammons, G., Bodik, R., Larus, J.: Mining specifications. In: Proceedings of 29th ACM Symposium on Principles of Programming Languages, pp. 4–16. ACM (2002)

[ACMN05] Alur, R., Cerný, P., Madhusudan, P., Nam, W.: Synthesis of interface specifications for Java classes. In: Proceedings of 32th ACM Symposium on Principles of Programming Languages, pp. 98–109. ACM (2005)

[AdRP13] Aarts, F., de Ruiter, J., Poll, E.: Formal models of bank cards for free. In: Proceedings of ICSTW 2013, pp. 461–468. IEEE (2013)

[AHK+12] Aarts, F., Heidarian, F., Kuppens, H., Olsen, P., Vaandrager, F.: Automata learning through counterexample guided abstraction refinement. In: Giannakopoulou, D., Méry, D. (eds.) FM 2012. LNCS, vol. 7436, pp. 10–27. Springer, Heidelberg (2012). https://doi.org/10.1007/978-3-642-32759-9_4

[AJUV15] Aarts, F., Jonsson, B., Uijen, J., Vaandrager, F.: Generating models of infinite-state communication protocols using regular inference with abstraction. Formal Methods Syst. Des. **46**, 1–41 (2015)

[AKT+12] Aarts, F., Kuppens, H., Tretmans, J., Vaandrager, F.W., Verwer, S.: Learning and testing the bounded retransmission protocol. J. Mach. Learn. Res. - Proc. Track **21**, 4–18 (2012)

[Ang87] Angluin, D.: Learning regular sets from queries and counterexamples. Inf. Comput. **75**(2), 87–106 (1987)

[ASV10] Aarts, F., Schmaltz, J., Vaandrager, F.: Inference and abstraction of the biometric passport. In: Margaria, T., Steffen, B. (eds.) ISoLA 2010 Part I. LNCS, vol. 6415, pp. 673–686. Springer, Heidelberg (2010). https://doi.org/10.1007/978-3-642-16558-0_54

[BHLM13] Bollig, B., Habermehl, P., Leucker, M., Monmege, B.: A fresh approach to learning register automata. In: Béal, M.-P., Carton, O. (eds.) DLT 2013. LNCS, vol. 7907, pp. 118–130. Springer, Heidelberg (2013). https://doi.org/10.1007/978-3-642-38771-5_12

[BJR08] Berg, T., Jonsson, B., Raffelt, H.: Regular inference for state machines using domains with equality tests. In: Fiadeiro, J.L., Inverardi, P. (eds.) FASE 2008. LNCS, vol. 4961, pp. 317–331. Springer, Heidelberg (2008). https://doi.org/10.1007/978-3-540-78743-3_24

[BPT10] Bertoli, P., Pistore, M., Traverso, P.: Automated composition of web services via planning in asynchronous domains. Artif. Intell. **174**(3–4), 316–361 (2010)

[CHJ15a] Cassel, S., Howar, F., Jonsson, B.: RALib: a LearnLib extension for inferring EFSMs. In: DIFTS 2015 (2015). http://www.faculty.ece.vt.edu/chaowang/difts2015/papers/paper_5.pdf

[CHJ+15b] Cassel, S., Howar, F., Jonsson, B., Merten, M., Steffen, B.: A succinct canonical register automaton model. J. Log. Algebr. Meth. Program. **84**(1), 54–66 (2015)

[CHJS16] Cassel, S., Howar, F., Jonsson, B., Steffen, B.: Active learning for extended finite state machines. Formal Asp. Comput. **28**(2), 233–263 (2016)

[DD17] Drews, S., D'Antoni, L.: Learning symbolic automata. In: Legay, A., Margaria, T. (eds.) TACAS 2017 Part I. LNCS, vol. 10205, pp. 173–189. Springer, Heidelberg (2017). https://doi.org/10.1007/978-3-662-54577-5_10

[EPG+07] Ernst, M.D., et al.: The Daikon system for dynamic detection of likely invariants. Sci. Comput. Program. **69**(1–3), 35–45 (2007)

[FH17] Fiterău-Broştean, P., Howar, F.: Learning-based testing the sliding window behavior of TCP implementations. In: Petrucci, L., Seceleanu, C., Cavalcanti, A. (eds.) FMICS/AVoCS -2017. LNCS, vol. 10471, pp. 185–200. Springer, Cham (2017). https://doi.org/10.1007/978-3-319-67113-0_12

[GHP02] Gery, E., Harel, D., Palachi, E.: Rhapsody: a complete life-cycle model-based development system. In: Butler, M., Petre, L., Sere, K. (eds.) IFM 2002. LNCS, vol. 2335, pp. 1–10. Springer, Heidelberg (2002). https://doi.org/10.1007/3-540-47884-1_1

[GIO12] Groz, R., Irfan, M.-N., Oriat, C.: Algorithmic improvements on regular inference of software models and perspectives for security testing. In: Margaria, T., Steffen, B. (eds.) ISoLA 2012 Part I. LNCS, vol. 7609, pp. 444–457. Springer, Heidelberg (2012). https://doi.org/10.1007/978-3-642-34026-0_33

[GRR12]   Giannakopoulou, D., Rakamarić, Z., Raman, V.: Symbolic learning of component interfaces. In: Miné, A., Schmidt, D. (eds.) SAS 2012. LNCS, vol. 7460, pp. 248–264. Springer, Heidelberg (2012). https://doi.org/10.1007/978-3-642-33125-1_18

[HHNS02] Hagerer, A., Hungar, H., Niese, O., Steffen, B.: Model generation by moderated regular extrapolation. In: Kutsche, R.-D., Weber, H. (eds.) FASE 2002. LNCS, vol. 2306, pp. 80–95. Springer, Heidelberg (2002). https://doi.org/10.1007/3-540-45923-5_6

[HIS+12] Howar, F., Isberner, M., Steffen, B., Bauer, O., Jonsson, B.: Inferring semantic interfaces of data structures. In: Margaria, T., Steffen, B. (eds.) ISoLA 2012 Part I. LNCS, vol. 7609, pp. 554–571. Springer, Heidelberg (2012). https://doi.org/10.1007/978-3-642-34026-0_41

[HJM05]   Henzinger, T.A., Jhala, R., Majumdar, R.: Permissive interfaces. In: ESEC/SIGSOFT FSE, pp. 31–40 (2005)

[HNS93]   Hungar, H., Niese, O., Steffen, B.: Domain-specific optimization in automata learning. In: Hunt, W.A., Somenzi, F. (eds.) CAV 2003. LNCS, vol. 2725, pp. 315–327. Springer, Heidelberg (2003). https://doi.org/10.1007/978-3-540-45069-6_31

[HSJC12] Howar, F., Steffen, B., Jonsson, B., Cassel, S.: Inferring canonical register automata. In: Kuncak, V., Rybalchenko, A. (eds.) VMCAI 2012. LNCS, vol. 7148, pp. 251–266. Springer, Heidelberg (2012). https://doi.org/10.1007/978-3-642-27940-9_17

[HSM11]   Howar, F., Steffen, B., Merten, M.: Automata learning with automated alphabet abstraction refinement. In: Jhala, R., Schmidt, D. (eds.) VMCAI 2011. LNCS, vol. 6538, pp. 263–277. Springer, Heidelberg (2011). https://doi.org/10.1007/978-3-642-18275-4_19

[Hui07]   Huima, A.: Implementing Conformiq Qtronic. In: Petrenko, A., Veanes, M., Tretmans, J., Grieskamp, W. (eds.) FATES/TestCom -2007. LNCS, vol. 4581, pp. 1–12. Springer, Heidelberg (2007). https://doi.org/10.1007/978-3-540-73066-8_1

[IHS14]   Isberner, M., Howar, F., Steffen, B.: Learning register automata: from languages to program structures. Mach. Learn. 96(1–2), 65–98 (2014)

[IHS15]   Isberner, M., Howar, F., Steffen, B.: The open-source LearnLib - a framework for active automata learning. In: Kroening, D., Păsăreanu, C.S. (eds.) CAV 2015. LNCS, vol. 9206, pp. 487–495. Springer, Cham (2015). https://doi.org/10.1007/978-3-319-21690-4_32

[JM09]   Jhala, R., Majumdar, R.: Software model checking. ACM Comput. Surv. 41(4), 1–54 (2009)

[LMP08]   Lorenzoli, D., Mariani, L., Pezzè, M.: Automatic generation of software behavioral models. In: ICSE, pp. 501–510 (2008)

[MM14]   Maler, O., Mens, I.-E.: Learning regular languages over large alphabets. In: Ábrahám, E., Havelund, K. (eds.) TACAS 2014. LNCS, vol. 8413, pp. 485–499. Springer, Heidelberg (2014). https://doi.org/10.1007/978-3-642-54862-8_41

[RS93]   Rivest, R.L., Schapire, R.E.: Inference of finite automata using homing sequences. Inf. Comput. 103(2), 299–347 (1993)

[SL07]   Shu, G., Lee, D.: Testing security properties of protocol implementations - a machine learning based approach. In: Proceedings of ICDCS 2007. IEEE Computer Society (2007)

[WBDP10] Walkinshaw, N., Bogdanov, K., Derrick, J., Paris, J.: Increasing functional coverage by inductive testing: a case study. In: Petrenko, A., Simão, A., Maldonado, J.C. (eds.) ICTSS 2010. LNCS, vol. 6435, pp. 126–141. Springer, Heidelberg (2010). https://doi.org/10.1007/978-3-642-16573-3_10

[WTD16] Walkinshaw, N., Taylor, R., Derrick, J.: Inferring extended finite state machine models from software executions. Empir. Softw. Eng. **21**(3), 811–853 (2016)

[XSL+13] Xiao, H., Sun, J., Liu, Y., Lin, S.-W., Sun, C.: TzuYu: learning stateful typestates. In: ASE, pp. 432–442. IEEE (2013)

Inferring FSM Models of Systems
Without Reset

Roland Groz[1(✉)], Adenilso Simao[2], Alexandre Petrenko[3], and Catherine Oriat[1]

[1] LIG, Computer Science Lab, Univ. Grenoble Alpes, Grenoble, France
{roland.groz,catherine.oriat}@imag.fr
[2] Universidade de São Paulo, São Carlos, Brazil
adenilso@icmc.usp.br
[3] CRIM, Montreal, Canada
Alexandre.Petrenko@crim.ca

Abstract. Active inference algorithms that are used to extract behavioural models of software systems usually assume that the System Under Inference (SUI) can be reset. Two approaches have been proposed to infer systems that cannot be reset. Rivest and Schapire proposed an adaptation of the L^* algorithm that relies on having a homing sequence for the SUI. We detail here another approach that is based on characterization sequences. More precisely, we assume classical testing hypotheses, namely that we are given a bound n on the number of states and a set W of characterizing sequences to distinguish states. Contrary to L^*, it does not require an external oracle to decide on equivalence. The length of the test sequence is polynomial in n and the exponent depends on the cardinality $|W|$ of the characterization set. For systems where resetting is impossible or expensive, this approach can be a viable alternative to classical learning methods.

1 Introduction

Query learning has received growing interest for software engineering. It is used to retrieve finite state models of software systems or components. These models can be used for various purposes: documentation as in "specification mining", verification with model checkers [14], test generation using model-based testing techniques [12,13], integration testing for modular and distributed systems [5,18], security analysis [3] etc. In this context, it makes sense to use active learning inference algorithms, because in many cases we can query the software system, by sending inputs to observe its outputs. The corresponding automata models are Mealy machines, often called FSM (Finite State Machines).

Most inference algorithms and techniques assume that the system can be reset, so that observed sequences can be rooted to a common initial state. However, in many black box contexts, typically when a system is queried over a network, the SUI cannot be reset. It may also be the case that a system could be reset, but it could take a very long time to do so. As a typical example, interacting over a local network for querying a web system packaged in a

© Springer International Publishing AG, part of Springer Nature 2018
A. Bennaceur et al. (Eds.): ML for Dynamic Software Analysis, LNCS 11026, pp. 178–201, 2018.
https://doi.org/10.1007/978-3-319-96562-8_7

virtual machine takes around a millisecond for a single input/output observation, whereas resetting a virtual machine takes typically almost over a minute, so the reset typically costs 10^5 more time than an I/O observation.[1]

The absence of a (reliable) reset is problematic for inference. When a system cannot be reset, only a single sequence can be observed, and it is more difficult to assign subsequences to inferred states of the system.

We assume that the SUI can be modelled, at some level of abstraction on its inputs and outputs, as a Finite State Machine. FSM-based testing theory has shown that an FSM can be identified, i.e., the SUI can be tested to be proven equivalent to it, with the help of state identifying (separating) sequences, constituting, e.g., a characterization set (W-set [20]) of input sequences.

The key difference between inference and testing is that classical testing methods start from a known specification machine, and just check whether the black box is equivalent (or conformant) to this specification. Therefore, those methods heavily rely on transfer sequences that make it possible to test a new state through a path known to transfer to the right state in the specification. In our context, since no specification is available, we cannot rely on known transfer sequences. Although the absence of reset had already been addressed by Hennie [9], the task is much harder in our context since we cannot return to a known state to compare the responses to input sequences of the W-set. Generating a checking sequence (without reset) from a known specification FSM with a characterization set is very costly, due to the fact that the sequences of this set have to be applied a number of times which is proportional to some exponential on the number of states in the specification [1]. We cannot expect better for infering a system without reset.

Rivest and Schapire [16] have addressed the problem of inferring without a reset by using a variant of the L^* algorithm and the assumption that a homing sequence was given. A homing sequence is a fixed input sequence such that the output observed completely determines the state reached at the end of the sequence (see [11]). We have proposed a new approach [8] that, instead of relying on a homing sequence, uses two classical assumptions from FSM-based testing. First, we assume a bound on the number of states of the SUI. Second, instead of a homing sequence, we start from a given characterization set The advantage as compared to Rivest and Schapire's approach is that this algorithm no longer requires an oracle. Implementing an oracle that can answer equivalence queries cannot be done for an unknown software system, so it is usually approximated. Therefore, being able to avoid an oracle or a counterexample generation process is a definite advantage. However, there is a difficulty: since the W-set could contain several sequences, it implies that for a system which cannot be reset, the algorithm must guarantee to return to a state where a previous sequence was applied. This is achieved by a recursive procedure called a localizer.

---

[1] The round trip time for a local network is usually between 0.1 and 1 ms. Resetting a virtual machine may depend on the type of virtualization and the speed of the underlying processor, but starting a Linux or Windows machine usually takes several tens of seconds.

The absence of an oracle is compensated by the fact that we assume we know a bound on the number of states as well as a characterization set (although the latter is a weaker compensation for a homing sequence). Such knowledge could be derived for instance from previous versions of the SUI (a frequent case is to use inference to get uptodate models of evolving systems).

In both approaches, Rivest and Schapire's and ours, there are strong assumptions that somehow contradict the idea that the SUI is a black box. Rivest and Schapire base inference on L^*, where an oracle is able to answer equivalence queries, i.e. telling whether the conjecture is equivalent to the SUI. Besides it assumes that this oracle can provide a counterexample that points to a difference between the conjecture and the SUI. It also assumes knowledge of a homing sequence for the SUI. Our assumptions (known bound on number of states and characterization set) are weaker than Rivest and Schapire's, but still questionable for a SUI that was supposed to be a black box.

Actually, the basic algorithms proposed by both approaches are proved to converge to a correct (equivalent) model in a polynomial number of queries under those assumptions. But it is possible to relax the assumptions. Rivest and Schapire [16] propose a probabilistic extension of the method that can be proved to converge in the limit. The probabilistic extension infers, with probability $1 - \delta$, a correct model of the SUI in polynomial number of queries in the size of the FSM, the length of the longest counterexample and $log(1/\delta)$. In [8], we do not develop a probabilistic approach, but give indications on how to deal with incorrect bounds or characterizing set. In both cases, the assumptions make it possible to propose core algorithms, from which extensions of the algorithms and heuristics can converge towards more precise models and learn in the limit.

In this paper, we compare the two algorithms: the $W - set$ based algorithm [8], and an implementation of Rivest and Schapire's approach for FSM. The rest of this paper is organized as follows. In Sect. 2, we give the formal notations and definitions used in the paper to describe the algorithms. In Sect. 3, we present a version of Rivest and Schapire's algorithm adapted to Mealy machines. In Sect. 4, we recall the algorithm for the general case defined in [8]. Section 5 develops two examples to show how the algorithm works. The following Sect. 6 provides preliminary statistical results on various kinds of machines. Finally, Sect. 7 concludes.

2   Definitions

In this section, we recall definitions for the type of automata we are considering here, namely Mealy machines, which we shall call indifferently Finite State Machines (FSMs for short).

A Finite State Machine is a complete deterministic Mealy machine. Formally, it is a 6-tuple $M = (Q, q_0, I, O, \delta, \lambda)$ where

- Q is a finite set of states with the initial state q_0,
- I is a finite set of inputs (the input alphabet), and O a finite set of outputs,

- $\delta : Q \times I \to Q$ is the transition mapping, and
- $\lambda : Q \times I \to O$ is the output mapping.

Notations δ and λ are lifted to sequences: $\delta(q, \epsilon) = q$, $\lambda(q, \epsilon) = \epsilon$, where ϵ is the empty sequence; and for $q \in Q$, $\alpha \in I^*$, $x \in I$, we have $\delta(q, \alpha x) = \delta(\delta(q, \alpha), x)$ and $\lambda(q, \alpha x) = \lambda(q, \alpha)\lambda(\delta(q, \alpha), x)$.

For inference without reset, we will assume that the FSM to be inferred is *strongly connected*, i.e. for all pairs of states (q, q') there exists an input sequence $\alpha \in I^*$ such that $\delta(q, \alpha) = q'$.

A homing sequence $h \in I^*$ for M is an input sequence such that the state reached by executing h from any state is uniquely determined by the output produced. h is a homing sequence iff

$$\forall q_1 \in Q, \forall q_2 \in Q[\lambda(q_1, h) = \lambda(q_2, h) \implies \delta(q_1, h) = \delta(q_2, h)].$$

Two states $q, q' \in Q$ are *distinguishable* by $\gamma \in I^*$ if $\lambda(q, \gamma) \neq \lambda(q', \gamma)$. γ is said to be a *separating* sequence. Two states are distinguishable by a set $H \subset I^*$ if there exists $\gamma \in H$ that distinguishes them. Otherwise the two states will be said *H-equivalent*. An FSM is *minimal* if all states are pairwise distinguishable. A set W of sequences of inputs (therefore conventionaly called a W-set, following [20]) is a *characterization set* for an FSM M if each pair of states is distinguishable by W.

A sequence of input/output pairs $\alpha \in (IO)^*$ is called a *trace*. Given a trace $\omega = \alpha\beta$ composed of a prefix α and suffix β, we will write $\alpha = \omega \setminus \beta$ and $\alpha \leq \omega$. $\omega \downarrow I$ will denote the projection of the trace on its input set, that is the sequence obtained by deleting all outputs from the trace. Given a machine $M = (Q, q_0, I, O, \delta, \lambda)$ and its current state q defined by the context, $tr(\alpha)$ will denote the trace from q such that $tr(\alpha) \downarrow I = \alpha$ and $tr(\alpha) \downarrow O = \lambda(q, \alpha)$. For a set of input sequences H, $Tr(H) = \{tr(h) \mid h \in H\}$. We overload the notation by defining $Tr(q)$ as the set of all traces of M from state q, i.e. $Tr(q) = \{tr(\alpha) \mid \alpha \in I^*\}$; and $Tr(M) = Tr(q_0)$. Finally, we define machine equivalence: $M \approx M'$ iff $Tr(M) = Tr(M')$.

Given a characterization set W, rather than naming or numbering states, we may refer to a state by its *state characterization* $Tr(W)$. A state characterization ϕ is actually a mapping from W to $(IO)^*$, such that $\phi(w) = tr(w)$. The set of all mappings $\Phi = \{\phi_1, ..., \phi_m\}$ corresponds to the set of states Q of the machine. Namely, for $\phi \in \Phi$ and $q \in Q$, we write $\phi \leftrightarrow q$ if $\forall w \in W, \phi(w) \downarrow O = \lambda(q, w)$. Thus, while inferring an unknown FSM with characterization set W, we will consider the set of mappings Φ as its set of states.

A checking sequence is defined w.r.t. a fault domain $\mathcal{F}$, which corresponds to the set of all possible correct or faulty implementations. A typical fault domain could be the set of all FSM with a number of states bounded by some n. Given an FSM M, a trace $\mathcal{T}$ is a *checking sequence* for M in $\mathcal{F}$ iff $\forall M' \in \mathcal{F}, \mathcal{T} \in Tr(M') \Leftrightarrow M' \approx M$. Conformance test generation consists in producing a checking sequence for a given reference machine (the specification), so that any implementation from $\mathcal{F}$ can be tested for conformance with the specification. A checking sequence is a perfect test that identifies a correct machine and detects all faulty implementations.

3   Rivest and Schapire's Algorithm

3.1   Approach and Algorithm

Rivest and Schapire [16] were the first to propose a query-based inference approach for machines that cannot be reset. Each query is therefore applied on a
SUI in its current state. As they base the approach on Angluin's L^* algorithm,
the main idea is that L^* cannot be applied in that case with sequences starting from the same initial state. Each state of the machine corresponds to one
instance of L^*. So there can be as many observation tables to be completed
as there are states. In order to know for which state an observation should be
recorded, Rivest and Schapire assume that a homing sequence is given for the
SUI. The approach consists in repeatedly applying a homing sequence, followed
by a query for the state reached at the end of the homing sequence, until one of
the observation tables is complete and the equivalence query confirms that the
SUI is correctly identified.

We assume here that the reader is familiar with L^*, so we do not detail the
steps of L^* and the queries. However, in order to describe the algorithm in a form
that makes it possible to understand the difference between the two approaches
and evaluate the results provided in Sect. 6, here are a few adjustments. Rivest
and Schapire's algorithm was given for a slightly different model of automata,
a Moore model where the output is completely determined by the (tail) state,
that is the output function was not λ as in our FSM Mealy model but a function
$\gamma : Q \to O$. Additionally, to be consistent with the DFA model used by L^*,
they considered that $O = \{0, 1\}$. For better comparison, we adapt it to the FSM
notations, and we implemented the algorithm by using a Mealy algorithm L_M^+
[17] instead of L^*.

The (deterministic version) algorithm assumes that

- the unknown automaton B is strongly connected,
- h is a homing sequence for B,
- B can be queried for outputs, by providing it an input sequence and observing
  the corresponding outputs
- an oracle can answer equivalence queries, i.e., a conjecture M can be provided
  to this oracle, that will answer with an input sequence (called a counterexample) distinguishing M from B (the two machines provide different output
  sequences for the same input sequence), if they are not equivalent.

3.2   Illustrating Rivest and Schapire Algorithm on Example 1

We consider the following three state automaton (cf. Fig. 1). a is a homing
sequence for it.

Let us illustrate the algorithm on this example, starting from initial state 1.
We start by applying the homing sequence a, and observe the output sequence 1.
So we are in state which we can call $a/1$, to which we associate a newly created
observation table $L_{a/1}$ as in L_M^+. This table has a single upper row labelled ϵ

```
 1  procedure RivestSchapire(B, h)
 2    repeat
 3      Apply h, producing output σ
 4      if it doesn't already exist, create L*σ, a new copy of L*
 5      simulate the next query of L*σ:
 6      if L*σ queries membership of a then
 7        | Apply a and supply L*σ with the output
 8      end
 9      if L*σ makes an equivalence query then
10        if the conjecture model M is correct then
11          | exit with M
12        else
13          | supply counterexample to L*σ
14        end
15      end
16
17  end
```

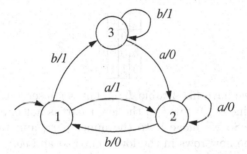

Fig. 1. Three state automaton

(empty sequence), and one column for each input. We apply a observing output 0. We can fill the corresponding cell of the observation table. At this point, we have applied two inputs: one for homing, and the second one to learn the output for input a (for state $a/1$).

We now need to repeat the cycle: applying again the homing sequence, in order to know to which state we should associate the next observation. In that case, we apply a and observe output 0. This indicates that we are in a state which we can call $a/0$. Actually, in this example, this is the same state as the one we called $a/1$, but we do not know it for a black box, and this is just coincidental for this example. Applying the algorithm, we create another observation table $L_{a/0}$. We again apply ϵa for this new table and observe 0.

$$1_0 \xrightarrow{a/1} 2_1 \xrightarrow{a/0} 2_2 \xrightarrow{a/0} 2_3 \xrightarrow{a/0} 2_4 \xrightarrow{a/0} 2_5 \xrightarrow{b/0} 1_6 \xrightarrow{a/1} 2_7 \xrightarrow{b/0} 1_8$$

In the trace above, positions are shown as indices of the states reached by the automaton. Of course, the inference algorithm only observes the positions and I/O pairs of transitions; it does not have access to the internal state: those are depicted for the reader to make it easier to follow the trace.

After 8 steps, we have filled the ϵ row with its two columns for both tables $L_{a/1}$ and $L_{a/0}$. Following Angluin's algorithm, we now need to fill the table for the rows of the lower half of the table, i.e. rows labeled with the concatenation of a label from the upper rows with one input (unless this concatenation was already in the upper rows). This means that for both tables, we need to complete cells for rows labelled a and b. Combining with the columns, we need to apply aa, ab, ba and bb, each time preceded by a homing sequence, until we complete at least one of the tables.

$$2_8 \xrightarrow{a/1} 2_9 \xrightarrow{a/0} 2_{10} \xrightarrow{a/0} 2_{11} \xrightarrow{a/0} 2_{12} \xrightarrow{a/0} 2_{13} \xrightarrow{a/0} 2_{14} \xrightarrow{a/0} 2_{15} \xrightarrow{a/0} 2_{16} \xrightarrow{b/0} 1_{17} \xrightarrow{a/1} 2_{18}$$

$$2_{18} \xrightarrow{a/0} 2_{19} \xrightarrow{b/0} 1_{20} \xrightarrow{a/1} 2_{21} \xrightarrow{b/0} 1_{22} \xrightarrow{a/1} 2_{23} \xrightarrow{a/0} 2_{24} \xrightarrow{b/0} 1_{25} \xrightarrow{a/1} 2_{26}$$

$$2_{26} \xrightarrow{a/0} 2_{27} \xrightarrow{b/0} 1_{28} \xrightarrow{b/1} 3_{29}$$

	a	b
ϵ	0	0
a	0	0
b	1	1

At this point, we have filled table $L_{a/0}$, but we observe that is it not closed (following L^* terminology): row b in the lower part is not equivalent to any row in the upper part. So we move it to the upper part, and table $L_{a/0}$ must be completed to fill the new rows in the lower part: ba and bb.

$$3_{29} \xrightarrow{a/0} 2_{30} \xrightarrow{b/0} 1_{31} \xrightarrow{a/1} 2_{32} \xrightarrow{a/0} 2_{33} \xrightarrow{a/0} 2_{34} \xrightarrow{b/0} 1_{35} \xrightarrow{a/1} 2_{36} \xrightarrow{b/0} 1_{37}$$

$$1_{37} \xrightarrow{a/1} 2_{38} \xrightarrow{b/0} 1_{39} \xrightarrow{b/1} 3_{40}$$

Now table $L_{a/0}$ is completely filled (it is the same table as above for $L_{a/0}$, since they correspond to the same state in the black box), but it has the same non-closed row b.

$$3_{40} \xrightarrow{a/0} 2_{41} \xrightarrow{b/0} 1_{42} \xrightarrow{b/1} 3_{43} \xrightarrow{a/0} 2_{44} \xrightarrow{a/0} 2_{45} \xrightarrow{b/0} 1_{46} \xrightarrow{b/1} 3_{47} \xrightarrow{b/1} 3_{48}$$

	a	b
ϵ	0	0
b	1	1
a	0	0
ba	0	0
bb	0	1

Now, we have again a non-closed completely filled table for $L_{a/0}$, and move row bb to the upper part. The sequence goes on with:

$$3_{48} \xrightarrow{a0b0b1a0a0} 2_{53} \xrightarrow{a0b0b1a0b0} 1_{58} \xrightarrow{a1b0a1a0} 2_{62} \xrightarrow{a0b0b1b1a0} 2_{67}$$

$$2_{67} \xrightarrow{a/0} 2_{68} \xrightarrow{b/0} 1_{69} \xrightarrow{b/1} 3_{70} \xrightarrow{b/1} 3_{71} \xrightarrow{b/1} 3_{72}$$

With this, we get a closed and compatible table for $L_{a/0}$.

	a	b
ϵ	0	0
b	1	1
bb	0	1
a	0	0
ba	0	0
bba	0	0
bbb	0	1

This enables to produce a three state conjecture. In order to search for a counterexample, we would need to apply from the initial state of $L_{a/0}$. So we have a final input to apply:

$$3_{72} \xrightarrow{a/0} 2_{73}$$

And the oracle would answer negatively to the counterexample query, since the conjecture is equivalent to the black box machine.

3.3 Complexity and Further Extensions

If n is the number of states of B, no more than n copies of L^* will be created. Thus, the algorithm will succeed in inferring B after no more than n times the complexity of the L^* algorithm. This complexity depends on the length m of the longest counterexample provided to the learner. Therefore, its complexity would be $O(|I|^2mn^2 + |I|mn^3)$ with a classical Mealy adaptation of L^*, and with the L_M^+ algorithm from [17], it would be $O(|I|^2n^2 + |I|mn^3)$. Actually, the paper that presented the inference without reset refered to the dichotomic search on counterexamples, so that the m factor could be reduced, yielding a complexity of $O(|I|n^3 + n^2 \log m)$. However, as shown later [2], this was flawed as a counterexample can still remain a counterexample in the updated conjecture. Therefore, in our experiments (see Sect. 6) we did not use dichotomic search, but a sound counterexample processing method that is efficient enough while keeping the observation table suffix-closed [10].

The original paper [16] also describes how to deal when it is provided with a sequence that is not homing. An incorrect homing sequence will lead to inconsistent behaviour in the tables of copies of L^* (one table for each output sequence in response to homing). Detecting the inconsistency makes it possible to extend h, until it becomes a real homing sequence. Each time an inconsistency is discovered, the existing copies of L^* are discarded and the algorithm is restarted. However, there is a possibility that no inconsistency is detected, and the algorithm will add rows to the tables of the copies of L^*. The authors propose a probabilistic approach that uses a bound on the number of states, which we do not detail here.

4   Algorithm Based on W-Set

We assume we are provided with a black-box FSM $B = (P, p_0, I, O, \delta, \lambda)$, and a characterization set for it $W \subset I^*$. We are also provided with a bound n on the number of states of B, so $|P| \leq n$.

Since we do not know B, we cannot compute a checking sequence using a test generation method. However, the inference algorithm will use the bound n and the knowledge that W is indeed a characterization set for B to derive

- a minimal FSM M that will be equivalent to B
- a sequence of inputs and observed outputs that in effect will be a checking sequence, with a unique solution $M \approx B$ up to equivalence, in the fault domain of all machines with up to n states.

A complete definition and proof of the algorithm can be found elsewhere [8]. In this section, we just provide the main description and results.

4.1   Data Records Used by the Algorithm

The algorithm will record deduced information in the following sets:

- $Q \subset 2^{W \mapsto (IO)^*}$ will denote states, defined by their characterizations. Each state is named by its traces recording its responses to the input sequences from W.
- $C : (IO)^* \mapsto Q \cup \{\bot\}$, actually defined on a subset of prefixes of ω will be used to *label* prefixes of the observed trace. For $\alpha \leq \omega$, we have $C(\alpha) = q \in Q$ when we have established that the machine B was in state p where $p \leftrightarrow q$ after observing α. $C(\alpha) = \bot$ when we do not know what is the state reached by B after α. C stands for "Characterized positions".
- $V \subseteq Q \times (IO)^* \times Q$ will record verified subtraces of ω, that is a subtrace is in V if its start and end "states" are labelled by C. Formally, $V' = \{(q, \alpha, q') \in Q \times (IO)^* \times Q \mid \exists \sigma \alpha \leq \omega, C(\sigma) = q, C(\sigma\alpha) = q'\}$. Actually, since the relation between states associated with V' would be transitively closed, the algorithm will maintain its transitive reduction V. V stands for "Verified sequences".
- R will record input verified transitions, those for which we define the start state and input, and we do not need to refer to the tail state. $R = \{(q, x) \in Q \times I \mid \exists o \in O, \exists q' \in Q, (q, xo, q') \in V\}$.
- $K \subseteq Q \times (IO)^+ \times (IO)^*$ keeps track of the applications of elements from W in a given state, followed by either a single transition or a non-empty trace of a sequence from W. $(q, \alpha, \gamma) \in K$ if $\exists \beta$ s.t. $\beta\alpha\gamma \leq \omega, C(\beta) = q, \alpha \downarrow I \in I \cup W$ and $\gamma \downarrow I \in W$. K stands for "Known applications of characterizing sequences".

Note that V, R and K can be derived from the knowledge of ω and C: they are data structures introduced to simplify the algorithm when it has to look up for sequences.

4.2   Localizer Procedure

The key element for the base algorithm is the localizer procedure, which makes it possible to ensure that we bring the machine to a state that is identified because its responses to all sequences in W have been ascertained. The localizer procedure is formulated for fixed input and output alphabets I and O, and an assumed bound n on the number of states in the black box. It takes as input the current observed trace ω and an ordered subset $Z \subseteq W$. The observed trace ω will be extended and updated as output when exiting the procedure. As originally defined in [8], it will append a fixed input sequence, a localizing sequence, to ω.

---

1 **procedure** $L(\omega, Z)$	**// returns** (ω', Tr, tr)
2	
3 **if** $\mid Z \mid= 1$, *i.e.* $Z = (w)$ **then**	
4 Apply w, observe $tr(w)$	
5 $\omega \leftarrow \omega tr(w)$	
6 **return** $(\omega, \{tr(w)\}, tr(w))$	
7 **else**	
8 **let** $Z = (w_1, ..., w_k), Z_1 = (w_1, ..., w_{k-2}, w_{k-1}), Z_2 = (w_1, ..., w_{k-2}, w_k)$	
9 **for** i **from** 0 **to** $2n - 2$ **do**	
10 $(\omega', Tr(Z_1), \tau_i) \leftarrow L(\omega, Z_1)$	**//** τ_i **is** $tr(w_{k-1})$
11 $\omega \leftarrow \omega'$	
12 **end**	
13 Find greatest j, $0 \leq j \leq n - 1$ s.t. for all $m \in [0, n - 2]$ $\tau_{j+m} = \tau_{n+m}$	
14 $(\omega', Tr(Z_2), tr(w_k)) \leftarrow L(\omega, Z_2)$	
15 **return** $(\omega', Tr(Z_2) \cup \{\tau_{j+n-1}\}, tr(w_k))$	
16 **end**	
17 **end**	

Regardless of the state in which the black-box machine B is, the localizer will ensure that just before applying the last w_k input sequence, B was in a state that can be characterized by the traces returned as second argument. This is captured by the following theorem.

Theorem 1. *When $Z = W$, from any starting state, the localizer will return (ω', X, β) such that $C(\omega' \setminus \beta) = X$ and $X \downarrow I = W$.*

The proof, and the explanation for this procedure are provided in the original paper [8]. Here we just provide an intuition on its structure and why it ensures the property.

If $W = \{w_1, w_2\}$, then, after applying w_1^n we can be sure that the state reached at the end of this sequence must be the same as one of the states reached after some prefix w_1^k with $k < n$, since there are at most n different states. Thus, the output sequence that will be observed after the $n + 1$ application of w_1 will necessarily be the same as a previously observed output sequence. However, we do not know on which previous state we have cycled. So it might be too early to be able to predict what would be this output. Nevertheless, after $n-1$ further applications, we have seen the cycle at least twice and we can indeed predict what would be the output of the $2n$ application of w_1. Actually, depending on the length of this cycle, we might be able to predict the output earlier, at some iteration between n and $2n-1$, but that would lead us to more complicate schemes when we have more than two sequences in W. Therefore, the procedure here is defined with a fixed number of iterations $2n-1$ that corresponds to the worst case.

In all cases, after $2n-1$ applications of w_1, we no longer need to apply it again, and we can apply w_2. We can say that, in the state reached after w_1^{2n-1}, we have somehow virtually applied w_1 and therefore, we know for that state its answers (output sequences) to both w_1 and now w_2. Once we have applied w_2, we have fully characterized the state we were in *before* applying it.

If we add one more sequence to W, the sequence becomes more complex. For $W = \{w_1, w_2, w_3\}$ the localizer would apply the following sequence: $(w_1^{2n-1}w_2)^{2n-1}w_1^{2n-1}w_3$. After each sequence $(w_1^{2n-1}w_2)$, we are able to predict what would be the answers of the state reached after the w_1^{2n-1} part to both w_1 and w_2. However, the states reached just before the application of w_2 after $(w_1^{2n-1}w_2)^k$ could be different, but again, after n iterations, we know we must have cycled. In order to recognize the length of the cycle, we go to $2n-1$ iterations. At this point, when we apply w_1^{2n-1} we know what would be the answer to w_1 *and* w_2: we virtually applied them at this point, and so we can now apply w_3.

Similarly, for $W = \{w_1, w_2, w_3, w_4\}$ the localizer would apply the following sequence: $((w_1^{2n-1}w_2)^{2n-1}w_1^{2n-1}w_3)^{2n-1}(w_1^{2n-1}w_2)^{2n-1}w_1^{2n-1}w_4$.

4.3   Main Procedure

The inference procedure assumes it is given a black-box machine B whose number of states is less or equal to n, and for which it is known that a set which we will order as $W = (w_1, ... w_p)$ is a characterization set. It can query B through the procedure <u>Apply</u> by submitting an input sequence and obtaining the corresponding output sequence from B, in the state it was left in following previous queries.

We have kept the traditional terminology of "conjecture", even though in the case of this algorithm under our assumptions, we only get a single final machine.

The sets K, T and R are updated to reflect the changes in C. This is done by applying the following rules as long as possible.

1. If $C(\beta) = q$, $C(\beta\alpha) = q'$, with $\beta\alpha \leq \omega$, then $(q, \alpha, q') \in V$.
2. If $C(\beta) = q$, $\beta\alpha \leq \omega$, and $(q, \alpha, q') \in V$ then $C(\beta\alpha) = q'$.
3. If $(q, x, q') \in V$ for $x \in I$, then $(q, x) \in R$.
4. If $C(\beta) = q$, $\beta\alpha\gamma \leq \omega$, $\alpha \downarrow I \in I \cup W$ and $\gamma \downarrow I \in W$, then $(q, \alpha, \gamma) \in K$.
5. If $\exists \alpha$ s.t. $\{w \in W \mid (q, \alpha, tr(w)) \in K\} = W$ then $\forall \beta\alpha \leq \omega$ s.t. $C(\beta) = q$, we have $C(\beta\alpha) = \{\gamma \mid (q, \alpha, \gamma) \in K\}$.

```
 1  procedure InferNoReset(B, W, n)
 2  │   Initialize K = R = V = ∅
 3  │   (ω, q₀, tr(w_p)) ← L(ε, W)                    // Home into a known state
 4  │   C(ω \ tr(w_p)) ← q₀
 5  │   Q_C ← {q₀}
 6  │   while ∃q' ∈ Q_C and x' ∈ I such that (q', x') ∉ R do
 7  │   │   if C(ω) = q ≠ ⊥ then
 8  │   │   │   Find a shortest α = α₁, ...α_k   // Move to unverified transition
 9  │   │   │       s.t. ∀i, (qᵢ, αᵢ, qᵢ₊₁) ∈ V, q₁ = q and x ∈ I s.t. (q_{k+1}, x) ∉ R
10  │   │   │   Apply α ↓ I, observe α
11  │   │   │   ω ← ωα ; χ ← ω
12  │   │   │   Apply x, observe xo                   // Observe transition
13  │   │   │   σ ← xo ; ω ← ωxo
14  │   │   else
                                                      // Use the latest known previous state
15  │   │   │   Find the shortest γ s.t. C(ω \ γ) ≠ ⊥   // Maybe shorter than w_p
16  │   │   │   χ ← ω \ γ ; σ ← γ
17  │   │   end
18  │   │   q ← C(χ)                                  // Here ω is unlabeled
19  │   │   Choose w ∈ W such that there is no tr(w) s.t. (q, σ, tr(w)) ∈ K
20  │   │   Apply w observe tr(w)        // Improve characterization of (q, σ)
21  │   │   ω ← ωtr(w) ; K ← K ∪ {(q, σ, tr(w))}
22  │   │   if {w ∈ W | (q, σ, tr(w)) ∈ K} = W then
                                                      // Full characterization reached
23  │   │   │   C(χσ) ← {tr(w) | w ∈ W and (q, σ, tr(w)) ∈ K}
24  │   │   │   Q_C ← Q_C ∪ {C(χσ)}
25  │   │   │   Update V, R, K, C
26  │   │   end
27  │   │   if C(ω) = ⊥ then
28  │   │   │   (ω, q', tr(w_p)) ← L(ω, W)        // Move to a characterized state
29  │   │   │   C(ω \ tr(w_p)) ← q' ; Q_C ← Q_C ∪ {q'}
30  │   │   │   Update V, R, K, C
31  │   │   end
32  │   end
33  │   Build the conjecture from Q_C and V ∩ (Q × (IO) × Q)
34  end
```

By definition, V is transitively closed, so in the implementation of the algorithm, we just need to keep a transitive reduction of it. Actually, this is sufficient for the algorithm, since we use V to find a shortest concatenation of sequences that would themselves be in V.

4.4   Illustrating on Example 1

4.5   Example 1

We consider again the three state automaton from Fig. 2. This machine has no distinguishing sequence. However, states can be fully characterized by their traces for sequences from the set $W = \{a, b\}$.

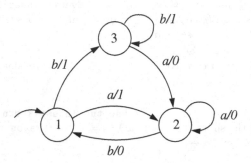

Fig. 2. Three state automaton

Let us illustrate our algorithm on this example. Assuming the bound is 3, the localizer procedure will generate the input sequence: a^5b. The algorithm will start by applying the localizer procedure on line 2, thus identifying a first state of the machine: $C(\omega \backslash b0) = q_0 = \{a0, b0\}$.

Thus, the prefix obtained in the 5th step is labelled by q_0. C is updated on the fourth line of the inference procedure.

$$1_0 \xrightarrow{a/1} 2_1 \xrightarrow{a/0} 2_2 \xrightarrow{a/0} 2_3 \xrightarrow{a/0} 2_4 \xrightarrow{a/0} 2_5 \xrightarrow{b/0} 1_6 \xrightarrow{a/1} 2_7$$
$$q_0$$

As in Sect. 3, positions are shown as indices of the states reached by the automaton. The states that can be inferred are shown below the positions. They are called q_i with a numbering i that starts from 0. Note that the states of the black-box machine are simply named with integers, starting at 1.

The algorithm then enters the main *while* loop in the inference procedure. As the last state of ω (6th step in the trace) is not yet labelled we proceed to the *else* part of the first *if* statement. Then $\gamma = b0$, $\chi = a1a0a0a0a0$ and $\sigma = b0$.

After the first *if* statement, $q = q_0$, K is empty, and we choose $w = a$. Applying a, we observe $a1$ and arrive at the 7th step. Now $K = \{(q_0, b0, a1)\}$, $V = R = \emptyset$.

Since the condition of the second *if* statement is false, the algorithm proceeds with the third *if* statement, which is true. It applies again the localizer procedure, and labels the state after $a0a0a0a0a0$ (12th step) with q_0: $C(12) = q_0$. At this point, the *while* loop is restarted.

$$2_7 \xrightarrow{a/0} 2_8 \xrightarrow{a/0} 2_9 \xrightarrow{a/0} 2_{10} \xrightarrow{a/0} 2_{11} \xrightarrow{a/0} 2_{12} \xrightarrow{b/0} 1_{13} \xrightarrow{b/1} 3_{14}$$
$$q_0 \qquad\quad q_1$$

The algorithm enters the *else* part of the *if* statement, with $\gamma = \sigma = b0$. Then $q = q_0$, and we choose $w = b$. Apply b, observe $b1$ and arrive at the 14th step. Now $K = \{(q_0, b0, a1), (q_0, b0, b1)\}$.

The condition of the second *if* statement is now true, we have thus identified a new state $q_1 = \{a1, b1\}$ and $C(13) = q_1$. Then $V = \{(q_0, b0, q_1)\}$, $R = \{(q_0, b)\}$ and $C(6) = q_1$. Thus $K = \{(q_0, b0, a1), (q_0, b0, b1), (q_1, a1, a0)\}$.

The algorithm now executes the third *if* statement: applying the localizer procedure and arriving at the 20th step. $C(19) = q_0$ and $C(20) = q_1$. K is unchanged.

$$3_{14} \xrightarrow{a/0} 2_{15} \xrightarrow{a/0} 2_{16} \xrightarrow{a/0} 2_{17} \xrightarrow{a/0} 2_{18} \xrightarrow{a/0} 2_{19} \xrightarrow{b/0} 1_{20} \xrightarrow{a/1} 2_{21} \xrightarrow{b/0} 1_{22}$$
$$q_0 \qquad\quad q_1 \qquad\quad q_0$$

Again restart the *while* loop. Since the last (20th) step is now labelled, the algorithm enters the *then* part of the first *if* statement. $\alpha = \epsilon$ and we choose $x = a$. Apply a, observe $a1$ and arrive at step 21. Now $\sigma = a1$, $q = q_1$, and we choose $w = b$, because $(q_1, a1, a0) \in K$. Apply b, observe $b0$ and arrive at step 22; so now $K = \{(q_0, b0, a1), (q_0, b0, b1), (q_1, a1, a0), (q_1, a1, b0)\}$.

Since the condition of the second *if* statement is true, we are now able to identify the tail state of the transition on input a from q_1: $C(21) = q_0 = \{a0, b0\}$. Update V, R, C and K:
$V = \{(q_0, b0, q_1), (q_1, a1, q_0)\}$, $R = \{(q_0, b), (q_1, a)\}$, $C(7) = q_0$, $C(22) = q_1$,
$K = \{(q_0, b0, a1), (q_0, b0, b1), (q_1, a1, a0), (q_1, a1, b0), (q_0, a0, a0), (q_1, b1, a0)\}$.
The trace at the last step (22) is labelled, and the condition of the third *if* statement is false.

$$2_{22} \xrightarrow{b/1} 3_{23} \xrightarrow{b/1} 3_{24} \xrightarrow{a/0} 2_{25} \xrightarrow{a/0} 2_{26} \xrightarrow{a/0} 2_{27} \xrightarrow{a/0} 2_{28} \xrightarrow{a/0} 2_{29} \xrightarrow{b/0} 1_{30}$$
$$q_1 \qquad\quad q_2 \qquad\qquad\qquad\qquad\qquad\qquad q_0 \qquad\quad q_1$$

The *while* loop is restarted, which allows to add $(q_1, b1, b1)$ to K, and thus to identify a new state $q_2 = \{a0, b1\}$ and label $C(23) = q_2$. The algorithm applies the localizer procedure and arrives at step 30. $C(29) = q_0$, $C(30) = q_1$. At this point,
$V = \{(q_0, b0, q_1), (q_1, a1, q_0), (q_1, b1, q_2), (q_2, b1a0a0a0a0a0a0, q_0)\}$,
$K = \{(q_0, b0, a1), (q_0, b0, b1), (q_1, a1, a0), (q_1, a1, b0), (q_0, a0, a0), (q_1, b1, a0),$
$\quad (q_1, b1, b1), (q_2, b1, a0)\}$,
$R = \{(q_0, b), (q_1, a), (q_1, b)\}$ and $C(14) = q_2$.

The *while* loop is restarted. As the last step (30) is labelled, it enters the *then* part of the first *if* statement. As all transitions from q_1 are now known, it must apply a transfer sequence to move to an unverified transition. We choose to go to q_0 with $\alpha = a1$ and $x = a$. Apply a, observe $a1$ (α), apply a again (as x), observe $a0$ and arrive at step 32. $\sigma = a0$.

We choose $w = b$, apply b, observe $b0$, arrive at step 33 and add $(q_0, a0, b0)$ to K. The condition of the second *if* statement is true, $C(32) = q_0$ and we add $(q_0, a0, q_0)$ to V. Now $R = \{(q_0, b), (q_1, a), (q_1, b), (q_0, a)\}$, $C(7) = C(8) = \ldots = C(11) = q_0$, $C(33) = q_1$.

After applying the *while* loop two more times, we obtain the trace below, with $V = \{(q_0, b0, q_1), (q_1, a1, q_0), (q_1, b1, q_2), (q_0, a0, q_0), (q_2, a0, q_0), (q_2, b1, q_2)\}$ and $R = \{(q_0, b), (q_1, a), (q_1, b), (q_0, a), (q_2, a), (q_2, b)\}$. All transitions are known and $C(38) = q_2$.

$$1_{30} \xrightarrow{a/1} 2_{31} \xrightarrow{a/0} 2_{32} \xrightarrow{b/0} 1_{33} \xrightarrow{b/1} 3_{34} \xrightarrow{a/0} 2_{35} \xrightarrow{b/0} 1_{36} \xrightarrow{b/1} 3_{37} \xrightarrow{b/1} 3_{38}$$
$$q_1 \quad\quad q_0 \quad\quad q_0 \quad\quad q_1 \quad\quad q_2 \quad\quad q_0 \quad\quad q_1 \quad\quad q_2 \quad\quad q_2$$

The algorithm now exits from the *while* loop and V gives us the inferred finite state machine, which is isomorphic to the FSM in Fig. 2.

The algorithm based on W-sets infer with a shorter sequence as compared to Rivest and Schapire's algorithm on this example. The behaviours of the two approaches will be discussed in Sect. 6, and a detailed analysis on a more complex example will be presented in Sect. 5.2.

4.6   Convergence and Complexity

The original paper [8] proved the following theorem and analyzed the complexity of the algorithm.

Theorem 2. *When W is a characterization set for B and the number of states of B is less than or equal to n, the inference procedure terminates and yields a conjecture that is isomorphic to the minimal FSM modelling B.*

The complexity of active learning algorithms based on queries is usually assessed in terms of the number and the length of queries. This makes sense in particular in the context of learning black-box software systems, especially when queried over a network or a bus, because remote interaction with the system takes much more time than the internal bookkeeping activities of the algorithm. In the case of algorithms that do not use reset and simply send inputs and observe outputs, the measure is quite simple: the total length of the trace until we can build the conjecture.

The algorithm uses the set W, whose cardinality is p, and n which is the given bound on the number of states. It also queries the machine by knowing its input set I. A coarse bound[2] for the length of the trace is $O(p(|I|+p)2^p n^{p+2})$. Actually this is a very coarse bound as it assumes that all characterization sequences would be of length n, whereas we would typically have in W much shorter sequences.

---

[2] The size of the output set does not play a role in this bound. The number of transitions is solely determined by the number of states and the number of inputs. In practice, a higher number of different outputs increases distinguishability and therefore can reduce the length and the number of separating sequences. The worst case in practice is for $|O| = 2$.

And it is also known that this length is asymptotically logarithmic in n (actually $log|I|log_{|O|}n$ [19]). Experiments showed that the average complexity for $p = 2$ (the most common case even for random machines with 2 inputs and 2 outputs) is $O((|I| + 2)n^{1.9})$. An interesting point worth mentioning is that the algorithm remains polynomial in n, although the degree of the polynomial depends on the number of sequences in W.

5   Example 2

5.1   Inferring with the W-Based Algorithm

Let us now consider in less detail a slightly more complex automaton, that will provide a more interesting basis for comparison. We consider the following 6-state automaton (Fig. 3), which is a product of a counter modulo 2 (on i) and a counter modulo 3 (on j). $I = \{i, j\}$ and $O = \{0, 1\}$. We choose as W-set the singleton $W = \{jji\}$. This will avoid recursive calls in the localizer procedure, so the example is easier to follow.

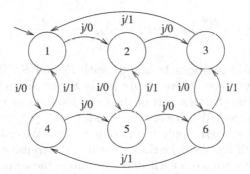

Fig. 3. Two-counters automaton

The W-based algorithm infers the automaton in 71 steps. The algorithm starts with the localizer, which consists in just applying the sequence jji. It gets the output sequence 000, and thus identifies a new state at position 0 of the trace: $S_0 = \{jji \mapsto j0j0i0\}$ which we shall simply write $\{j0j0i0\}$. Since the states of the black box machine are discovered progressively in an order that is not related to their numbering, state S_i does not correspond in general to state i or $i + 1$.

$$1_0 \xrightarrow{j/0} 2_1 \xrightarrow{j/0} 3_2 \xrightarrow{i/0} 6_3 \xrightarrow{j/1} 4_4 \xrightarrow{j/0} 5_5 \xrightarrow{i/1} 2_6 \xrightarrow{j/0} 3_7 \xrightarrow{j/1} 1_8 \xrightarrow{i/0} 4_9$$
$$\underset{S_0}{} \qquad\qquad\qquad \underset{S_1}{} \qquad\qquad\qquad \underset{S_2}{}$$

The algorithm enters the main *while* loop. The current state is unknown, so the algorithm enters the *else* part of the first *if* statement and gets $\sigma = j0j0i0$. We choose $w = jji$, apply w and observe 101.

Now $K = \{(S_0, j0j0i0, j1j0i1)\}$, and the algorithm discovers a new state $S_1 = \{j1j0i1\}$ and get $V = \{(S_0, j0j0i0, S_1)\}$. As the last position is unknown, it enters the last *if* statement and applies the localizer procedure. Notice that states are not discovered in the order of their "names" in the automaton. We first found state 1 which was called S_0, then discovered state 3 which is called S_1.

Now $K = \{(S_1, j1j0i1, j0j1i0)\}$. A new state $S_2 = \{j0j1i0\}$ is discovered, $V = \{(S_0, j0j0i0, S_1), (S_1, j1j0i1, S_2)\}$ and we label position 6 of the trace with S_2.

The *while* loop is restarted and yields the trace

$$4_9 \xrightarrow{j/0} 5_{10} \xrightarrow{j/0} 6_{11} \xrightarrow{i/1} 3_{12} \xrightarrow{j/1} 1_{13} \xrightarrow{j/0} 2_{14} \xrightarrow{i/0} 5_{15} \xrightarrow{j/0} 6_{16} \xrightarrow{j/1} 4_{17} \xrightarrow{i/1} 1_{18}$$
$$S_3 \qquad\qquad\qquad S_4 \qquad\qquad\qquad S_5$$

At this point, we have identified the states $S_3 = \{j0j0i1\}$, $S_4 = \{j1j0i0\}$ and $S_5 = \{j0j1i0\}$. Now $K = \{(S_4, j1j0i0, j0j1i0)\}$ and $V = \{(S_0, j0j0i0, S_1), (S_1, j1j0i1, S_2), (S_2, j0j1i0, S_3), (S_3, j0j0i1, S_4)\}$.
We still do not know where we are, so we apply the localizer again.

$$1_{18} \xrightarrow{j/0} 2_{19} \xrightarrow{j/0} 3_{20} \xrightarrow{i/0} 6_{21} \xrightarrow{i/1} 3_{22} \xrightarrow{j/1} 1_{23} \xrightarrow{j/0} 2_{24} \xrightarrow{i/0} 5_{25}$$
$$S_0 \qquad\qquad\qquad S_1 \quad S_4 \qquad\qquad\qquad S_5$$

We can now label positions 18 and 21 with S_0 and S_1. We can notice that for the first time, we know where we are (state S_1) at the end of the trace. The algorithm thus enters the *then* part of the first *if* statement in order to move to an unverified transition. We choose $\alpha = \epsilon$ and $x = i$, apply x and observe 1. At step 22, we choose $w = jji$, apply w and observe 100. We can now label step 22 with S_4 and 25 with S_5. We have thus identified the transition $(S_1, i1, S_4)$.

The same process can go on until all transitions of the automata are identified. Since we now know all 6 states, and V contains all start and end states of each application of the DS jji, this is a rather straightfoward process now. There are 11 remaining transitions to identify, for each one of them the algorithm just needs to apply it and then jji, and at a few points just needs to transfer with an α sequence that is not the empty string.

$i/1\ j/0\ j/1\ i/0\ i/1\ j/0\ j/0\ i/0\ j/1\ j/0\ j/0\ i/1\ i/0\ j/1\ j/0\ i/1\ i/0$
$j/0\ j/1\ i/1\ i/0\ j/0\ j/0\ i/1\ j/1\ j/0\ j/0\ i/0\ j/1\ j/0\ j/0\ j/1\ i/1\ j/0\ j/0$
$j/1\ i/0\ j/0\ j/0\ j/1\ j/0\ i/1\ j/0\ j/1\ j/0\ i/0$

The total length of the inference process consists of 71 inputs to be applied. We observe that in this particular example, we have first identified all states and then all transitions, which is not the case in general.

Actually, more information could be extracted from the prefixes of the trace, and a recent paper [6] shows how this could be done by combining passive inference (with a notion of compatibility) with the active W-based inference method. In that case, the inference can be done with a trace reduced to 41 steps (down from 71 as above).

5.2   Example 2: Comparison with Rivest and Schapire's Algorithm

The algorithm by Rivest and Schapire requires an oracle to answer equivalence queries. In our black-box testing context, we need to define a realistic way of implementing an oracle to provide counter-examples. As we have no information on the black box except for a bound on its number of state (to compare with the W-based algorithm), we look for a counterexample by heuristics based on random walks. This introduces a higher degree of nondeterminism or choices in the algorithm, so that we do not have a fixed number for the length of the trace needed to infer the example. For better efficiency, we also consider cases where random walks are interrupted to avoid cycling in non-productive parts of the FSM, then restarted in a different direction.

In the W-based algorithm, although there are a few choices (choice of the input x and of α on lines 8–9 and of a w on line 19), those can easily be determinized by choosing a lexical order on the input alphabet (as we did above) and of the order defined on W by the localizer (irrelevant in our example since $|W| = 1$). Similar choices are made in L^* as used by Rivest and Schapire's algorithm.

Our experiments with various parameters for the heuristics gave a mean of 1750 inputs to infer the 6 state machine of the example with Rivest and Schapire's algorithm. This went down to around 1500 when L^* was provided with shortest counter-examples (which we could find since in that case, the 6-state target machine is known).[3]

Therefore, Rivest and Schapire's algorithm is vastly more expensive than the W-based algorithm on this example, and the experiments with large samples of random machines presented in Sect. 6 show that this would be the normal case for low cardinality of W. More detailed analysis of the behaviour of the algorithms shows that there are two major causes for the high number of inputs required by Rivest and Schapire's algorithm.

- It requires creating n copies of L^* observation tables, and filling them. Although a natural idea would be to try and avoid some redundancy by deducing some information from one table to the other, this idea seems difficult to concretize, and Rivest and Schapire informed that they had not found a way to do it [16].
- The processing of counter-examples introduces a factor m in the complexity, corresponding to the maximal length of a countexample, because all suffixes would be added to columns, therefore expanding the observation table by this factor.

---

[3] Since we have a bound on the number of states, another method for searching counterexamples could be used: enumerating sequences of increasing length up to the given bound. This would be an exponential search, but with a low bound it could be viable. However, this would still be longer than the shortest counterexamples to which we compared for reference.

This implies that Rivest and Schapire's algorithm incurs at least an nm multiplicative factor that the W-based algorithm avoids. In our example, the typical length of optimal counterexamples would be between 2 and 4, so the factor would be around 18 or 20, which accounts for a large part of the difference between 71 and 1500.

6   Experimental Results

It is difficult to compare algorithms based on different assumptions. Knowing a homing sequence could be similar to knowing a W-set, but whereas there is a single homing sequence, the size of the W-set would be a parameter. However the main differing assumption is that the algorithm by Rivest and Schapire heavily relies on an oracle able to provide counterexamples to equivalence queries.

We still give elements of comparisons, based on experiments where we assume that all assumptions are satisfied. In active learning contexts, the time or space complexity of the algorithms is not the main factor to be considered. Instead, we compare algorithms on the length of the sequence needed to infer an equivalent model of the black-box. In a software testing context, as described in this paper, the critical factor would be the length of the sequence, as each interaction with the system is usually more costly in time than the book-keeping activities of the algorithm. The number of queries is not considered here. Each query generates a subsequence of inputs, so they are assessed through the length of the sequence generated. Equivalence queries could add extra costs, but since the results are already in favour of the W-based algorithm, we do not provide any specific analysis on equivalence queries.

We experimented with random machines, with a low level of state distinguishability (input and output sets of sizes 2) so as to consider inference without reset in unfavourable conditions for the W-based algorithm. Of course, an input set of size 2 also reduces the number of transitions, but an increase in the input size would simply add a linear factor to the W-based algorithm, and a quadratic one for Rivest and Schapire's.

In a first experiment, we considered a few hundred (random) machines, to compare the average complexity of Rivest and Schapire's algorithm with the W-based method. Actually, we also compared with a brute force combinatorial approach that would do some enumeration of possible solution machines; such a method rapidly blows up in computing time, but it is a good reference as a baseline method. Figure 4 shows the average trace length for variants of the algorithms. For the W-based algorithm, we distinguish between $p = 1$ and $p = 2$ (remember that $p = |W|$), because the length of the localizer, that depends exponentially on p, has a high impact on the complexity. For random machines, some of them may have a distinguishing sequence ($p = 1$ in that case), otherwise we were able to find W-sets of cardinality 2 for most of the others.

Note that the vertical axis (length of trace, i.e. number of inputs required to infer) has a logarithmic scale. Both the combinatorial algorithm and Rivest and Schapire's blew up for n reaching 10 states. Although a more careful implementation (with optimized memory usage) of those algorithms could have gone

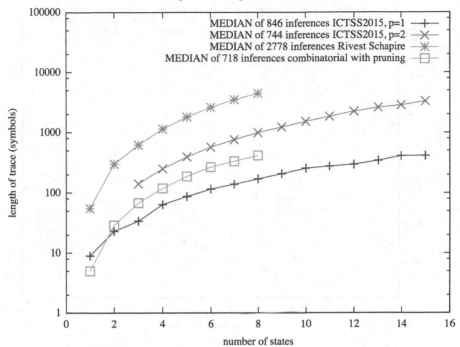

Fig. 4. Comparison of algorithms

a little further, this would not change the overall growth and ranking of the curves. The average complexity of the W-based algorithm lies between 1 and 2 order of magnitude below Rivest and Schapire's.

In order to better assess the average complexity of the W-based algorithm w.r.t. to our very coarse complexity bound, we conducted another experiment with ca. 500 random machines (Fig. 5). The upper, dotted curve shows the shape of the complexity bound $O(p(|I|+p)2^p n^{p+2})$, in that case, since $p = 2$ and $|I| = 2$, reduced to $O(32n^4) = O(n^4)$. In order to better fit in the chart, we plot the function $0.2n^4$, which keeps the shape of the curve in a linear scale. A polynomial regression on the average complexity shows that it follows a curve that has an exponent of 1.9 instead of 4. The actual curve for the average complexity is $20n^{1.9}$.

From these experiments, it appears that the W-based algorithm outperforms significantly the approach by Rivest and Schapire on random machines, even though it has weaker assumptions (no equivalence queries). It also scales up better, at least for W-sets that do not have too many sequences.

When assessing inference algorithms, although random machines are an easy way to have statistical results on a large number of machines, it is known that they are not typical of real software models. Collecting evidence on a large set

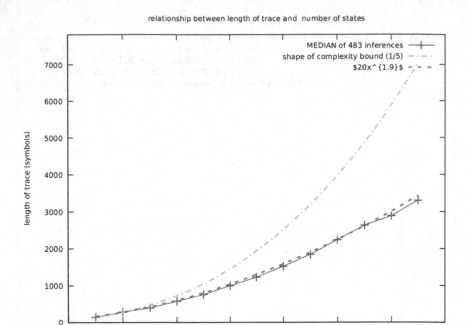

Fig. 5. Length of trace as function of number of states for W-based algorithm

of real systems would provide more relevant results. It is unlikely however that it would change the main comparison results between the two algorithms, given the wide difference. Note that example 2 is a 2-counter system, and counters are typical elements of programs. The detailed analysis of the example provided in Sect. 5 provides good indications on the difference between the performances of the two algorithms.

7   Conclusion

This paper revisits the problem of inferring FSM models of black box systems when those systems cannot be reset. It compares an algorithm proposed by Rivest and Schapire based on Angluin's L^*, and a new method proposed by the authors. This new method uses weaker assumptions than those used by L^*; no oracle is needed. Instead, it uses classical elements used in software testing, namely a characterization set W and an assumed upper bound n on the number of states. The method requires a number of interactions with the system that is polynomial in n. The degree of the polynomial is bounded by the cardinality of W (plus 2). Although this might be crippling for machines with large characterization sets, it seems that most machines have characterization sets of at most 2 elements that can be found relatively easily with heuristics (as are implemented in our Simpa tool).

Although the assumptions used by the W-based algorithm are weaker than those used by Rivest and Schapire, the length of the trace is much shorter as long as $|W| \leq 3$ in our experiments.

The localizer procedure presented in Sect. 4.2 is the main contributor to the length of the trace. There are many ways for reducing its complexity. Instead of using a fixed sequence, the length of the sequence can be dramatically reduced by producing an adaptive sequence [4].

It is worth pointing out that if we assume that we know both a homing sequence and a characterization set, then the lengthy localizing sequences can be just replaced by a homing sequence. A very straightforward adaptation of the algorithm in Sect. 4.3 yields a simplified algorithm that easily improves on the other algorithms. There is no need for an oracle, and it is not even necessary to know a bound on the number of states. The most interesting path for better applicability would be the possibility to alleviate the key assumption that we know a characterization set of a black box FSM. We have started recently investigating those ideas, with an adaptive heuristic approach. The key idea is to start from an approximate homing sequence (as Rivest and Schapire did in the probabilistic version of their algorithm) as well as an approximate W-set that will be refined when inconsistencies are detected. Preliminary results [7] indicate that such an approach could perform much better than the more deterministic methods presented in this paper. And it scales up to machines that may have thousands of states. On random machines, it converges fast to a correct model of the system with an average trace length that is around $O(n^{1.3})$, a very low polynomial in the number of states.

Finally, another recent paper proposes an approach that requires no specific assumption apart from a bound on the number of states [15]. This approach looks quite promising since it could be used on a black box with a tentative bound that could be extended if the model proves inaccurate, and it does not require assumptions on the black box, such as a homing sequence, a W-set, or an oracle for equivalence queries. The approach is based on the ability to derive alternative solutions from an existing prefix trace (passive inference), and extending the sequence in order to eliminate wrong conjectures. The implementation of that paper [15] uses a constraint solver to derive alternative conjectures. The main drawback is that even though the length of the sequence remains polynomial in n, the time used by the algorithm for solving the constraints grows rapidly with the length of the sequence, thus limiting the number of states that can be inferred. However its potential of applicability is still interesting since experiments have shown that the implementation could infer machines with up to 13 states. An even newer publication [21] proposes an approach that does not require any a priori knowledge on the black box SUI, and can work with an approximated oracle such as a random walk on the conjectured model. This approach scales up to hundreds or thousands of states, and seems quite promising. This shows that model inference of non-resettable systems is a problem that can yield new solutions, with new efficient algorithms to come.

Acknowledgements. The authors acknowledge the work of Nicolas Bremond, master student from Enseirb-Matmeca who implemented the algorithms.

References

1. Ural, H., Rezaki, A.: Construction of checking sequences based on characterization sets. Comput. Commun. **18**(12), 911–920 (1995)
2. Balcazar, J.L., Diaz, J., Gavalda, R.: Algorithms for learning finite automata from queries: a unified view. In: Du, D.Z., Ko, K.I. (eds) Advances in Algorithms, Languages, and Complexity, pp. 53–72. Springer, Heidelberg (1997). https://doi.org/10.1007/978-1-4613-3394-4_2
3. Büchler, M., Hossen, K., Mihancea, P.F., Minea, M., Groz, R., Oriat, C.: Model inference and security testing in the spacios project. In: CSMR-WCRE, Antwerp, Belgium (2014)
4. Groz, R., Simao, A., Oriat, C.: Adaptive localizer based on splitting trees. In: Yevtushenko, N., Cavalli, A.R., Yenigün, H. (eds.) ICTSS 2017. LNCS, vol. 10533, pp. 326–332. Springer, Cham (2017). https://doi.org/10.1007/978-3-319-67549-7_21
5. Groz, R., Li, K., Petrenko, A., Shahbaz, M.: Modular system verification by inference, testing and reachability analysis. In: Suzuki, K., Higashino, T., Ulrich, A., Hasegawa, T. (eds.) FATES/TestCom -2008. LNCS, vol. 5047, pp. 216–233. Springer, Heidelberg (2008). https://doi.org/10.1007/978-3-540-68524-1_16
6. Groz, R., Oriat, C., Bremond, N.: Inferring non-resettable mealy machines with n states. In: Proceedings ICGI 2016, pp. 30–41 (2016)
7. Groz, R., Simao, A., Bremond, N., Oriat, C.: Revisiting AI and testing methods to infer FSM models of black-box systems. In: AST 2018, Göteborg, May 2018
8. Groz, R., Simao, A., Petrenko, A., Oriat, C.: Inferring finite state machines without reset using state identification sequences. In: El-Fakih, K., Barlas, G., Yevtushenko, N. (eds.) ICTSS 2015. LNCS, vol. 9447, pp. 161–177. Springer, Cham (2015). https://doi.org/10.1007/978-3-319-25945-1_10
9. Hennie, F.C.: Fault-detecting experiments for sequential circuits. In: Proceedings of Fifth Annual Symposium on Circuit Theory and Logical Design, pp. 95–110 (1965)
10. Irfan, M.N., Oriat, C., Groz, R.: Angluin style finite state machine inference with non-optimal counterexamples. In: MIIT, pp. 11–19. ACM, New York (2010)
11. Lee, D., Yannakakis, M.M.: Principles and methods of testing finite state machines - a survey. Proc. IEEE **84**(8), 1090–1123 (1996)
12. Margaria, T., Niese, O., Raffelt, H., Steffen, B.: Efficient test-based model generation for legacy reactive systems. In: High-Level Design, Validation, and Test Workshop. IEEE (2004)
13. Meinke, K.: CGE: a sequential learning algorithm for mealy automata. In: Sempere, J.M., García, P. (eds.) ICGI 2010. LNCS (LNAI), vol. 6339, pp. 148–162. Springer, Heidelberg (2010). https://doi.org/10.1007/978-3-642-15488-1_13
14. Peled, D., Vardi, M.Y., Yannakakis, M.: Black box checking. In: Wu, J., Chanson, S.T., Gao, Q. (eds.) Formal Methods for Protocol Engineering and Distributed Systems. IAICT, vol. 28, pp. 225–240. Springer, Boston, MA (1999). https://doi.org/10.1007/978-0-387-35578-8_13

15. Petrenko, A., Avellaneda, F., Groz, R., Oriat, C.: From passive to active FSM inference via checking sequence construction. In: Yevtushenko, N., Cavalli, A.R., Yenigün, H. (eds.) ICTSS 2017. LNCS, vol. 10533, pp. 126–141. Springer, Cham (2017). https://doi.org/10.1007/978-3-319-67549-7_8

16. Rivest, R.L., Schapire, R.E.: Inference of finite automata using homing sequences. In: Hanson, S.J., Remmele, W., Rivest, R.L. (eds.) Machine Learning: From Theory to Applications. LNCS, vol. 661, pp. 51–73. Springer, Heidelberg (1993). https://doi.org/10.1007/3-540-56483-7_22

17. Shahbaz, M., Groz, R.: Inferring mealy machines. In: Cavalcanti, A., Dams, D.R. (eds.) FM 2009. LNCS, vol. 5850, pp. 207–222. Springer, Heidelberg (2009). https://doi.org/10.1007/978-3-642-05089-3_14

18. Shahbaz, M., Groz, R.: Analysis and testing of black-box component-based systems by inferring partial models. Softw. Test. Verif. Reliab. **24**(4), 253–288 (2014)

19. Trakhtenbrot, B.A., Barzdin, Y.M.: Finite Automata, Behaviour and Synthesis. North Holland, Amsterdam (1973)

20. Vasilievskii, M.P.: Failure diagnosis of automata. Cybernetics **9**, 653–665 (1973)

21. Groz, R., Simao, A., Bremond, N., Oriat, C.: Revisiting AI and testing methods to infer FSM models of black-box systems. In: Proceedings of the 13th International Workshop on Automation of Software Test, AST 2018, Gothenburg, Sweden, 28–29 May 2018, pp. 16–19 (2018). https://doi.org/10.1145/3194733.3194736

Integrative Approaches

Constraint-Based Behavioral Consistency of Evolving Software Systems

Reiner Hähnle[1][(✉)] and Bernhard Steffen[2]

[1] Department of Computer Science, Technische Universität Darmstadt,
64289 Darmstadt, Germany
haehnle@cs.tu-darmstadt.de
[2] Department of Computer Science, Technische Universität Dortmund,
44221 Dortmund, Germany
steffen@cs.tu-dortmund.de

Abstract. Any complex software system exhibits a tension between the technical perspective required for its realization and the user-level perspective. We term this the "how-what gap", represented by the questions "*how* is a system implemented" vs. "*what* is its functionality/usage". The normative, *anticipated* behavior of a software system as envisaged during its *development* and the de facto, *observed* behavior emerging after its continued *operation* tends to drift apart, resulting in *behavioral inconsistency*. We discuss how behavioral consistency in software systems can be captured in technical and formal terms, we sketch a possible tool chain that could support it, and we describe some of the research challenges that must be solved. Our main idea is to combine software analysis approaches represented by various forms of static analysis and formal verification with runtime verification, monitoring, and automata learning in order to optimally leverage the de facto observed behaviour of the deployed systems.

1 Introduction

Any complex software system exhibits a tension between the technical perspective required for its realization and the user-level perspective at which the primary concerns of the client/customer are evaluated. We term this the "how-what gap", represented by the questions "*how* is a system implemented" vs. "*what* is its functionality/usage". In more precise terms, the normative, *anticipated* behavior of a software system as envisaged during its *development* and the de facto *observed* behavior emerging after its continued *operation* tend to drift apart, resulting in *behavioral inconsistency*.

The how-what gap recently gained prominence under the heading *DevOps* [40]. Here, it manifests itself in terms of an often serious and with time increasing mismatch between design and implementation artifacts. While the

---

The research reported in this article has been partially supported by Deutsche Forschungsgemeinschaft (DFG) under grant nr. HA 2617/7-1.

© Springer International Publishing AG, part of Springer Nature 2018
A. Bennaceur et al. (Eds.): ML for Dynamic Software Analysis, LNCS 11026, pp. 205–218, 2018.
https://doi.org/10.1007/978-3-319-96562-8_8

problem is well recognized by practitioners, there is little systematic research and, as far as we are aware, no tool support to help maintaining behavioral consistency.

In this article we discuss how behavioral consistency in software systems can be captured in technical and formal terms, we sketch a possible tool chain that could support it, and we describe some of the research challenges that must be solved.

Our main idea is to combine software analysis approaches represented by various forms of static analysis and logical inference with runtime verification, monitoring, and automata learning in order to optimally leverage the de facto observed behaviour of the deployed systems. All of these approaches require suitable abstraction techniques for scaling, but they have complementary strengths and weaknesses when it comes to their predictive power: the results of glass box approaches are typically provably correct, but they are restricted to a certain level of modeling (specification). In contrast, the results of black-box, or learning approaches reflect the actual runtime behaviour, and therefore comprise the whole system, including compilers, runtime environment, hardware, etc. On the other hand, these results have the status of a hypothesis. Predictions for not explicitly observed runs are mere "best guesses" according the principle of Occam's razor [44, 48]: they are true according to the simplest explanation/model for the concretely observed phenomena.

We suggest to achieve behavioral consistency by automated, iterative refinement steps. These maintain a formal specification model, technically realized as a *common global constraint model*, that represents the accumulated knowledge about a given system at a given time during its operation. Consistency is then established by comparing the specification of the system with its operation, i.e., comparing static constraints against a model obtained by active automata learning by way of model checking.

To the best of our knowledge, there is no previous work that systematically enforces (behavioral/operational) consistency of knowledge gained through (static or symbolic) analysis at the normative how-level and operation-based knowledge at the what-level, obtained by active automata learning. To do so requires a common abstraction level on the basis of extended finite state machines, tailored to support an adequate notion of "learning modulo theories".

In the following section we explain the problem and its ramifications in greater detail. In Sect. 3 we make a detailed proposal, based on state-of-art research results and tools, for a technology that may represent behavioral consistency of a piece of software in a unified manner and that is robust in the presence of evolution. In Sect. 4 we draw some conclusions.

2   The Problem of Deteriorating Specifications

During the course of any complex software development project, a large amount of diverse knowledge from a wide variety of sources is accumulated. This knowledge is crucial for producing a correctly working, usable, and maintainable product in timely fashion. Close analysis of catastrophic software errors and failed projects repeatedly shows that lack in the ability to make crucial connections among diverse knowledge artifacts is at the heart of the matter [25].

Even for less critical software development projects it is of paramount importance to systematically integrate knowledge and project artifacts. This is strongly suggested by the frame conditions of contemporary software development: rapid time-to-market with changing, unanticipated requirements; very long-lived usage of some components; incremental, cyclic ("agile") development processes. Specifically, recent software engineering trends such as DevOps call for a systematic and continuous connection between runtime and design time information [40, 51].

In current practice, however, the integration of design knowledge and the knowledge gained from operation is rather limited. Merely a few updates are often sufficient to separate a running system from its design artifact and documentation. A conceptual explanation for this phenomenon is the fact that the design phase is typically dominated by a *how* perspective, describing the system to be developed in terms of its software architecture, whereas post-deployment is characterized by a *what* perspective describing the system in terms of what it actually does.

Table 1. The how-what dichotomy

	How perspective	*What* perspective
Development phase	Design	Deployment
Purpose	System specification	System understanding
Behavioral aspect	Instruction-level behavior	User experience
Description artifacts	Architectural diagrams	Test models, use cases
Formal result (cf. Sect. 3)	Executable specifications	Behavioural automata

Table 1 summarizes the *how-what* distinction. Whereas the how perspective addresses the system builder, supporting her with means for system specification, in terms of, for example, class diagrams, abstract algorithms, contracts, that help capturing the envisioned instruction-level behaviour, to ultimately construct executable specifications, the what perspective aims at user-level system understanding: What does the user experience when interacting with the deployed system? Test models and use case diagrams often serve as basis for a systematic, test-based investigation of running systems.

The longer systems live, the looser becomes the connection to their design models (which are hardly ever kept up to date in current practice) and, as a consequence, quality control is mostly confined to merely *testing* the current product. In addition, test models—the basis for model-based testing—hardly ever enter industrial practice. In those rare cases where they are constructed during development time, they typically suffer the same fate as their design counter parts. In short, what is lacking in contemporary development practice is the ability to automatically maintain behavioral consistency between design artifacts and the actual system implementation. Active automata learning is an ideal means to aggregate test-based knowledge in order to provide behavioural automata that are suitable for "closing the loop" and (re-)establishing behavioural consistency, i.e. consistency between the how and the what.

3   Representation of Behavioral Consistency

We propose to combine software analysis approaches represented by various forms of static analysis and formal verification with runtime verification, monitoring, and automata learning in order to optimally leverage the de facto observed behaviour of the deployed systems. Iterative refinement steps build a behavioral and specification model backed by a common global constraint model representing the knowledge about the underlying system. This knowledge is constantly refined and updated and can be used to automatically enforce behavioral consistency.

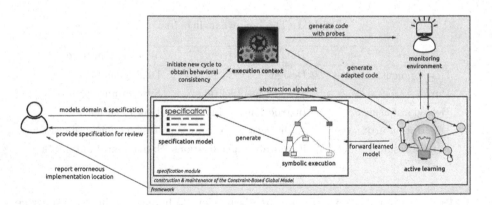

Fig. 1. Life cycle of automatically gaining or maintaining behavioral consistency

The envisaged user workflow and consistency maintenance cycle is sketched in Fig. 1. The activities involved in it are described in the following.

3.1   Constraint-Based Global Model

The backbone of the considered notion of consistency is the *Constraint-Based Global Model*, our main data structure. It collects all knowledge gained during design, analysis, and execution of a software system. The central design decision is to use *logic-based constraints* to represent that knowledge. Specifically, we use two basic building blocks: *typed first-order logic* (FOL) with a number of built-in theories to represent constraints; and a symbolic representation of sets of computation states, variously called *updates* [52] or *explicit substitutions* [3]. Both are implemented in the KeY system ([4], see also sidebar). These basic constraint types are closed under the usual logical composition operators, such as conjunction or functional composition.

On this basis one can define different *kinds* of logic-based constraints. Obviously, we envisage first-order assertions that hold relative to a symbolic state. Additionally, any constraint can be relativized with a symbolic path condition, essentially a constraint on the input variables of a program, given as a quantifier-free first-order formula. Such relative constraints can be generated (and understood) by, for example, deductive symbolic execution [12]. They can also be used to generate test cases [6, 22] or monitors [17].

Hence, logic constraints enable one to *uniformly* express the essential common properties of the rather heterogeneous

KeY [4] is a state-of-the-art deductive software analysis tool based on symbolic execution of source code and invariant reasoning. It can be used for functional verification [19], code-based test case generation [6, 22], certification of resource analysis [8], information flow analysis [21, 53], visualization of control flow and symbolic data structures [29], and for verified code compilation and program optimization [41]. Its currently supported languages are JAVA [4] and ABS [20].

artifacts obtained from symbolic execution, from user input, and from active learning and monitoring. The decision to employ FOL constraints and symbolic states has a number of important advantages:

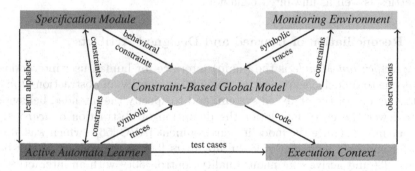

Fig. 2. Data flow among different components around the *Constraint-Based Global Model*.

- **Simplicity:** typed FOL is a very well understood formalism with undisputed semantics.
- **Flexibility:** the expressiveness of FOL ensures that we are not tied to specific kinds of semantic information that is exchanged.

- **Formal semantics:** the inputs/outputs of all environments mentioned in Fig. 1 can be given a formal semantics in terms of FOL in a straightforward manner. This is essential for ensuring correct interoperability among different analysis methods and tools.
- **Scalable automation:** SMT solvers and automated theorem provers can be employed to simplify logic-based constraints aggressively and continuously. This is feasible, because those tools have achieved a degree of maturity that lets them cope even with large formulas [18,58]. Another reason why it can be expected that the analysis scales is that in practice path conditions and assertions are mostly quantifier-free.
- **Incrementality/Looseness:** the constraint-based setting permits to start with arbitrarily partial information about a system (in the extreme case, with the empty constraint) which can be incrementally augmented by logical conjunction in the guise of [55].
- **Bidirectionality:** it is not merely possible to *import* information in the form of adding constraints, but also to *export* it using well-understood methods and tools, such as first-order model generation, projection (substitution), consistency checking, inference, abduction, etc.

The main task of the consistency maintenance framework illustrated in Fig. 1 is to forward incoming information and to update and maintain the *Constraint-Based Global Model*, which is not simply one large, monolithic FOL formula, but structured to reflect the specifics of the various tasks detailed below.

The categories processed by this framework include sets of constrained symbolic computation states, symbolic transition systems, test oracles, concrete system configurations, etc. Important is here the ability to model both, desired properties as well as unwanted behaviour.

3.2   Reconciliation of Learned and Designed Artifacts

The *Specification Module* is the (main) interface for human user interaction. It allows one to model the application domain, to identify an abstraction alphabet, i.e. the actions of the analyzed system, and to specify the intended behavior.

To lower the entry hurdle for the definition of abstraction or *learn* alphabets one may enhance the modeling environment jABC [56]—which was already used for end-user modeling of learn alphabets [50] in the context of risk-based testing [23] and active continuous quality control [60]—with an interactive user interface.

A suitable technology for the specification module that supports abstract, human-readable, formal models, is available as the *abstract behavioral specification* (ABS) language (see side bar). ABS permits precise modeling of distributed and highly variable software systems from the *how* perspective. ABS models can be partially obtained by specification generation techniques based on deductive symbolic execution [59] and invariant generation [45]. They are complemented by hand-crafted models supplied by domain experts. The result is an executable specification structure resembling information both from top-down and bottom-up reasoning similar to the *One Thing* in the eXtreme Model Driven Development paradigm [46,47].

The *Specification Module* feeds into the *Constraint-Based Global Model* by generating behavioral constraints. (The data flow between the *Constraint-Based Global Model* and the other components is illustrated in Fig. 2.) Constraints can be used for test case generation, for code generation (in the *Execution Context*), or for adequate (aspect-oriented) probing to support automata learning and monitoring. The implementation of the constraint generation facilities is based on the deductive analysis tool KeY-ABS [20], the ABS version of the KeY tool described in Sect. 3.1.

The *Specification Module* receives symbolic traces indicating constraint violations observed by the *Execution Context* at runtime in the *Monitoring Environment* or from the *Active Automata Learner* (details see Sects. 3.3 and 3.4 below). This information can be used for error location/diagnosis. Vice versa, the *Specification Module imposes* constraints in the form of symbolic execution paths enriched with state constraints such as strongest post-conditions or signaled exceptions (representing implementation errors). These are *consumed* by the *Active Automata Learner* to improve the efficiency of learning and the precision of the learned models as well as by the *Monitoring Environment* to speed up monitoring in the style of [5,17]. In particular, this interplay addresses one of the major challenges of automata learning, how to adequately realize the so-called equivalence query in practice [30,32].

Instantiation constraints, typically derived by model finding from pre-conditions and path conditions, are used by both, the *Specification Module* and *Active Automata Learner*, to relate abstract and concrete behavior: for example, glass-box test case generation in the *Specification Module* relies on the ability to produce such constraints [10]. There is, however, a considerable degree of freedom in solving them. Ideally, test case generation should be combined with information from the *Active Automata Learner* to produce relevant test cases.

> The ABS language[a] [27,42] is a behavioral modeling language. It supports modeling of variability and provides a uniform basis for the modeling of features, behavior, and data. ABS is a mature technology for behavioral modeling and analysis of industrial systems [9] and is also used to model inherently concurrent physical systems as diverse as railways [28] or biological organisms.[b] ABS was developed with the explicit goal to support scalable analysis. It comes with an extensive toolbox [14,61], including test case generation [10], resource analysis [7], deadlock detection [24], and functional verification [20].
>
> [a] www.abs-models.org.
> [b] www.compugene.tu-darmstadt.de/compugene/welcome.

3.3 Automata Learning

The *Active Automata Learner* uses the learn alphabet defined in the *Specification Module* together with other static constraints (if available) to infer a behavioral model via systematic, feedback-guided testing of the system provided by the *Execution Context*. There is a large body of existing research [15,31,33,35,36,39] and tools (see LearnLib sidebar) that form the basis. Most promising is a novel algorithm called TTT [34,37], which is also a part of LearnLib. It was designed to optimally deal with excessively long counter examples as they appear in the envisioned monitoring-based learning scenario.

One pressing question in automata learning is how to deal with data. While automata learning is a technology that matches perfectly the control perspective, it has to comprise strategies for handling data flow in practice. State-of-the-art solutions consist in defining the abstraction of the learned model at a granularity where the model is based on a regular language and the states do not contain structured data. Bridging the gap to a real system is commonly achieved by *hand-crafted* so called mappers [2,26,43] or via automated alphabet abstraction refinement [1,33,35].

The open-source LearnLib [38,49] is a library for active automata learning [11]. It has a high degree of flexibility and extensibility, while at the same time providing a performance that allows for large-scale applications. It comprises numerous algorithms for inferring behavioral models via system testing, technology to automatically adapt abstractions of the alphabet and to optimize the exploitation of domain characteristics during the learning process.

Recently, also more ambitious automata learning techniques have been developed that explicitly deal with data [15,36]. In particular the SMT-solver-based approach presented in [15,16,31] nicely fits into the ABS/KeY landscape and will enable the automatic construction of data flow-sensitive behavioral models of black-box systems based on knowledge from the *Constraint-Based Global Model*.

In practice, automata learning is characterized by the fact that the learning process is continuous and can never be assumed to have completed [13,30]. The interplay with the other analysis and validation techniques employed here drives this continuous process. In particular, monitoring is ideal to providing execution sequences that can be turned into counter examples for the learner to start a new learning phase. The TTT algorithm is the only known algorithm capable of dealing with counter examples of the length typical for monitoring-generated counter examples [37].

In our setting, after each learning phase, the obtained behavioral information needs to be incorporated into the *Constraint-Based Global Model*, e.g., the monitoring observations or (parts of) the ABS specification. This resembles a kind of "equivalence query" from classical active automata learning, but is in fact a more general approach. Consequently, the task of analyzing and exploiting counter examples to refine the learned behavioral model is considerably more challenging in this setting. To realize this vision we plan to generalize the TTT algorithm [37] to cover the learning of register automata and extended finite state machines.

3.4   Runtime Monitoring

Monitoring observes the actual runtime behavior of the system under analysis to detect violations against the *Constraint-Based Global Model*. The monitor usually works on a monitoring model comprising the properties under observation, which is generated from the behavioral model obtained from the *Active Automata Learner* by a certain set of rules. If system behavior is observed that is not in compliance with the model, then the latter has to be adapted by restarting the learning process with the newly found information. If the system behavior is also not compliant with the *Constraint-Based Global Model*, this hints at inconsistencies in the global model, which in turn have to be fixed, either through automatic handling strategies or explicit user input.

To detect non-compliance, the incoming observations have to be matched against the monitoring model. If the monitoring component detects a mismatch, i.e., a violation of one or more constraints in the global model, it generates a "witness" for this anomaly. A witness is a sequence of observations made by the monitor which leads to the point where a mismatch was detected. This is a more general notion of what in automata learning is called a "counter example": The witness can be regarded as a further constraint in the model (e.g., "the behavioral model has to contain some additional trace"), and actions have to be taken in order to reconcile the global model and resolve inconsistencies.

Since the constraints that are monitored originate from various sources, there is a large heterogeneity in how this reconciliation can be achieved: As long as the learned behavioral models are incorrect, the witnessing constraint is used to construct a counter example which is then fed to the counter example-handling facility of some learning algorithm. A violation of the constraints imposed by the ABS specification, in contrast, would trigger some notification in the design environment.

Two different model representations for the behavioral model suggest themselves: Mealy Machines and extended finite-state machines. Especially the interplay between symbolic execution, monitoring and extended finite-state machines learning, which form the conceptual basis for "learning modulo theories" [15], is promising as these approaches seem able to complement each other well. Knowledge about data values might be preserved in the learned extended finite-state machines, which are also more concise and scale better for large applications. To further exploit the incremental nature of the approach, behavioral models of former versions could be used to find counter examples more quickly, which would speed up the overall learning process [60].

3.5   The Execution Context

The *Execution Context* is augmented by code generation from the constraints provided by the *Specification Module*, for example, following the sound code transformation paradigm developed in [41].

For monitoring-based anomaly detection to work reliably, the generated code has to incorporate instrumentation and monitoring facilities that provide suitable observations for this purpose. High-level constructs that are to be monitored have to be identifiable in the generated code. For instance, observations must contain information on the system actions at an abstraction level that can be mapped to the monitored model. In particular, actions have to be related to the notions used in the actively learned model, in order to be able to automatically relate system actions to the correct alphabet symbols.

4   Conclusion

The interplay between the different components described above establishes a framework for controlling software evolution by synchronizing the traceable *how* and the learning-based and, therefore, self-adapting *what* perspective to obtain and maintain an overall coherent system knowledge. Thus it automatically bridges the inevitable semantic gap in software engineering in a way that requires interaction only at the specification level. This is possible due to the looseness of behavioral consistency, which does not reflect syntactic features but focuses on runtime behavior, the true primary concern.

As a consequence, the constraint-based behavioral consistency framework proposed in this paper will establish the theoretical and practical basis for a software development framework that is holistic in the following sense:

- Knowledge artifacts obtained during analysis, modeling, coding, as well as runtime knowledge gained through log data, testing and monitoring are consistently combined in an integrated, semantic framework.
- Tools for symbolic static analysis, test case generation, automata learning, and code generation are integrated on the basis of a common behavioral understanding [54,57].

Synchronizing the knowledge about changes in model, code and system behavior maintains the consistency between the perspectives of the different people involved in the system life-cycle independently of who and where the change happened. This makes the software evolution process transparent and counter-acts the usual tendency of software to turn into legacy.

Acknowledgments. We would like to thank Falk Howar and Karl Meinke and for their constructive criticism which helped to improve our paper.

References

1. Aarts, F., Heidarian, F., Kuppens, H., Olsen, P., Vaandrager, F.: Automata learning through counterexample guided abstraction refinement. In: Giannakopoulou, D., Méry, D. (eds.) FM 2012. LNCS, vol. 7436, pp. 10–27. Springer, Heidelberg (2012). https://doi.org/10.1007/978-3-642-32759-9_4
2. Aarts, F., Jonsson, B., Uijen, J., Vaandrager, F.W.: Generating models of infinite-state communication protocols using regular inference with abstraction. Formal Methods Syst. Des. **46**(1), 1–41 (2015)

3. Abrial, J.-R.: The B Book: Assigning Programs to Meanings. Cambridge University Press, Cambridge (1996)
4. Ahrendt, W., Beckert, B., Bubel, R., Hähnle, R., Schmitt, P., Ulbrich, M. (eds.): Deductive Software Verification-The KeY Book: From Theory to Practice. LNCS, vol. 10001. Springer, Cham (2016). https://doi.org/10.1007/978-3-319-49812-6
5. Ahrendt, W., Chimento, J.M., Pace, G.J., Schneider, G.: Verifying data- and control-oriented properties combining static and runtime verification: theory and tools. Formal Methods Syst. Des. **51**(1), 200–265 (2017)
6. Ahrendt, W., Gladisch, C., Herda, M.: Proof-based test case generation. In: Ahrendt et al. [4], chap. 12, pp. 415–451
7. Albert, E., et al.: SACO: static analyzer for concurrent objects. In: Ábrahám, E., Havelund, K. (eds.) TACAS 2014. LNCS, vol. 8413, pp. 562–567. Springer, Heidelberg (2014). https://doi.org/10.1007/978-3-642-54862-8_46
8. Albert, E., Bubel, R., Genaim, S., Hähnle, R., Díez, G.R.: A formal verification framework for static analysis—as well as its instantiation to the resource analyzer COSTA and formal verification tool KeY. Softw. Syst. Model. **15**(4), 987–1012 (2016)
9. Albert, E., de Boer, F.S., Hähnle, R., Johnsen, E.B., Schlatte, R., Tarifa, S.L.T., Wong, P.Y.H.: Formal modeling of resource management for cloud architectures: an industrial case study using real-time ABS. J. Serv.-Oriented Comput. Appl. **8**(4), 323–339 (2014)
10. Albert, E., Gómez-Zamalloa, M., Isabel, M.: SYCO: a systematic testing tool for concurrent objects. In: Zaks, A., Hermenegildo, M.V. (eds.) Proceedings of the 25th International Conference on Compiler Construction, CC, Barcelona, Spain, pp. 269–270. ACM (2016)
11. Angluin, D.: Learning regular sets from queries and counterexamples. Inf. Comput. **75**(2), 87–106 (1987)
12. Beckert, B., Klebanov, V., Weiß, B.: Dynamic logic for Java. In: Ahrendt et al. [4], chapt. 3, pp. 49–106
13. Bertolino, A., Calabrò, A., Merten, M., Steffen, B.: Never-stop learning: continuous validation of learned models for evolving systems through monitoring. ERCIM News **2012**(88), 28–29 (2012)
14. Bubel, R., Montoya, A.F., Hähnle, R.: Analysis of executable software models. In: Bernardo, M., Damiani, F., Hähnle, R., Johnsen, E.B., Schaefer, I. (eds.) SFM 2014. LNCS, vol. 8483, pp. 1–25. Springer, Cham (2014). https://doi.org/10.1007/978-3-319-07317-0_1
15. Cassel, S., Howar, F., Jonsson, B., Steffen, B.: Learning extended finite state machines. In: Giannakopoulou, D., Salaün, G. (eds.) SEFM 2014. LNCS, vol. 8702, pp. 250–264. Springer, Cham (2014). https://doi.org/10.1007/978-3-319-10431-7_18
16. Cassel, S., Howar, F., Jonsson, B., Steffen, B.: Extending automata learning to extended finite state machine. In: Bennaceur, A., Hähnle, R., Meinke, K. (eds.) ML for Dynamic Software Analysis. LNCS, vol. 11026, pp. 149–177. Springer, Cham (2018)
17. Chimento, J.M., Ahrendt, W., Pace, G.J., Schneider, G.: STaRVOOrS : a tool for combined static and runtime verification of Java. In: Bartocci, E., Majumdar, R. (eds.) RV 2015. LNCS, vol. 9333, pp. 297–305. Springer, Cham (2015). https://doi.org/10.1007/978-3-319-23820-3_21

18. Cok, D.R., Griggio, A., Bruttomesso, R., Deters, M.: The 2012 SMT competition. In: Fontaine, P., Goel, A. (eds.) 10th International Workshop on Satisfiability Modulo Theories, SMT, Manchester, UK, EPiC Series in Computing, vol. 20, pp. 131–142. EasyChair (2013)

19. de Gouw, S., Rot, J., de Boer, F.S., Bubel, R., Hähnle, R.: OpenJDK's Java.utils.collection.sort() is broken: the good, the bad and the worst case. In: Kroening, D., Păsăreanu, C.S. (eds.) CAV 2015. LNCS, vol. 9206, pp. 273–289. Springer, Cham (2015). https://doi.org/10.1007/978-3-319-21690-4_16

20. Din, C.C., Bubel, R., Hähnle, R.: KeY-ABS: a deductive verification tool for the concurrent modelling language ABS. In: Felty, A.P., Middeldorp, A. (eds.) CADE 2015. LNCS (LNAI), vol. 9195, pp. 517–526. Springer, Cham (2015). https://doi.org/10.1007/978-3-319-21401-6_35

21. Do, Q.H., Bubel, R., Hähnle, R.: Exploit generation for information flow leaks in object-oriented programs. In: Federrath, H., Gollmann, D. (eds.) SEC 2015. IAICT, vol. 455, pp. 401–415. Springer, Cham (2015). https://doi.org/10.1007/978-3-319-18467-8_27

22. Engel, C., Hähnle, R.: Generating unit tests from formal proofs. In: Gurevich, Y., Meyer, B. (eds.) TAP 2007. LNCS, vol. 4454, pp. 169–188. Springer, Heidelberg (2007). https://doi.org/10.1007/978-3-540-73770-4_10

23. Felderer, M., Ramler, R.: A multiple case study on risk-based testing in industry. Int. J. Softw. Tools Technol. Transf. **16**(5), 609–625 (2014)

24. Giachino, E., Laneve, C., Lienhardt, M.: A framework for deadlock detection in core ABS. Softw. Syst. Model. **15**(4), 1013–1048 (2016)

25. Glass, R.L.: Software Runaways: Monumental Software Disasters. Prentice Hall, Upper Saddle River (1997)

26. Hagerer, A., Hungar, H., Niese, O., Steffen, B.: Model generation by moderated regular extrapolation. In: Kutsche, R.-D., Weber, H. (eds.) FASE 2002. LNCS, vol. 2306, pp. 80–95. Springer, Heidelberg (2002). https://doi.org/10.1007/3-540-45923-5_6

27. Hähnle, R.: The abstract behavioral specification language: a tutorial introduction. In: Giachino, E., Hähnle, R., de Boer, F.S., Bonsangue, M.M. (eds.) FMCO 2012. LNCS, vol. 7866, pp. 1–37. Springer, Heidelberg (2013). https://doi.org/10.1007/978-3-642-40615-7_1

28. Kamburjan, E., Hähnle, R.: Uniform modeling of railway operations. In: Artho, C., Ölveczky, P.C. (eds.) FTSCS 2016. CCIS, vol. 694, pp. 55–71. Springer, Cham (2017). https://doi.org/10.1007/978-3-319-53946-1_4

29. Hentschel, M., Bubel, R., Hähnle, R.: Symbolic execution debugger (SED). In: Bonakdarpour, B., Smolka, S.A. (eds.) RV 2014. LNCS, vol. 8734, pp. 255–262. Springer, Cham (2014). https://doi.org/10.1007/978-3-319-11164-3_21

30. Howar, F., Steffen, B.: Active automata learning in practice: an annotated bibliography of the years 2011 to 2016. In: Bennaceur, A., Hähnle, R., Meinke, K. (eds.) ML for Dynamic Software Analysis. LNCS, vol. 11026, pp. 123–148. Springer, Cham (2018)

31. Howar, F., Steffen, B., Jonsson, B., Cassel, S.: Inferring canonical register automata. In: Kuncak, V., Rybalchenko, A. (eds.) VMCAI 2012. LNCS, vol. 7148, pp. 251–266. Springer, Heidelberg (2012). https://doi.org/10.1007/978-3-642-27940-9_17

32. Howar, F., Steffen, B., Merten, M.: From ZULU to RERS. In: Margaria, T., Steffen, B. (eds.) ISoLA 2010. LNCS, vol. 6415, pp. 687–704. Springer, Heidelberg (2010). https://doi.org/10.1007/978-3-642-16558-0_55

33. Howar, F., Steffen, B., Merten, M.: Automata learning with automated alphabet abstraction refinement. In: Jhala, R., Schmidt, D. (eds.) VMCAI 2011. LNCS, vol. 6538, pp. 263–277. Springer, Heidelberg (2011). https://doi.org/10.1007/978-3-642-18275-4_19

34. Isberner, M.: Foundations of active automata learning: an algorithmic perspective. Ph.D. thesis, TU Dortmund University (2015)

35. Isberner, M., Howar, F., Steffen, B.: Inferring automata with state-local alphabet abstractions. In: Brat, G., Rungta, N., Venet, A. (eds.) NFM 2013. LNCS, vol. 7871, pp. 124–138. Springer, Heidelberg (2013). https://doi.org/10.1007/978-3-642-38088-4_9

36. Isberner, M., Howar, F., Steffen, B.: Learning register automata: from languages to program structures. Mach. Learn. **96**(1–2), 65–98 (2014)

37. Isberner, M., Howar, F., Steffen, B.: The TTT algorithm: a redundancy-free approach to active automata learning. In: Bonakdarpour, B., Smolka, S.A. (eds.) RV 2014. LNCS, vol. 8734, pp. 307–322. Springer, Cham (2014). https://doi.org/10.1007/978-3-319-11164-3_26

38. Isberner, M., Howar, F., Steffen, B.: The open-source LearnLib. In: Kroening, D., Păsăreanu, C.S. (eds.) CAV 2015. LNCS, vol. 9206, pp. 487–495. Springer, Cham (2015). https://doi.org/10.1007/978-3-319-21690-4_32

39. Isberner, M., Steffen, B.: An abstract framework for counterexample analysis in active automata learning. In: Proceedings of the 12th International Conference on Grammatical Inference, volume 34 of JMLR Workshop & Conference Proceedings, pp. 79–93 (2014)

40. Jabbari, R., Bin Ali, N., Petersen, K., Tanveer, B.: What is DevOps? A systematic mapping study on definitions and practices. In: Proceedings of the Scientific Workshops of XP 2016, Edinburgh, Scotland, UK, p. 12. ACM (2016)

41. Ji, R., Hähnle, R., Bubel, R.: Program transformation based on symbolic execution and deduction. In: Hierons, R.M., Merayo, M.G., Bravetti, M. (eds.) SEFM 2013. LNCS, vol. 8137, pp. 289–304. Springer, Heidelberg (2013). https://doi.org/10.1007/978-3-642-40561-7_20

42. Johnsen, E.B., Hähnle, R., Schäfer, J., Schlatte, R., Steffen, M.: ABS: a core language for abstract behavioral specification. In: Aichernig, B.K., de Boer, F.S., Bonsangue, M.M. (eds.) FMCO 2010. LNCS, vol. 6957, pp. 142–164. Springer, Heidelberg (2011). https://doi.org/10.1007/978-3-642-25271-6_8

43. Jonsson, B.: Learning of automata models extended with data. In: Bernardo, M., Issarny, V. (eds.) SFM 2011. LNCS, vol. 6659, pp. 327–349. Springer, Heidelberg (2011). https://doi.org/10.1007/978-3-642-21455-4_10

44. Gauch Jr., H.G.: Scientific Method in Practice. Cambridge University Press, Cambridge (2003)

45. Kovács, L.: Symbolic computation and automated reasoning for program analysis. In: Ábrahám, E., Huisman, M. (eds.) IFM 2016. LNCS, vol. 9681, pp. 20–27. Springer, Cham (2016). https://doi.org/10.1007/978-3-319-33693-0_2

46. Margaria, T., Steffen, B.: Business process modelling in the jABC: the one-thing-approach. In: Handbook of Research on Business Process Modeling, IGI Global (2009)

47. Margaria, T., Steffen, B.: Service-orientation: conquering complexity with XMDD. In: Hinchey, M., Coyle, L. (eds.) Conquering Complexity, pp. 217–236. Springer, London (2012). https://doi.org/10.1007/978-1-4471-2297-5_10

48. Maurer, A.: Ockham's razor and dialectical reasoning. Pontifical Institute of Mediaeval Studies (1996)

49. Merten, M., Steffen, B., Howar, F., Margaria, T.: Next generation LearnLib. In: Abdulla, P.A., Leino, K.R.M. (eds.) TACAS 2011. LNCS, vol. 6605, pp. 220–223. Springer, Heidelberg (2011). https://doi.org/10.1007/978-3-642-19835-9_18

50. Neubauer, J., Windmüller, S., Steffen, B.: Risk-based testing via active continuous quality control. Int. J. Softw. Tools Technol. Transf. **16**(5), 569–591 (2014)

51. Pérez, J.F., Wang, W., Casale, G.: Towards a DevOps approach for software quality engineering. In: Proceedings of Workshop on Challenges in Performance Methods for Software Development, WOSP-C 2015, Austin, TX, USA, pp. 5–10. ACM (2015)

52. Rümmer, P.: Sequential, parallel, and quantified updates of first-order structures. In: Hermann, M., Voronkov, A. (eds.) LPAR 2006. LNCS (LNAI), vol. 4246, pp. 422–436. Springer, Heidelberg (2006). https://doi.org/10.1007/11916277_29

53. Scheben, C., Greiner, S.: Information flow analysis. In: Ahrendt et al. [4], chap. 13, pp. 453–472

54. Steffen, B.: Unifying models. In: Reischuk, R., Morvan, M. (eds.) STACS 1997. LNCS, vol. 1200, pp. 1–20. Springer, Heidelberg (1997). https://doi.org/10.1007/BFb0023444

55. Steffen, B., Margaria, T., Claßen, A., Braun, V.: Incremental formalization: a key to industrial success. Softw. Concepts Tools **17**(2), 78–95 (1996)

56. Steffen, B., Margaria, T., Nagel, R., Jörges, S., Kubczak, C.: Model-driven development with the jABC. In: Bin, E., Ziv, A., Ur, S. (eds.) HVC 2006. LNCS, vol. 4383, pp. 92–108. Springer, Heidelberg (2007). https://doi.org/10.1007/978-3-540-70889-6_7

57. Steffen, B., Rüthing, O.: Quality engineering: leveraging heterogeneous information. In: Jhala, R., Schmidt, D. (eds.) VMCAI 2011. LNCS, vol. 6538, pp. 23–37. Springer, Heidelberg (2011). https://doi.org/10.1007/978-3-642-18275-4_4

58. Sutcliffe, G., Urban, J.: The CADE-25 automated theorem proving system competition: CASC-25. AI Commun. **29**(3), 423–433 (2016)

59. Wasser, N.: Generating specifications for recursive methods by abstracting program states. In: Li, X., Liu, Z., Yi, W. (eds.) SETTA 2015. LNCS, vol. 9409, pp. 243–257. Springer, Cham (2015). https://doi.org/10.1007/978-3-319-25942-0_16

60. Windmüller, S., et al.: Active continuous quality control. In: 16th International ACM Sigsoft Symposium on Component-Based Software Engineering, Vancouver, Canada (2013)

61. Wong, P.Y.H., Albert, E., Muschevici, R., Proença, J., Schäfer, J., Schlatte, R.: The ABS tool suite: modelling, executing and analysing distributed adaptable object-oriented systems. STTT **14**(5), 567–588 (2012)

Logic-Based Learning: Theory and Application

Dalal Alrajeh(✉) and Alessandra Russo

Department of Computing, Imperial College London, 180 Queen's Gate, London, UK
{dalal.alrajeh,a.russo}@imperial.ac.uk

Abstract. In recent years, research efforts have been directed towards the use of Machine Learning (ML) techniques to support and automate activities such as specification mining, risk assessment, program analysis, and program repair. The focus has largely been on the use of machine learning black box methods whose inference mechanisms are not easily interpretable and whose outputs are not declarative and guaranteed to be correct. Hence, they cannot readily be used to inform the elaboration and revision of declarative software models identified to be incorrect or incomplete. On the other hand, recent advances in ML have witnessed the emergence of new *logic-based machine learning* approaches that overcome such limitations and which have been proven to be well-suited for many software engineering tasks. In this chapter, we present a survey of the state-of-the-art of logic-based machine learning techniques, highlight their expressivity, define their different underlying semantics, and discuss their efficiency and the heuristics they adopt to guide the search for solutions. We then demonstrate the application of this type of machine learning to (declarative) specification refinement and revision as a complementary task to program analysis.

1 Introduction

Machine Learning (ML) has been shown to provide a promising approach to support and automate various software engineering (SE) activities. Numerous (traditional) ML techniques have been used for modelling and predicting software costs, predicting software defects [13], performing program repair [43], improving software reliability [22], and mining (quantitative) knowledge from data on past software engineering projects [52]. They have been shown to have the potential of reducing human effort and human-driven errors. They have also been used as components of software systems themselves, giving, for instance, the software the ability to model the environment in which they operate and to adapt its behaviour at run-time in response to changes in its environment (e.g., [21]). However, as noted in [32], most of these applications of ML are mainly optimisation tasks. The synergy between ML techniques and SE has the potential to go beyond this.

Software engineering activities are predominately knowledge-intensive. Some of this knowledge is explicit at design time whilst some becomes apparent only

© Springer International Publishing AG, part of Springer Nature 2018
A. Bennaceur et al. (Eds.): ML for Dynamic Software Analysis, LNCS 11026, pp. 219–256, 2018.
https://doi.org/10.1007/978-3-319-96562-8_9

after the deployment of the software within its environment. For example, in requirements engineering, knowledge about the domain is key to the development of correct specifications with respect to given system goals, and its absence may lead to significant system failures [40]. Domain knowledge is also relevant at run-time. Complex software systems are increasingly required to be context-aware and self-adaptive. In other words, they must be sufficiently intelligent, i.e., to know when and how to evolve in response to changes in the environment. To demonstrate intelligent behaviour, software needs to be able to: (*i*) *learn* and react to new knowledge, exhibited once it interacts with its environment, in order to improve over time and with experience, and (*ii*) be *analysable*, so that the evolved behaviours can be verified with respect to overall (domain-specific) properties (e.g., safety, security, correctness and completeness properties) [51]. But the integration of "black box" ML in software development tasks and in software systems may reduce the transparency of the (evolved) software models, thus jeopardising their correct use, analysis and deployment. So the question that we address in this chapter is *how can relevant knowledge be automatically learned at both design and run-time expressed in a way that can be amenable to analysis, and human inspection, where required.*

Recent advances in Artificial Intelligence have witnessed the development of new ML approaches, called *logic-based machine learning* methods [30]. They differ from traditional ML approaches in that (*i*) observations, prior knowledge and learned outcomes are all represented within the same declarative formalism, hence making the learned outcomes interpretable, and, due to their precise semantics, easier to inspect and analyse; (*ii*) they allow for declarative specification of the space of possible outcomes; (*iii*) guaranteeing correctness of the learned outcomes with respect to given constraints, observations and prior knowledge; (*iii*) they do not suffer from the problem of overfitting when handling small number of examples due to their ability of generalising; and (*iv*) they may produce alternative solutions if any exist, with possible ranking (if needed).

This chapter surveys key recent advances in logic-based machine learning over the last fifteen years. It presents different types of learning tasks, including non-monotonic learning and learning-based revision, their underlying semantic assumptions, expressivity, and the common heuristics they use to guide the search for solutions. A case study is then explored to illustrate how logic-based machine learning can be used to support the task of software specification refinement and revision. We discuss some of the recent research trends in logic-based ML as well as some promising applications in formal software analysis.

2 Background

2.1 Notation and Terminology

We summarise here the terminologies and notations that will be used throughout this chapter. These are adapted from Lloyd [46], and Nienhuys-Cheng and de Wolf [59]. First-order logic is a formalism characterised by a first-order language $\mathcal{L}$ and a formal model-theoretic semantics. The language $\mathcal{L}$ consists of quantifiers,

$\forall$ and $\exists$, logical connectives $\land$, $\lor$, $\leftarrow$ and $\neg$, logical constants $\top$ and $\bot$, a set Σ^p of predicate symbols, with specified arities, a set Σ^f of function symbols, with specified arities, and a set Σ^v of variables. We denote a *predicate* (resp. *function*) p (resp. f) with arity n as p/n (resp., f/n). Function symbols with arity 0 are also called *constants*. Throughout the chapter, we adopt the standard convention of denoting variables as strings of letters and digits starting with an uppercase letter (e.g., X, X_1, C, $C1$ etc.); and predicate, function and constant symbols as strings of letters and digits starting with a lowercase letter (e.g., c, l_1, etc.). A *term*, t, is either a constant, a variable or a construct of the form $f(t_1, \ldots, t_n)$, where f is an n-ary function and t_1, ..., t_n are terms. A term is said to be *ground* if it contains no variable. For instance, c is a ground term, $f(c, d)$ is also a ground term, whereas $g(X, c)$ is not. An *atomic formula* (also called *atom*) is composed of a predicate symbol, say p/n, of arity n, and a tuple of n terms, say t_1, ..., t_n. We denote such an atom as $p(t_1, \ldots, t_n)$. Similarly to terms, we say that an atom is *ground* if it does not include any variable. For example, $p(f(c), d)$ is a ground atom whereas $p(f(X), d)$ is not. The notion of a *formula* is recursively defined as follows. A formula is either an atom or one of the following expressions, where α_1 and α_2 are themselves formulae.

$$\neg\alpha_1 \mid \alpha_1 \lor \alpha_2 \mid \alpha_1 \land \alpha_2 \mid \alpha_1 \leftarrow \alpha_2 \mid \forall X(\alpha_1) \mid \exists X(\alpha_1)$$

A *literal* is either an atom or a *negated* atom. Given a formula $\forall X(\alpha)$ (resp. $\exists X(\alpha)$), α is the scope of the quantifier $\forall X$ (resp. $\exists X$). Occurrences of the variable X in α are said to be *bound* as they are within the scope of a quantifier. A formula whose variables are all bound is said to be *closed*. For example, the formula $p(X)$ is not closed because X does not occur within the scope of a quantifier, whereas the formula $\forall X(\forall Y(p(X, Y)))$ is a closed formula. Close formulae are also called *sentences*. In the rest of this chapter, we assume all formulae to be closed and use the terms formula and sentence interchangeably.

Another important notion in classical logic is that of *substitution*. A *substitution*, θ, is a finite set of the form $\{X_1/t_1, \ldots, X_n/t_n\}$ where each X_i is a different variable and each t_i is a term distinct from X_i. We call each element of the set a *binding*. θ is called a *ground substitution* if all t_i are ground terms. Given a sentence f and a substitution $\theta = \{X_1/t_1, \ldots, X_n/t_n\}$, the instantiated sentence $f\theta$ is obtained by replacing each variable X_i with the term t_i. $f\theta$ is a ground instantiation of f, or simple an *instance* of f, if θ is a ground substitution.

The *model-theoretic* semantics of first-order logic assumes a semantic structure comprising of an interpretation, I, and a non-empty domain of discourse, D. Given first-order language $\mathcal{L}$, the interpretation assigns each constant c to an element c^I in D; each n-ary function g in $\mathcal{L}$ to a function g^I from D^n to D; each n-ary predicate p in $\mathcal{L}$ to a function p^I from D^n to the Boolean set {true, false}. Given an arbitrary sentence α and a semantic structure (I, D), the truth value of α is defined inductively as follows. The atom $p(t_1, \ldots, t_n)$ is true (resp. false) if and only if the value of $p^I(t_1^I, \ldots, t_n^I)$ is true (resp. false). The truth value of a complex sentence α follows the conventional semantics of the connectives (truth tables) and quantifiers that appear in α (see [46] for further details). Finally, an interpretation I is a *model* of a sentence α if α is true with respect to I. Similarly an interpretation I is a model of set S of sentences if each sentence in S is true with respect to I, i.e., I is a model of every sentence in S. A sentence is *consistent* (satisfiable) if and only if it has at least one model, *inconsistent* (unsatisfiable) if it has no models, *valid* if every interpretation is a model. Let S be a set of sentences, and α be a sentence. We say α is a *logical consequence* of S, denoted $S \models \alpha$, if for every interpretation I that is a model of S, I is also a model of α. In this case we also say that S *logically entails* α.

2.2   Logic Programming

We have introduced basic notions of first-order logic. *Logic programming* is a programming paradigm based on a subset of first-order logic that is computationally tractable. Programs, written in a logic programming language, are sets of specific types of sentences for which various formal framework and algorithms have been developed to support different forms of computational inference (e.g., deductive, abductive and inductive). Various families of logic programming languages have been proposed in the literature, each with different level of expressivity. The basic language represents a problem in terms of *definite clauses*. Definite clauses are first-order sentences of the form $\forall \overline{X}(h \vee \neg b_1 \vee \ldots \vee \neg b_n)$ where $\forall \overline{X}$ is a shorthand for $\forall X_1, .., \forall X_n$ of all variables $X_1, .., X_n$ appearing in the clause, h and every b_i are positive atoms. Such clauses are also written in rule form as $h \leftarrow b_1, \ldots, b_n$ where h is the *head* of the rule and $b_1, \ldots, b_n$ is the *body* of the rule, consisting essentially of conjunction of atoms. Definite clauses with empty body are called *facts* whereas definite clauses with empty head are called *denial constraints*. A definite logic program Π is a conjunction of definite clauses.

Example 1. Consider a basic electric circuit consisting of a single light bulb and a single switch connected in series. We want to describe the property "it is always the case that flicking the switch may turn the light on" as a logic program Π. We can use the constant *lightOn* to refer to the light being on, and the constant *flickSwitch* to express the event of flicking the switch. We can also assume a notion of time as additional type of constant (and variable) in our domain. We can use the predicate *happens*/2 to express the occurrence of an event at a specific time, the predicate *initiates*/3 to express the effect that an event may have, and the predicate *holdsAt*/2 to express what is true at any given time point. To represent the above property, we can write the following definite logic program where the fact states that at any time point T, *flickSwitch* may have the effect of *lightOn*, and the rule captures the general property that the occurrence of an event that may have an effect causes that effect to be true after the event has occurred.

$$\Pi = \left\{ \begin{array}{l} initiates(flickSwitch, lightOn, T) \\ holdsAt(F,T) \leftarrow happens(E,T_1), initiates(E,F,T_1), time(T), time(T_1), T > T_1) \end{array} \right\}$$

A model of the definite program Π is constructed by first considering the *Herbrand domain* of the program as domain of discourse, denoted as U. This is the set of all ground terms that can be constructed using constants and functions that occur in Π. If we assume the program Π in the example above extended with facts about time points (i.e., $time(0)$. $time(1)$. $time(2)$.) then the Herbrand domain of Π would be $U(\Pi) = \{flickSwitch, lightOn, 0, 1, 2\}$. The *Herbrand base* of the program Π, denoted $HB(\Pi)$, is instead the set of all ground atoms constructed using the predicates in Π and ground terms in $U(\Pi)$. For the program Π given in the above example, the Herbrand base $HB(\Pi)$ is the following set of ground atoms extended with the ground atoms about time $time(0), \ldots, time(2)$.

$$HB(\Pi) = \left\{ \begin{array}{l} initiates(flickSwitch, lightOn, 0), initiates(flickSwitch, lightOn, 1), \\ initiates(flickSwitch, lightOn, 2), happens(flickSwitch, 0), \\ happens(flickSwitch, 1), happens(flickSwitch, 2), \\ holdsAt(lightOn, 0), holdsAt(lightOn, 1), holdsAt(lightOn, 2) \end{array} \right\}$$

An *Herbrand interpretation* I of a given definite program is a subset of the Herbrand base of the program. Ground atoms in I are assumed to be true and any other ground atoms in $HB(\Pi) \setminus I$ is assumed to be false. An *Herbrand interpretation* is an *Herbrand* model of a definite program Π if and only if it makes all the clauses in Π true. For instance, the following Herbrand interpretation, extended with ground atoms $time(0), \ldots, time(2)$, is an Herbrand model of Π.

$$HM(\Pi) = \left\{ \begin{array}{l} initiates(flickSwitch, lightOn, 0), initiates(flickSwitch, lightOn, 1), \\ initiates(flickSwitch, lightOn, 2), happens(flickSwitch, 0), \\ holdsAt(lightOn, 0), holdsAt(lightOn, 1), holdsAt(lightOn, 2) \end{array} \right\}$$

Definite programs have the appealing property of accepting a unique minimal Herbrand model, called the *least Herbrand model* (LHM). For a given definite program Π, the $LHM(\Pi) \subseteq HB(\Pi)$ such that any other Herbrand interpretation I, $I \subset LHM(\Pi)$ is not an Herbrand model of Π. In other words, $LHM(\Pi)$ is the smallest set of ground positive atoms from the Hebrand base that satisfy a given program Π. For instance, the $HM(\Pi)$ given above is an Herbrand model of Π, but it is not a $LHM(\Pi)$. This is because the strict subset $HM(\Pi) \setminus holdsAt(lightOn, 0)$ is also a Herbrand model of Π, and it is actually the $LHM(\Pi)$. The least Herbrand model of a program can be computed using a notion of *immediate consequence operator* T_Π. Starting from an empty interpretation, the T_Π operator iteratively adds to the interpretation immediate consequences of the program until no new consequence (ground atom) is generated (i.e., a *fixed point* of the operator is reached). At each iteration, assuming I to be the interpretation constructed so far, $T_\Pi(I) = \{h\theta | h \leftarrow b_1, \ldots, b_n \in \Pi$ and $b_1\theta, \ldots, b_n\theta \in I\}$ [46]. Essentially, for every rule $h \leftarrow b_1, \ldots, b_n \in \Pi$ and for all ground substitutions θ, $\{b_1\theta, \ldots, b_n\theta\} \subseteq I$ implies $h\theta \in I$. Given a definite logic program Π and a ground atom α, $\Pi \models \alpha$ if and only if $\alpha \in LHM(\Pi)$.

The notion of entailment under the least Herbrand model semantics essentially equates the entailment of a ground atom from a program to the notion of *provability* of that ground atom from the program. The least Herbrand model semantics imposes the implicit assumption that ground atoms that are true are also *known* to be true, that is they are computationally provable. Adding rules or facts to a given definite program can therefore only allow the derivation of additional ground atoms whilst preserving the entailment of all the ground atoms that are already provable from the initial program. The entailment based on least Herbrand model semantics is therefore *monotonic*. This is not the case for logic programs that include negation as failure, called *normal logic programs*. Normal logic programs are programs consisting of rules of the form $h \leftarrow b_1, \ldots, b_n, not\ c_1, \ldots, not\ c_m$, where h, b_i, and c_j are all atoms, and *not* is a *negation as failure* (NAF) operator. This operator interprets the notion of negation as *failure to prove*. The semantics of negation as failure reflect the notion of Closed World Assumption (CWA) [53]. A ground atom f that is not provable is not currently known to be true, therefore it is false and *not f* is true. Conversely, a ground atom f that is true, is provable and therefore currently known to be true, so *not f* is false. The semantic interpretation of *not f* can therefore be defined as follows:

  not f is true if and only if f is not provable

  not f is false if and only if f is provable

Different formal semantics have been proposed in the literature for normal logic programs (see [6] for a survey). One of the most established is the *stable model* semantics [28]. This is based on the concept of *grounding* of a program. Given a normal logic program Π, the grounding of Π, written $ground(\Pi)$, is given by $ground(\Pi) = \cup_{r \in \Pi}\ ground(r)$, where $ground(r)$ is obtained by substituting the variables occurring in r with all possible elements in the Herbrand domain of Π. Consider the program Π given in Example 1 and let r be the first rule in Π.

$ground(r) = \{initiates(flickSwitch, lightOn, 0), initiates(flickSwitch, lightOn, 1),$
$\qquad\qquad initiates(flickSwitch, lightOn, 2).\}$

The computation of a stable model of a normal logic program Π is based on the notion of a *reduct* of the program with respect to a given set of ground atoms. The reduct is essentially a transformation of the normal program into a definite program for which a unique least Herbrand model exists. If such a least Herbrand model is equal to the chosen set of ground atoms than the chosen set of ground atoms constitutes the stable model of the initial normal program. More formally, let Π be a normal program, for any rule $r \in ground(\Pi)$ let $head(r)$ be the head of r, $body^+(r)$ and $body^-(r)$ be respectively the set of positive atoms and the set of negated (by NAF) atoms in the body of r. Let I be a chosen set of ground atoms. Then the *reduct* of $ground(\Pi)$ relative to I is defined as $\Pi^I = \{head(r) \leftarrow body^+(r) \mid r \in ground(\Pi)$ and $body^-(r) \cap I = \emptyset\}$. A set of ground atoms I is a *stable model* of Π if it is the case that I is the least Herbrand model of Π^I.

Example 2. Consider a modified version of the electric circuit given in Example 1 where the required properties are (*i*) "flicking the switch may turning the light on if the switch is not already on"; (*ii*) "flicking the switch may make the switch on if the switch is not on"; and (iii) "flicking the switch may make the switch not on if the switch is already on". We need to use a new constant $switchOn$ to refer to the switch being already on. Let's also assume that at time 0 the switch is not on and that the $flickSwitch$ happens at time 0. The program will now be

$$
\Pi = \left\{
\begin{array}{l}
initiates(flickSwitch, lightOn, T) \leftarrow not\ holdsAt(switchOn, T) \\
initiates(flickSwitch, switchOn, T) \leftarrow not\ holdsAt(switchOn, T) \\
terminates(flickSwitch, switchOn, T) \leftarrow holdsAt(switchOn, T) \\
holdsAt(F, T) \leftarrow happens(E, T_1), initiates(E, F, T_1) \\
\qquad\qquad\qquad not\ clipped(T_1, F, T), T > T_1 \\
clipped(T_1, F, T) \leftarrow happens(E, T_2), terminates(E, F, T_2), T_1 \leq T_2, T_2 < T \\
happens(flickSwitch, 0)
\end{array}
\right\}
$$

Consider the set

$$
\begin{array}{l}
I = \{\ happens(flickSwitch, 0), holdsAt(switchOn, 1), holdsAt(switchOn, 2), \\
\quad holdsAt(lightOn, 1), holdsAt(lightOn, 2), initiates(flickSwitch, lightOn, 0), \\
\quad initiates(flickSwitch, switchOn, 0), terminates(flickSwitch, switchOn, 1), \\
\quad terminates(flickSwitch, switchOn, 2)\}
\end{array}
$$

Part of the reduct of Π with respect to I is given by:

$$
\Pi' = \left\{
\begin{array}{l}
initiates(flickSwitch, lightOn, 0) \\
initiates(flickSwitch, switchOn, 0) \\
terminates(flickSwitch, switchOn, 1) \leftarrow holdsAt(switchOn, 1) \\
terminates(flickSwitch, switchOn, 2) \leftarrow holdsAt(switchOn, 2) \\
holdsAt(lightOn, 1) \leftarrow happens(flickSwitch, 0), \\
\qquad\qquad\qquad initiates(switchOn, lightOn, 0), 1 > 0 \\
holdsAt(switchOn, 1) \leftarrow happens(flickSwitch, 0), \\
\qquad\qquad\qquad initiates(flickSwitch, switchOn, 0), 1 > 0 \\
holdsAt(lightOn, 2) \leftarrow happens(flickSwitch, 0), \\
\qquad\qquad\qquad initiates(switchOn, lightOn, 0), 2 > 0 \\
holdsAt(switchOn, 2) \leftarrow happens(flickSwitch, 0), \\
\qquad\qquad\qquad initiates(flickSwitch, switchOn, 0), 2 > 0 \\
happens(flickSwitch, 0)
\end{array}
\right\}
$$

The $LHM(\Pi')$ is equal to the given set I. So I is the stable model of Π. As no other $flickSwitch$ event occurs, the $lightOn$ and $switchOn$ preserve their truth value, from time point 1 onwards. This is because the predicate $clipped$ is not provable. But if $happens(flickSwitch, 1)$ is added to Π the ground atom $holdsAt(switchOn, 2)$ would not be provable from Π, since $clipped(0, switchOn, 2)$ would be now true. Similarly, the ground facts $initiates(flickSwitch, lightOn, 2)$ and $initiates(flickSwitch, switchOn, 2)$ become provable as $holdsAt(switchOn, 2)$ would be false and, for the same reason, the fact $terminates(flickSwitch, switchOn, 2)$ becomes no longer provable. In this case the given interpretation I would not be a stable model.

The above example demonstrates how the use of NAF and CWA makes the entailment relation of a given program (defined in terms of provability), non-monotonic (i.e., entailment of ground atoms are no longer preserved as new information is added to or deleted from the program).

3   A Survey on Logic-Based Learning

In the early 1970s, contributions to the area of resolution theorem proving prompted many research activities in the area of automated inference, which led to the definition and development of three main research fields, logic programming for deductive inference [38], abductive logic programming for abductive inference [63] and inductive logic programming for inductive inference [62]. The main distinction between deduction, on the one hand, and abduction and induction on the other hand, lays on the fact that the former is a *necessary* inference, whereas the latter are *ampliative* inferences. In a deductive inference step, what is inferred is necessarily true if the premises from which it is inferred are true, that is the truth of the premises guarantees the truth of the conclusion. In syllogistic terms, deductive inference is the process of deriving results by applying general rules to specific cases. Abduction and induction are instead ampliative forms of inferences, as they generate knowledge that is not explicitly included in the premises of the inference process. Specifically, abduction is the process of reasoning from observations to possible causes. It starts from general rules and observations (or results) and finds possible cases for which the general rules, if applied, would lead to the given observations. These cases are the explanations of the given observations. Induction is also an ampliative reasoning mechanism, but it aims at discovering new general rules from samples of cases and related results, in a way that the learned general rule when applied to the given cases would prove the given results. In summary, abduction is the process of *explanation*—reasoning from effects to possible causes, whereas induction is the process of *generalisation* – reasoning from specific cases to general *hypothesis*.

Inductive Logic Programming (ILP) is the study of frameworks and algorithms for performing the inductive reasoning task of *learning* logic programs, in the form of hypotheses, from given observations. ILP approaches can be grouped into two main types: *descriptive ILP* and *predictive ILP* [23]. The former is designed to 'discover clausal regularities from unclassified data' [1]. Observations are full Herbrand interpretations, and the task is to learn a *descriptive* hypothesis, as a set of clauses, that accepts each observation as a model. More formally, given as set O of observations, such that each element $o \in O$ is an Herbrand interpretation with respect to a given language, an hypothesis H is a set of definite clauses such that $\forall o \in O$, we have $o \models H$. The symbols used to construct the hypothesis are limited to those found in the given set of observations.

In contrast, predictive ILP aims to learn rules that define a classification of given observations. A predictive task takes a set E of observations, called *examples*, labelled according to some predetermined labelling, together with a background theory B (if any), and *searches* for a set of rules, H that, together with B, assigns the correct labels to the given observations as well as to unseen observations. We refer to the notion of assigning correct labels to given observations as *coverage* of the learned hypothesis H, denoted as $c(B \cup H, E)$, and correctly labelling unseen examples as *predictive accuracy* of the hypothesis H. Predictive ILP differs from other machine learning techniques in that the hypothesis is represented as a logic program and the classification of the examples may rely upon an existing background theory also expressed as a logic program that defines relevant concepts for the learning task. These characteristics give predictive ILP two main advantages. Firstly, it can be applied to complex domains where entities are (to be) modelled using complex rule-based models. Secondly, the outcome of the learning is readable and can be interpreted by domain experts or by end users.

The most common framework for predictive ILP is *learning from entailment*. In a learning from entailment, examples are ground literals. Positive literals are examples labelled as true (i.e., *positive* examples), whereas atoms that are negated are examples labelled as false (i.e., *negative examples*). The background theory, examples and hypotheses are all expressed using a common logic programming language with a specific underlying semantics and entailment relation. Hypotheses are assumed to belong to a given search space of possible logic programs, called *hypothesis space*. Not all the logic programs in the hypothesis space are *solutions* of a given learning task. The goal of a learning task is to find a hypothesis in the hypothesis space that together with the given background theory *entails* each positive examples and *does not entail* any of the negative examples. Such an hypothesis is referred to as a *solution* of a learning task. Coverage of examples is, therefore, defined in terms of the *entailment* relation of the chosen logic program's semantics considered in the learning task. This is formalised as follows.

Definition 1 (Learning from entailment). *A learning from entailment task is a tuple $T = \langle B, L_H, E \rangle$, where B is a logic program, called the* background *theory, L_H is a set of logic programs, called the* hypothesis space *and E is a set of positive and negative literals, called* examples. *An inductive solution of T is a logic program $H \in L_H$ such that $B \cup H \models E$.*

Different algorithms have been proposed in the literature to address the problem of how to solve a learning from entailment task. Such task could be seen as a search problem, i.e., search within a given hypothesis space for solutions that classify (or cover) the given examples correctly. In the above definition, coverage has to be *perfect*, that is, all examples must be entailed by a solution. Perfect coverage is appropriate in learning tasks that have examples perfectly labelled. But the search may lead to multiple hypotheses with perfect coverage. So often ILP algorithms use a *quality measure* for which more *compact* solutions are preferred[1]. The notion of compact solution is often given in terms of size of the solution, computed as the number of different literals that appear in the

---

[1] This follows the standard Occam's razor principle for which simpler hypotheses are better.

solution. In practice, examples are not perfectly labelled. In this case, the quality measure of a solution has to take into account the number of examples that are covered. An example of such measure is given by the following function [18], where $|r|$ is the number of literals that appear in a rule of H.

$$score(B, H, E) = - \sum_{r \in H} |r| + |\{e \in E | B \cup H \models e\}| - |\{not\ e \in E | B \cup H \models e\}|$$

The above function, referred to as *score* of an hypothesis, can be defined as the number of positive examples correctly covered minus the number of negative examples covered and the number of literals in the hypothesis. So, when an hypothesis H has perfect coverage, the number of negative examples covered is 0 and the number of positive examples is equal to the given set of positive examples. So if few hypotheses with perfect coverage exist in the hypothesis space, the most preferred one will be the hypothesis with highest score, which corresponds to the hypothesis with less number of literals.

As shown in Definition 1 one of the components of a learning task is the hypothesis space L_H. In practice, the hypothesis space, provided as input to a learning task, is defined in the form of a specification language, called *mode declarations*, first introduced in [58]. In brief, a set M of mode declarations is composed of two subsets, M^+ and M^-, called *head* and *body* declarations, respectively. Each of these declarations consists of a *scheme*. A scheme is an atom that may contain special terms called *placemarkers*. It can be thought of as a "template" with placemarkers as its "slots". Placemarkers can be of three different *modes*: input (denoted as $+$), output (denoted as $-$), or ground (denoted as $\sharp$). Intuitively, input and output placemarkers stand for variables, while ground placemarkers stand for ground terms. Head declarations are denoted as $modeh(s)$, where s is a scheme, and body declarations are denoted as $modeb(s)$ where s is a scheme. An example of a mode head declaration is $modeh(terminates(+action, +fluent, +time))$, where the scheme is the predicate *terminates* which has three placemarkers (*action*, *fluent* and *time*) of mode input. An instance of this mode declaration is a predicate of the form $terminates(X, Y, T)$ where X is a variable of type *action*, Y is a variable of type *fluent* and T is a variable of type *time*. Being an head mode declaration means that such a predicate may appear in the head of a rule defining the solution of a learning task. Similarly, for mode body declarations. So given a set M of mode declarations, the hypothesis space specified by M is $L_H = \mathcal{P}(S)$ where S of the set of clauses $a_0 \leftarrow a_1, a_2, \dots, a_n$ for which there is a mode head declaration $m_0 \in M^+$, and mode body declarations $m_1, m_2, \dots, m_n$ in M^- such that a_i is an instance of m_i for every $0 \leq i \leq n$, and every variable v with an input occurrence in a_i has an input occurrence in a_0 or an output occurrence in a_j for some $0 < j < i$.

Example 3. Consider the following set M of mode declarations, h_1, and h_2 are examples of two hypotheses in the hypothesis space L_H specified by M.

$$M = \left\{ \begin{array}{l} modeh(p(+type1)) \\ modeb(r(+type1, \sharp type2)) \\ modeb(q(+type1, -type1)) \end{array} \right\} \qquad \begin{array}{l} h_1 = \left\{ \begin{array}{l} p(X) \leftarrow r(X, c) \\ p(X) \leftarrow q(X, Y), r(Y, d) \end{array} \right\} \\[1em] h_2 = \left\{ \begin{array}{l} p(X) \leftarrow r(X, c) \\ p(X) \leftarrow q(X, Y), r(X, d) \end{array} \right\} \end{array}$$

Existing ILP approaches, which fall within the framework of learning from entailment, can be grouped into two main classes: *monotonic ILP* and *non-monotonic ILP*. The former assume a background theory and hypothesis space expressed only in terms of definite logic programs with the notion of entailment based on the least Herbrand model semantic. The latter, on the other hand, are capable of handling learning tasks where both the background theory and hypothesis space are expressed as normal logic programs. The underlying semantics and entailment relation is that of stable model semantics. Within each of these classes, ILP approaches can be further characterised into *top-down*, *bottom up* and *meta-level* learning, depending on the type of search algorithm used to compute solutions within the given hypothesis space. The following two subsections survey the most established ILP approaches, specifying in particular the type of input and output that they accept, the algorithmic approach they adopt to learn correct solutions, and current limitations.

3.1   Monotonic ILP

Traditionally, ILP has addressed the problem of learning definite logic programs. As this class of programs does not allow any form of negation, the notion of learning from entailment given in Definition 1 is reformulated as follows. A learning from entailment task for definite logic programs is a tuple $\langle B, L_H, E^+, E^- \rangle$, where B is a definite logic program, the hypothesis space L_H is also a set of definite logic programs, and E^+ and E^- are respectively the set of positive and of negative examples, each consisting of ground atoms. An inductive solution of such a task is a definite logic program $H \in L_H$ such that $B \cup H \models e$, for each $e \in E^+$ and $B \cup H \not\models e$ for each $e \in E^-$, where the entailment relation is under the least Herbrand model semantics. An example of an ILP task for definite logic programs is given below, where the function symbol s returns the successor of a given number.

Example 4. Consider the ILP task $T = \langle B, L_H, E^+, E^- \rangle$ where B, E^+, E^- are defined below, and L_H is the hypothesis space specified by the following set M of mode declarations:

$$B = \left\{ \begin{array}{l} even(0) \\ nat(0) \\ nat(s(X)) \leftarrow nat(X) \end{array} \right\} \quad M = \left\{ \begin{array}{l} modeh(even(+nat)) \\ modeh(odd(+nat)) \\ modeb(+nat = s(-nat)) \\ modeb(even(+nat)) \\ modeb(odd(+nat)) \end{array} \right\}$$

$$E^+ = \{ odd(s(s(s(s(s(0)))))) \}$$

$$E^- = \left\{ \begin{array}{l} odd(s(s(0))) \\ odd(s(s(s(s(0))))) \end{array} \right\}$$

A solution to the above task would be the following definite logic program. It is easy to see that H is an element of an hypothesis space L_H.

$$H = \left\{ \begin{array}{l} odd(X) \leftarrow X = s(Y), even(Y) \\ even(X) \leftarrow X = s(Y), odd(Y) \end{array} \right\}$$

Due to the monotonicity of the entailment relation for definite logic programs, the hypothesis space of an ILP task can be seen as a lattice structure, whose top node is the empty clause (i.e., inconsistency from which everything is provable), and the bottom nodes are the given positive examples. Nodes in this lattice structure are definite logic programs corresponding to hypotheses in the hypothesis space, and the relation between nodes is defined in terms of θ-subsumption between two definite logic programs. Informally, an hypothesis h_1 θ-subsumes an hypothesis h_2 if it is the case that every positive ground atom that is provable by h_2 is also provable by h_1, but h_1 proves also ground atoms that are not provable by h_2. Hypothesis h_1 is therefore said to be *more general* than hypothesis h_2 if h_1 θ-subsumes h_2. Solving an ILP task can therefore be seen as searching over this lattice for a node corresponding to a definite logic program that together with the given background theory entails all positive examples and none of the negative examples. Walking the lattice from "bottom-to-top" means searching for more general solutions. This is needed when the logic program at a current node does not entail some positive example (i.e., the program is too specific and needs to be generalised further). Because of the θ-subsumption property every positive example entailed by such current program will still be entailed by a more general program that θ-subsumes it. So the generalisation step is in order to expand the entailment of positive examples. Walking the lattice from "top-to-bottom" means searching for more specialised solutions. This is needed when the logic program at the current node entails some negative examples (i.e., the program is too general). So specialising such a program means restricting its entailment relation to eliminate the negative examples that are currently proved.

Algorithms that adopt the first type of search are called *bottom-up* algorithms. A first renown algorithm of this type was that proposed by Plotkin in [62]. It was based on the notion of *least general generalisation* operator [61]. The algorithm starts from two bottom nodes (i.e., two given positive examples), and generalises them by applying a least general generalisation operator, which computes a more general logic program that θ-subsumes the chosen current programs and does not entail any negative example. This process is repeated until all positive examples are covered. Another bottom-up approaches is GOLEM [56], which generalises pairs of current definite clauses into a *relative least general generalisation*, relative to the given background theory. GOLEM greedily selects the clause with best coverage over those created by relative least general generalisation.

Algorithms that adopt the "top-to-bottom" search are called *top-down* algorithms. A first algorithm of this kind was proposed in the early 1980s by Shapiro (e.g., [72]). The approach uses an oracle that knows which examples are positive or negative. The search is a top-down search that uses a *downward subsumption operator* [72]. Given the set of clauses at a current node of the hypothesis space, this operator produces the set of all set of clauses that are subsumed by it. So, starting from a very general set of clauses (e.g., the node in the lattice that corresponds to a single clause with just an unground head atom), the oracle confirms whether any negative example is entailed. If this is the case, then this current set of clauses is refined by replacing some clauses with the clauses generated by the downward subsumption operator. This process is repeated until no further negative example is entailed. Another top-down algorithm proposed in the literature is FOIL (First Order Inductive Learning) [65]. It specialises rules according to an *information based* search heuristic. As it adopts a greedy search strategy, it is suitable for learning tasks where suboptimal hypotheses are acceptable. These are solutions that do not need to entail all positive examples and none of the negative example, but minimise the number of examples that are wrongly classified.

In the mid 90s, a new approach for solving monotonic ILP tasks, called *Induction by Bottom Generalisation*, was proposed based on the idea of *inverse entailment* [55], which states that given a positive example e, $B \cup h \models e$ if and only if $B \cup \neg e \models \neg h$. Using this property, the algorithm assumes a lattice structure where every node is a single clause, and solves a monotonic ILP task in two steps. Firstly, given a positive example e, called *seed example*, and the background theory B, the negation of an hypothesis, $\neg h$ is inferred deductively from B and the negation of the seed example. The inferred $\neg h$ is denoted as $\overline{Bot(B, e)}$ and defined as $\overline{Bot(B, e)} = \{l \mid B, \neg e \models l\}$. Given that B is a definite logic program and $\neg e$ is the only negated fact, it is easy to see that $\overline{Bot(B, e)}$ is essentially a set of positive ground atoms, provable from B and $\neg e$, together with the negated e. Then a ground define clause is constructed, denoted as $Bot(B, e)$ by negating all the ground literals in $\overline{Bot(B, e)}$, i.e., $Bot(B, e) = \{\neg l \mid B, \neg e \models l\}$. This is clearly a ground definite clause as it includes only one positive ground atom (i.e. e) and the rest are all negated ground atoms. The algorithm calls such a clause the ground *Bottom clause* as it is the most specific clause in the lattice that explains the seed example e with respect to the given background theory B. The second step of the algorithm searches the lattice in a top-down fashion for a clause that θ-subsumes $Bot(B, e)$ and does not entail the negative examples. Two ILP systems were developed based on this algorithm: Progol [57] and Progol5 [58]. The former was only able to learn single definite clauses per seed example, whose head predicate was the predicate of the example itself. This type of learning is referred in the literature as *observation predicate learning* as the learned rule defines the predicate whose instances are observed as positive and negative examples. The second algorithm was also able to learn only single define clauses per seed example but with the extended capability of learning definite rules that define predicates that are not directly observed as examples but "linked" to the examples via rules in the background theory. This type of learning is referred in the literature as *non-observation predicate learning*. A further algorithm, also based on the idea of Bottom Generalisation, was subsequently proposed [54]. This approach, called ALECTO, uses abduction, instead of the deductive step of PROGOL, to learn predicates that are not directly observed and therefore supporting non-observation predicate learning.

All ILP systems based on Bottom Generalisation share the same computational method described in Algorithm 1, referred in the literature as *coverage loop*. The coverage loop method takes as input an ILP learning task $\langle B, L_H, E^+, E^- \rangle$ for definite programs. At each loop iteration a seed example $e_i \in E^+$ is chosen. This is a positive ground atom. A definite clause h is learned that satisfies the conditions $B \cup h \models e_i$ and $B \cup h \not\models e_k$ for any ground atom $e_k \in E^-$. The coverage of h is then checked (line 9) and all ground atoms in E^+ that are also entailed by the learned clause, together with the background theory B, are removed (line 10). Different monotonic ILP algorithms for learning definite programs may use different "LearningStep" procedures based on any of the learning approaches described so far (i.e., bottom-up generalisation, top-down specialisation or inverse entailment). What is crucial of the coverage loop method is the monotonicity property that is typical of learning definite logic programs. Whenever a new definite clause is added (line 8) to the current hypothesis, it is safe to remove all positive examples that have been entailed so far from the set of positive examples since they will still be entailed by the rules learned in the subsequent iterations.

In summary, existing ILP algorithms that use the coverage loop method have the advantage of be able to learn from reasonably large set of positive examples, since the learning is iterative. However they suffer of the following limitations. First of all, only one single definite clause can be learned per seed example. Although this seems to be reasonable for learning tasks where the solution is a single definition of a predicate that is observed, it is very limited in cases when multiple predicates need to be learned to entail the given positive examples. A simple instance of such cases is learning recursive definitions. So they cannot do multiple clause learning from single seed examples. A second limitation is the inability to learn from negative examples. In all the methods described above, negative examples are only used to reject possible candidate solutions, as the learning process is solely driven by the seed examples that are

---

Algorithm 1. Coverage Loop

1: Inputs: E^+ positive examples, E^- negative examples, L_H hypothesis space,
   B background theory
2: Outputs: H hypothesis
3: $E_{curr} = E^+$
4: $H = \emptyset$
5: **while** $E_{curr} \neq \emptyset$ **do**
6:     *Select* $e_i \in E_{curr}$
7:     $h = LearningStep(B, e, E^-)$
8:     $H = H \cup \{h\}$
9:     $E_{cov} = \{e_j \in E_{curr} | B \cup H \models e_j\}$
10:     $E_{curr} = E_{curr} \setminus E_{cov}$
11: **end while**
12: **return** H;

---

encountered. It makes for instance difficult to compute solutions that are specifically learned to reject a negative example. The third most relevant limitation is the inability of learning logic programs that have negation as failure either in the background theory or in the actual learned program. The first limitation has been addressed and resolved by a new hybrid abductive inductive learning algorithm, called HAIL, proposed in [68]. This algorithm is still based on the coverage loop method, but it uses a more general *LearningStep* procedure, which combines abductive, deductive and inductive reasoning in a seamless manner. The abductive reasoning step identifies a set of ground predicates that together with the background theory explain a chosen seed example. These ground predicate instances constitute the head predicates of the set of definite clauses to be learned in a single loop iteration. The deductive step computes ground literals, to add to the body of these definite clauses, which are derivable from the given background theory B. These two steps together generate a set of ground definite clauses that are guaranteed to entail the given seed example. Such a set is called ground *Kernel Set*. Finally, the inductive step searches for a set of unground clauses, with a minimal number of literals, that θ subsume the ground Kernel Set and does not entail the negative examples. The HAIL algorithm has been the first learning algorithm to show how the three forms of reasoning, abduction, deduction and induction, can be integrated to enable a more powerful learning of definite logic programs. Although limited to definite clauses, HAIL has also been shown to generalise the PROGOL algorithm and to resolve a well known incompleteness problem of PROGOL5 [77].

The monotonicity assumption that underpins the coverage loop method for learning, no longer holds in the case when the background theory and/or the hypothesis space is expressed in terms of normal logic programs, i.e., programs that include negation as failure. This is because the underlying semantics of normal logic programs (e.g., stable model semantics) is non-monotonic. Adding new normal clauses to a given normal logic program may stop the entailment of some of the positive atoms that are initially entailed by the program. Consider, for instance, the simple learning task where the background theory $B = \{p \leftarrow not\ q, r\}$ and examples $E^+ = \{p, q\}$ and $E^- = \emptyset$. The hypothesis space can include any normal logic program written using propositions p, q, and r. The coverage loop approach would start with choosing a seed example, let's say p. In this case a learner should be able to compute, as first hypothesis, the single fact r, since $B \cup \{r\} \models p$, under the stable model semantics. What is learned does not explain the second positive example q so after the first iteration $E_{curr} = \{q\}$ and the current hypothesis is $H = \{r\}$. In the second iteration the new chosen seed example is q and the only possible hypothesis for it is q itself. However, when we add q to the current hypothesis H, the new updated hypothesis H' will no longer be able to entail the previous example p, since $B \cup \{r\} \cup \{q\} \not\models p$. This example, although simple and propositional, shows that the coverage loop method cannot be used by ILP algorithms targeted to learn normal logic programs.

3.2   Non-monotonic ILP

Learning normal logic programs brings new challenges to the task of logic-based learning. Firstly, the coverage loop method, described in the previous section, that learns iteratively from selected seed examples cannot be used when learning normal logic programs. As illustrated above, applying this method to the problem of learning normal logic programs leads to incorrect solutions, as the entailment of ground atoms may not be guaranteed to be maintained when new learned normal clauses are added to the solution during the iterative process. The second challenge is that normal logic programs may accept multiple stable models. So the notion of learning from entailment given in Definition 1 may be too strong (i.e., requiring that positive examples are satisfied in all stable models of $B \cup H$), as in some applications it might be sufficient to require that positive examples are satisfied in at least one stable model of $B \cup H$. In what follows we present recent advancements in the area of non-monotonic ILP frameworks for learning normal logic programs that, together with existing background theory, cover given examples, and learning revisions of existing programs, which is one of the typical application of non-monotonic ILP.

Learning Normal Logic Programs. In contrast to what we have seen in Sect. 3.1, when learning normal logic programs positive and negative examples have to be considered all together in order to guarantee their coverage by the final solution. So a learning task can be formalised as a tuple $\langle B, L_H, E \rangle$, where E is a set of positive ground atoms (positive examples) and negated ground atoms (negative examples), as given in Definition 1 – no need to split the set of examples into two sets of positive and negative examples. We denote $E = \{e_1^+, \ldots, e_n^+, not\ e_1^-, \ldots, not\ e_m^-\}$. The background theory B is assumed to be a normal logic program and the hypothesis space L_H a set of normal logic programs, specified by a set of mode declarations with mode body declarations referring to scheme that can include also negation as failure. When a solution H is computed, the extended program $K \cup H$ may accept more than one stable model. So to fully define the notion of learning from entailment in the case of non-monotonic learning, we need to specify a notion of example *coverage*. In the literature two different semantic notions of entailment have been proposed, *brave entailment* ($\models_b$) and *caution entailment* ($\models_c$), which have given rise to two notions of non-monotonic learning, *brave induction* and *caution induction* respectively, initially defined in [70]. The notion of coverage for each of these two types of non-monotonic learning is captured by the following definitions.

Definition 2 (Cautious induction). *A cautious induction task is a tuple* $T = \langle B, L_H, E \rangle$, *where* B *is a normal logic program,* L_H *is a set of normal logic programs, and* $E = \{e_1^+, \ldots, e_n^+, not\ e_1^-, \ldots, not\ e_m^-\}$ *is a set of positive and negative examples. A normal logic program* $H \in L_H$ *is a cautious inductive solution of* T *if and only if for every stable model* M_s *of* $B \cup H$ *it is the case that* $e_i^+ \in M_s$, *for every* $1 \leq i \leq n$, *and* $e_j^- \notin M_s$ *for every* $1 \leq j \leq m$.

Definition 3 (Brave induction). *A brave induction task is a tuple* $T = \langle B, L_H, E \rangle$, *where* B *is a normal logic program,* L_H *is a set of normal logic programs, and* $E = \{e_1^+, \ldots, e_n^+, not\ e_1^-, \ldots, not\ e_m^-\}$ *is a set of positive and negative examples. A normal logic program* $H \in L_H$ *is a brave inductive solution of* T *if and only if there exists a stable model* M *of* $B \cup H$ *such that* $e_i^+ \in M$, *for every* $1 \leq i \leq n$, *and* $e_j^- \notin M$ *for every* $1 \leq j \leq m$.

Early approaches to non-monotonic ILP adopted cautious induction, as this notion is closer to the notion of learning from entailment (Definition 1), where examples must be covered in every model. In [70] it was argued that in some cases cautious induction can be too strong, and that a weaker form of induction – brave induction – is more appropriate. In the rest of this chapter we will refer mainly to non-monotonic ILP approaches for brave induction.

One of the first recently proposed algorithms for non-monotonic ILP is XHAIL [67]. It generalises the HAIL approach, described in Sect. 3.1, to the case of brave induction for non-monotonic learning. Similarly to HAIL, XHAIL computes brave inductive solutions in three steps: abductive, deductive and inductive steps. In the first step, a set Δ of ground atoms such that $B \cup \Delta \models_b e$ for every $e \in E$ is computed. These atoms are required to conform to mode head declarations defined in the learning task, and constitute the heads of ground instances of rules in the final brave inductive solution. In the deductive step, XHAIL finds the set of ground literals that could go in the body of the rules in the final brave solution. Each of these body literals l are such that $B \cup \Delta \models_b l$ and conform to at least one mode body declaration of the task. These first two steps generate together what is called the ground Kernel set, that is a set of ground normal rules whose head atoms are the elements in Δ and body literals are those computed in the deductive step. Such ground Kernel set K has already the property that $B \cup K \models_b e$, for every $e \in E$, but may not belong to the hypothesis space L_H. The final step of XHAIL, the inductive step, computes a set of normal rules, H that (i) is in the hypothesis space, $H \in L_H$, (ii) it subsumes the Kernel set, and (iii) bravely entails the examples. The computation also guarantees that if there were two solutions H_1 and H_2, which satisfy these three conditions, then the solution with the minimal number of literals would be returned, referred to as the *most compressed* solution. The XHAIL approach is an example of a non-monotonic ILP algorithm that uses a mixture of bottom-up and top-down search. The construction of the Kernel Set can be seen as a bottom-up process that looks for the most specific normal logic program that bravely entails the examples. The inductive step could be seen instead a form of top-down search that looks for most compressed solutions, starting from those that have only head predicates. We omit here the description of how the search for most compressed solution is performed in XHAIL. The reader is referred to [67] for further details.

Several other approaches have been recently proposed in the literature for non-monotonic learning, which adopt different strategies for resolving brave induction tasks. The *Top-directed Abductive Learning* (TAL) approach [16], for instance, makes use of a top-down meta-level search that aims to solve a brave induction task by automatically translating it into an equivalent abductive task for which a top-down search algorithm is used [60]. The transformation relies upon a one-to-one mapping function from the mode declarations, which specify the hypothesis space of the brave induction task, to the set of possible abductive solutions and vice-versa[2]. So, solutions generated by the abductive task are translated back into solutions of the given brave induction task. The transformation of an brave induction task to an equivalent abduction task, translates each normal rule that could appear in the hypothesis space into a meta-level representation and generates a normal logic program that reasons over possible ways of constructing such rules using this meta-level representation [16]. This abductive reasoning process can be seen essentially as a "meta-level" search over the hypothesis space. The main advantage of this approach is its generality and ability to compute brave inductive solutions that can include recursive rules, definition of multiple predicates and rules that are interdependent (i.e., predicates that appear in the body of a rule can also appear in the head of another rule belonging to the same solution). Finally, it has been shown to support both observation and non-observation predicate learning [18]. The generality of this non-monotonic learning approach has been evaluated in practice in various application domains (e.g., [3,36,69]), demonstrating the advantage of adopting such a meta-level strategy for solving brave induction tasks [18].

However, a drawback of this approach is its scalability. The abductive reasoning engine used by TAL is implemented in Prolog and as such its computational time is affected by the size of the hypothesis space and the number of examples of a given brave induction task. Furthermore, non-monotonic ILP systems based Prolog, including TAL, are not declarative enough. The order of the normal rules in the background theory can affect not only the efficiency of the computation, but also its termination. In addition, whenever the brave induction task is particularly knowledge-intensive (i.e., it relays a lot on the background theory), Prolog based ILP systems tend to perform redundant computations and

---

[2] We omit a full definition of an abductive algorithm as this would fall outside the scope of this chapter. The reader is referred to [20] for further details.

particularly heavy inferences which are responsible for a high share of the total time needed to compute a brave inductive solutions. Answer Set Programming [34] provides a natural solution to these computational problems, which can be more adequately solved by SAT-based techniques rather than resolution.

To combine the theoretical advantages of the meta-level abductive learning approach used by TAL with computational efficiency, the ASPAL system has been proposed in [17]. This system adapts the meta-level abductive learning approach of TAL to the computational environment of Answer Set Programming (ASP), a knowledge representation technique oriented towards declarative problem solving [11]. ASP combines a rich modelling language with powerful solving mechanisms based on satisfiability testing. ASP, unlike Prolog, resulted from the line of research regarding stable models [34]. Its language combines that of normal logic programming with ASP constructs like aggregates and optimisation statements [2]. ASP solvers make use of a grounder that derives the grounding of a given ASP program using optimisation techniques to reduce the instantiations whilst maintaining logical equivalence with the original program. Given an ASP program, an ASP solver computes all the answer sets of the program.

The ASPAL algorithm is based on the TAL approach of converting an ILP task to a meta-level logic program, but with the difference that such meta-level program is an ASP program. Given an brave induction task $T = \langle B, L_H, E \rangle$, where L_H is specified by a given set of mode declarations M, the first step of the algorithm is to compute a set Sk of *skeleton rules*. Consider, for instance, the set M of model declarations. Sk is the corresponding set of skeleton rules:

$$M = \left\{ \begin{array}{l} modeh(penguin(+bird) \\ modeb(not\ can(+bird, \natural ability) \end{array} \right\} Sk = \left\{ \begin{array}{l} penguin(X) \leftarrow bird(X) \\ penguin(X) \leftarrow not\ can(X, C_1) \end{array} \right\}$$

Each skeleton rule R is associated with a unique atom $rule(R_{id}, C_1, \ldots, C_n)$, denoted as R_{meta}, where $C_1, \ldots, C_n$ are the "constant placemarker" variables in R. Given a brave induction learning task, $T = \langle B, L_H, E \rangle$, where L_H is specified by a set M of mode declarations, and $E = \{e_1^+, \ldots, e_n^+, not\ e_1^-, \ldots, not\ e_m^-\}$, the set Sk of skeleton rules is generated from M. Then ASPAL automatically constructs an ASP meta-level representation of the learning task by adding to the background theory B, the set $\{h \leftarrow b_1, \ldots b_{n1}, R_{meta}|$ for each rule $R \in Sk\}$, of rules that could possibly appear in a solution, together with the following ASP constructs:

1. $0\{R_{meta_1}, \ldots R_{meta_k}\}n$ for each R_{meta_i} associated to the each skeleton rule.
2. $goal \leftarrow e_1^+, \ldots, e_n^+, not\ e_1^-, \ldots, not\ e_m^-$
3. $\leftarrow not\ goal$

The statement (1) is an ASP *aggregation*. This groups together all the ground instances of atoms $rule(R_{id}, C_1, \ldots, C_n)$ associated with the skeleton rules. Statement (2) groups together all the examples (positive and negative) given in the task, and statement (3) defines a constraint which states that the atom *goal* must be satisfied. The atoms in the aggregation are not defined in the program (i.e., they don't appear in the head of any rule) so their truth value is guessed by the ASP solver. In this process the solver computes a stable model of the ASP program by assigning true to a minimal number of atoms in the aggregation such that the constraint is satisfied. The satisfiability of the constraint guarantees that the Answer Set solution bravely entails all the positive examples and does not entail any of the negative examples. The guess of minimal assignment of true value to the atoms in the aggregation corresponds essentially to an *optimal abductive solution*. So each answer set computed by the ASP solver comes with a specific optimal assignment of true value to the atoms in the aggregate, which in turn corresponds to the optimal set of rules in the hypothesis space that bravely entail all the positive examples and none of the negative examples. The overall procedure is described in Algorithm 2.

Algorithm 2. FIND-HYPOTHESIS

1: Inputs: E examples; B background theory; M mode declarations; γ penalisation function
2: Outputs: H hypotheses
3: $MNC = 0$
4: $H = \emptyset$
5: **while** $\langle$ *termination_condition* $\rangle$ **do**
6:     $Q, A =$ DERIVE-SKELETON-RULES$(M,$ MNC$)$
7:     $\{\Delta_1, ..., \Delta_n\} =$ ASP-ABDUCE$(Q \cup B, E, A, \gamma)$
8:     $H = H \cup$ TRANSLATE-SOLUTIONS$(\{\Delta_1, ..., \Delta_n\}, M)$
9:     $\langle$ increase MNC $\rangle$
10: **end while**
11: **return** H;

Given the explicit representation of the rules present in an hypothesis space, the ASPAL algorithm uses an incremental approach over the maximum number of conditions (MNC) that can appear in the rules of a brave inductive solution. The loop terminates when a condition is met, e.g., when a satisfactory number of solutions is generated or when an optimal solution is found. Optimisation statements of ASP are used to find an optimal abductive solution (in ASP) within each iteration (see line 7). This corresponds to the $\{\Delta_1, \ldots, \Delta_n\}$ generated by the ASP-ABDUCE function (line 7) in the algorithm, which are then translated back into a solution (set of normal rules) of the original brave inductive learning task, by the function TRANSLATE-SOLUTIONS. ASPAL's top theory could in principle grow exponentially with respect to the length of rules that may appear in an inductive solution. This is why the algorithm adopts an iterative way for searching for solutions, where the iteration takes into account the length of rule that maybe learned as part of inductive solution. To analyse the space of possible skeleton rules for a given language bias M, consider M_h to be the number of head mode declarations in M, M_b to be the number of body mode declarations, max_o and max_i to be respectively the largest number of output and input variables in the body mode declarations, d_{max} to be the maximum number of body literals allowed in the rules of an inductive solution, and max_i^h to be the largest number of input variables in all head mode declarations. The upper bound for the size $|Sk|$ of the non-ground set of skeleton rules can be estimated to be defined as follows[3]:

$$|Sk| \leq \sum_{d=0}^{d_{max}} |M_h| \times (|M_b| \times (max_i^h + max_o \times (d-1))^{max_i})^d$$

It is easy to see that even for a small learning task, the size of Sk increases exponentially with an increase in the maximum number of body literals in a rule d_{max}. This may cause problems with the grounding step of the ASP program, as one of the main factors in the size of this grounding is the number of body literals that are allowed to appear in a rule in the hypothesis space. So although ASPAL is computationally more efficient than TAL, the meta-level representation in ASP of a brave inductive learning task scales poorly with respect to the size of the grounding of $B \cup L_H$ [8]. To overcome this bottleneck, a different meta-level approach for brave induction, called RASPAL, was recently proposed [8]. This approach breaks the learning process into small manageable steps and uses a notion of *hypothesis revision*. The learning process iteratively refines a hypothesis until all of the examples in an given brave induction task are covered. At each step, the number of literals that are allowed to be added to the hypothesis is restricted, meaning that the grounding is often significantly smaller than the meta-level program in ASPAL. In [9] it was shown that RASPAL significantly outperforms ASPAL on some learning tasks with large problem domains and large hypothesis spaces.

Model Revision. The task of learning revisions has been applied not only for scaling up learning algorithms, as it is the case for the RASPAL algorithm, but also for revising logic-based theories, specifications and models. Theory revision is a particular case of the problem known as theory refinement, "the problem of improving the quality of a given theory" [76]. In general, a theory can be either restructured, i.e., its entailment relation does not change but it is only modified for efficiency, elegance or understanding, or changed so that its entailment relation is changed. Non-monotonic ILP has full power over the semantic changes of a given theory. By definition, non-monotonic learning is capable to learn a hypothesis H such that the consequences of an existing background theory B is changed once B is extended with H. That is the entailment relation of $B \cup H$ is not necessarily a superset of the entailment relation of B only. Change of the entailment relation is essentially the objective of a learning revision task, but with the difference that what is learned are not necessarily new clauses but rather retraction or addition of literals to existing clause.

---

[3] The parameter max_i^h is included as variables in a body literal can either be from input variables in the head literal or output variables in other body literals, giving $max_i^h + max_o \times (d-1)$ as the total number of variables that can serve as a inputs to a body literal.

In [18] it has been shown that theory revision can be solved in terms of a non-monotonic brave induction learning task. Such a task can be automatically generated from a given theory revision problem and solutions are *prescriptions for changes* in the original theory of the revision problem. Performing such changes leads to a revised theory that satisfies the requirements of the theory revision problem. Typical prescriptions for changes that can be learned include addition or deletion of entire rules, and/or addition and deletion of literals in the body of existing rules. Algorithm 3 shows how a non-monotonic ILP system can be used to learn a set of revisions to apply to a given theory.

Algorithm 3. FIND-HYPOTHESIS

1: Inputs: E examples; B background theory; R revisable program; M mode declarations
2: Outputs: R' revised program
3: $(\tilde{R}, L_{\tilde{R}}) = pre\text{-}processing(\text{R}, \text{M})$
4: $H = ILP(B \cup \tilde{R}, L_{\tilde{R}}, E)$
5: $R' = post\text{-}processing(\text{R}, \text{H})$
6: **return** $B \cup R'$

The input of the algorithm is a theory revision task $\langle B, R, L_R, E \rangle$. B is a background theory, which is not revisable, R is a *revisable program*, L_R is the search space of possible revised programs generated from R after applying revision operations to it, and E is a set of literals expressing what is expected to be entailed and not entailed from the revised program. A solution to a theory revision task is a revised program R' such that (i) $R' \in L_R$, (ii) $B \cup R' \models E$, and (iii) if there exists another revised program $S \in L_R$ that satisfies conditions (i) and (ii), then the distance $d(R, S) \geq d(R, R')$, where d defines the number of revision operations applied to R to generate the revised program. The third condition essentially captures the notion of *minimal changes* to R to generate R'. The search space L_R is specified by a set of mode declarations that define the literals that are allowed to be in the head and body of the learned and/or revised rules.

Let us assume for simplicity that the theories B and R of our revision task are expressed already as sets of normal clauses. In principle, Algorithm 3 can be applied to other types of logic-based theories but translations of these theories into normal logic programs would need to be provided, as the learning approach is a non-monotonic ILP approach. The algorithm resolves a theory revision task using a non-monotonic brave induction approach. It consists of three phases. The first phase is called *pre-processing*. It transforms the rules of the revisable program R into a meta-level representation $\tilde{R}$ to allow reasoning about the literals in the rules in R that should be kept or deleted during the revision process. An extra condition is added to the body of each rule in R, using a predicate called *extension*() which represents a placeholder for possible literals that need to be added to the rule. Learning definitions of each of these *extension* predicates correspond basically to learning the "extra" conditions to add to the body of the corresponding rule in R. Using the same transformation process, the space L_R of possible revised programs is mapped into a hypothesis space $L_{\tilde{R}}$ of possible revisions that can be learned. The output of this phase is the pair $(\tilde{R}, L_{\tilde{R}})$. The second phase is called *learning phase*. At this point a non-monotonic brave induction task has been automatically generated. The background theory is $B \cup \tilde{R}$, the hypothesis space is $L_{\tilde{R}}$ and the examples are the same examples E of the revision task. The learner (e.g., RASPAL) computes a brave inductive solution. This may include information about what literal to delete from existing rules, what new literals to add to existing rules (through the learned definitions of the *extension* predicate), as well as what rules to add to or to delete from the given program. The third phase is called *post-processing*. It takes the learned inductive solution and the initially given set R of revisable rules and performs the changes that are specified in the learned solution. The result is a revised theory $B \cup R^-$ which is guaranteed now to entail the given set E of literals.

Example 5. Consider the following theory revision task $\langle B, R, L_R, E \rangle$ where B is the set of rules

$$B = \left\{ \begin{array}{l} c_2(X) \leftarrow c_3(X) \\ c_3(b) \\ c_2(a) \end{array} \right\}$$

R is the revisable program $R = \{p(X) \leftarrow c_1(X), c_2(X)\}$ and the mode declaration $M = \{modeb(c_1(+any)), modeb(c_2(+any)), modeb(c_3(+any))\}$, indicating that literals c_1, c_2, c_3 could be added to the body of the rules in the revisable program R. Note that the *any* type that appear in the mode declaration indicates that variables of any type could appear as arguments of the predicates in a learned solutions. E is the set $\{p(a), not\ p(b)\}$ that must be entailed by the revised program. Given this task, it is easy to see that $B \cup R \not\models E$. So R needs to be revised. The pre-processing step generates the following re-written revisable program $\tilde{R}$ and mode declarations $\tilde{M}$.

$$\tilde{M} = M \cup \{modeh(extension(1, p(+any), []), modeh(del(1,1)), modeh(del(1,2))\}$$

$$\tilde{R} = \left\{ \begin{array}{l} p(X) \leftarrow try(1,1,c_1(X)), try(1,2,c_2(X)), extension(1, p(X), []). \\ try(1,1,c_1(X)) \leftarrow use(1,1), c_1(X). \\ try(1,1,c_1(X)) \leftarrow not\ use(1,1). \\ try(1,2,c_2(X)) \leftarrow use(1,2), c_2(X). \\ try(1,2,c_2(X)) \leftarrow use(1,2). \\ use(X,Y) \leftarrow not\ del(X,Y). \end{array} \right\}$$

The learning phase uses now a non-monotonic ILP system to compute a set of hypotheses for the task $\langle B \cup \tilde{R}, L_{\tilde{R}}, E \rangle$, where $L_{\tilde{R}}$ is the hypothesis space specified by the set $\tilde{M}$ of mode declarations. Learning a most compressed hypothesis would correspond in this case to learn minimal changes to be made to the revisable theory R. Let the following H be the brave inductive solution of the generated learning task:

$$H = \left\{ \begin{array}{c} del(1,1). \\ extension(1, p(X), []) \leftarrow not\ c_3(X). \end{array} \right\}$$

The post-processing phase takes the initial revisable program R, the learned hypothesis H and applies the changes that appear in the learned solution. Each del facts instructs a deletion of a literal (indicated by the second argument of the del fact) from a rule indexed by the first argument of the del fact. So, for instance $del(1,1)$ instructs deletion of first body literal from first rule in R. For each rule with head predicate $extension$ the literals that appear in this rule are added to the body of a rule indexed by the first argument of $extension$. So the learned rule $extension(1, p(X), []) \leftarrow not\ c_3(X)$ instructs the addition of the literals $not\ c_3(X)$ to the first rule in R. By performing these two learned changes, the post-processing phase generates the revised theory:

$$R' = \left\{ p(X) \leftarrow c_2(X), not\ c_3(X). \right\}$$

So the algorithm returns the program $B \cup R'$, which clearly entails E.

4   ILP for Specification Refinement and Revision

Correct and complete specifications provide significant aid in the formal analysis of software, enabling tasks such as verification [49], program synthesis [31], program analysis [19] and software maintenance [47]. However obtaining such specifications remains a fundamental challenge [7]. Their manual construction requires immense effort in identifying the right level of abstraction and considerable expertise in the formal languages and semantics deployed. There have been continual efforts to develop rigorous, automated mechanisms for generating such specifications, of which dynamic approaches specifically have gained growing attention in recent years [26,27].

In general, dynamic approaches to specification generation (also referred to as specification mining and inductive synthesis) provide means for inferring specifications automatically from execution traces (e.g., program runs, use-cases, system logs). Existing approaches mainly differ in the input they require (e.g., traces, domain knowledge, input/output examples), their method of computation (e.g., user-driven interaction, SMT solver, machine learning), the type of specification generated (e.g., automata, declarative logical assertion, sequence charts), the features they guarantee (e.g., domain consistency, completeness) and the function the specifications serve (e.g., controller synthesis, program verification).

There have been several applications of monotonic ILP to support specification generation including specification recovery [15], requirement elaboration [5] and interface (APIs) specifications mining [71]. These approaches, however, presume the input traces provide complete knowledge of the intended specification and hence are not well-suited for exploratory and incremental specification generation.

In this section, we demonstrate the use of non-monotonic learning for such task, specifically for refining partial specification and revising incorrect ones. We focus on a goal-oriented requirements elaboration framework which is founded on the idea that requirements are derived from stakeholders' goals and that these requirements must be fulfilled by the software being developed [40].

4.1 Notation and Terminology

We begin with some basic definitions of terms and notations. In what follows, we consider the Event Calculus (EC) formalism [39] (a logical framework for representing and reasoning about states, actions, and time) as the specification language $\mathcal{L}$. For convenience, our illustration adopts the EC formulation of [3], which includes three types of terms: *time-points* (with variables $T, T_1, T_2, \ldots$) represented by the domain of integers; *events* (with variables $E, E_1, E_2, \ldots$) capturing actions that happen at various time-points; *fluents* (with variables $F, F_1, F_2, \ldots$) marking propositional atoms whose values change over time; and *scenarios* (with variables $S, S_1, S_2, \ldots$) denoting linear-time sequences. The main EC predicates considered are $holds(f, t, s)$ and $nholds(f, t, s)$ to mean that a fluent f holds and does not hold respectively at time-point t in scenario s. Thus, for a given system, the Herbrand domain U comprises event constants, fluent constants, scenario constants and the set of natural numbers. The Herbrand base HB contains the set of ground *holds* and *nholds* atoms and type declarations for elements in U, e.g., $event(e)$ and $fluent(\mathsf{f})$. We write HB^* to denote HB excluding the type declarations.

Given a background theory B, a Herbrand universe U and a Herbrand base HB from which a set of examples $E \subseteq HB^*$ are drawn, a specification is a set of logic programs Φ such that $I \subseteq HB$ for every stable model I of $\phi \in \Phi$. We sometime write $I[\phi]$ to denote the stable model of program ϕ.[4]

In our setting, examples are sets of ground facts within the domain of discourse collectively representing partial executions of a system (i.e., traces). These are defined using 2 or more arity predicates over time-point and scenario sorts (i.e., in addition to the two, it may contain arguments over other sorts). A single trace is a set of ground atoms which have the same scenario constant. It is said to be a positive example, denoted ω^+, iff $\omega^+ \subseteq I[\phi \cup B] \cap E$. Conversely, it is said to be a negative example, denoted ω^-, iff $\omega^- \subseteq E$ and $\omega^- \not\subseteq I[\phi \cup B]$ for all $\phi \in \Phi$. Since there may be several correct specifications in Φ that guarantee goals' achievement, our aim is to learn at least one correct specification ϕ definable within the language L_Φ.

---

[4] We focus here on specifications with a single stable model.

Let ψ be a candidate specification, Ω_ψ a set of traces accepted by ψ, ϕ a target specification and Ω_ϕ a set of traces accepted by ϕ. We say that ψ is an *over-approximation* of ϕ with respect to Ω_ϕ if $\Omega_\phi \subset \Omega_\psi$. Conversely, ψ is said to be an *under-approximation* of ϕ if $\Omega_\psi \subset \Omega_\phi$.

4.2   Requirement Specification Refinement

The formalisation and refinement of requirement specifications are fundamental problems of requirements engineering [35]. A requirement specification is a set of prescriptive expressions, typically expressed in a temporal logic, that describe the objectives to be achieved by a system being developed [45]. The use of a temporal formalism enables the deployment of automated analysis and refinement tools, but is not directly accessible to most stakeholders with a non-technical background. In practice, stakeholders tend to convey their requirements through more intuitive narrative-style scenarios of desirable and undesirable interactions between system objects rather than temporal assertions [74]. Because scenarios are inherently *partial* descriptions about specific system behaviours, they leave requirements implicitly defined, some of which may be inconsistent. It is therefore necessary to be able to infer declarative specifications of these requirements which would admit the desired behaviours while rejecting the undesired ones, and at the same time are consistent with any available domain knowledge. The requirement inference task may be defined as follows.

Given: A set of desirable scenarios Ω^+, and undesirable scenarios Ω^- and domain knowledge D;
Find: a requirement specification ψ such that:

$$\omega^+ \subseteq I[\psi \cup D] \; for \; all \; \omega^+ \in \Omega^+$$
$$\omega^- \nsubseteq I[\psi \cup D] \; for \; all \; \omega^- \in \Omega^-$$

To illustrate how non-monotonic ILP may be deployed to achieve this task, we first introduce the example below.

Example 6. Consider a simple example of a driver assistance system [29] in which a car driver, cars' control software and a construction control software must interact to avoid collision on two-lane road. We describe here two scenarios which illustrate what should happen when a car approaches a construction site on the road. The first scenario captures a desirable case of when a car approaches a construction site blocking its lane. The car control detects the obstruction by communicating with the construction control and overtakes the construction site using the lane for oncoming traffic to avoid unnecessary hold-up. The second scenario describes an undesirable situation where the car approaches the construction site, and as it attempts to overtake, collides with an oncoming car.

We assume the following constants: c_1 and c_2 representing two car controllers; r for the construction controller; and l_1 and l_2 for the two lanes. We further consider fluents capturing the location of the car and construction site which are represented by ground terms: $overtaking/2$ (for a car overtaking a construction site), $approaching/2$ (for a car approaches a construction site), $on/2$ (for a car/construction site is on a lane), $safe\_passage/1$ (when a car has safely passed a construction site) and $collided/2$ (when two cars collide). Auxiliary predicates are introduced to define a total order over time points, e.g., $next(2,1)$ meaning 2 is the next timepoint following 1, and over locations such as $next(l_2, l_1)$. Given this language, we assert the following type declarations and facts as part of D.

$car(c_1)$. $car(c_2)$. $construction(r_1)$. $lane(l_1)$. $lane(l_2)$.

$fluent(overtaking(c_1, r))$. $fluent(overtaking(c_2, r))$. $fluent(collided(c_1, c_2))$.

$fluent(collided(c_2, c_1))$.$safe\_passage(c_1)$. $safe\_passage(c_2)$. $\qquad\qquad$ (1)

$fluent(approaching(c_1, r))$. $fluent(approaching(c_2, r))$. $fluent(on(r, l_1))$. $fluent(on(r, l_2))$.

$fluent(on(c_1, l_1))$. $fluent(on(c_2, l_1))$. $fluent(on(c_1, l_2))$. $fluent(on(c_2, l_2))$.

$time(0)$. $time(1)$. $time(2)$. $time(3)$.$time(4)$. $time(5)$.

$next(1, 0)$. $next(2, 1)$. $next(3, 2)$. $next(4, 3)$. $next(5, 4)$. $next(l_1, l_2)$. $next(l_2, l_1)$.

In addition to this, suppose that the controllers keep track of the locations of the cars and construction sites over time which are recorded as the following facts in D. (We consider only finite observations to be recorded.) The constants s_1 and s_2 denote two distinct scenarios.

$holds(on(c_1, l_1), 0, s_1)$. $holds(on(r_1, l_1), 0, s_1)$.

$holds(on(c_1, l_1), 1, s_1)$. $holds(on(r_1, l_1), 1, s_1)$. $holds(approaching(c_1, r_1), 1, s_1)$.

$holds(on(c_1, l_2), 2, s_1)$. $holds(on(r_1, l_1), 2, s_1)$. $\qquad\qquad$ (2)

$holds(on(r_1, l_1), 3, s_1)$. $holds(on(c_1, l_1), 3, s_1)$. $nholds(collided(c_1, c_2), 3, s_1)$

$holds(on(r_1, l_1), 0, s_2)$. $holds(on(c_1, l_1), 0, s_2)$. $holds(on(c_2, l_2), 0, s_2)$.

$holds(on(r_1, l_1), 1, s_2)$. $holds(on(c_1, l_1), 1, s_2)$. $holds(approaching(c_1, r_1), 1, s_2)$. $\qquad\qquad$ (3)

$holds(approaching(c_2, r_1), 1, s_2)$.

$holds(on(r_1, l_1), 2, s_2)$. $holds(on(c_1, l_2), 2, s_2)$. $holds(approaching(c_2, r_1), 2, s_2)$.

$holds(on(r_1, l_1), 3, s_2)$. $holds(on(c_1, l_2), 3, s_2)$. $holds(collided(c_1, c_2), 3, s_2)$.

The first observation (2), for instance, indicates that there is a construction site r_1 on lane l_1. A car c_1 is detected on lane l_1 at start after which it moves at time point 2 to lane l_2 and then returns afterwards to lane l_1 at time point 3. The second observation (3) records a situation where a construction site r_1 is on lane l_1, c_1 is on lane l_1 and c_2 is on lane l_2 for the first two time points. At time point 3, both cars are detected on l_2 and collide.

We further include the following domain-independent and dependent rules in D with which ϕ must be consistent.

$$nholds(F, T, S) \leftarrow not\ holds(F, T, S). \tag{4}$$
$$\leftarrow holds(F, T, S), nholds(F, T, S). \tag{5}$$
$$\leftarrow holds(collided(C, C), T, S). \tag{6}$$
$$\leftarrow holds(collided(C1, C2), T, S), holds(safe\_passage(C1), T, S). \tag{7}$$
$$\leftarrow holds(collided(C1, C2), T, S), holds(safe\_passage(C2), T, S).$$

The first expression (4) provides a default definition for $nholds$ in terms of the negation (as failure) of $holds$, whilst the second (5) is an integrity constraint stating that fluents cannot both hold and not hold at the same time in a scenario. Rule (6) states a car cannot collide with itself, whilst the last two constraints (7) state that cars cannot pass safely if they have collided.

The two scenarios described in Example 6 can be represented as the following sets. They capture the consequence of the cars movements on the two lanes.

$$\omega_1^+ = \{holds(overtaking(c_1, r_1), 2, s_1), holds(safe\_passage(c_1), 3, s_1)\}$$
$$\omega_1^- = \{holds(overtaking(c_1, r_1), 2, s_2), nholds(safe\_passage(c_1), 3, s_2),$$
$$nholds(safe\_passage(c_2), 3, s_2)\}$$

The task we aim to achieve here is *learning a specification ψ that exactly matches a target requirements specification $\phi \in \Phi$, that is consistent with D, from partial scenarios*. Given the above rules, we can define a learning task $\langle D, L_\Phi, \Omega^+ \cup \Omega^- \rangle$ where D corresponds to the background knowledge B and comprises the programs (1)–(7), and $\Omega^+ = \{\omega_1^+\}$, $\Omega^- = \{\omega_1^-\}$. We define L_Φ to be the set of clauses that can be constructed using the following mode declaration M.

$modeh(holds(safe\_passage(+car), +time, +scenario))$.
$modeh(holds(overtaking(+car, +construction), +time, +scenario))$.
$modeh(nholds(safe\_passage(+car), +time, +scenario))$.   (8)
$modeh(nholds(overtaking(+car, +construction), +time, +scenario))$.
$modeb(next(+lane, -lane))$. $modeb(next(-lane, +lane))$.
$modeb(next(+time, -time))$.
$modeb(holds(on(+car, -lane), +time, +scenario))$.
$modeb(holds(on(-car, -lane), +time, +scenario))$.
$modeb(holds(on(+construction, -lane), +time, +scenario))$.
$modeb(holds(approaching(+car, +construction), +time, +scenario))$.
$modeb(holds(approaching(-car, +construction), +time, +scenario))$.   (9)
$modeb(holds(overtaking(+car, +construction), +time, +scenario))$.
$modeb(holds(overtaking(+car, -construction), +time, +scenario))$.
$modeb(holds(overtaking(-car, -construction), +time, +scenario))$.
$modeb(nholds(on(+car, -lane), +time, +scenario))$.
$modeb(nholds(on(-car, -lane), +time, +scenario))$.
$modeb(nholds(on(+construction, -lane), +time, +scenario))$.
$modeb(nholds(approaching(+car, +construction), +time, +scenario))$.
$modeb(nholds(approaching(-car, +construction), +time, +scenario))$.
$modeb(nholds(overtaking(+car, +construction), +time, +scenario))$.
$modeb(nholds(overtaking(+car, -construction), +time, +scenario))$.
$modeb(nholds(overtaking(-car, -construction), +time, +scenario))$.

The above restricts the class of requirements to safety properties over a fixed
bound of consecutive states. Other classes including liveness are discussed in [4].
To compute a solution, we use the system ASPAL described in [16] as our
learning engine. The learning task is non-monotonic since the program itself
(owing to (4) is non-monotonic). The specification learned comprises the following candidate requirements.

$$\psi = \left\{ \begin{array}{l} holds(overtaking(C1, R), T, S) \leftarrow holds(on(C1, L), T, S), nholds(on(C2, L), T, S). \\ holds(safe\_passage(C), T, S) \leftarrow holds(overtaking(C, R), T, S). \end{array} \right\}$$
(10)

The first states that a car overtakes a construction site whenever another
car is not on the same lane as it does so. The second says that whenever a car
overtakes a construction site, the car safely passes the contraction site. Since
the program, as demonstrated in [4], is locally stratified, $\psi \wedge D$ has a single
stable model in which traces in Ω^+ are consistent with the specification but not
those in Ω^-. In [4], we showed how the output could be soundly translated into
temporal logic making it amenable to further analysis (e.g., model checking).

For instance, each of the expressions above can be rewritten in Linear Temporal Logic as follows respectively. (The G is a temporal operator that stands for *always*.)

$$\forall c_1, c_2 : Car, \ r : Construction, \ l : Lane. \ \ \mathsf{G}((on(c_1, l) \land \neg on(c_2, l)) \to overtaking(c_1, r)) \tag{11}$$

$$\forall c : Car, \ r : Construction. \ \ \mathsf{G}(overtaking(c, r) \to safe\_passage(c)) \tag{12}$$

Though the above assertions are consistent with scenarios given, they may not reflect the behaviour intended by the target specification (either an over- or under-approximating the behaviour prescribed by the target specifications). In what follows, we discuss how learning-based revision can also be used to modify goals in light of new observations.

4.3   Requirements Specifications Revision

Requirements elicitation is an incremental process. Requirements (as described for above for instance) are extracted from partial descriptions, in this case scenarios. As further scenarios are identified, and the extracted requirements are merged, inconsistencies may arise and obstacles to their achievement may emerge. Consider the first requirement in ψ (10) above. This states that cars shall not be allowed to overtake if there are other cars on the same lane been though these may not be close to the construction site and hence do not pose a collision risk. Of course it would be desirable to allow cars to overtake when oncoming cars are at a safe distance. Since this desirable behaviour is not consistent with the learned requirement, we say that the extracted requirement is an under-approximation of the target specification.

When such cases are identified, requirements need to be revised in such a way that ensures that their preservation of all the desirable behaviour identified thus far and none of the undesirable ones, they are consistent amongst each other and they are feasible to achieve within their domain.

Such assurances can be met by either: (i) retracting the current requirements and re-instigate the inference process from the start with the extended set of desirable and undesirable scenarios, or (ii) revising the problematic requirements, and retain all the valid ones. Though both processes lead to correct requirements specifications, we adopt the latter approach as we argue that the former requires engineers to abandon any development activities they may have started based on the earlier specification. The general task of revising requirements is formulated as follows.

Given: A set of desirable scenarios Ω^+, undesirable scenarios Ω^-, domain knowledge D, a requirements specification $\varphi \in 2^{\Psi}$ and a revision function $f : 2^{\Psi} \to 2^{\Psi}$ such that:

$$\omega^+ \not\subseteq I[\varphi \cup D] \ for \ some \ \omega^+ \in \Omega^+$$
$$\omega^- \subseteq I[\varphi \cup D] \ for \ some \ \omega^- \in \Omega^-$$

Find: a revision $\varphi' = f(\varphi)$ such that:

$$\omega^+ \subseteq I[\varphi' \cup D] \qquad \qquad for\ all\ \omega^+ \in \Omega^+$$
$$\omega^- \not\subseteq I[\varphi' \cup D] \qquad \qquad for\ all\ \omega^- \in \Omega^-$$
$$The\ distance\ d(\varphi, \varphi')is\ minimal$$

Since there might be multiple revisions that satisfy the conditions above, f may return instead a set $\{\varphi'_i\}$ where each φ'_i meets the conditions above.

Let us go back to our running example. In addition to (1)–(7), we consider D to include the following facts about the cars' locations from the new observation s_3.

$$holds(on(r_1, l_1), 0, s_3).holds(on(c_1, l_1), 0, s_3).holds(on(c_2, l_2), 0, s_3).$$
$$holds(on(r_1, l_1), 1, s_3), holds(on(c_1, l_1), 1, s_3).holds(on(c_2, l_2), 1, s_3).$$
$$holds(approaching(c_1, r_1), 1, s_3). \qquad\qquad\qquad (13)$$
$$holds(on(r_1, l_1), 2, s_3).holds(on(c_1, l_2), 2, s_3).holds(on(c_2, l_2), 2, s_3).$$
$$holds(on(r_1, l_1), 3, s_3).holds(on(c_1, l_2), 3, s_3).nholds(on(c_2, l_2), 3, s_3)$$
$$nholds(collided(c_1, c_2), 3, s_3).$$

We extend the set of positive examples to $\Omega^+ = \{\omega_1^+, \omega_2^+\}$ where ω_2^+ is

$$\omega_2^+ = \{holds(overtaking(c_1, r_1), 2, s_3),$$
$$holds(safe\_passage(c_1), 3, s_3), nholds(safe\_passage(c_2), 4, s_3)\} \qquad (14)$$

To generate revisions for ψ, we define a theory revision task as $\langle D, \psi, L_\Phi, \Omega^+ \cup \Omega^- \rangle$ in which ψ of (10) is the revisable program. M is defined as before (8 and 9).

The learning algorithm aims to find within the space of possible revisions L_Φ definable by M for variant rules of ψ (obtainable by adding/deleting literals or rules from ψ) that yield a correct solution with the smallest distance (i.e., the least number of revision operator applications), i.e., minimize $|d(\psi, \psi')|$. Since, given the new observation (13), the revisable rule

$$holds(overtaking(C1, R), T2, S) \leftarrow holds(on(C1, L), T1, S),$$
$$nholds(on(C2, L), T1, S).$$

is the only rule in the program $D \cup \psi$ that defines *overtaking* and for which $nholds(on(C2, l_2), 2, s_3)$ does not hold for any car constant in U, we have that $holds(overtaking(c_1, r_1), 2, s_3) \notin I[\psi \cup D]$. Thus $\omega_2^+ \notin I[\psi \cup D]$ and therefore (10) must be revised.

We use the learning-based revision system RASPAL, described in Sect. 3.2, to compute revisions for this rule. The learning procedure seeks to find which literals may be added or deleted for the examples to be entailed. In this case, both literals $holds(on(C1, L), T1, S)$ and $nholds(on(C2, L), T1, S)$ are removed from the body of (10) and the literals $next(T2, T1)$ and $nholds(approaching(C2, R), T1, S)$ are added instead. The output of the learning is:

$$\psi' = \left\{ \begin{array}{l} holds(overtaking(C1, R), T2, S) \leftarrow next(T2, T1), \\ \qquad\qquad\qquad\qquad nholds(approaching(C2, R), T1, S). \\ holds(safe\_passage(C), T, S) \leftarrow holds(overtaking(C, R), T, S). \end{array} \right\}$$

From the solution, we see that the only goal that is revised is the first. The goal about safe passing remains unchanged. The revised goal now states that a car overtakes the construction site, if at the previous time-point, a car is not approaching the site. (Note that the solution is correct given that the language only considers two cars.) The distance $|d(\psi, \psi')| = 4$. The revised assertions can be expressed in LTL as follows. (The X is a temporal operator that stands for *next*.)

$$\forall c_1 : Car, r : Construction\mathsf{G}((\exists c_2 : Car.\neg approaching(c_2, r)) \rightarrow \mathsf{X} overtaking(c_1, r)) \tag{15}$$

$$\forall c : Car, r : Construction.\mathsf{G}(overtaking(c, r) \rightarrow safe\_passage(c)) \tag{16}$$

5   Research Trends and Promising Applications

The learning approaches described in this chapter assume correct labelling of examples. In practise, labelled examples might be noisy either because they are wrongly labelled by humans, or because their are data generated by devices, such as sensors, that operate often within a certain margin of error and/or approximation. A future venue of research is how to make such logic-based learning approaches resilient to noise in the labelled examples, e.g. when not all examples are correctly labelled. This open problem has given raise to two new research trends in the area of logic-based learning.

A first trend is the combination of probabilistic and logic-based learning. First attempts have been proposed in [66], where the notion of probabilistic Inductive Logic Programming was first proposed. This combines ILP with probabilistic reasoning. The learning task combines structural learning, where an underlying logic program is learned, and parameter estimation or weight learning, where the probabilities associated to the rules in the program are also learned so to minimise the errors between the a posterior (conditional) probability of the entailed examples and those given as labelled examples. But results so far are limited to the case of probabilistic definite clauses. Possible directions on how to extend these approaches to probabilistic non-monotonic ILP would be to build upon recent results in [50] that provide a first ever framework for integrating parameter learning with abductive logic programming in the context of normal logic programming. The abductive logic programming approach used in this approach is the same as that used by the meta-level abductive learning methods such as TAL and ASPAL described in Sect. 3.2. So an immediate research challenge would be to explore how the probabilistic non-monotonic learning could be defined in terms of meta-level probabilistic abductive learning.

A second trend for supporting logic-based learning from noisy data is through Inductive Learning Answer Set Programs (ILASP) [42]. This has recently been applied to learn non-deterministic concepts, such as the possible of two outcomes of tossing a coin. Although different from probabilistic ILP settings where the focus is on learning the probabilities of the outcomes of an event, learning non-deterministic concepts corresponds to learning programs that represent the set of possible instances of a problem. Such type of learning takes as positive and negative examples, instance of possible (highly probable) and impossible (highly improbable) instances of a problem. Learning answer set programs has also very recently shown the possibility of learning from noisy examples by defining a notion of *weights* over labelled examples and *penalty score* over hypotheses. An hypothesis that does not cover an example has to pay the penalty of that example. Solutions are learned by considering optimisation statements (e.g., minimisation of the penalty score) over the penalty score of the hypothesis.

The approach of inductive learning of answer set programs has also open up a new opportunity for learning preference models from examples that are pairwise ordered. Recent results in [41] have shown how such an approach can be used for performing preference learning. Machine learning solutions to preference leaning aim at *learning to rank* any two objects given some examples of pairwise preferences [24]. Previous attempts of applying ILP to preference learning has been limited to addressing just the problem of learning ratings, such as *good*, *poor* and *bad*, rather than rankings over the examples (e.g., [33]). But ratings are not expressive enough if we want to find an optimal solution, as we may rate many objects as good when some are actually better than others. Answer Set Programming, on the other hand, allows for declarative expression of preferences in terms of constructs called *weak constraints*. Results in [41] have recently proposed a learning approaches for learning ASP program containing weak constraints and it has been successfully applied to the problem of learning user's preferences in journey planning to provide personalised recommendations. Learning preference models from pairwise ordered examples provides also new opportunity for learning norms and arguments in legal reasoning (e.g., [37]), as well as application opportunity in any areas where policy, norms and strategies need to be learned.

Finally, the big underpinning challenge to all these methods is how to increase the scalability of existing state of the art systems with respect to large hypothesis spaces. One possible direction is to provide mechanisms for constraining the hypothesis space using domain-specific knowledge. Some preliminary results have been proposed in [25], where the notion of constraint-bias has been proposed and formalised as an additional input to a non-monotonic brave induction task. It has also been shown to be particular useful not only in controlling the size of the hypothesis space during the learning process and at the same time guaranteeing that what is learned is close to the intended program.

We outline below also some of the promising areas in applying ILP to software development.

Oracle-guided Inductive Synthesis. Inductive synthesis seeks to find software artefacts (such as programs, automata, specifications) from a given set of example (e.g., input/output, counterexamples, execution traces). Oracle guided inductive synthesis is a class of techniques that emphasises the use of an oracle to both check the correctness of the candidate artefact and to generate examples that can further guide the synthesis process. Examples of such methods have been developed for the purpose of program synthesis (e.g., [73]), model abstraction refinement (e.g., [14]), assume-guarantee reasoning (e.g., [64]) and assumption refinement (e.g., [12]). The work presented in [4] shows how model checking and ILP can be used in tandem to support the inductive synthesis of specification refinements. In this setting non-monotonic ILP is used to incrementally learn specifications from counterexamples generated by a model checker. The key advantage in using ILP here is that it ensures the consistency of candidate artefacts (in the case of [4] specification) with previously synthesised ones and with the available domain knowledge. Though this integration has been shown to be promising, there remains a number of open questions to be addressed. On the theoretical side, it is yet to be understood how much the quality of artefacts and rate of convergence to target artefact is improved by using ILP. Furthermore the application of ILP in other OGIS setting is yet to be explored.

Program Repair. Program repair is concerned with finding fixes to erroneous programs. In recent years, techniques such as machine learning (including genetic programming [75]) and SAT solving (e.g., [10]) have been applied to support the automation of such process. Machine learning based approaches typically formulate a program repair task as a learning task requiring the computation of fixes for faulty programs from passing and failing test cases (such as [44]) or human-written patches (e.g., [48]) or other forms of input. One of the major limitation of existing methods however is the huge search space for candidate programs. These are typically handled by either limiting the class of programs (e.g., loop-free programs), restricting the repair operations to be applied (e.g., change to variables only), or deploying a pre-defined set of templates to the faulty programs. A limiting factor in existing methods is that they do not allow for conditional repairs, i.e., if one part of the program is changed, then other parts of the programs should also be modified (consider the case of replacing an *if* condition and needing to update *else if* conditions dependent on it). ILP methods that allow for semantic and syntactic constraints to be defined over the language bias could potentially provide repair methods with the capability of enforcing such constraints on the forms of acceptable repair.

6   Summary

This Chapter outlines recent advances in the area of logic-based learning. It defines two main learning tasks, non-monotonic learning and theory revision, and reviews some algorithms for solving them. In contrast to other forms of learning, logic-based learning computes declarative hypotheses—expressed as logic programs—that are guaranteed to be consistent with a given background theory from a set of examples. The learning setting provides syntactic and semantic control over the set of computable hypotheses. We have illustrated their use in the context of dynamic specification inference and revision.

Acknowledgement. We would like to acknowledge Duangtida Athakravi, Krysia Broda, Domenico Corapi, Tim Kimber, Jeff Kramer, Jiefei Ma, Oliver Ray and Sebastián Uchitel for their contributions to the material presented in this Chapter.

References

1. Clausal discovery. Mach. Learn. **26**, 99–146 (1997)
2. Gebser, M., et al.: Potassco: the Potsdam answer set solving collection. AI Commun. **24**, 107–124 (2011)
3. Alrajeh, D., Kramer, J., Russo, A., Uchitel, S.: Learning operational requirements from goal models. In: 31st International Conference on Software Engineering, ICSE 2009, Vancouver, Canada, Proceedings, 16–24 May 2009, pp. 265–275 (2009)
4. Alrajeh, D., Kramer, J., Russo, A., Uchitel, S.: Elaborating requirements using model checking and inductive learning. IEEE Trans. Softw. Eng. **39**(3), 361–383 (2013). https://doi.org/10.1109/TSE.2012.41
5. Alrajeh, D., Russo, A., Uchitel, S.: Inferring operational requirements from scenarios and goal models using inductive learning. In: Proceedings of the 2006 International Workshop on Scenarios and State Machines: Models, Algorithms, and Tools, pp. 29–36 (2006)
6. Apt, K.R., Bol, R.: Logic programming and negation: a survey. J. Log. Program. **19**, 9–71 (1994)
7. Asteasuain, F., Braberman, V.: Declaratively building behavior by means of scenario clauses. Requir. Eng. 1–36 (2016). https://doi.org/10.1007/s00766-015-0242-2
8. Athakravi, D., Corapi, D., Broda, K., Russo, A.: Learning through hypothesis refinement using answer set programming. In: Zaverucha, G., Santos Costa, V., Paes, A. (eds.) ILP 2013. LNCS (LNAI), vol. 8812, pp. 31–46. Springer, Heidelberg (2014). https://doi.org/10.1007/978-3-662-44923-3_3
9. Athakravi, D.: Inductive logic programming using bounded hypothesis space. Ph.D. thesis, Imperial College London (2015)
10. Attie, P., Cherri, A., Bab, K.D.A., Sakr, M., Saklawi, J.: Model and program repair via sat solving. In: 2015 ACM/IEEE International Conference on Formal Methods and Models for Codesign (MEMOCODE), pp. 148–157 (2015)
11. Baral, C.: Knowledge representation, reasoning and declarative problem solving. Cambridge University Press (2003)
12. Cavezza, D.G., Alrajeh, D.: Interpolation-based GR(1) assumptions refinement. In: Legay, A., Margaria, T. (eds.) TACAS 2017. LNCS, vol. 10205, pp. 281–297. Springer, Heidelberg (2017). https://doi.org/10.1007/978-3-662-54577-5_16
13. Challagulla, V., et al.: Empirical assessment of machine learning based software defect prediction techniques. Int. J. Artif. Intell. Tools **17**, 389–400 (2008)
14. Clarke, E., Grumberg, O., Jha, S., Lu, Y., Veith, H.: Counterexample-guided abstraction refinement for symbolic model checking. J. ACM **50**(5), 752–794 (2003)
15. Cohen, W.W.: Inductive specification recovery: understanding software by learning from example behaviors. Autom. Softw. Eng. **2**(2), 107–129 (1995)
16. Corapi, D., Russo, A., Lupu, E.: Inductive logic programming as abductive search. In: Technical Communications of the 26th International Conference on Logic Programming, Schloss Dagstuhl Leibniz-Zentrum fuer Informatik, vol. 2010, pp. 54–63 (2010)

17. Corapi, D., Russo, A., Lupu, E.: Inductive logic programming in answer set programming. In: Muggleton, S.H., Tamaddoni-Nezhad, A., Lisi, F.A. (eds.) ILP 2011. LNCS (LNAI), vol. 7207, pp. 91–97. Springer, Heidelberg (2012). https://doi.org/10.1007/978-3-642-31951-8_12

18. Corapi, D.: Nonmonotonic inductive logic programming as abductive search. Ph.D. thesis, Imperial College London (2011)

19. David, C., Kroening, D., Lewis, M.: Using program synthesis for program analysis. In: Davis, M., Fehnker, A., McIver, A., Voronkov, A. (eds.) LPAR 2015. LNCS, vol. 9450, pp. 483–498. Springer, Heidelberg (2015). https://doi.org/10.1007/978-3-662-48899-7_34

20. Denecker, M., Schreye, D.: SLDNFA: an abductive procedure for abductive logic programs. J. Log. Program. **34**(2), 111–167 (1998)

21. Ding, Z., Zhou, Y., Zhou, M.: Modeling self-adaptive software systems with learning petri nets. IEEE Trans. Syst. Man Cybern. Syst. **46**(4), 483–498 (2016)

22. Fenton, N., et al.: On the effectiveness of early life cycle defect prediction with Bayesian nets. Empir. Softw. Eng. **13**, 499–537 (2008)

23. Flach, P., Lavrač, N.: Learning in clausal logic: a perspective on inductive logic programming. In: Kakas, A.C., Sadri, F. (eds.) Computational Logic: Logic Programming and Beyond. LNCS (LNAI), vol. 2407, pp. 437–471. Springer, Heidelberg (2002). https://doi.org/10.1007/3-540-45628-7_17

24. Fürnkranz, J., Hüllermeier, E.: Pairwise preference learning and ranking. In: Lavrač, N., Gamberger, D., Blockeel, H., Todorovski, L. (eds.) ECML 2003. LNCS (LNAI), vol. 2837, pp. 145–156. Springer, Heidelberg (2003). https://doi.org/10.1007/978-3-540-39857-8_15

25. Athakravi, D., Alrajeh, D., Broda, K., Russo, A., Satoh, K.: Inductive learning using constraint-driven bias. In: Davis, J., Ramon, J. (eds.) ILP 2014. LNCS (LNAI), vol. 9046, pp. 16–32. Springer, Cham (2015). https://doi.org/10.1007/978-3-319-23708-4_2

26. Gabel, M., Su, Z.: Symbolic mining of temporal specifications. In: 2008 ACM/IEEE 30th International Conference on Software Engineering, pp. 51–60 (2008). https://doi.org/10.1145/1368088.1368096

27. Gabel, M., Su, Z.: Testing mined specifications. In: Proceedings of the ACM SIGSOFT 20th International Symposium on the Foundations of Software Engineering, pp. 4:1–4:11 (2012). https://doi.org/10.1145/2393596.2393598

28. Gelfond, M., Lifschitz, V.: The stable model semantics for logic programming. pp. 1070–1080. MIT Press, Cambridge (1988)

29. Greenyer, J., Gritzner, D., Glade, N., Gutjahr, T., König, F.: Scenario-based specification of car-to-x systems. In: Gemeinsamer Tagungsband der Workshops der Tagung Software Engineering 2016 (SE 2016), Wien, 23–26 February 2016, pp. 118–123 (2016)

30. Gulwani, S., et al.: Inductive programming meets the real world. Commun. ACM **58**(11), 90–99 (2015)

31. Gulwani, S., Jha, S., Tiwari, A., Venkatesan, R.: Synthesis of loop-free programs. SIGPLAN Not. **46**(6), 62–73 (2011)

32. Harman, M.: The role of artificial intelligence in software engineering. In: Proceedings of the 1st International Workshop on Realizing AI Synergies in Software Engineering (2012)

33. Horvath, T.: A model of user preference learning for content-based recommender systems. Comput. Inform. **28**(4), 453–481 (2012)

34. Lifschitz, L.: What is answer set programming? In: AAAI, pp. 1594–1597 (2008)

35. Jackson, M.: The meaning of requirements. Ann. Softw. Eng. **3**, 5–21 (1997). http://dl.acm.org/citation.cfm?id=590564.590577
36. Kimber, T., Broda, K., Russo, A.: Induction on failure: learning connected horn theories. In: Erdem, E., Lin, F., Schaub, T. (eds.) LPNMR 2009. LNCS (LNAI), vol. 5753, pp. 169–181. Springer, Heidelberg (2009). https://doi.org/10.1007/978-3-642-04238-6_16
37. Kowalski, B., Satoh, K.: Obligation as optimal goal satisfaction. J. Philos. Log. 1–31 (2017)
38. Kowalski, R., Kuehner, D.: Linear resolution with selection function. Artif. Intell. **2**, 227–260 (1971)
39. Kowalski, R., Sergot, M.: A logic-based calculus of events. New Gener. Comput. **4**(1), 67–95 (1986)
40. van Lamsweerde, A.: Requirements Engineering: From System Goals to UML Models to Software Specifications. Wiley, Hoboken (2009)
41. Law, M., Russo, A., Broda, K.: Learning weak constraints in answer set programming. TPLP **15**, 511–525 (2015)
42. Law, M., Russo, A., Broda, K.: The complexity and generality of learning answer set programs. Artif. Intell. **259**, 110–146 (2018)
43. Le Goues, C., et al.: A systematic study of automated program repair: fixing 55 out of 105 bugs for $8 each. In: Proceedings of the 34th International Conference on Software Engineering, pp. 3–13 (2012)
44. Le Goues, C., Nguyen, T., Forrest, S., Weimer, W.: GenProg: a generic method for automatic software repair. IEEE Trans. Softw. Eng. **38**(1), 54–72 (2012)
45. Letier, E., Lamsweerde, A.V.: Deriving operational software specifications from system goals. In: Proceedings of 10th ACM FSE Symposium, pp. 119–128 (2002)
46. Lloyd, J.W.: Foundations of Logic Programming. Springer, Heidelberg (1987). https://doi.org/10.1007/978-3-642-83189-8
47. Lo, D., Khoo, S.C., Liu, C.: Mining temporal rules for software maintenance. J. Softw. Maint. Evol. Res. Pract. **20**(4), 227–247 (2008)
48. Long, F., Rinard, M.: Automatic patch generation by learning correct code. SIGPLAN Not. **51**(1), 298–312 (2016)
49. Lorenzoli, D., Mariani, L., Pezzè, M.: Automatic generation of software behavioral models. In: Proceedings of the 13th international conference on Software engineering (2008). https://doi.org/10.1145/1368088.1368157, http://portal.acm.org/citation.cfm?doid=1368088.1368157
50. Turliuc, C.R., Dickens, L., Russo, A., Broda, K.: Probabilistic abductive logic programming using Dirichlet priors. Int. J. Approx. Reason. **78**, 223–240 (2016)
51. Markitanis, A., et al.: Learning user behaviours in real mobile domains. In: Latest Advances in Inductive Logic Programming, pp. 43–51. Imperial College Press (2015)
52. Menzies, T.: Practical machine learning for software engineering and knowledge engineering. In: Handbook of Software Engineering and Knowledge Engineering (2001)
53. Minker, J.: An overview of nonmonotonic reasoning and logic programming. J. Log. Program. Spec. Issue **17**, 95–126 (1993)
54. Moyle, S.: Using theory completion to learn a robot navigation control program. In: Matwin, S., Sammut, C. (eds.) ILP 2002. LNCS (LNAI), vol. 2583, pp. 182–197. Springer, Heidelberg (2003). https://doi.org/10.1007/3-540-36468-4_12
55. Muggleton, S.: Inverse entailment and progol. New Gener. Comput. Spec. issue Inductive Log. Program. **13**, 245–286 (1995)

56. Muggleton, S., Feng, C.: Efficient induction of logic programs. In: ALT (1990)
57. Muggleton, S.: Inductive logic programming. New Gener. Comput. **8**(4), 295–318 (1991). https://doi.org/10.1007/BF03037089
58. Muggleton, S.: Inverse entailment and progol. New Gener. Comput. **13**(3&4), 245–286 (1995). https://doi.org/10.1007/BF03037227
59. Nienhuys-Cheng, S., de Wolf, R.: Foundations of Inductive Logic Programming. LNAI, vol. 1228. Springer, Heidelberg (1997). https://doi.org/10.1007/3-540-62927-0
60. Nuffelen, B.V.: Abductive constraint logic programming: implementation and applications. Ph.D. thesis, K.U. Leuven (2004)
61. Plotkin, G.: A note on inductive generalization. Mach. Intell. **5**, 153–163 (1969)
62. Plotkin, G.: A further note on inductive generalization. Mach. Intell. **6**, 101–124 (1971)
63. Pople, H.: In the mechanization of abductive logic. In: Proceedings of the 3rd International Joint Conference on Artificial Intelligence, pp. 147–152 (1973)
64. Păsăreanu, C.S., Giannakopoulou, D., Bobaru, M.G., Cobleigh, J.M., Barringer, H.: Learning to divide and conquer: applying the l* algorithm to automate assume-guarantee reasoning. Form. Methods Syst. Des. **32**(3), 175–205 (2008)
65. Quinlan, J.R., Cameron-Jones, R.M.: Induction of logic programs: foil and related systems. New Gener. Comput. **13**, 287–312 (1995)
66. De Raedt, L., Kersting, K.: Probabilistic inductive logic programming. In: Ben-David, S., Case, J., Maruoka, A. (eds.) ALT 2004. LNCS (LNAI), vol. 3244, pp. 19–36. Springer, Heidelberg (2004). https://doi.org/10.1007/978-3-540-30215-5_3
67. Ray, O.: Nonmonotonic abductive inductive learning. J. Appl. Log. **7**, 329–340 (2009)
68. Ray, O., Broda, K., Russo, A.: A hybrid abductive inductive proof procedure. Log. J. IGPL **12**(5), 371–397 (2004)
69. Ray, O.: Automated abduction in scientific discovery. In: Magnani, L., Li, P. (eds.) Model-Based Reasoning in Science, Technology, and Medicine. SCI, vol. 64, pp. 103–116. Springer, Heidelberg (2007). https://doi.org/10.1007/978-3-540-71986-1_5
70. Sakama, C., Inoue, K.: Brave induction: a logical framework for learning from incomplete information. Mach. Learn. **76**(1), 3–35 (2009)
71. Sankaranarayanan, S., Ivančić, F., Gupta, A.: Mining library specifications using inductive logic programming. In: Proceedings of the 30th International Conference on Software Engineering, pp. 131–140 (2008)
72. Shapiro, E.Y.: An algorithm that infers theories from facts. In: Proceedings of the 7th International Joint Conference on Artificial Intelligence, vol. 1, pp. 446–451 (1981)
73. Solar-Lezama, A., Tancau, L., Bodik, R., Seshia, S., Saraswat, V.: Combinatorial sketching for finite programs. SIGOPS Oper. Syst. Rev. **40**(5), 404–415 (2006)
74. Sutcliffe, A., Maiden, N.A.M., Minocha, S., Manuel, D.: Supporting scenario-based requirements engineering. IEEE TSE J. **24**, 1072–1088 (1998)
75. Weimer, W., Nguyen, T., Le Goues, C., Forrest, S.: Automatically finding patches using genetic programming. In: Proceedings of the 31st International Conference on Software Engineering, ICSE 2009, pp. 364–374. IEEE Computer Society, Washington, DC (2009)
76. Wrobel, S.: First order theory refinement. In: Advances in Inductive Logic Programming, pp. 14–33 (1996)
77. Yamamoto, A.: Which hypotheses can be found with inverse entailment? In: Lavrač, N., Džeroski, S. (eds.) ILP 1997. LNCS, vol. 1297, pp. 296–308. Springer, Heidelberg (1997). https://doi.org/10.1007/3540635149_58

Author Index

Printed in the United States
By Bookmasters